COLD WAR SPY STORIES FROM EASTERN EUROPE

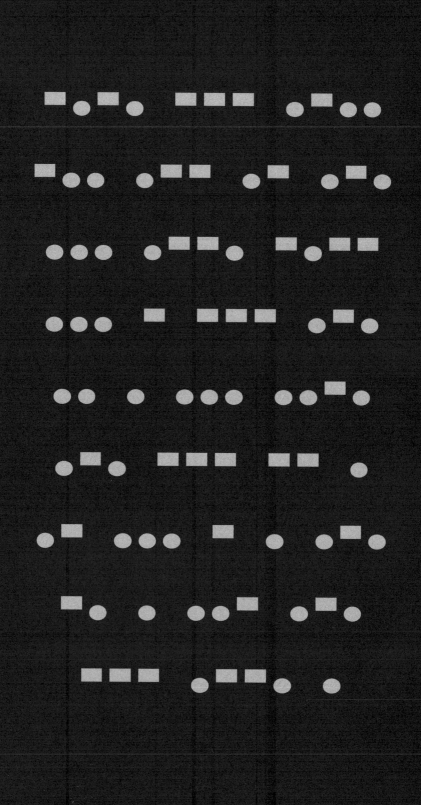

COLD WAR
SPY STORIES
FROM EASTERN EUROPE

EDITED BY
VALENTINA GLAJAR, ALISON LEWIS,
AND CORINA L. PETRESCU

POTOMAC BOOKS

AN IMPRINT OF THE UNIVERSITY OF NEBRASKA PRESS

Library of Congress Cataloging-in-Publication Data
Names: Glajar, Valentina, editor. | Lewis, Alison, 1958– editor. |
Petrescu, Corina L., editor.
Title: Cold War spy stories from Eastern Europe / edited by
Valentina Glajar, Alison Lewis, and Corina L. Petrescu.
Description: Lincoln: Potomac Books, an imprint of the
University of Nebraska Press, [2019] | Includes bibliographical
references and index.
Identifiers: LCCN 2018036252
ISBN 9781640121874 (cloth: alk. paper)
ISBN 9781640121980 (epub)
ISBN 9781640121997 (mobi)
ISBN 9781640122000 (pdf)
Subjects: LCSH: Espionage—Europe, Eastern—History—20th
century. | Espionage—Communist countries—History. | Spies—
Europe, Eastern—History—20th century. | Spies—Europe,
Eastern—Biography. | Cold War. | Espionage in literature. |
Espionage in motion pictures. | Cold War in literature. | Cold
War in motion pictures. | Europe, Eastern—History—1945-1989.
Classification: LCC DJK50 .C65 2019 |
DDC 327.1247009/045—dc23
LC record available at https://lccn.loc.gov/2018036252

Set in Lyon Text by Mikala R. Kolander.

Sergio and Aki

CONTENTS

ILLUSTRATIONS

ACKNOWLEDGMENTS

Valentina Glajar and Corina L. Petrescu would like to thank CNSAS for its continued support of their research of Romanian secret police files. Special thanks go to Silviu Moldovan, who tirelessly deals with their requests and exceeds their expectations every time they visit the Securitate archives in Bucharest. Alison Lewis would also like to thank the BStU for allowing her access to the Stasi files.

Corina L. Petrescu is grateful to the Alexander von Humboldt Foundation for its generous financial support that afforded her the means to conduct the research and the leisure to work on this project. Valentina Glajar would like to acknowledge funding from her institution that helped produce this volume. Alison Lewis would like to acknowledge the financial assistance of the Australian Research Council and its Discovery Project scheme, which funded the research.

COLD WAR SPY STORIES FROM EASTERN EUROPE

Introduction

ALISON LEWIS, VALENTINA GLAJAR, AND CORINA L. PETRESCU

If the Great War belonged to the soldier in the trenches, the Cold War surely belonged to the spy: the shadowy soldier on the invisible front fighting behind the scenes in the service of Communism or the free world. During the Cold War, spy stories became popular on both sides of the Iron Curtain, capturing the imaginations of readers and filmgoers alike, as secret police outfits quietly went about their business of espionage and surveillance, under the shroud of utmost secrecy. Curiously, in the post–Cold War period there are no signs of this enthusiasm diminishing. Indeed, the advent of what is often called a postpolitical world order (cf. Taşkale 2016) and a "politics without frontiers" (Laclau and Mouffe 2001, xiv) has opened up exciting opportunities to tell these spy stories anew. We can now recompose these tales of collusion and complicity, betrayal and treason, right and wrong, good and evil in light of new ways of thinking as well as new evidence from declassified archival sources. We can read Cold War modes of storytelling differently—remaining attentive to the fictional subtexts in factual spy narratives and the factual underpinnings of fictional works about espionage.

With the opening of the secret police archives in many countries in Eastern Europe, moreover, comes the unique chance to excavate forgotten accounts of espionage and tell them for the first time. Spy stories told through the prism of the secret police conveyed as "file stories" (Glajar 2016, 57)—about the top-secret lives of intelligence officers, their agents or informers as well as their targets—represent one distinct mode of Cold War spy story, a mode based on "factual or forensic truth" (Lewis 2016, 215) but undergirded by ideological fantasies and paranoid fictions. The opening of the files has also led to the rediscovery of curious or enigmatic espionage events, which are being told in interconnected multimodal webs of narration—whether as memoirs of notorious spymasters or as recent fictions and feature films about complex and hitherto unexplained Cold War incidents. Finally, the opening of the Iron Curtain has challenged old Cold War antagonisms such as the friend/foe binary, which is in turn recasting espionage scripts and the very character of the spy and double agent, as witnessed in new styles of spy films such as *Bridge of Spies* (2015) and television dramas such as *Weißensee* (2010–), *The Americans* (2013–18), *Deutschland 83* (2015–), and *Berlin Station* (2016–) made for a global, postpolitical audience.

This book is concerned with the stories we tell about lives lived during the Cold War. Stories are, according to Paul Ricoeur, what mediates between the past and the present and a fundamental means of how we make sense of experience. The act of narrating is how we assimilate "a life to a history" (Valdés 1991, 425). Put simply, without stories, lives would remain untold and hidden in dusty archives. While Ricoeur speaks here about the world of fiction, as that which "helps to make life—in the biological sense of the world—human" (Valdés 1991, 425), his analysis of the relation between stories and lives can be extended to all forms of storytelling from the stories of history and personal memory to the stories in secret police files. Individuals seem "entangled in stories that happen" to them, according to Ricoeur (Valdés 1991, 435), even historical individuals, and through their telling of stories we can understand them. Narration, narratives, and plots are fundamental ways of making sense of the world: "By means of the plot, goals, causes, and chance are brought together within the temporal unity of a whole and complete action" (Ricoeur 1990, ix).

The Cold War stories in this book are complex amalgams of fact and fiction, history and imagination, past and present. They refer to the secret lives of spies, referring backward to the time of the

Cold War, but like all texts in Ricoeur's hermeneutics, they also have a life beyond the historical time of writing. They come to life through the reader or spectator who refigures the author's configurations (Ricoeur 1990, 9) against the backdrop of his or her own needs and understandings. Thus these narratives narrated during the Cold War can be read against the grain from a post–Cold War perspective. Above all, they can be read with the hindsight that enables us to reassess many aspects of the Cold War and its facts and fictions about espionage.

The Cold War

The joyous celebrations of victory over National Socialist Germany lay less than a year behind him when Sir Winston Churchill delivered his speech at Westminster College, Missouri, on March 5, 1946, and deplored the Iron Curtain that had descended on Europe and closed its eastern territories behind it. While his hope that the world would not see another world war came true, instead a passive-aggressive confrontation between the former allies emerged and materialized into what has been called poetically the Cold War. When trying to explain this rapid deterioration of the Grand Alliance, historian John Lewis Gaddis points out that the Second World War "had been won by a coalition whose principle members were already at war—ideologically and geopolitically if not militarily—with one another," and this alliance's triumph had been possible because of "the pursuit of compatible objectives by incompatible systems" (2007, 6). Once the coalition reached its main common objective—National Socialist Germany's defeat—the victors had "either to cease to be who they were, or to give up much of what they had hoped . . . to attain" (6). As neither the Western allies nor the Soviet Union were ready to renounce their principles, the coalition's division along ideological lines and Europe's ensuing division into two camps was imminent. Equally true was the fact that neither party wanted a new, direct war, so the other available option was an "indirect warfare" (Krieger 2014, 251), in which propaganda and operations carried out by or with the blessing of the two superpower's secret services played a major role. According to Wolfgang Krieger, secret services were never as important for the national and international history of states as they were during the Cold War: "They were no longer an *extension* to other instruments of power politics but became a *substitute* for the war of the superpowers, which no one wanted to fight, and which simply could not be fought given the [superpowers'] growing nuclear arsenals" (251–52).

Carrying the laurels for the success of the war on the European western front, the United States approached the postwar era cautiously, not completely sure of the part it would play in Europe. That security in the homeland was a priority was undebatable, but how the United States would go about transplanting it to Europe was less certain. In breaking with its traditional isolationism during times of peace, the United States embraced its victor role and put forth a strategy that allowed it not only to restore peace to its European sphere of influence but also to secure its postwar development. George F. Kennan formulated this strategy better than anyone else when he proclaimed that all that was needed from the United States when dealing with the Soviet Union was a "long-term, patient but firm and vigilant containment of Russian expansive tendencies" (1947, 575). The best way to achieve this was through closely monitoring and surveilling the enemy; the best place to do so was certainly Germany where the United States and the Soviet Union faced each other not only along the country's inner border but more intimately and directly along the inner-city frontier of Berlin.

Having carried the largest burden for the war in terms of human and material losses, the Soviet Union expected nothing less than goodwill from its former allies and compliance from its satellites to ensure peace in the world and its own prosperity. Relying on Marxism-Leninism, which taught him that sooner or later greed would make it impossible for capitalists to cooperate, Joseph Stalin counted on "the inevitability of wars between capitalist countries" (quoted in Gaddis 2007, 14) to give him the upper hand internationally. Within his own sphere of influence, the Eastern Bloc, he made sure to install political leaders loyal to him, who thought to replicate his regime in their countries. Whether Walter Ulbricht in East Germany, Gheorghe Gheorgiu-Dej in Romania, or Bolesław Bierut in Poland—the leaders of the three satellite states at the core of this project—they all embraced Stalinism and promoted it in their respective countries at great cost. To ensure their peoples' submission, the authorities in each of the three countries established powerful state police forces replicating the Soviet chekist model.

The secret services of both camps had to figure out a modus operandi for the times of peace since they could not carry on with their previous practices. While in the United States and the Soviet Union the transition was more fluid as the state leadership did not change as dramatically as it did in defeated Germany or satellite Romania and Poland, it nonetheless involved changes even if they were primarily structural—departments were renamed, integrated or subordinated to other offices without really changing their duties (see Krieger 2014, 252–57). Collectively speaking, secret services are charged with identifying, containing, and disciplining or dealing with state enemies. The extent to which each secret service carries out these tasks and the way it does depend on the nature of the state they serve. During the Cold War both the U.S. and the Soviet secret services also had to train the secret forces of their respective allies/satellites. The U.S. military helped establish the BND (Bundesnachrichtendienst [Federal Intelligence Service]) (Krieger 2014, 264–74), and the KGB (Komitet gosudarstvennoĭ bezopasnosti [Committee for State Security]) helped with the birth of the Stasi (Ministerium für Staatssicherheit [Ministry for State Security]), the Securitate (Departamentul Securității Statului [Department of State Security]), and the UB (Urząd Bezpieczeństwa [Department of Security], 1945–54). While according to Krieger the exact extent of American influence on the BND cannot be fully analyzed yet (2014, 273–74), insights into the Soviet method of forming the secret police forces of its allies are accessible in the archives of the respective forces (see Gieseke 2000 for the Stasi; Oprea 2008 for the Securitate, and Szwagrzyk 2005 for the UB).

Ultimately, each secret police agency was charged with detecting activities of hostile powers and unmasking enemies of the state at home and threats abroad. Whatever the reason, once an individual attracted the secret police's attention, she or he entered a surveillance network of an interpersonal, political, and bureaucratic nature that reduced one to a target: a person of interest to the secret police and categorized according to enemy types. While these types varied from country to country, they were deemed equally dangerous in all the countries represented in this book.

The Soviet Union was wary of the Zionist Jew, the old Russian elite, the wealthy peasant (kulak), the religious leader, and the dissident intellectual. In East Germany the enemy bore the face of the West German spy and saboteur, the land-owning aristocrat (*Junker*), the cosmopolitan youngster with a preference for American culture, the "deserter from the republic" (*Republikflüchtling*), and the critical or reform-socialist writer or intellectual. Poland was equally at odds with the wealthy peasant and the Western spy and saboteur but also with the meat black-marketer (*Fleischspekulant*), the American instigator, the neo-Nazi, and the Jew as Zionist and revisionist (Satjukow and Gries 2004). The Romanian state combated the intellectual and political opponent of the prewar era, the religious leader, the land-owning peasant, and among its national minorities particularly the ethnic German as nationalist, the Hungarian as irredentist, and the Jew as Zionist (Tismaneanu 2016, 9–19). Unmasking these troublemakers was essential to the secret police, whose agents and informants pursued their targets relentlessly.

Cold War Propaganda and Covert Operations

In the struggle between the two superpowers, propaganda was the main weapon of choice, deployed mercilessly by both sides. Propaganda was produced and reproduced across each of the two spheres of influence from the dominant power down to its smallest ally or satellite state. For many years in the West, the Cold War was seen as a war of words. As Martin J. Medhurst writes: "A Cold War is, by definition, a rhetorical war, a war fought with words, speeches, pamphlets, public information (or disinformation) campaigns, slogans, gestures, symbolic actions, and the like" (1997, xiv). All these media could and did morph into propaganda. Propaganda was not something the West readily admitted to using, nor did it like to regard itself as participating in mutual struggles over ideology—ideology was after all what the Soviets used, not the United States or its NATO partners (W. S. Lucas 1999, 12). Yet propaganda was, as W. Scott Lucas has forcefully argued, rife on both sides, not just as "an adjunct to policies but [as] an integral part of a strategy to win hearts and minds as well as acquire territory and attain economic supremacy" (1999, 17). As research has shown, U.S. information officials had already launched the first peacetime propaganda offensive in 1945 (Belmonte 2008, 4), and the United States' first two Cold War presidents used propaganda (Parry-Giles 2000, 95). As post–Cold War studies have increasingly concluded, propaganda was most definitely not the exclusive provenance of the Soviet Union and its satellites; rather both parties relied on it, openly and covertly. It infused political rhetoric and foreign policy, but more importantly for our context, it underpinned mass culture, such as films, and to a lesser extent literature.

Critics of U.S. foreign policy during the Cold War have since drawn attention to its moralistic, ideological underpinnings and reminded us that it hid behind the pragmatic-sounding notion that it was merely serving the interests of national security (W. S. Lucas 1999, 14). In the United States, the focus of Cold War information programs and their public diplomacy efforts was, as Laura Belmonte has argued, "selling America to foreign audiences" (2008, 2). Radio was central to these efforts, for example, and the United States' foreign intelligence agency, the CIA, sought to spread democratic values behind the Iron Curtain through funding European radio services such as Radio Free Europe and Voice of America (Risso 2013). The key to selling the West abroad was to "explain . . . its values and notions of freedom to the world" (Belmonte 2008, 2). This was not only the task of espionage agencies such as the CIA but also of NATO. Although NATO was primarily a military and political alliance, its cultural programs—such as the NATO Information Service NATIS (Risso 2014, 5)—provided crucial support for its operations through fostering mutual understanding and a sense of community. As a "security community," NATO sought to "extend beyond its geographical area and seek to influence neighboring countries to ensure political stability and good governance" (Risso 2014, 1). While the Warsaw Pact did not have a similar tool of propaganda, it had in effect no need for one since it fell to the Cominform (Risso 2014, 5) to provide consistent uniform propaganda across the Warsaw Pact. The Cominform—the Communist Information Bureau—was established in 1947 by the Soviet Union for the purpose of coordinating activities across Communist Parties around the world. Its first objective was to launch a propaganda "peace" offensive against the West (Wettig 2008, 197–98).

From 1960 on NATO responded to attacks from the Soviet Union by openly declaring it would engage in psychological warfare, even in peacetime (Risso 2014, 93-94). Communist propaganda depicted the West as imperialistic and a plausible, real threat to national security, particularly in those satellite states close to the Cold War fault lines. According to NATO this propaganda portrayed West Germany as a "warmonger, a hotbed of Nazism, revanchism and anti-Semitism" (95). To the Soviet Union, NATO was a "colonial and economic imperial organization" that happily exploited West Germany's weakness as a divided country (95). In the United States and the West, anti-Communist propaganda worked in a similar fashion and portrayed the West and its values as under threat from the "red peril." These threats varied in type and scale from Communists at home in the labor movement to the specter of a Communist nuclear attack during the Cuban missile crisis and later from Reagan's so-called evil empire in the eighties. The West's response to the "red scare" ranged accordingly over the course of the Cold War from McCarthyist inquisitions and religious crusades against Communists (Jenkins 1999, 166–67) to the purging of the teaching profession (118). On the other side of the Iron Curtain, the Soviet Union and its satellite regimes railed unrelentingly against the evils of Western imperialism and capitalism, invoking all the while the menace of a rebirth of Nazism and fascism. These putative evils posed a similarly wide range of threats to security from the various specters of invasion and war—which during the Berlin blockade and the building of the Berlin Wall was a genuine possibility—to the threat of a NATO nuclear strike in 1983.

Although there was a remarkable degree of symmetry in these perceived threats, one area of propaganda warfare was asymmetrical: the one-way population movements from East to West. The West scored painful political victories over the Soviet Union in the continuous exodus of its populations from Eastern Europe, including ethnic Germans from Romania, Jews from Romania and the Soviet Union, and refugee dissidents and intellectuals from the counter-revolutionary flashpoints of Hungary in 1956, Czechoslovakia in 1968, and Poland in 1956, 1968, and 1981 (Ardittis 1994, xvii). Despite prevailing restrictions on migration provided by the Iron Curtain, the persistence of sizable numbers of political and economic migrants from East to West came at a considerable economic cost to the Eastern Bloc, which lost valuable labor power and human resources. In the case of dissident intellectuals and political refugees there were damaging symbolic losses as well. East Germany suffered in particular from successive waves of emigration to the West, mostly before the closing of the borders and the erection of the Berlin Wall, when 3.5 million, or one in six, East Germans left or "absconded" from the German Democratic Republic (GDR) (Major 2010, 56). After the closing of the borders in 1961, the flow of refugees to the West continued, albeit radically reduced. Some fled in spectacular and often doomed escapes via hot-air balloons, tunnels, hidden compartments in cars, and even airplane hijackings (cf. Major 2010, 144). There were in total 136 deaths at the Berlin Wall; 98 of the victims were shot dead (Hertle and Nooke 2011, 21). Other Eastern Bloc citizens left involuntarily and were forcibly sent into exile by their respective regimes, stripped of their citizenship, like Wolf Biermann in the GDR in 1976 and prominent Soviet dissident Petr Grigorenko in late 1977, or banished, as Andrei Sakharov, who was sent to Gorki in 1980 while under KGB surveillance. Dissidents and victims of the gulag system who were allowed to travel to the West, such as Alexander Solzhenitsyn, Lew Kopelew, and Efim Etkin, subsequently found themselves forced into exile, falling victim to standoffs between the superpowers that no diplomatic negotiations could ameliorate at the start of the second Cold War in the early eighties.

Cold War propaganda relied on the aforementioned national

enemy types, which were upheld in strict binaries of enemy and friend that allowed for few shades of gray. Propaganda was an important way of "making sense" of the Cold War (Rawnsley 1999, 2), and it suffused everyday life and culture, implicating everyone from those close to the center of power to those at the periphery. For the intelligence agencies at the epicenter of the Cold War, propaganda was of course part and parcel of a wide-ranging arsenal of instruments at the disposal of both democratic and totalitarian regimes. Intelligence agencies had recourse to far greater types of propaganda, including "gray" propaganda of questionable origin and accuracy and even "black" propaganda, which is false information from a hostile source parading as though it were from a friendly source (Del Pero 2003, 68). In addition to this gambit, intelligence availed itself of clandestine actions, or "covert operations," which were an "indispensable instrument" in foreign policy and foreign intelligence agencies during the Cold War (Del Pero 2003, 68). In the early years, covert operations became important instruments on both sides of "containment," justified by the rapidly deteriorating relations between the West and the Soviet bloc and the ideological "cold" nature of the Cold War (Del Pero 2003, 69–70). In fact, the fifties in particular were for the CIA a "golden age" for covert operations (Callanan 2010, 5).

In domestic intelligence, covert operations were also widespread during the Cold War particularly in the Eastern Bloc. While secret operations on foreign soil generally enjoy a greater degree of acceptance, when used against a country's own citizens, there is far less tolerance for the secret tracking or surveillance of internal enemies. Yet both sides engaged in covert action against their own citizens and justified doing so by invoking counterintelligence or security arguments, namely, that the domestic population was in danger from internal enemies or threats. On both sides of the Cold War, nation-states conducted covert operations against suspected Communists in the West and anti-Communists in the East. Secrecy was regarded as necessary for the success of a covert operation, even though there were risks, for example, that dysfunctional operations might not be detected in time "whether in democratic or authoritarian systems" (Reisman and Baker

1992, 14–15). There are by the same token obvious political advantages to secrecy: "it enhances the power of the party using it, and where power sharing is called for, secrecy circumvents it" (141).

Propaganda, Truth, and the "Curtain of Lies"

The performative structure of statements in the media shape the world, according to John Frow's analysis of discourses, in particular news (2006, 17). In few instances has that worked more efficiently than during the Cold War, on both sides of the Iron Curtain. The text of news, for example, can be analyzed according to the three dimensions Frow distinguishes: the attitude toward it, the evaluative tone, and the rhetorical channel or deictic signs, such as the bold print or color (17–18). These dimensions evoke, according to Frow, background knowledge (18), which during the Cold War was shaped by significant propaganda, as each side was in constant search for evidence to support its ideology and thus "its version of the truth" (Feinberg 2017, x). Melissa Feinberg coins the term "curtain of lies"—the title of her recent book—and indicates that both sides were entangled in a struggle to prove their own rightness and thus used the concepts of "truth" and "lies" as signifiers of their particular ideology (xi).

Evidence to support their "truth" came from various sources. Evidence meant intelligence about life behind this curtain of lies that could support the opposing views and that shaped what Feinberg calls the Cold War political culture (2017, xiv). In the early Cold War years, émigrés and refugees who brought their stories and firsthand knowledge about Communist societies to the West, were some of the first sources of information. However, the layers of background knowledge that Frow presupposes in his analysis of news (2006, 18) were activated in the minds of the journalists who interviewed these refugees and émigrés. As Feinberg indicates, Western analysts read these stories against the background of constant polarizing propaganda "in ways that upheld their existing beliefs" (2017, xxi). As Cheryl Dueck shows in her chapter in this book, the film *Westen* (*West*, 2013) sheds some light on life in transitional refugee camps and draws a comparison between the interviews and the surveillance these refugees were subjected to by the Americans and West Germans agents with that of the Stasi in East Berlin.

Mistrust and fear were two other important components of this Cold War political culture in the race for "truth." In the East there was the fear of imperialists who infiltrated the Communist societies and were attempting to usurp the accomplishments of these new peoples' democracies. As a result Communists closely monitored their own populations in order to find and neutralize any sources of imperialist propaganda, and it comes as no surprise that most foreigners were viewed as potential infiltrators and spies. Especially in the Stalinist years, individuals were expected to denounce any traitors—a category that was wide-ranging during this time and also included citizens who expressed any opinions opposing the regimes in power. As we will see in Valentina Glajar's chapter, the case against the Romanian Securitate officer Samuel Feld was built on various evidence that included offending a Soviet officer, failure to denounce his own uncle, and having relatives in Western enemy countries.

In the West the fear resulted both from the lack of information and the misleading, often false media reports (the equivalent of today's "fake news") that in Feinberg's words "exemplified the dual moral economy of Cold War politics" (2017, x). To counter this lack of "real" news, the West projected and broadcasted in part its own fears and propaganda through its radio stations Radio Free Europe, Voice of America, and the BBC. The information these broadcasters transmitted was often meant to counter the Eastern propaganda with their own (106) and to rectify and counter the "lies" spread through the censored regime-controlled radio stations in the East. Westerners received in part their information from the aforementioned Eastern émigrés and refugees, who brought their individual stories to the West that painted everyday life in the grayish colors Western analysts were expecting. These Easterners described, as prompted, their fear of spies and informers, of war, and of scarcity (xvii). The Western-broadcasted "real" news was so efficient, and in many cases the only more reliable source of information, that a very large number of Easterners relied on it. As the refugees' interviews discussed in Feinberg's *Curtain of Lies* reveal, many Easterners listened at night to the various broadcasters and discussed the news with friends and coworkers the following day despite fears of being under surveillance, while others took precautions to avoid being reported to the secret service. Yet some interviewees claimed they avoided listening to these Western broadcasters and instead developed a system of reading the officially transmitted fake news against the grain to excavate the pieces of embellished or tarnished nuggets of real news (106–8).

Cold Warriors, Spies, Agents, and Intelligence Officers

As Eva Horn claims, the most important weapon is knowledge about the enemy, and thus in her opinion the Cold War was not an "arms race" but rather "a knowledge race" (2013, 231). While the refugees' and émigrés' stories helped create a Cold War culture shaped by fear and truth (or lack of it) (Feinberg 2017, xxi), scientists came to the West as bearers of secrets about arsenals, nuclear and otherwise (Horn 2013, 231). In Horn's opinion the real "Cold Warriors" were civilians—secret agents, physicists, mathematicians, computer scientists, economists, and other experts who allowed university research, espionage, and military war games to speculate jointly about the enemy (232). These "warriors" presented a security risk on both sides of the Iron Curtain, as each side was in the pursuit of knowledge and intelligence. There are lists of mathematicians, physicists, and secret agents or officers who crossed the Iron Curtain: some over Western Europe to the United States, and others from the United States to the Soviet Union, the People's Republic of China, and East Germany, among other countries. As farfetched as the U.S. TV show *The Americans* may seem, the KGB spies portrayed in this highly successful series are based on true stories that are stranger than fiction. An almost carbon-copy story is that of the KGB spies Andrei Bezrukov ("Donald Heathfield") and Elena Vavilova ("Tracey Foley"), who like the protagonists of *The Americans* led normal American lives but were part of a Soviet program that dispatched deep-cover agents called "illegals." However, after the fall of Communism, they continued to spy for the SVR (Sluzhba vneshney razvedki

[Foreign Intelligence Service of the Russian Federation]), the successor of the KGB in modern Russia. As occurred so many times with exposed agents, Bezrukov and Vavilova were swapped for Russians who were spying for the United States (Walker 2016).

Two of the most important defectors to the West who inflicted serious blows to their respective Cold War intelligence agencies were the East German Werner Stiller and the Romanian Ion Mihai Pacepa. The East German double agent Stiller left with a briefcase full of top-secret files and documents that were meant to assure his survival but also to allow him to prove his worth to the West. Most notably, the information that Stiller gave to the West German secret service helped visually identify Markus Wolf, the long-time director of the Stasi's Main Directorate for Reconnaissance, until then known as "the man without a face" (see Mary Beth Stein's chapter in this book). Stiller eventually also collaborated with the CIA and made it to the United States, where he lived the American dream for a while under a new identity as an investment broker. Before he died at the age of sixty-nine in Budapest, he was eager to talk about his life as a spy and his fear for his life (Stiller and Adams 1992; Heim 2017). Pacepa was a Securitate general, head of Romanian industrial espionage, and personal adviser to Nicolae Ceauşescu. After his defection in 1978, he worked with the CIA on various operations against the Eastern Bloc, and the agency described his contribution as "important and unique" (Borchgrave 2004). His first book, *Red Horizons: Chronicles of a Communist Spy Chief* (1987), in which according to other former Securitate officers he laid bare truths, half-truths, and outright fiction about the Communist regime in Romania, the Ceauşescu couple, and covert Eastern Bloc operations, was serialized on Radio Free Europe in 1988. Pacepa was sentenced to death twice in absentia and continues to live in hiding in the United States (Hossu-Longin 2009).

While many of these defection and spy stories are still veiled in secrecy due to security concerns, the end of the Cold War presented a unique opportunity in the East: the opening of the secret police files, which helped researchers unearth stories of victims and collaborators but also of secret operations. Yet the lustration process in the various former Eastern Bloc countries did not evolve without glitches and in some cases serious hurdles (see Stan and Nedelsky 2013). The former Communist secret services did not surrender power without a last attempt to cover their traces. For instance, both the East German Stasi and the SRI (Serviciul Roman de Informații [Romanian Service of Information]), the successor of the Romanian Securitate, proceeded to destroy files in 1989 and 1991, respectively. The shredded Stasi files are currently undergoing a meticulous process of recovery that began with the ePuzzler, a reconstruction software that uses complex image processing and pattern-recognition algorithms to reconstruct scanned shreds of paper into complete pages, and has now switched to manual mending (Oltermann 2018). The partially burned and buried Romanian Securitate files, uncovered by Romanian journalists, could only be recovered to some extent, and the irremediable loss of information remains to be assessed (Botez 2011).

Yet the remaining almost intact files allow us rare insight into the life and activity of various intelligence officers and informers, as discussed in part 1. Chapter 1 focuses on the former Securitate officer Samuel Feld, who on February 29, 1960, was discharged from MAI (Ministerul Afacerilor Interne [Ministry of Internal Affairs]). Feld's file story, as composed by Valentina Glajar, reveals a fragmented, often embellished, other times conflicting account that retraces his eleven-year career as a Securitate officer and the two investigations into his life and activity that eventually led to his dismissal. Based on Feld's cadre file (D102) and his surveillance files (I 259048 and I 259049), opened under the code name "Dayan" after his dismissal from MAI, Glajar's analysis exposes, in part, the inner workings of the Securitate at its core but also offers a slice of Jewish Romanian personal history that speaks of antisemitism, persecution, and ultimately false hopes. The case against Major Feld was based on informers' reports, characterizations by his colleagues, anonymous denouncements, and interrogations that are only alluded to but most likely removed from or never included in this file. Yet like an apt chess player, he anticipated his investigators' moves, always ready to provide them with elaborate explanations for his activities and often successfully outmaneuvering them. As Glajar shows, Feld knew how to skillfully influence the unfolding of his own story, at least up to the point when it inescapably slipped out of his hands and followed his investigators' desired trajectory. Several years after his dismissal, Feld managed to emigrate with his family to the United States—after several failed attempts to emigrate to Israel. While he expressed regrets about having been entangled with the Securitate, he also requested that his real name be obscured in this chapter.

In chapter 2, Mary Beth Stein tackles the story of East Germany's greatest spymaster, Markus Wolf, whom Western intelligence agencies simply dubbed "the man without a face" for twenty-five years. Unlike in Feld's case, though, Wolf's three personnel files comprise roughly one hundred pages, and the information they entail hardly allows one to evaluate truth claims about him or espionage operations in his autobiographies. As Stein claims, the man without a face might have remained the man without a *trace* had it not been for his many autobiographical publications. In this chapter Stein focuses specifically on Wolf's 1997 English language autobiography coauthored with Anne McElvoy *The Man without a Face*, and a revised and expanded German edition published in 1997 under the title *Spionchef im geheimen Krieg: Erinnerungen*. Like other Stasi officers who penned their autobiographical stories (Kopp 2016), Wolf's German and English-language editions are critical in his own campaign for personal redemption and a more positive assessment of the East German state. Drawing on Phillipe Lejeune's "autobiographical pact," Stein explores truth claims about Wolf himself and the controversial espionage practice of using "Romeo spies" and his reflections on the legacy of East German socialism at a time when he and the system he served were on trial.

In chapter 3 Alison Lewis turns to the role of Stasi informers in the Stasi's secret war on books, namely, informers who wrote reader's reports on a clandestine basis for the Stasi, as the "fifth censor" (Walther 1996) of literature. In the absence of autobiographical testimony, the Cold War spy story of Stasi informer and minor poet Uwe Berger, namely, IM (*inoffizieller Mitarbeiter*)

"Uwe," is composed mainly from the extensive and telling traces left behind in his file in the Stasi archives. Enlisted in 1972, Berger reviewed and mostly tried to sabotage the publication of works by a string of notable East German writers: Sarah Kirsch, Paul Wiens, Monika Maron, Günter Kunert, Klaus Poche, Erich Loest, Lutz Rathenow, Wolfgang Hilbig, Eva Strittmatter, Jurek Becker, and Bettina Wegner. Lewis discusses the various facets of this informer's self-ascribed role as an aesthetic gatekeeper and an ideological "policeman" in the field of literature, as well as "Uwe's" role as a secret agent. As she argues in this chapter, working undercover as a freelance reader for the Stasi provided Berger with a chance to work off personal grievances and resentments as well as to bank greater symbolic, albeit secret, capital for himself, as a member of what he and others saw as an elite secret surveillance society.

Part 2 explores the making of targets by two secret police forces: Romania's Securitate and the Soviet Union's KGB. Instrumental in the process through which an individual metamorphosed into a target was information gathered from informers. Collected in classified files, it provided the secret police with intelligence on the persons under observation and aided in building a case against these targets. In chapter 4, for example, Corina L. Petrescu focuses on the French Romanian writer Ana Novac and analyzes how she became a Securitate target in the early 1960s. Petrescu proposes the term "target identity" to describe the specific features and particular behaviors that the Securitate pieced together in individuals' files, and which allowed the Securitate to treat these individuals as suspicious and surveil them. By analyzing in detail the reports that two informers, called "sources" in the Romanian context, produced about Novac, she showcases the role these sources played in the criminalization of targeted regime critics. Irrespective of Novac's true nature, sources "Magda" and "Karl Fischer" first painted and then cemented "target Novac" into an enemy of the state both ideologically (through her openly articulated criticism) and personally (in terms of lifestyle and expectations). While Novac was able to escape Romania due to her intuition that she would be able to do so only if she thwarted the Securitate, Petrescu's engagement with her files also illustrates how persistent secret police forces could be in their pursuit of targets. As a French citizen in the 1980s, Novac captured the Securitate's attention again due to her collaborations with Radio Free Europe, and the reports of sources "Magda" and "Karl Fischer" gained relevance anew.

In chapter 5 Julie Fedor shows how in 1980 the KGB stage-managed the case of Orthodox priest Father Dmitrii Dudko so as to recast the heroic image of the dissident into that of a marionette of Western secret services. By examining the worldview of the chekist and the manner in which he conceived of and categorized Soviet citizens, Fedor retraces the distinctive moral universe of the KGB. She focuses on Dudko as a KGB target and approaches the topic from his perspective as a victim by examining a series of autobiographical writings in which Dudko attempted to come to terms with his past decades after his direct confrontation with the Soviet system. Dudko's ultimate conversion into a regime loyalist allows Fedor to scrutinize his works for insights into the categories that fueled the chekist discourse of the Cold War and how they permeated Dudko's own thinking. The trope of "repentance" becomes a key element not only of this discourse but also of Dudko's autobiographical output and of the accounts put forth by his contemporaries. In an attempt to further explain Dudko's actions, Fedor also explores the post-Soviet life of Dudko's story and its appropriation by contemporary Russian nationalists. With the set goal of recasting Cold War history in the service of a grand Russian narrative dominated by the confrontation between Russia and the West, these nationalists refashion the KGB—and implicitly also the Cheka—as a valiant protector of Russian spirituality.

Part 3 is devoted to Cold War stories with a transnational East-West European focus. Most Cold War studies proceed from the assumption that the Iron Curtain was impassable and that there was a strict bipolarity between East and West superpowers (Autio-Sarasmo and Miklóssy 2011, 1). However, as recent research in Finland shows, there was a far greater degree of "multilevel interaction . . . between the different types of actors, between people, institutions and states" (2) that belies this view. Satellite states did not always act in monolithic ways, and parts of Europe, such as the two Germanies, served as an "arena of collaboration" (6) rather than confrontation, as we shall see in the next two chapters, by Jennifer Miller and Axel Hildebrandt. The motif of the Iron Curtain implies a rigid impassable physical border as well as a "metal-like mental border" (Autio-Sarasmo and Miklóssy 2011, 6), yet for many, the Iron Curtain "leaked" (6) and was passable both physically and ideologically. This applied particularly to those residents of both East and West Berlin living geographically in close proximity to the wall as a physical edifice or to those living along the internal border in Germany, a country that shared the same language and cultural traditions.

In chapter 6 Jennifer Miller unearths a little known "area of collaboration" during the Cold War involving espionage and Turkish nationals. This East-West spy story—or rather this interlocking web of intriguing smaller spy narratives—allowed for a more intimate kind of "collaboration" at a grassroots level among residents of divided Berlin. As Miller reveals, "West Berlin–residing Turkish nationals built social lives, business deals, intimate relationships, and transnational families across divided Berlin," offering new perspectives on the lived experience of divided Berlin and the Cold War from a German perspective. For Germans and their respective governments, Turkish guest workers presented, as Miller argues, a "paradox" since they were seen as suspicious on both sides: foreign in the West and a security risk in the East. For the East German Stasi, moreover, they posed a new kind of capitalist threat, especially the many regular border crossers among Turks who formed relationships with East German women, often as a prelude to helping the women escape. For the Turks the East seemed to offer a "space to explore and enjoy greater social autonomy and acceptance among Germans." As Miller explores through close analysis of various sources, including personal and departmental Stasi files, Turkish border crossers were kept under strict surveillance on their sojourns in the East, often as targets under suspicion of some illicit activity, but sometimes as enlisted collaborators spying on fellow countrymen or East German women.

In chapter 7 Axel Hildebrandt excavates another unknown Cold War spy story and another "area of collaboration" between

East and West Germans, this time one that extended to the United States and Poland. This chapter tells the backstory behind a major Cold War international incident in August 1978 involving terrorism and an illegal escape across the Iron Curtain. The story of a spectacular hijacking of a Polish airplane headed to East Berlin by two East Germans desperate to escape to the West, and helped by a West German accomplice, was well publicized in the West German media at the time. Hildebrandt composes a multimedial account from the memories of eyewitnesses, including the U.S. judge at the trial and the extensive Stasi records on each of the participants, who were under constant surveillance. Hildebrandt compares factual and fictional versions of the event and analyzes the unique perspectives offered by each of the different types of narratives—the secret police files, the accounts of eyewitnesses, and some of the newer fictional treatments of the historical material such as the novel *Tupolew* (2004) by Antje Rávic Strubel. Rather than regarding one source as more truthful or accurate than the other, Hildebrandt explores instead how each source and narrative—the factual and the fictional—has contributed to our understanding of the Cold War along the frontier between East and West and has shaped our memory of this remarkable event.

Part 4, "Spies on Screen," focuses on fictional representations in film and television at the height of the Cold War and beyond. For the West films were pivotal to exporting democracy and the values of freedom to the rest of the world, not just for the United States but for NATO-member countries as well. Nothing did this better than the spy film. The gentleman-like screen character of British secret agent James Bond has come to epitomize the figure of the Cold War spy, and the British-American film franchise has come to typify the genre of the spy thriller. Yet Eastern Bloc audiences were largely unfamiliar with Bond, and "Bondmania" remained a Western phenomenon. In the Eastern Bloc a rather different kind of spy movie gained popularity. In chapter 8 Carol Anne Costabile-Heming focuses on two lesser known spy films made in the GDR: *For Eyes Only—streng geheim* (1963) and *Chiffriert an Chef—Ausfall Nr. 5* (Coded message for the boss, 1979), produced by the state-owned film studio, the Deutsche Film-

Aktiengesellschaft (DEFA). Set in divided Berlin just prior to the building of the Berlin Wall, at a time of heightened tensions, both films modified the genre of the spy film and "domesticated" the figure of the double agent. They did so not as a form of escapism but to lend support to dominant East German belief systems and the specific fear that East Germany was under threat of invasion from NATO forces. Moreover, as Costabile-Heming notes, GDR espionage films were tasked with "clearly marking the rival, while working to exclude and contain the enemy." As she shows, although set some sixteen years apart, both films served to reactualize the threat from the U.S. enemy around the time of the Cuban missile crisis and the Berlin crisis (1958–61) to shore up support for GDR domestic politics, particularly the regime's intransigent stance on its closed borders.

In chapter 9 Lisa Haegele explores West German film perspectives on the spy genre and turns to a critically acclaimed but little-known example of New German Cinema and spy film *Der Willi-Busch-Report* (The Willi Busch report, 1979) by Swiss-born Niklaus Schilling. Schilling chooses a decidedly atypical setting for his espionage film in an uneventful fictional town along the inner-German frontier. The film relocates the conflict from the international to the (West German) national. At the same time, it serves to refocus the problems of the Cold War from a novel perspective, which is not "them" but rather "us," the Germans. As a "spy story *about* spy stories," *Der Willi-Busch-Report* provides a humorous, close-up, German view of the Cold War and of the spy genre. It takes an ironic approach both to Cold War politics and to espionage, offering a "counter-aesthetic" not only to the Bond films of the time but also to post–Cold War Hollywood-style productions such as Florian Henckel von Donnersmarck's Oscar-winning *Das Leben der Anderen* (*The Lives of Others*, 2006). By creating narrative ambiguities and subverting spy film tropes, the film draws attention to the issues of surveillance, hysteria, and paranoia in West Germany shortly after the German Autumn in 1977, when West Germany was shaken by the terrorist attacks of the Red Army Faction.

Chapter 10 by Cheryl Dueck moves from the Cold War to the post–Cold War era, in which films and television series about Cold

War espionage—many of which are transnational productions—are enjoying a renaissance. As she shows, rather than expressing a nostalgia for Cold War certainties and old binaries between friend and foe, many filmic variations of the spy thriller such as *Westen*, *Bridge of Spies* (2015), and *Deutschland 83* (2015–) muddy the waters of the old dichotomies between East and West, enemy and friend. They speak to the changed geopolitical situation after 1990, and to the new concerns of a postpolitical era. In her readings of spy films since 2010, she reveals how the aesthetics of surveillance provide a conduit for national stories to travel internationally, which in turn allows these works to make meaningful contributions to current post–Cold War debates about surveillance. The principal means by which they do so is the use of political and moral ambiguity, conveyed through filmic devices such as blurring, framing, reflections, and representation of affect, as well as narrative. They thus have a double referent in the Cold War past and the post–Cold War present, addressing memories of the all-pervasive climate of fear and mistrust during the Cold War and our current concern with *all* mechanisms of surveillance. However, as Dueck argues, the politics of surveillance has indeed changed since the end of the Cold War as have its means and forms. Anxieties about spying and surveillance too have shifted, and as she argues, if the spy comes from within, spy thrillers about internal surveillance "speak compellingly to contemporary anxieties about the kind of 'liquid surveillance' that is conducted worldwide through digital monitoring."

If the Cold War from a U.S. perspective was about "defense of the West," in the post–Cold War era U.S. foreign policy was about "the political and ideological extension of the West" (Mandelbaum 2016, 5). Despite U.S. hopes that the dissolution of the Soviet Union would lead to a lasting transformation of Russian society that would also see Russia become a friendly power, after 2000 relations between the United States and Russia soured, as "Russia went backward politically, becoming a less open, less tolerant, less democratic, more repressive place" (Mandelbaum 2016, 354). With NATO's expansion eastward in particular, Vladimir Putin began to see the United States and NATO as rivals again, and Russia moved to aggressively protect what it saw as its interests in its region, which culminated in its 2014 invasion of neighbor and former Soviet republic Ukraine (354). As Michael Mandelbaum writes: "Russian resentment, in concert with Russian autocracy, put an end to the peaceful post–Cold War era on the European continent" (357).

While the post–Cold War era challenged many of the certainties of the Cold War and its binaries, sometimes inverting fixed reference points of friend and foe, it has also revealed some uncomfortable continuities with the past. As we shall show, there are many constants such as the "shared belief in the universality of American freedom, democracy, and free enterprise" that link both the Truman and the George W. Bush eras of foreign policy (Belmonte 2008, 3). In post-Soviet Russia as well, the Soviet past, in particular, is being rehabilitated as Putin, who was a colonel in the KGB, has surrounded himself with "secret police veterans" who "form the core of Putin's new, authoritarian, Russian political system" (Mandelbaum 2016, 357). Moreover, as Russian interference in the 2016 U.S. elections has revealed, we are in many ways witnessing a revival of the information wars of the Cold War, which are now being fought through the new social media. These ideological front lines continue to run between NATO and Warsaw Pact member states, albeit along a frontier that has now moved eastward, and continues to shape political and cultural life in the United States, Europe, and Russia. This is nowhere more evident than in the phenomenon of so-called fake news, which is nothing more than what during the Cold War went under the epithet of disinformation. Similarly, in Russia today in what is now being dubbed a "new Cold War" (E. Lucas 2008), there are attempts to resume past cultural wars, especially the wars against church-led dissidents, which the Soviet Union lost to the West, and to try to win back the hearts and minds of former dissenters.

Yet, despite the *Sonderweg* taken by Russia under Putin with regard to the KGB, the remainder of the former Soviet bloc states have embraced lustration in dealing with former elites and its secret police forces, making their archives available to researchers and victims. This open and democratic approach to the past has allowed the forensic search for the truth to proceed unimpeded, fostering the work of historians and other researchers. By the same token, the declassification of archival sources has also allowed other kinds of mediation of the Cold War past to flourish. Especially in recent years we have seen a wide array of new types of stories—films, television series, and works of fiction—that have continued the search for truth into other media and fora and experimented with new interpretations and perspectives on the past. Espionage was undoubtedly a rich field to mine during the Cold War, although much of this field was obscured from view. The exposure of this explosive seam of facts and fiction, truth and lies has revealed a fascinating and productive source of knowledge about espionage. For both the historian and the creator of fictional works in the post–Cold War period, this presents both a formidable challenge and a unique opportunity.

References

Ardittis, Solon. 1994. "General Introduction." In *The Politics of East-West Migration*, edited by Solon Ardittis, xvii–xxiii. Houndmills, Basingstoke: Macmillan.

Autio-Sarasmo, Sari, and Katalin Miklóssy. 2011. *Reassessing Cold War Europe*. London: Routledge.

Belmonte, Laura A. 2008. *Selling the American Way: U.S. Propaganda and the Cold War*. Philadelphia: University of Pennsylvania Press.

Borchgrave, Arnaud de. 2004. "Red Past in Romania's Present." *Washington Post*, January 13. https://www.washingtontimes.com/news/2004/jan/13/20040113-085236-5919r/.

Botez, Cristian. 2011. "Cazul Berevoiești dupa 20 de ani." *Ziariști* Online, May 27. http://www.ziaristionline.ro/2011/05/27/cazul-berevoiesti-dupa-20-de-ani-dan-voinea-a-ingropat-documentele-securitatii-si-ale-sri-la-parchetul-militar-exclusiv-cristian-botez-ziarul-timpul/.

Callanan, James. 2010. *Covert Action in the Cold War: U.S. Policy, Intelligence and CIA Operations*. London: Tauris.

Churchill, Winston. 1946. "The Sinews of Peace." March 5. http://www.winstonchurchill.org/wp-content/uploads/1946/03/1946-03-05_BBC_Winston_Churchill_The_Sinews_Of_Peace.mp3.

Del Pero, Mario. 2003. "The Role of Covert Operations in U.S. Cold War Foreign Policy." In *Secret Intelligence in the Twentieth Century*, edited by Heike Bungert, Jan G. Heitmann, and Michael Wala, 66–80. London: Frank Cass.

Feinberg, Melissa. 2017. *Curtain of Lies*. Oxford: Oxford University Press.

Frow, John. 2006. *Genre: The New Critical Idiom*. New York: Routledge.

Gaddis, John Lewis. 2007. *The Cold War: A New History*. New York: Penguin Books.

Glajar, Valentina. 2016. "'You'll Never Make a Spy out of Me!'—The File Story of 'Fink Susanne.'" In *Secret Police Files from the Eastern Bloc: Between Surveillance and Life Writing*, edited by Valentina Glajar, Alison Lewis, and Corina L. Petrescu, 56–83. Rochester NY: Camden House.

Gieseke, Jens. 2000. *Die DDR-Staatssicherheit: Schild und Schwert der Partei*. Bonn: Bundeszentrale für Politische Bildung.

Heim, Wolfgang. 2017. "Peter Fischer: Ex-Spion über Stasi, Frauen und Abenteuer." *SWR1 Leute Night*, June 27. https://www.youtube.com/watch?v=fFaV4-TPXCw.

Hertle, Hans-Hermann, and Maria Nooke, eds. 2011. *The Victims at the Berlin Wall, 1961–1989*. Berlin: Links.

Horn, Eva. 2013. *The Secret War: Treason, Espionage, and Modern Fiction*. Evanston IL: Northwestern University Press.

Hossu-Longin, Lucia. 2009. *Față în față cu generalul Ion Mihai Pacepa*. Bucharest: Humanitas.

Jenkins, Philip. 1999. *The Cold War at Home: The Red Scare in Pennsylvania*. Chapel Hill: University of North Carolina Press.

[Kennan, George F.]. 1947. "The Source of Soviet Conduct." *Foreign Affairs* 25 (July): 566–82.

Kopp, Horst. 2016. *Der Desinformant*. Berlin: Das Neue Berlin.

Krieger, Wolfgang. 2014. *Geschichte der Geheimdienste*. Munich: C. H. Beck.

Laclau, Ernesto, and Chantal Mouffe. 2001. *Hegemony and Socialist Strategy: Towards a Radical Democratic Politics*. London: Verso.

Lewis, Alison. 2016. "Confessions and the Stasi Files in Post-Communist Germany: The Modest Scales of Memory and Justice in *Traitor to the Fatherland*." *Australian Humanities Review* 59 (April/May): 209–22.

Lucas, Edward. 2008. *The New Cold War: Putin's Russia and the Threat to the West*. London: Palgrave Macmillan.

Lucas, W. Scott. 1999. "Beyond Diplomacy: Propaganda and the History of the Cold War." In *Cold-War Propaganda in the 1950s*, edited by Gary D. Rawnsley, 11–30. London: Macmillan.

Major, Patrick. 2010. *Behind the Berlin Wall: East Germany and the Frontiers of Power*. Oxford: Oxford University Press.

Mandelbaum, Michael. 2016. *Mission Failure: America and the World in the Post-Cold War Era*. Oxford: Oxford University Press.

Medhurst, Martin J. 1997. Introduction to *Cold War Rhetoric: Strategy, Metaphor, and Ideology*, edited by Martin J. Medhurst, Robert J. Ivie, Philip Wander, and Robert L. Scott, xiii–xv. East Lansing: Michigan State University Press.

Oltermann, Philip. 2018. "Stasi Files: Scanner Struggles to Stitch Together Surveillance State Scraps." *Guardian*, January 3. https://www.theguardian.com/world/2018/jan/03/stasi-files-east-germany-archivists-losing-hope-solving-worlds-biggest-puzzle.

Oprea, Marius. 2008. *Bastionul cruzimii: O istorie a Securității (1948-1964)*. Iași: Polirom.

Pacepa, Ion Mihai. 1987. *Red Horizons: Chronicles of a Communist Spy Chief*. Washington DC: Regnery.

Parry-Giles, Shawn J. 2000. "Militarizing America's Propaganda Campaign." In *Critical Reflections on the Cold War: Linking Rhetoric and History*, edited by Martin J. Medhurst and H. W. Brands, 95-134. College Station: Texas A&M University Press.

Rawnsley, Gary D. 1999. Introduction to *Cold-War Propaganda in the 1950s*, edited by Gary D. Rawnsley, 1-10. London: Macmillan.

Reisman, W. Michael, and James E. Baker. 1992. *Regulating Covert Action: Practices, Contexts and Policies of Covert Action Abroad in International and American Law*. New Haven CT: Yale University Press.

Ricoeur, Paul. 1990. *Time and Narrative*. Vol. 1. Chicago: University of Chicago Press.

Risso, Linda. 2013. "Radio Wars: Broadcasting in the Cold War." *Cold War History* 13 (2) (May): 145-52.

———. 2014. *Propaganda and Intelligence in the Cold War*. London: Routledge.

Satjukow, Silke, and Rainer Gries. 2004. *Unsere Feinde: Konstruktionen des Anderen im Sozialismus*. Leipzig: Leipziger Universitäts-Verlag.

Stan, Lavinia, and Nadya Nedelsky, eds. 2013. *Encyclopedia of Transitional Justice*. Cambridge: Cambridge University Press.

Stiller, Werner, and Jefferson Adams. 1992. *Beyond the Wall: Memoirs of an East and West German Spy*. Washington DC: Brassey's.

Szwagrzyk, Krzysztof, ed. 2005. *Aparat Bezpieczenstwa w Polsce: Kadra kierownicza*. Vol. 1, *1944-1956*. Warsaw: Institute of National Remembrance. https://web.archive.org/web/20120104082816/http://www.ipn.gov.pl/ftp/pdf/Aparat_kadra_kier_tom%20I.pdf.

Taşkale, Ali Riza. 2016. *Post-Politics in Context*. New York: Routledge.

Tismăneanu, Vladimir, coordinator. 2016. *Raport final—Comisia Prezidențială pentru Analiza Dictaturii Comuniste din România*. Bucharest. https://www.wilsoncenter.org/sites/default/files/RAPORT%20FINAL_%20CADCR.pdf.

Valdés, Mario J., ed. 1991. *A Ricoeur Reader: Reflection and Imagination*. Translated by Kathleen McLaughlin and David Pellauer. Toronto: University of Toronto Press.

Walker, Shaun. 2016. "The Day We Discovered Our Parents Were Russian Spies." *Guardian*, May 7. https://www.theguardian.com/world/2016/may/07/discovered-our-parents-were-russian-spies-tim-alex-foley.

Walther, Joachim. 1996. *Sicherungsbereich Literatur: Schriftsteller und Staatssicherheit in der Deutschen Demokratischen Republik*. Berlin: Links.

Wettig, Gerhard. 2008. *Stalin and the Cold War in Europe: The Emergence and Development of East-West Conflict, 1939-1953*. New York: Rowman & Littlefield.

I.----

Intelligence Officers and Informers

1 The File Story of the Securitate Officer Samuel Feld

VALENTINA GLAJAR

On February 29, 1960, Major Samuel Feld, a Jewish-Romanian secret police officer, was discharged from MAI (Ministerul Afaceri-lor Interne [Ministry of Internal Affairs]) Region Stalin (Brașov).[1] The decision number 1426 to release him cites the Statute of the Officers' and Generals' Corps, Article 52, paragraph d. Up until his discharge, he had been the chief of the counterespionage and interrogation services. A closer look at his file explains this dismissal and the reasons behind the official citation as "grave transgressions" that are now partly redacted in his file.[2] His failure to denounce crimes, joining the Securitate under false pretexts, his disrespect for the workers' and peasants' classes, his Zionist ties, and his relatives abroad were among the main accusations that led to Feld's downfall. As was customary in such cases, Feld was also expelled from the Romanian Communist Party and had to return all the medals and honors he had received during his eleven-year career in the service of the Securitate. Finally, he also signed a statement that he would not divulge any professional secrets he had been privy to as an officer and interrogation expert of MAI Region Stalin.

Feld belonged to the first generation of Romanian secret service (Securitate) agents during the Stalinist years of the Cold War. The political changes in Romania at that time called for a restructuring of the intelligence organizations that would reflect the needs of the newly proclaimed People's Republic in 1947 and the demands of the Soviet military presence on its territory. Thus the Securitate had a particular type of spy in mind: young individuals (up to thirty years of age) with a "healthy" (nonbourgeois) social origin, who exhibited feelings of "devotion" to the Communist cause and "manifested love" and appreciation for the Soviet Union (Banu 2001, 89). These criteria are not surprising, as Soviet officers— also called counselors or advisers (*consilieri*)—closely supervised the selection and recruitment of this first generation of Securitate officers. These new agents came mainly from poor working-class families, and their education level was in many cases very low, at times just a handful of elementary classes.[3] As a result obedient and uneducated individuals from a politically "healthy" social background joined the secret service and were later promoted less on the value of their achievements but rather on the desired characteristics and aforementioned credentials on their résumés. As historian Florian Banu shows, the above qualifications proved an ill-fated combination that, coupled with frequent moves and a sense of careerism, led in many cases to extraconjugal affairs (in the lingo of the Securitate: "deviation from the proletarian moral") and chronic alcoholism (2001, 90). This, as Banu further explains, led in turn to the violence and brutality that would come to characterize Securitate officers of the Romanian Stalinist era. As I will show in this chapter, Samuel Feld's background fitted the required profile only to some extent, as his own Securitate files reveal.[4] While he could claim a healthy social background and an apparent devotion to the Communist Party, his education and superior intelligence, coupled with his Jewish origins, later proved to have fateful consequences for his career and, indeed, his life.

When read meticulously and against the grain, Feld's Securitate files reveal a multilayered story in the highly politicized context of Stalinist Romania. The reality of this story was shaped and re-created by various actors, not least by our protagonist, who tailored his biography in favorable ways to fit ideologies at certain times during his career. Denouncers or fellow Securitate officers contributed to this story and were instrumental in undoing our protagonist's version of events. The deictic presence of investigators exemplified through the red markings on the documents reveal a third dimension to the story, one that at times invoked their attitude toward the content or a general sense of urgency (see figs. 1.3–1.7). They all tell a story about Feld's opportunity to join the secret service, his rise to power, his false sense of invulnerability, pronounced hubris, and ultimately his retrospectively inevitable dismissal. His story, like other stories one can excavate from files, contains life segments, factual and skewed as viewed through the eyes of the secret police, which allow us rare insight into an officer's life—an officer who was both the subject and the object of surveillance and investigation. In John Frow's words, genres create the effects of reality and truth that are central to the different ways one understands the world in writing of history (2005, 19). Feld's story is neither entirely false nor true. It is simply a "file story" whose performative structure, as Frow reminds us, shapes the world and truth of an individual life. A "file story," as I define it, is a form of "remedial" life writing, one that unravels skewed life segments coded and recorded in secret police files and recovers them through a multilayered and polyphonic biographical act. In order to compose a file story, one needs to interpret not only the often-disjointed pieces afforded in a file (documents, informers' notes, officers' reports, denunciations, investigations, interrogations, phone tapping transcripts, etc.) but also the "omissions, distortions, and insinuations," as Igal Halfin points out in his study of red autobiographies and the Bolshevik self (2011, 44). Connecting the dots and fording the various gaps entails also interpreting parties' attitudes, veiled hostility, and purpose. The result is a precarious and capricious collage that represents a compelling life story, yet any overlooked or missing detail has the potential of disturbing or rearranging the life fragments of this volatile file story.[5] In the same vein, the central character of such a file story cannot necessarily be equated with the historical person but must rather be regarded as the protagonist abstracted from his files and the lead performer in our file story.[6]

Feld's records reveal a rather complicated file story, one that exposes, in part, the inner workings of the Securitate at its core, but also one that offers a slice of a Jewish-Romanian personal history that speaks of antisemitism, persecution, and ultimately false hopes, during a period the political scientist Vladimir Tis-maneanu calls "Stalinism unbound" (2003, 107–35). While the material comprised in his files reflects a fragmented, often embel-lished, other times conflicting account of his activity, the Securi-tate investigations into Feld's activity allow us rare insights into the life of a disgraced officer. Similar to the incriminating cases in strictly victim files, the case against Major Feld was based on informers' reports, characterizations by his colleagues, anony-mous denunciations, and interrogations that are only alluded to but most likely removed from or never included in this file. His cadre file story ends with an arrest, also absent from the files, and his discharge from MAI, in spite of several commendations and medals received for outstanding work in the service of MAI Timișoara and Orașul Stalin.[7] At the core of this investigation lies also a pronounced antisemitism that, on the one hand, motivated young Feld to join the Communist Party in 1945 and then the Secu-ritate in 1948 and, on the other, likely played a role in his eventual dismissal from the MAI and his exclusion from the party in 1960.[8]

His cadre file, like a captivating detective novel, begins with the denouement and invites the intrigued reader to discover how the case against this officer had been built and how the story unfolded. The protagonist comes to life through the eyes of others but also through his own self-fashioning narratives, the intervallic "auto-biographies" he had to compose for the purpose of record keep-ing. At times, depending on the political requirements of any given day, these bureaucratic "autobiographies" allowed new details to emerge, like short, precise brushstrokes refining a painter's self-portrait. If one understands autobiographical storytelling as "a rec-itation of a recitation" (Smith 1998, 111) and an autobiography as "a story of a story" (Eakin 1993, 120), then Feld was a master at tell-ing and retelling his life story. He polished his memories to reflect his background in the most favorable light and to highlight each accomplishment to his utmost advantage. He knew how to adapt to the various political requirements of the changing times, and like a chess player, he anticipated his investigators' moves, always ready to provide them with elaborate explanations for his activ-ities and often successfully outmaneuvering them. He created a self-censored, self-fashioned, and politically expedient personal history that allowed him to rise from wretched conditions and to remain in the elite service of the Securitate for eleven years.[9]

Feld, who would become the "victim" in this case, unlike average citizens who were often unaware that they had become targets of the Securitate, knew how to skillfully influence the unfolding of his own story, at least up to the point when it inescapably slipped out of his hands and followed his investigators' desired trajectory. Not only was our protagonist informed about the various accusations brought against him at certain points in his career; he was also allowed to react to them by manipulating the information and choreographing a new advantageous version of events that, as I will show, often barely corresponded to or predictably contradicted the already-staged reality. He deftly and cunningly exploited his own investigative skills and experience, which, at least in his opinion, were superior in competence and aptitude to those of his colleagues and certainly to those of the lower-ranked officers, whom he apparently treated with conceit and disdain.

Filed Autobiographical Sketches

From the various mandatory "autobiographies" and "biographical questionnaires" Feld drafted or filled out over the years for the Securitate, a compelling story unfolds—one he sometimes specifically altered by adding or leaving out various details pertaining to him or his family. From an autobiography drafted in 1948, we learn that he was born in Uzhhorod, then in the Soviet Union, on April 30, 1927, but moved with his family to the city of Timișoara in western Romania at a very early age.[10] About his parents, a mandatory topic in these autobiographies, we learn that his father, Jacob, had been deported to Buchenwald, and his mother, Ella, had been residing in a village in the then-newly founded state of Israel since 1946. Feld explained that he had attended the Israelite primary school in District 4 in Timișoara (interestingly, he wrote and crossed out the first three letters of Josefin, the original name of the neighborhood, and then added the new official name; D102, 86), where he did not have to pay school taxes and could also benefit from consistent warm meals.

He went on to enroll in the "Israelite Lycée," a reputable high school in Timişoara, and graduated the first four years in 1942. During the summer of the same year, he found employment with two well-to-do Jewish families, Csendes and Fischoff, where he performed odd jobs such as splitting wood or peeling vegetables.[11] In 1943, at the age of sixteen, he replaced his older brother Arthur, who along with other Jewish men between the ages of eighteen and forty-five, had been enlisted in so-called work teams that were in reality forced labor squads.[12] In spite of his age, Feld worked at the town's nursery in his brother's stead, while Arthur looked for black-market employment opportunities in order to support their family.[13] After having established his "healthy" social background, as he came from a very poor rather than a bourgeois capitalist family, Feld highlighted his brief yet substantial activity within the Communist Party organizations up to 1948. His résumé included joining Uniunea Tineretului Comunist (UTC, Union of the Communist Youth) in January 1944, organizing the Jewish youth at the Israelite Lycée, and joining the Communist Party in 1945. The same year he began his career with the secret police as commissar aid at the Siguranţa Timişoara.[14] In 1946, he joined the Information Bureau at the Communist Party Committee Timişoara. A year later, he was in charge of propaganda at the Tineretul Progresist (Progressive Youth), which was dissolved a few months later.[15] After passing the entrance examination at the law school in Cluj, he requested to be allowed to join the work force in order to save money for college.[16] He was thus allowed to transfer to the Federation of Cooperatives Banat, where his financial situation apparently worsened due to a lower-than-expected salary, and where he faced antisemitic remarks from the president himself, who allegedly stated that "a Jew had no place at Federală" (D102, 87). Evidently remaining determined to serve the Communist cause, the young Feld went on to organize the youth at the Federală within Uniunea Tineretului Muncitoresc (UTM, Union of the Working Youth), where he rose through the ranks all the way to the regional UTM committee.[17] His biography depicts a confusing and meandering path that reflects the rapid changes within and dissolutions of the Communist youth organizations but at times also his exuberant and vivacious view of the world. One sentence in particular strikes one as offbeat in this serious world of rapid life-altering transformations and allows us to see him as just a young man who saw girlfriends as a distraction from his important work in the service of the party: "I decided to abandon . . . a bourgeois girl who took too much of my time" (D102, 88). While it seems odd that he, the party enthusiast, could become entangled with a "bourgeois girl," he knew to sacrifice this relationship for the sake of the party.

In another rendition of his past, an autobiography dated April 11, 1951, further details about his life and activity emerge in a comprehensive account that comprises more than six typed pages. For the most part, it reiterates the political engagement in the Communist organizations but offers more details about Feld's family and a list of most likely mandatory references for each segment of his life and each work place. While in his 1948 biographical story he indicated that his father had been killed in Buchenwald, he rectified this by merely alluding to his death, as he simply indicated that his father had been deported and never returned. We further learn that his father had worked for many years as a day laborer, but since he had a beautiful singing voice, he joined a church choir. There is no mention of a temple or synagogue, although Feld never actively denied his Jewish origins. Furthermore, he related that his father had abandoned the family—his mother and his other siblings—when Feld was eight. The father then moved from Romania to Northern Transylvania, which after 1940 became part of Hungary, remarried, and was deported with his new family to a Nazi extermination camp.[18] Some details about the other members of Feld's family, including his mother, earned some red, blue, and pencil underlining, as they were apparently of interest to Feld's superiors who reviewed his autobiography: first, the fact that Feld, a Securitate officer, had been writing to his mother in Israel. Also significant to his future investigators was Feld's intention to marry a UTM member, whose background he intended to investigate prior to asking for the Securitate's approval (D102, 79). In a "Fişă individuală" (Individual chart, D102, 72–78) that Feld signed on May 28, 1952, we learn that he had married A.C. (D102, 76), the aforementioned UTM member, whose family strongly opposed the marriage. According to the information in this chart, A.C.'s family had in fact an undesirable social and political background that would prove to be consequential in Feld's investigation: they had been closely associated with the historical parties and owned various properties in Bucharest prior to August 23, 1944, when Romania joined the Allies and declared war on Nazi Germany.

In a biographical questionnaire (D102, 63–70) that Feld filled out and signed on November 16, 1955, new details surface, including his complete name, Samuel *Iacob* Feld. In addition to his baccalaureate obtained at the Israelite Lycée, he had also attended a Marxist-Leninist school at the University of Timişoara from 1949 to 1951. We learn that he actually wanted to become a doctor but due to his active role in the party, he abandoned the idea of higher education, which contradicts his earlier statement that he abandoned his law studies in Cluj due to financial difficulties. By November 1955 he had been promoted to the rank of captain and transferred to Region Stalin (D102, 63b). As his résumé details (see fig. 1.1; D102, 63b), Feld had enrolled in the Securitate as *sublocotenent* (second lieutenant), at the recommendation of officer Martin Schnellbach, on February 14, 1949.[19]

For the previous year, he had offered his services as "Informatorul nr. 2" (Informer number 2), of which several informative notes are included in his cadre file (D102, 263–68). By April 1951, he had been promoted twice already: to *locotenent* (first lieutenant) in February 1950, and the same year on August 23 to *locotenent-major* (senior lieutenant). We also learn that he was an athletic type, and he participated as a rower and a rowing trainer in the organization Regatta in Timişoara from 1946 to 1947, which coincides with the time he worked as *lucrător de informaţii* (information worker) at the Information Bureau of the regional Communist Party committee. He was fluent or conversant in several foreign languages: Hungarian, his native tongue, German, French, Italian, and Hebrew.

The last autobiography in Feld's cadre file is dated September 3, 1958, around the time that the second investigation into his past and career was initiated, and comprises thirteen handwritten pages (D102, 92–105). Among the new details regarding his

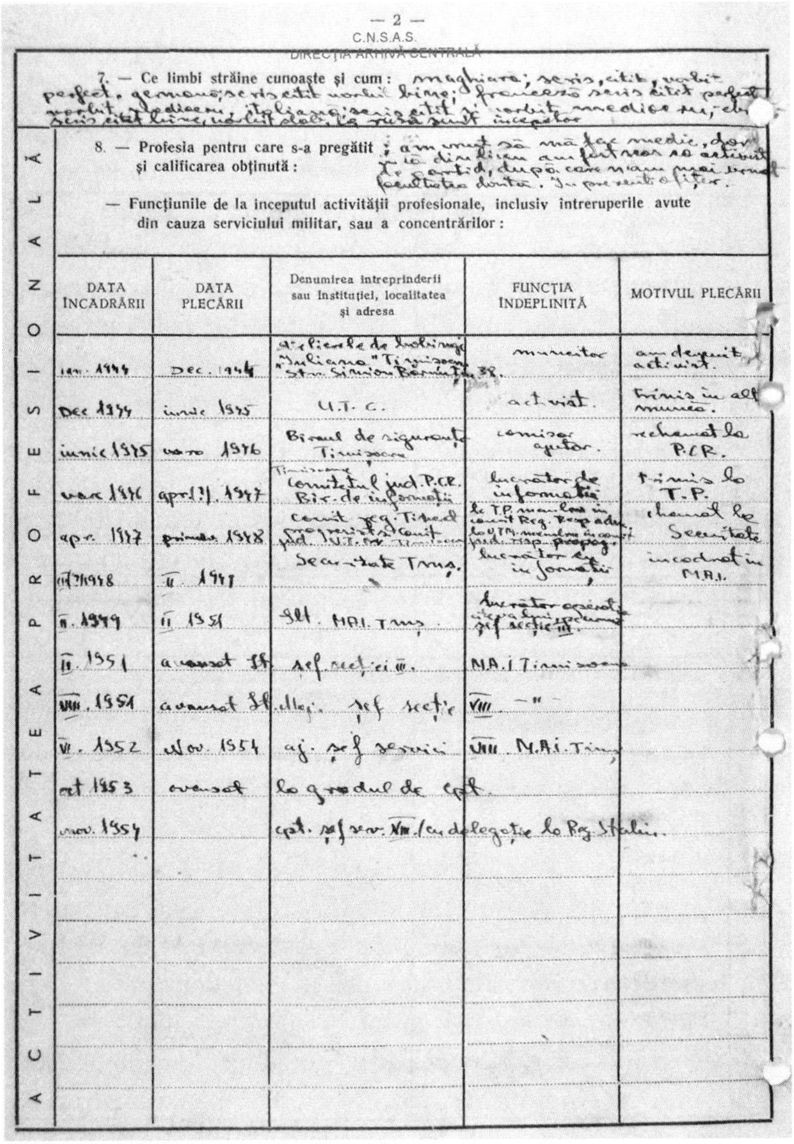

— 2 —

C.N.S.A.S.
DIRECŢIA ARHIVĂ CENTRALĂ

7. — Ce limbi străine cunoaşte şi cum: maghiara; scris, citit, vorbit perfect. germana; scris citit vorbit bine; franceza scris citit perfect vorbit mediocru. italiana; scris citit şi vorbit mediocru; ebraica scris citit bine, vorbit slab, la rusă sunt începător

ACTIVITATEA PROFESIONALĂ

8. — Profesia pentru care s-a pregătit şi calificarea obţinută: am vrut să mă fac medic, dar ... după care nu am mai urmat facultatea ... În prezent ofiţer.

— Funcţiunile de la inceputul activităţii profesionale, inclusiv întreruperile avute din cauza serviciului militar, sau a concentrărilor:

DATA ÎNCADRĂRII	DATA PLECĂRII	Denumirea intreprinderii sau Instituţiei, localitatea şi adresa	FUNCŢIA ÎNDEPLINITĂ	MOTIVUL PLECĂRII
ian. 1944	Dec. 1944	Atelierele de ... "Iuliana" Timişoara Str. Simion Bărnuţiu 38	muncitor	am devenit activist.
Dec 1944	iunie 1945	U.T.C.	activist.	trimis în altă muncă.
iunie 1945	vara 1946	Biroul de siguranţă Timişoara	comisar ajutor.	rechemat la P.C.R.
vara 1946	apr. [?] 1947	Timişoara Comitetul jud. P.C.R. Bir. de informaţii	lucrător de informaţii	trimis la T.P.
apr. 1947	primăvara 1948	comit. reg. Timiş ...	la T.P. ... lucrător ...	chemat la Securitate
... 1948	II. 1949	Securitate Tmş.	lucrător de informaţii	încadrat în M.A.I.
II. 1949	II 1951	Sft. MAI. Tmş.	lucrător operativ ... şef secţie III.	
II. 1951	avansat Slt.	şef secţiei III.	M.A.I. Timişoara	
VIII. 1951	avansat Slt. Maj.	şef secţie	VIII. —"	
VI. 1952	Nov. 1954	aj. şef serviciu	VIII. M.A.I. Tim.	
oct 1953	avansat	la gradul de cpt.		
nov. 1954		cpt. şef serv. XIII. (cu delegaţie la Reg. Stalin.		

FIG. 1.1. Feld's professional activity résumé from 1944 to 1954 (CNSAS, Bucharest, Romania, D102, 63b).

marital status, Feld also addressed the recurring lines of inquiry into the whereabouts of his father and his correspondence with his family residing in "unfriendly" (non-Communist) countries like Israel. He carefully crafted an explanation to distance himself from his Jewish family. About his father he specified for the first time that he was brutal and unfaithful to his mother, which led to the parents' divorce in 1936. Feld cautiously stuck with the vague formulation of "he never returned" from the extermination camps, rather than that he died there, which later proved to be untrue and, according to the red markings, did not escape his investigators. Feld attempted to fend off any suspicions regarding his ongoing correspondence with his mother, an Israeli citizen. He vehemently denied it and indicated that he did not even know her address but would inquire about it and provide it at a later time. His brother Arthur, who was also residing in Israel, appears as an undesired afterthought. As Feld claimed, he had cut any ties with his brother after he had deserted one of the aforementioned "work teams" and fled to British Palestine in 1944.

In this same last biographical sketch, Feld addressed accusations pertaining to his relationship with Zionist organizations dating back to 1939 and with other "imperialist" organizations from 1947 to 1949. Simple math would solve his predicament. As Feld reminded his superiors and investigators, he could not have been a Zionist at the age of twelve. While various Zionist organizations were present and active among the Jewish community, he spent time with these organizations as a child to benefit from free meals and clothes. Regarding the second accusation about his relationship with Western ("imperialist") organizations, he cleverly veered the conversation toward his accomplishments as Securitate "informer number 2": "I succeeded within several months to bring valuable informative materials [intelligence] from the English Library, from 'America's Friends,' from the 'inst. [institute] of Italian culture' and from the Zionist organizations of Timişoara. The materials had been exploited in [the Securitate's] activity" (D102, 100).[20] Therefore, he had to visit the various places and get in touch with members of these organizations in order to provide the "valuable" intelligence he acquired from them (see fig. 1.2).[21]

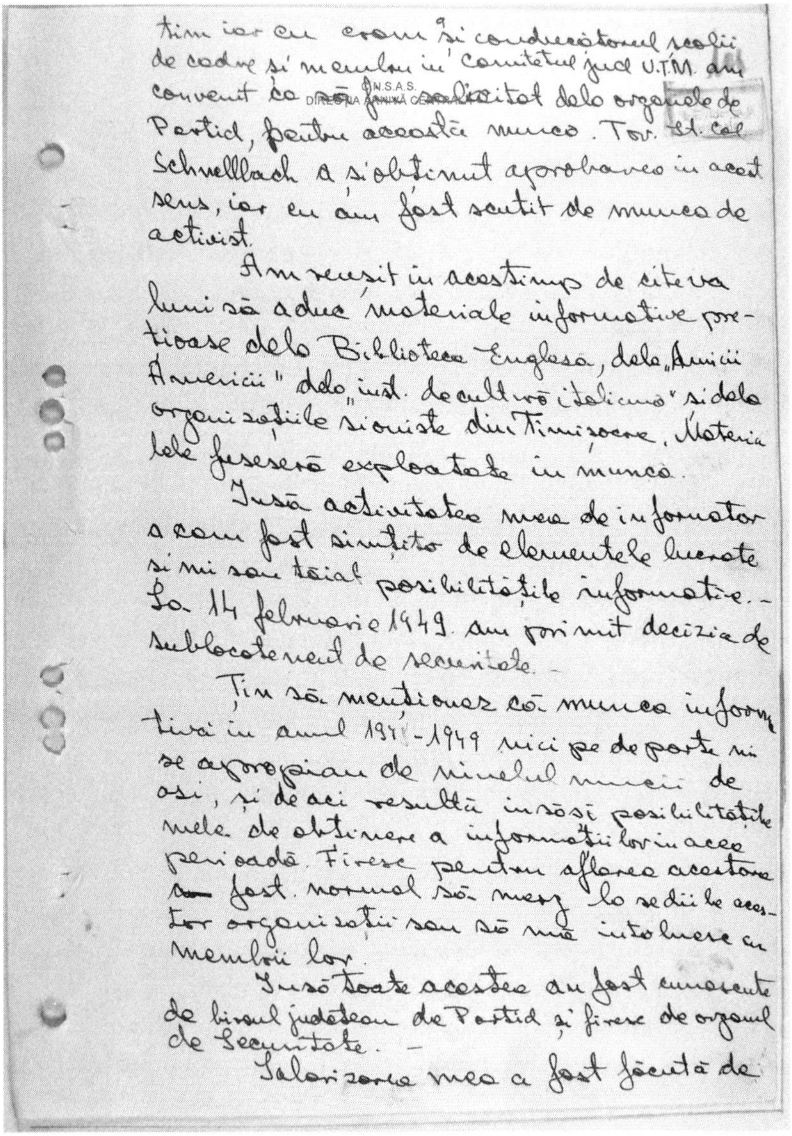
tim iar eu eram și conducătorul școlii
de cadre și membru în Comitetul jud. U.T.M. am
convenit ca să fiu solicitat dela organele de
Partid, pentru această muncă. Tov. Lt. Col.
Schnellbach a și obținut aprobarea în acest
sens, iar eu am fost scutit de munca de
activist.
Am reușit în acest timp de câteva
luni să aduc materiale informative pre-
țioase dela Biblioteca Engleză, dela „Amicii
Americii" dela „Inst. de cultură italiano" și dela
organizațiile sioniste din Timișoara. Materia-
lele fuseseră exploatate în muncă.
Însă activitatea mea de informator
a cam fost simțită de elementele lucrate
și mi s-au tăiat posibilitățile informative. –
La 14 februarie 1949. am primit decizia de
sublocotenent de securitate. –
Țin să menționez că munca informativă în anul 1948-1949 nici pe departe nu
se apropiau de nivelul muncii de
azi, și de aci rezultă însăși posibilitățile
mele de obținere a informațiilor în acea
perioadă. Firesc pentru aflarea acestora
a fost normal să merg la sediile aces-
tor organizații sau să mă întâlnesc cu
membrii lor.
Însă toate acestea au fost cunoscute
de biroul județean de Partid și firesc de organul
de Securitate. –
Salarizarea mea a fost făcută de

FIG. 1.2. Feld's statement about his accomplishments as "informer number 2" in his own handwriting (CNSAS, Bucharest, Romania, D102, 101).

In more detail Feld highlighted his aversion to the former bourgeois system and the way he was exploited from an early age. As with the explanation for his involvement in the Zionist movement above, Feld returned to his childhood and youth to dispel accusations about his bourgeois lifestyle—a time, when his profile still mostly fitted the desired social and ideological background of a Securitate officer. As such, his story appears as a carbon copy of that of numerous Romanian Jews who were lured into the party by what Liviu Rotman has called "the siren's song" (2003, 8). While at times Feld's narrative seems forced and sounds disingenuous, his recollections of his poverty-stricken childhood in a profoundly antisemitic society further cemented and legitimized by racial laws sound genuine and heartfelt.[22] He was fifteen in 1942, when he began to work from 6:00 a.m. to 2:00 p.m. while also attending school in the afternoons from 3:00 p.m. to 10:00 p.m.[23] His experiences working for the aforementioned rich Jewish families or at the spool factory Iuliana, where he was paid less because as a Jew he could not be employed with proper paperwork, evolved into "hatred for the regime of bourgeois and landowners that was hitting [him] with full force" (D102, 97).

In this last autobiographical rendition of his life, Feld spares no details in his attempt to construct a persuasive portrayal of a zealous Communist by reminding his investigators of his very poor beginnings and the antisemitic persecution he had faced. As expected Feld associates the new Communist regime with equality and prosperity for the working class. However, by the time he wrote this last autobiography in 1958, Feld's situation had changed considerably, as he then belonged to the elite and powerful organization of Securitate officers rather than to the poor working class he evoked in his autobiography. Yet his storytelling proved to be a futile exercise in the eyes of his investigators, whose particular accusations Feld could not counter by simply invoking his early credentials, no matter how persuasive his plea.

The First Investigation, 1952–54

On May 14, 1952, Lieutenant Sabin Roman wrote a report on an order he had received to investigate two specific issues relating to then-Senior Lieutenant Feld: whether he was corresponding with his relatives living in Israel, which he determined was unfounded; and how he was related to H. Feld (D102, 53–54). H. and his wife P. Feld, relatives on his father's side, had been shot while attempting to cross the border into Hungary illegally on March 22, 1948.[24] Not only did Feld have to explain his relationship with the couple, given their common surname, but also a photograph found on the body of H. Feld. The photograph, signed "Samuel," included a brief message in Hungarian and was dated March 21, just one day before the couple was shot by the border guards (D102, 38). There is no document in this file that shows what prompted this inquiry, and the name of the lieutenant who had requested this investigation is not mentioned either. Lieutenant Roman gathered his information from a Dr. Kleici and from other neighbors of H. and P. Feld. This Dr. Kleici reported that the Feld couple had moved to Timişoara with little more than a few belongings but were able to furnish their apartment and even purchase jewelry and other expensive objects shortly after their move. The same source related that H. Feld was involved in black-market schemes and as such had crossed the border into Hungary on a regular basis between 1945 and 1947. Dr. Kleici also knew to report that the couple had applied for emigration but grew impatient and decided to cross the border illegally. Dr. Kleici was not aware of any relatives the couple might have had in Timişoara. From conversations with Captain Martin Schnellbach and Senior Lieutenant Iosif Stepunyak, who were both involved in the investigation of the couple's death, Roman also learned that H. was indeed a paternal relative of Samuel Feld but could not specify whether H. was his father's brother or cousin (D102, 53).

However, H.'s tragic fate could not be buried easily, and it resurfaced in the form of an anonymous incriminating note from December 2, 1953, along with the following other grave accusations against Feld and his family (D102, 137–37b). According to the information included in this note, the source seemed to have been well acquainted with the Feld siblings and the deceased Feld couple. In broken Romanian the source divulged that the entire family believed the new regime to be worse than the one before, even worse than the Antonescu years. Apparently, the Felds were pro-American and would not be afraid if the Americans were to arrive as liberators—a decades-long dream for many Romanians. First, they believed that Samuel Feld's in-laws (A.C.'s bourgeois parents) would save them, and second, Feld was careful not to cause any harm as a Securitate officer in anticipation of the Americans' arrival. He would rather keep this job because of the good salary and in order to help other Jews. In regard to H. Feld, the source related that he or she had seen Samuel Feld numerous times at his uncle's residence, including just a few days before the couple was shot on the border. According to this source, Feld was sad about their deaths but was more preoccupied with seizing the valuables that had been found on the corpses of the deceased Feld couple. To further demonstrate the dishonesty and subversive attitude of the Feld family, the source disclosed that the Feld siblings were indeed in touch with their relatives in Israel but corresponded clandestinely through others.

It is not surprising that this condemnatory note earned blue underlining and red marks from Feld's investigators, as it had ample incriminating information that at the very least threatened to end Feld's career if proven accurate. Yet, Feld was given the opportunity to respond to these grave accusations, and he crafted a statement explaining, justifying, and rationalizing facts, events, and actions on January 8, 1954, roughly a month after the aforementioned note had been registered. Feld was asked first to clarify the nature and extent of his relationship with H. Feld and the recurring question about his knowledge of H.'s plan to leave Romania illegally. In his response Feld appears to be unaware of the denunciatory note's exact content because his answers were so improbable in light of the details the source had divulged that they raised several red flags, based on the underlining and marks on his statement. He described, for example, H. Feld as a casual acquaintance and in terms so general and vague that they could have passed as believable had the denunciatory note not existed. As things in fact were, the two versions of the events stood in too sharp a contrast to allow for any shred of credibility on Feld's side. He wrote simply, "Feld H. was a distant relative on my father's side. He was something of a cousin of my father's" (see fig 1.2; D102, 89). However, the more he tried to distance himself from his uncle, the more suspicious his statements appeared to his investigators, even more so when he described how he had met his uncle: "I met him (F.H.) by chance after August 23, [19]44 in the street, I believe. We couldn't have any intimate conversation because it made no sense" (D102, 89). What struck the investigators was the farfetched scenario Feld created to introduce his uncle, according to their markings and question marks in the margins, but they did not have any issue with his vague and baffling statement that a conversation with his long-lost uncle "made no sense." Feld did, however, admit that he might have met him accidentally a few more times when they allegedly engaged in trivial small talk. Feld went so far as to claim that he was ashamed they bore the same name since he was a party activist and his uncle was known as "Feld, the racketeer with a mustache" (D102, 89). After having set the stage, Feld addressed the grim incident of H.'s death in the same vague, matter-of-fact, and indifferent style. He claimed that he could not remember exactly when—perhaps "in the beginning of 1948" (D102, 89b)—he had learned from an announcement in the newspaper or maybe from Captain Schnellbach that H. Feld had been killed while crossing the border. He stopped short of saying that his uncle deserved it, when he stated that he was not surprised at the news of his uncle's death because at that time Jewish racketeers in particular were trying to leave the country daily. Regarding whether he knew about the planned escape, he denied it categorically: the logical conclusion he must have hoped his investigators would reach by accepting his version of events as described in his cleverly drafted statement. The following paragraph functions as the climax of his carefully crafted denial, and unsurprisingly it earned the most vigorous underlining: "Categorically, had I known about these intentions, that he wanted to leave, definitely, without any hesitation, I would have arrested him or informed comrade Colonel Mois or comrade Cpt. Schnellbach, who were my superiors" (D102, 89b). It is not clear whether the investigative markings on this particular statement were made during the first investigation in 1954 or the second one in 1958 to 1960, when H.'s story resurfaced. Yet two different readers marked this statement; one used a regular pencil and the other, more vigorously, a red-colored one, both indicating their respective reactions to Feld's statement. One could assume that the insistent red marks oozed disbelief at Feld's audacious lies.

This statement, which eventually proved to be untrue, as attested to by the documents pertaining to Feld's dismissal and confirmed by Feld in correspondence with the author, attracted attention that, at the very least, led to the investigators' request for more information.[25] They wanted to know specifics about how Feld carried out the investigation of this tragic event at the behest of his superior, officer Schnellbach. Schnellbach's order to involve Feld in the investigation of his own uncle's death seems puzzling and raises additional questions that seem to point to Feld's voluntary request to join the operation. Whether in order to influence the outcome or to cover up any traces leading to his own involvement or prior knowledge of the uncle's intentions to leave, Feld took charge of the case and was able to find the alleged facilitator and to coerce him into admitting his involvement: "[While] investigated, the individual (I believe Punici) [correction added: Putici] denied everything at first, but after much insistence, he recognized that he was the facilitator, identifying the guide with imprecision, [but revealing] some helping facts" (D102, 91). In spite of Feld's zealous dedication to this investigation, he must not have been aware of his photo found on the victim, nor was he asked to explain its existence in his statement of January 1954.

Yet, during this investigation of then-Captain Feld, he apparently did admit in the end that he knew about his uncle's intentions to cross the border fraudulently. The file does not include any transcripts of any interrogations that might have shed more light on the outcome of the investigation. In one of the final documents summarizing his activity and the accusations against Feld, his involvement is elucidated: "Since 1945, the month of August, he had been a collaborator of Bureau 2 of the Siguranţa Inspectorate Timişoara; during which period we cannot say that he carried out the tasks he had been entrusted with, as he did not pass on to the bodies of the Siguranţa information that his uncle

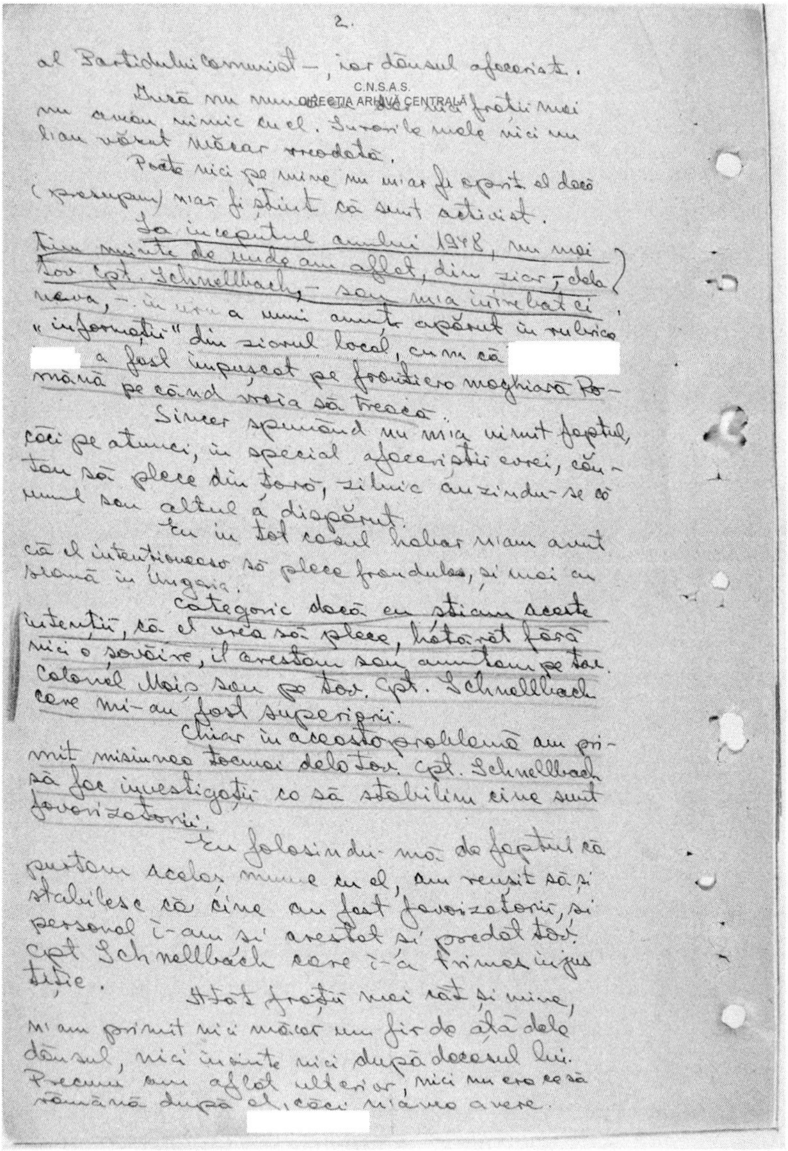

FIG. 1.3. Feld's statement about denouncing his uncle (CNSAS, Bucharest, Romania, D102, 89b).

FELD H. was intending to cross the border fraudulently, [though] the officer [Feld] knew about it, and when he was asked why he did not denounce his uncle, he replied that he did not denounce [him] for sentimental reasons" (D102, 18). Despite Feld's previous statements, in which he tried desperately to portray his uncle as some acquaintance or distant relative he had accidentally met on the streets of Timişoara, he must have eventually recanted and admitted his lies, though it is not clear from the file when and how that took place.

A closer look at Feld's activity in Timişoara raises questions about his Jewishness and his bourgeois inclinations, as first exemplified in his marriage to A.C. From the various officers' reports, we learn that he was vigilant and efficient in his work as an informer and later as an officer. A party member since 1945, Feld had been responsible for Communist agitation and propaganda, recruiting new members, and organizing them at various levels ranging from local to regional. Regarded as a devoted Communist, the young Feld seemed to have had a clear agenda in terms of capturing enemies of the working class and thus of the people. He targeted especially those who participated in or were supporters of the previous regime, which promoted racial laws and officially endorsed antisemitism and the persecution of Jews in Romania. It comes as no surprise that "legionnaires," members or supporters of the fascist-nationalist Romanian organization Iron Guard, ranked high on his list of enemies who had to be brought to justice. His superior officers had only words of praise in this respect: "He participated in tracking down the enemies of the working class and in capturing a subversive legionnaire organization, where he had good results, as he succeeded in capturing the head [leader] of that organization. In these operations he showed initiative and determination in his work" (D102, 19). Furthermore, the names of the captured enemies are showcased like trophies in his cadre file: "He took part in the operation of capturing the bandit CRETU and the war criminal LAZARUICA IOAN, as well as the fugitive bandit Dr. VUC LIVIU" (D102, 19).[26]

One can find manifold justifications and explanations for his ardor and dedication in pursuing these operations against those he found responsible for his own difficult childhood and the circumstances that led to family members perishing in Nazi concentration camps.[27] Yet surprisingly, according to the information in his cadre file, Feld also turned against Zionist organizations, which presents an obvious contradiction. One may surmise that his strong Communist convictions or brainwashing let him equate Zionists with "nationalist extremists" or even "fascists," as the regime in power did.[28] His superiors highlighted the following as one of Feld's most important accomplishments at the beginning of his career: "Even though he was young, he coped well with the difficult tasks he was entrusted with by the comrades he was working with, he offered precious assistance in uncovering both legal and subversive Zionist organizations, his best results, as he was able to obtain the organizations' structure and the lists of names from the entire Zionist organization of the Region Timișoara; in the surveillance work he succeeded in organizing a good network of informers in various target areas" (D102, 20). Whether exposing and sacrificing Zionists was the loyalty test he had to pass in order to be considered worthy of the Securitate's trust is not clear from the documents in the file.[29] Feld used his involvement in these operations to prove that he had never been a Zionist, and in the process, he seems to have rejected what was most dear to his family and his relatives, who were all members of the Zionist organization Ichud: his mother and his brother Arthur, who had escaped to British Palestine, and several other relatives. H. and P. Feld were also carrying Ichud and America's Friends membership cards during their ill-fated attempt to cross the border into Hungary.[30]

More contradictions arise when considering the political background of Feld's first wife that question his devotion to party ideals and his prior activity of hunting down legionnaires and other enemies of the working class. In fact in the final paragraph of the decision to dismiss Feld in 1954, the officers referred precisely to Feld's wife: "He still made the wrong choice in marriage, although he knew that his wife came from an unfit family and that she had a series of relatives who in the past had important posts in the bourgeois regime . . . , and that one of his wife's uncles hosted the legionnaire leader HORIA SIMA at his residence" (D102,

21).[31] Aside from the ironic detail that Lieutenant Colonel Aurel Moiş, the signatory and Securitate chief of the Region Timişoara, had been at Feld's wedding and played the role of godfather—a rough Romanian approximation of a best man—this last paragraph raises questions about Feld's aforementioned bourgeois aversion but also about the very core of his apparent conviction to bring legionnaires and other persecutors to justice. While his wife was evidently not responsible for her family's actions, Feld was responsible for investigating her background, and his superiors for giving their final approval for his marriage. During the time of this investigation, Feld divorced his first wife for personal and professional reasons.

What had begun as a vicious denunciation by an anonymous yet seemingly informed source led to this full-blown investigation and an initial decision to discharge him as an unfit MAI officer. Yet for reasons undocumented in the file, the decision was overturned. More importantly, the fact that the anonymous denunciation turned out to be true raises questions about Feld's dedication to the secret service, whether to the Siguranţa at the beginning or the Stalinist Securitate for the rest of his career. His motives for joining and pursuing a job at the Securitate seem to indicate a sense of careerism rather than loyalty and conviction. The answers these questions beg might lie behind the source's impetus to denounce Feld and his siblings and Feld's desperate struggle to defend his career, shield his family, and secure his freedom. While this first dismissal could have been his chance to escape this organization that was growing increasingly antisemitic, he was offered and accepted a transfer to Oraşul Stalin and a promotion to the rank of captain in the fall of 1954.[32]

The Second Investigation, 1958–60

The second and final investigation led to Feld's irrevocable dismissal in 1960. It rehashed several points from the 1954 one, especially his Zionist relatives, the Feld couple shot while attempting to cross the border, and certainly the bourgeois background of his first wife, which spoke to his own bourgeois mentality. However, in a report from Securitate Timişoara, a new detail about his father's situation and whereabouts surfaced for the first and only time in the file, which apparently presented new challenges for Feld as it contradicted his previous statements about his father either being dead or never having returned to Romania: "In 1945–1946 he [the father] came to Timişoara to visit his family, and because his wife didn't want to receive him, he visited his children, of which some were married. He lived for about a month with his daughter S. [Feld's sister], married G., and left Timişoara again afterward, but it is unknown where he has settled" (my redactions; D102, 33). As many reports seem to be absent from the file, the one the officer from Timişoara alluded to is missing as well. However, the story line drafted and insisted on by Feld in his earlier biographical reports must have been proven false at some point of the investigation. While his father had indeed been deported to Auschwitz from Northern Transylvania along with his wife and two young children, he had managed to survive while his new family perished. The same report claims that his father went to England after liberation from the extermination camps.

Apart from the various misleading facts about his background and his family and relatives, and in spite of the Timişoara investigation, Feld continued to be negligent and careless in several situations. The most reckless and far-reaching one, which in fact initiated a request for a complete verification of Major Feld on June 9, 1958, was his comment pertaining to the Soviet counselor, Colonel Mihailov, who was returning home. On May 3, 1958, on his way from Timişoara to Bucharest, Mihailov stopped in Oraşul Stalin to say farewell to the chief officers he knew there. Feld apparently searched the car (a Soviet "Pobeda") and engaged in conversation with the counselor's chauffeur inquiring about the rest of the luggage, insinuating that he must have already shipped the things acquired in Romania to the Soviet Union. The chauffeur evidently reported the conversation to the Soviet counselor, who complained about it at the Cadre Directorate in Bucharest. Sergeant Marin Alecu, the chauffeur, reproduced the following dialogue, which he framed as a swipe at Mihailov's integrity: "'Hey, you, is this all the luggage he has? Has he sent the rest by train?' saying these words with irony and an implied meaning. I would like to point out that I replied the following to this affirmation: He doesn't have any other luggage than the one in the car, to which he replied ironically: '. . . As if you'd know what he has done?'" (D102, 212). Lieutenant Victor Crețu of Timișoara also confirmed the veracity of Alecu's statement, declaring that Alecu had described the incident to him in similar terms: "'What, as if this is the only luggage? . . . Has he sent the rest clandestinely?' . . . Here he referred to the personal luggage of comrade Counselor Mihailov" (see fig. 1.4; D102, 213).

Feld was allowed to offer his perspective in a statement, which constitutes another rhetorical exercise through which he attempted to exonerate himself by reinterpreting and casting the existing facts in a favorable light. Thus, on September 3, 1958, he gave the story a "scientific" twist, alluding to a Marxist scientific interpretation of the event that seemed to have puzzled his investigators as well. "Astonished because I had seen the empty car, I asked him [Alecu] about the comrade Counselor's family and maybe even about the luggage (because naturally when somebody is moving one also says, 'He takes his luggage and his family'—), to which the comrade [Alecu] replied that he is leaving by himself, I don't know what he was saying about the family. 'As you can see'—perhaps" (see fig. 1.4; D102, 240).

As Feld was asked to report to the Securitate Headquarters in Bucharest, where he also wrote this statement, he could not have had enough time to think everything through. Yet intelligently he moved the main focus from the luggage, which would have indeed implied that Mihailov had clandestinely sent goods acquired during his five-year stay in Romania, to his family, who was not accompanying him. To sound more convincing, Feld highlighted his admiration for Mihailov, who apparently had taught Feld a lot in terms of his Securitate work and whose departure he pretended to regret: "Therefore, I consider that giving my natural and comradely questions an interpretation 'with hidden connotations'—'an ironic look' etc., is a purely personal and subjective affirmation, which had nothing to do with my thoughts" (D102, 241). The quotes from other accusatory reports, especially "with hidden connotations" and "ironic look," are not accidental.

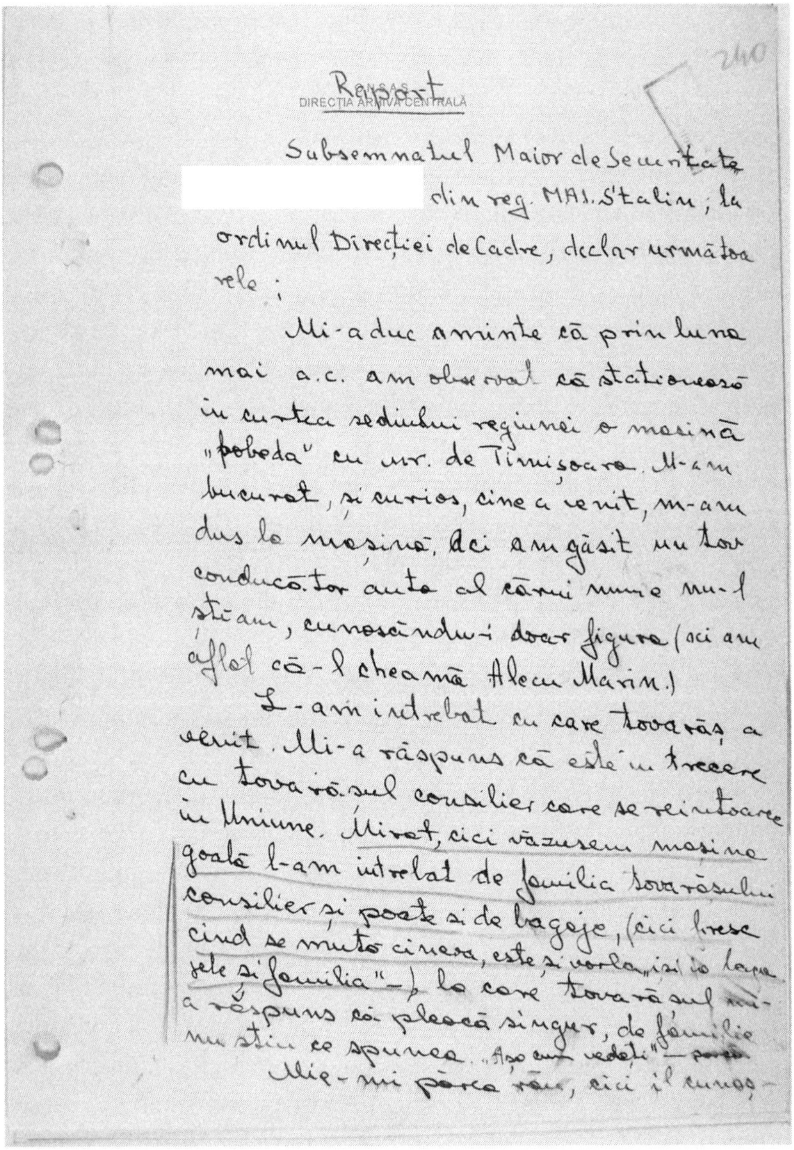

Subsemnatul Maior de Securitate ████████████████ din reg. MAI. Stalin; la ordinul Direcției de Cadre, declar următoarele:

Mi-aduc aminte că prin luna mai a.c. am observat că staționează în curtea sediului regiunei o mașină "pobeda" cu nr. de Timișoara. M-am bucurat, și curios, cine a venit, m-am dus la mașină. Aci am găsit un tov. conducător auto al cărui nume nu-l știam, cunoscându-i doar figura (aci am aflat că-l cheamă Alecu Marin.)

L-am întrebat cu care tovarăș a venit. Mi-a răspuns că este în trecere cu tovarășul consilier care se reîntoarce în Uniune. Mirat, căci văzurem mașina goală l-am întrebat de familia tovarășului consilier și poate și de bagaje, (căci trebuie cînd se mută cineva, este și vorba, "își ia cu el și familia"-) la care tovarăș ul mi-a răspuns că pleacă singur, de familie nu știu ce spunea. "Așa am vedeți" —

Mie-mi părea rău, căci îl cunoș-

FIG. 1.4. Excerpt from Feld's handwritten statement about the Mihailov incident with green and red markings (CNSAS, Bucharest, Romania, D102, 240).

They demonstrate that Feld either had access to the actual statements or was precisely informed about their content. Feld's last attempt to exonerate himself seems less logical and earned a red question mark from one of the investigators.

"Allow me to report that my personal opinion [Feld's underlining] is that one has sought to misconstrue and to give my questions an absolutely unscientific meaning with negative connotations and thus turned them against me" (D102, 241). As "scientific" was the buzzword of the Romanian Stalinist era, and Feld had graduated from the "Marxist-Leninist university," he tried to impress his investigators with his "scientific" approach, which turned the tables on his accuser, Sergeant Alecu. As in other instances when he had to explain difficult situations he had created for himself, he reinterpreted facts by dissecting and spinning the information he had received from his investigators (see fig. 1.5).

Unlike in Timişoara, where Martin Schnellbach and Aurel Moiş vouched for Feld's exemplary activity in the service of the Securitate, in Oraşul Stalin he apparently made few friends, if any, among his superiors and barely any among his subordinates at the Securitate. This speaks especially to the character traits pointed out by every character reference in his file, ranging from his early years at UTC in Timişoara to his years in Oraşul Stalin: adjectives like "conceited" and "self-important" and everything in between seemed to spring readily to his referees' minds when asked to evaluate Feld's character. He apparently had explained to his peers (or subordinates) that they needed to have obtained at least a baccalaureate degree in order to carry out a successful investigation. Indeed, many of his peers did not have a high school diploma because a "healthy" social background was essential and oftentimes sufficient for new hires in the early years of the Securitate. Feld's haughty attitude and his disparaging remarks irritated many peers and subordinates, who undoubtedly resented and dreaded Feld's intellect and education. They saw their chance to avenge these humiliations during the investigation of Feld's activity in Oraşul Stalin.

During this investigation the anonymous denunciation that almost brought Feld down in 1954 continued to be an important

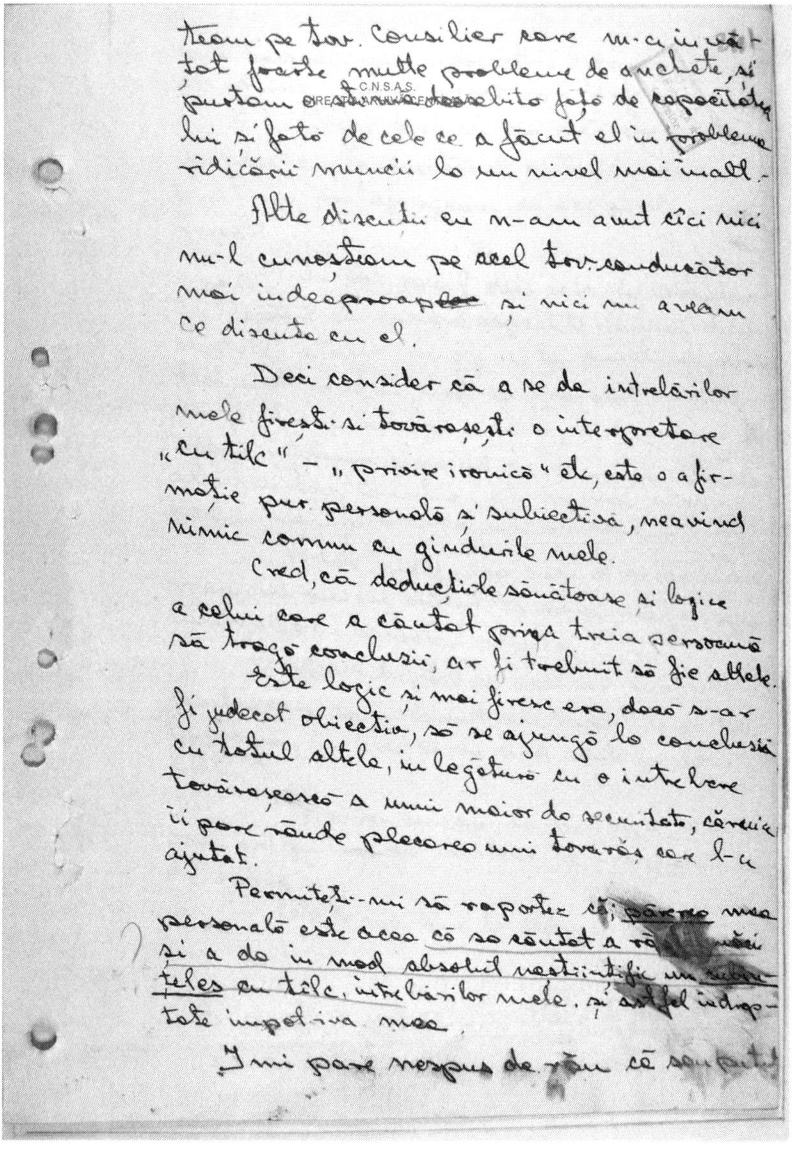
teau pe tov. Consilier care m-a învăţat
tot foarte multe probleme de anchete, şi
purtam o stimă deosebită faţă de capacităţile
lui şi faţă de cele ce a făcut el în problema
ridicării muncii la un nivel mai înalt.

Alte discuţii cu n-am avut căci nici
nu-l cunoşteam pe acel tov. conducător
mai îndeaproape şi nici nu aveam
ce discuta cu el.

Deci consider că a se da întrebărilor
mele fireşti şi tovărăşeşti o interpretare
„cu tâlc" – „privire ironică" etc, este o afir-
maţie pur personală şi subiectivă, neavînd
nimic comun cu gîndurile mele.

Cred, că deducţiile sănătoase şi logice
a celui care a căutat prin a treia persoană
să tragă concluzii, ar fi trebuit să fie altele.

Este logic şi mai firesc era, dacă s-ar
fi judecat obiectiv, să se ajungă la concluzii
cu totul altele, în legătură cu o întrebare
tovărăşească a unui maior de securitate, căruia
îi pare rău de plecarea unui tovarăş care l-a
ajutat.

Permiteţi-mi să raportez că; părerea mea
personală este aceea că s-a căutat a ră[illegible]ci
şi a da în mod absolut neştiinţific un subîn-
ţeles cu tâlc, întrebărilor mele, şi astfel îndrep-
tate împotriva mea.

Îmi pare nespus de rău că s-a căutat

FIG. 1.5. Feld accusing his accusers (CNSAS, Bucharest, Romania, D102, 241).

link in the web of lies and deceit that was slowly closing its grip around Feld, foreshadowing the end of his MAI career. Already then the denouncer had related that the Feld siblings were hoping for a regime change facilitated by the arrival of the Americans and acting accordingly during the interim. This theme of anticipating a regime change reemerged in 1958, as Alexandru Suciu, one of Feld's subordinates in Oraşul Stalin, reported to his superiors about a discussion that had taken place in Feld's office, during which Feld had asked him: "Do you think that you will still be an engineer if the regime changed?" (D102, 214). Apparently, this was the second time in about a week that Feld had talked to Suciu about a regime change. Though Feld's statement was reckless enough to attract Suciu's attention, Suciu did not report it for weeks on the advice of another fellow officer "because when comrade Feld would be asked, him being a very intelligent person, he would know how to explain things so that he would come out on top" (D102, 220). In fact, Feld attempted to do just that and explained the context of the question by chastising his accuser and also infuriating his superiors. Suciu, according to Feld, had neglected his duties as a Securitate officer while pursuing a long-distance-learning college degree in forestry—one that was not relevant to his work for the agency, as Feld eagerly emphasized. Suciu also repeatedly asked for time off in order to prepare for his exams and thus neglected his professional responsibilities. He failed to recruit any informers and to assist in an operation pertaining to intelligence that the CIA had infiltrated American spies in the proximity of Făgăraş, a town sixty kilometers east of Oraşul Stalin. The following excerpt illustrates how Feld tried to twist and spin the facts and to create a context in which his rather audacious statement could appear justifiable: "I showed that the imperialists want to restore the bourgeois regime of landowners, and if the people and their secret police didn't do their duty, then we could encounter hardship, so his [Suciu's] duty was to acquit himself of his tasks as a Securitate officer first and not of those as a student" (D102, 229–30). In spite of Feld's innuendo, his intention was to attack and expose Suciu's lack of competence and aptitude. In the process he ended up treating a member of the working class with disdain and criticizing the quality of college education obtained by Securitate officers—both consequential offences. Whether Feld was indeed still hoping for a regime change becomes almost secondary in this problematic context. His apology, a mandatory self-critical reflection, did not achieve the desired result either: "I regret profoundly. My intentions were good but badly interpreted. I was wrong to discuss such problems at an undesired level and with comrades who did not think maturely enough" (D102, 232). The investigators, not all as brainless as Feld apparently considered them, did not appreciate his heavy-handed apology and overt arrogance, as the comment in the margin illustrates: "A way of making fools of people" (see fig. 1.6; D102, 232). Feld's fate at the MAI might have been already sealed by then, and the documentation that followed served only to justify his investigators' decision.

Suciu's statement allowed various other officers to step forward and voice their discontent about Feld as a colleague and as a superior officer. Among these Captain Octavian Iordănescu wrote the longest (twelve single-spaced, typed pages) and most unfavorable report regarding Feld's personal transgressions and his attitude and activity as a Securitate officer. Iordănescu, who himself had earlier been accused of stealing money from the informer recompense fund, described Feld on December 1, 1958, as follows: "From the very beginning I express my view that Major FELD SAMUEL is a rotten element, morally degenerate, without scruples, consumed by careerist tendencies and void of any love for human beings" (D102, 248). Due to privacy concerns, CNSAS has redacted sensitive personal parts of Iordănescu's statement that describe Feld's moral transgressions. In fact, page 12 is almost completely obscured although it reveals several such cases. As per Romanian legislation, these indiscretions cannot be disclosed, even though they refer to a Securitate officer and were allegedly instrumental in his dismissal. They were ranked as the number one reason for his dismissal in the various documents archived in his cadre file. However, one can still glean that some of Iordănescu's accusations corroborate other officers' statements, while others shed new light on Feld's activity, viewed from Iordănescu's evidently biased perspective.

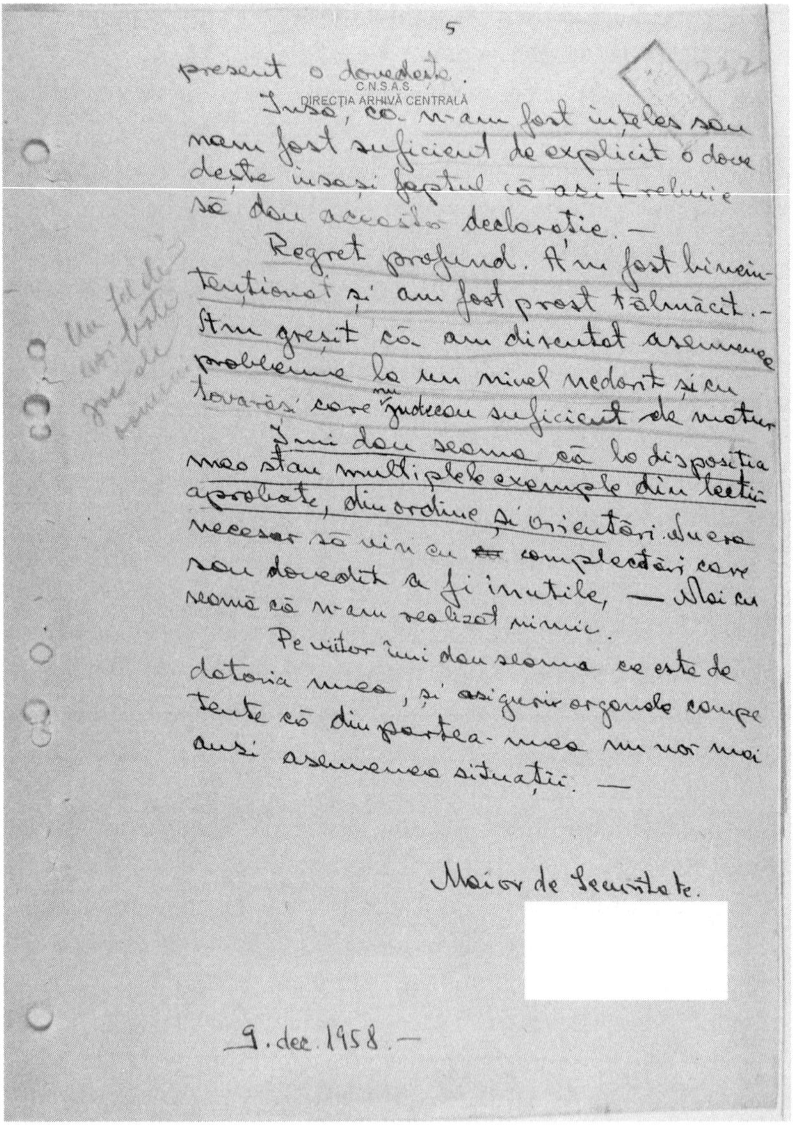

FIG. 1.6. Feld's self-critical reflection marked by his investigators (CNSAS, Bucharest, Romania, D102, 232).

Iordănescu's no-holds-barred report paints a picture of Feld as a superior Securitate officer who was interested in the benefits his position offered him rather than the work it entailed. The advantages appeared to have been numerous and his power commensurate, including an entry pass into the high society of Orașul Stalin, college graduates and professionals, whom he saw as his peers in terms of education and culture, although he himself never finished college.[33] According to Iordănescu and other officers who were also asked for statements, Feld had repeatedly abused his power in aiding friends, informers, and even the Zionist organization in Orașul Stalin, sometimes for a recompense. The first consequential accusation in this respect was about one of Feld's friends, Dr. Molnar, a physician from Orașul Stalin, who had received Feld's approval to travel to East Germany on a tourist visa, although his application was initially rejected. Molnar had already tried to escape Stalinist Romania in October 1956 during a trip with a group of physicians to Hungary. Based on the statements in the file, Molnar had even simulated an operation to be able to stay in Hungary and not return to Romania, but he was forced to return when the unrests erupted in Hungary.[34] Evidently, Molnar needed a friend to help him leave a second time, as the Securitate would not approve his application following that failed attempt. After his arrival in West Germany, the actual goal of his trip, Molnar stated during a phone conversation with his father that he hoped Feld would not be mad at him (D102, 136).

Further, in terms of his attitude toward his job at the Securitate and the officers in his department, Feld's apathy was evident. Apparently, Feld exhibited disinterest in operational work and claimed other people's results as his own; he favored interrogations over the more involved work of recruiting informers. Feld had recruited only two during his time at MAI Region Stalin, and both were of "bad quality" because they did not provide any significant intelligence. Moreover, according to Iordănescu, by abusing his power Feld was stealing other officers' recruited informers, whom he then paraded through several safe houses, which was against the Securitate's regulations. At the same time, though, according to Iordănescu, Feld knew to exploit the perks that came with being a high-ranked officer: he used his chauffeur for personal matters, had a very flexible schedule that allowed him to be late every day, and did not offer any help or assistance unless pushed by his superiors. "Regarding the help that Major FELD SAMUEL ought to grant the workers . . . this is inexistent, and if it is said that he sometimes tries to help a worker, one can observe how he shows boredom, impatience, and much superficiality" (D102, 251). Feld's disdain for his subordinates manifested itself in his openly calling them "dirty" (D102, 253) and "untidy" (D102, 253). Women apparently earned even starker epithets: "About the women comrades, respectively about comrades T. and M. [my redaction], he stated that they were whores" (D102, 253).

The last far-reaching accusation in Iordănescu's statement connected Feld again to the Zionist movement, as it did during the first investigation of 1954. A female agent under the code name "Vasiliu Panea," who had infiltrated the Zionists of Oraşul Stalin, related to Iordănescu the following: "A Securitate major of Jewish nationality who works at MAI Region Stalin had communicated to some nationalist Jewish elements in town that there was insufficient evidence on the group of arrested Zionists for them to be sent to trial, and for this reason some of the arrested would be released" (D102, 256). "Vasiliu Panea" had learned about this from a former Zionist member of the organization Bethar, P.M. (my redaction), from Oraşul Stalin, who was already in the operational system of the Securitate (D102, 256). Divulging information about an ongoing case certainly sparked the interest of Feld's investigators and allowed them to link his behavior and favoritism to earlier accusations regarding his ties to Zionist organizations.

Iordănescu's zealous attempt to bring down Feld, although more detailed and sophisticated, compares in scope to the anonymous denunciation that prompted the first investigation that ended in 1954. It allowed investigators to establish consistency of behavior and to connect the dots between the older and more recent accusations. They revisited the grounds for the first dismissal, requested new statements from Timişoara, and together with the new material Iordănescu and other fellow officers provided, they were able to ultimately discharge Feld. However, the file does not provide information describing in any detail what transpired after Iordănescu's incriminating letter. In fact, a gap in his cadre file transports us to Feld's next job in a leading position at a construction firm in Braşov. A favorable characterization from his boss, the director of this firm, describes Feld as a capable and reliable leader who had been able to reorganize his sector very ably. As to his dismissal from MAI and exclusion from the Communist Party, Feld explained to his new boss that it happened due to his departure from the "proletarian morals" and his relatives living in Israel (D102, 378).

Postdismissal, 1960–84

During the postdismissal period, Feld's activity was closely monitored, as well as his entourage and his relationship with his relatives in Israel and his brother in West Germany. The Securitate's most significant concern was Feld's intimate knowledge of the agency, the secret operations he had been privy to, as well as the informers from before 1960 who were still active in the network. As he had worked in counterespionage before his dismissal from MAI, he apparently knew various agents who at that time were active in West Germany (I 259049, vol. 1, 32). As a result, his applications for emigration to Israel were repeatedly rejected between 1970 and 1974 because the Securitate continued to see him as a threat, imagined or real, due to the intelligence he had obtained during his years in its service (see fig. 1.7).[35]

His surveillance file erroneously states that the former Securitate officer Samuel Feld was finally allowed to immigrate to Israel in 1974 and had been living in the United States since 1977, as the proposal to close and archive his file indicates (I 259049, vol. 1, 1). There is no information concerning how the Securitate's decision came about and why it determined that Feld posed no more threats and allowed him to emigrate.[36] Several other documents in his surveillance file present contradictory information regarding his emigration, indicating both 1974 or 1975 as the year he left Romania (I 259048, 8–8b). Yet in the same file, informers' notes situate Feld still in Braşov in 1975. According to the wiretappings archived in his surveillance file, in February 1976 Feld was try-

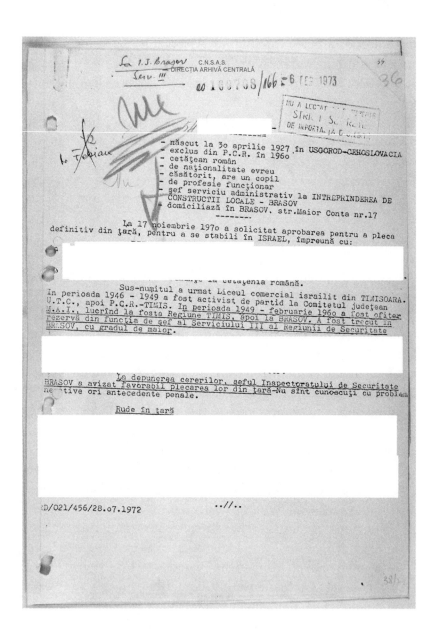

- născut la 30 aprilie 1927 în USGOROD-CEHOSLOVACIA
- exclus din P.C.R. în 1960
- cetățean român
- de naționalitate evreu
- căsătorit, are un copil
- de profesie funcționar
- șef serviciu administrativ la INTREPRINDEREA DE CONSTRUCTII LOCALE - BRASOV
- domiciliază în BRASOV, str.Maior Conta nr.17

        La 17 noiembrie 1970 a solicitat aprobarea pentru a pleca definitiv din țară, pentru a se stabili în ISRAEL, împreună cu:

                                ...je la cetățenia română.
        Sus-numitul a urmat Liceul comercial israilit din TIMISOARA. În perioada 1946 - 1949 a fost activist de partid la Comitetul județean U.T.C., apoi P.C.R.-TIMIS. In perioada 1949 - februarie 1960 a fost ofiter M.A.I., lucrînd la fosta Regiune TIMIS, apoi la BRASOV. A fost trecut în rezervă din funcția de șef al Serviciului III al Regiunii de Securitate BRASOV, cu gradul de maior.

        La depunerea cererilor, șeful Inspectoratului de Securitate BRASOV a avizat favorabil plecarea lor din țară-Nu sînt cunoscuți cu problem negative ori antecedente penale.

        Rude în țară

RD/021/456/28.07.1972   ..//..

FIG. 1.7. The emphatic *nu* (no) in red on Feld's application for emigration to Israel (CNSAS, Bucharest, Romania, I 259049, vol. 1, 36).

ing to liquidate his property in anticipation of his emigration (I 259049, vol. 2, 2–3). Well aware of the fact that his apartment was wiretapped, in his conversation with a buyer he expressed political views in line with the Cold War climate; he criticized, for example, Radio Free Europe (I 259049, vol. 2, 5–5b).[37] In his transparent opinion, he lamented the fact that Romania did not put an end to it and would transmit more detailed news on Radio Bucharest. In a conversation with another potential buyer, Feld narrowed down the date of his emigration to May 16 of the same year (I 259049, vol. 2, 2). In 1977 the Feld family was living in Forest Hills, New York, according to several informative notes and intercepted correspondence between Feld's family and friends and relatives in Romania. Finally, source "Traian Ionescu" provides the last piece of information about Feld on May 29, 1985. The source reported that Feld owned a small furniture store, enumerated the various Romanian friends belonging to his inner social circle, and stated that the Feld couple traveled frequently (I 259048, 22).

The elusive nature of a file story extends to the nature of its protagonist. It begs the question: who is Samuel Feld? Is he the person he described himself to be or the person his denouncers and investigators portrayed? Each version of his past and of his actions plays a different role in his overall file story, which is undeniably colored by hindsight knowledge and the historical actor's own contributions. And each needs to be read with a grain of salt given the political context and the stakes for the protagonist and possibly for the denouncers as well. On the one hand, we have Samuel Feld's autobiographical texts, mandatory sketches in which he tirelessly highlighted his credentials for joining the Securitate. There are accurate facts but also omissions and performative utterances whose purpose is self-evident now but convinced many of his superiors in the 1940s and 1950s. There are also his deftly crafted statements that performed yet another role: to deflect accusations in order to save his career and secure his safety and that of his family. Yet most or all of these accusations proved to be true, and thus his statements were utter lies, albeit elaborate and sophisticated ones—a trait of a Cold War spy no doubt. On the other hand, the text of his Securitate life is also composed by his denouncers and his investigators. The most influential and consequential are the anonymous denunciation and that of Iordănescu, his fellow officer. They played a major role in prompting the ensuing investigations, but more essential for our file story is the picture they paint of our protagonist. This portrayal does not necessarily contradict Feld's own autobiographical texts; it rather tackles his omissions and complements it simultaneously. Yet these biographical segments also have to be challenged, taking into account the denouncers' resentment and jealousy and a veiled antisemitism never voiced outright in them. One also has to question at times the spontaneous character and timing of these denunciations, which could point to various purges in the ranks of the Securitate.

His file story, however, exemplifies the text of a life in the higher echelons of the Securitate, from multiple perspectives, told as narratives of denunciation, indictment, and defense in a web of deceit and falseness, sprinkled with rare instances of humanity and apparent sincerity. This text about Samuel Feld's eleven years at the Securitate thus attempts to offer some interpretative coherence and structure to what would otherwise be a sequence of disjointed life segments and accusations archived between the grayish covers of a file. Does this file story imply that these years are the most important part of the historical actor's life, as he himself mused? This job elevated him to a socioeconomic position he could only dream of in his childhood. He surpassed the Csendeses and Fischoffs of his world and certainly the Cernescu brothers, who had harassed and beaten him as a young boy. This position also afforded him power—the power and means to avenge his childhood and teenage years and the persecution and humiliation he had experienced. But at what price? At the age of eighty-eight, reflecting on his career he remarked: "Nine and a half years at the Securitate—is this the most important part of my life?" (Samuel Feld, phone conversation with the author, December 2015).[38] Maybe the "nine and a half years" in the service of the Securitate are, for our protagonist himself, not the most important part of his long life, but they undoubtedly affected, altered, or curtailed the lives of many in a period of terror in Communist Romania, even if inside he must have felt at times like the poor boy whose feet were always frozen in the winter and who learned from his brother-in-law to alternate cold and hot foot baths every night to relieve the pain and cold. He still remembers in astonishing detail his first-ever wool coat and leather boots that finally kept him warm: his Securitate uniform.

Notes

This is an updated and expanded version of an article published in *Caietele CNSAS* (2018).

1. The protagonist allowed me to use information from our December 2015 phone conversation and his written replies to my questions from 2017 under the condition that I replace his name with the pseudonym Samuel Feld throughout my study. I have thus honored his request. I have also altered the names of his family members or used initials. From 1950 to 1960, both the Transylvanian town and the region of Brașov (German: Kronstadt; Hungarian: Brassó) were renamed in honor of the Soviet leader.

2. Unless otherwise noted all translations are mine.

3. In 1949, for example, the social origin of the Securitate recruits was stated as follows: 64 percent unskilled workers, 4 percent peasants, 28 percent white-collar workers, 2 percent intellectuals, and 2 percent unspecified origin (Banu 2001, 82).

4. I would like to thank CNSAS for allowing me access to Feld's cadre (officer) file D102 (397 leaves) and his surveillance files I 259048 (22 leaves) and I 259049 (volume 1: 190 leaves; volume 2: 163 leaves). His surveillance files were opened under the code name "Dayan" after his dismissal from MAI. The cadre file (D102), more organized than many victim or informer files, is carefully divided into nine parts: the dismissal decision and severance forms (1–5); reports (6–26); investigations (27–62); autobiographies and biographical questionnaires (63–118); references and characterizations (119–209); investigative materials (210–350); verification materials for marriage (351–88); MAI appointment forms (389–90); and miscellaneous (381–401). The surveillance files (I 259048 and I 259049) document aspects of his life, carefully followed until 1976, when he left Romania, and sporadically until 1985, when he was already living in the United States.

5. Angela Brintlinger uses the metaphor of quilt making for the writing of history and that of a quilter for the historian, who stitches together pieces of material from incomplete archives and other sources in order to present a coherent and convincing historical narrative (2008, 2). While the metaphor of a quilt resembles that of a collage or montage, it does not allow for the volatility that a file story implies and focuses on history rather than life writing. Yet to allow for a more readily "stitchable" version of events, I elucidate some incomplete and confusing aspects rendered in the file through the historical actor's own

recollections, well aware, though, that his statements might have the opposite effect—namely, to add to the precariousness of his file story and produce further imbalance of the life fragments. As Ulric Neisser reminds us, "remembering is not like playing back a tape" (2008, 88). The historical actor's narrative will stay in the endnotes while his file story will unfold in the main text.

6. I am indebted to Igal Halfin's inspiring work on red autobiographies. In his analysis he also views the autobiographer as the protagonist abstracted from an autobiography rather than the historical actor (2003, 44).

7. In a letter to the author from September 2017, Feld explained that he was handcuffed, blindfolded, and taken to the Jilava prison, one of MAI's most infamous interrogation sites. He was released three weeks later after intense interrogations.

8. In fact as the *Raport Final* shows, Romanian Jews became for the first time involved in the state apparatus in 1948, but Romanians considered them undesired though necessary "temporary companions" and their joining the Communist Party just provisory (Comisia Prezidențială pentru Analiza Dictaturii Comuniste din România 2007, 364–65).

9. I am indebted to Angela Brintlinger's interpretation of the term "usable past" and have adapted it to the personal and political context of this file story (2008, 7).

10. The name of the town appears as "Uzgorod" in Feld's file. Nowadays, Uzhhorod is in western Ukraine at the border with Slovakia and near the border with Hungary.

11. According to Tiberiu Mozes, the Csendes family owned a large transport company in Timişoara (2014, 265). An interview with and two photos of Magdalena Csendes Holender, who married into this family, are featured in Smaranda Vultur's *Memoria salvată* (Saved memory, 2002, 134–44, 183).

12. These "work teams" were instated in July 1942 in Romania. See "Munca forțată sub regimul Antonescu" (Forced labor under the Antonescu regime) in *Raport Final* (Comisia Prezidențială pentru Analiza Dictaturii Comuniste din România 2007, 116–17).

13. All his other older brothers and sisters had been fired from their jobs because of the racial laws in place. For antisemitic legislation in Romania, see Benjamin 1993. See also Jădăneanț 2015.

14. Siguranța or Siguranța Statului was the secret police of the Kingdom of Romania. It was founded in 1908 and dissolved in 1948 in favor of the newly established Securitate. On the predecessors of the Securitate between 1944 and 1948, see Banu n.d.

15. There is scarce information on this Communist youth organization. Vladimir Tismaneanu calls it a "short-lived experiment" after which the UTC was reestablished (2003, 92). However, the UTC was reestablished only in 1965.

16. Feld apparently attended just one semester in Cluj and had to abandon his studies due to persistent financial difficulties that plagued his childhood and youth.

17. UTM was the main Communist youth organization from 1947 to 1965, when it was renamed UTC. See http://www.cercetare-memorialulrevolutiei1 989.ro/wp-content/uploads/2016/05/Uniunea-Tineretului-Comunist.pdf.

18. Northern Transylvania (Transilvania de Nord) was a region of the Romanian Kingdom that after the Second Vienna Award of August 1940 became part of the Kingdom of Hungary. Once Hungary implemented the final solution, the Jewish population from Northern Transylvania was also deported to Nazi extermination camps. Most famously Elie Wiesel and his family were deported from Sighet to Auschwitz in May 1944, months after Nazi Germany occupied Hungary.

19. Martin Schnellbach (1912–84) was one of the very few ethnic German officers in the Securitate. See Totok 2015. According to Radu Ioanid's statistics regarding the ethnic distribution of the Securitate employees in 1948, Schnellbach must have been part of the "other" category that comprised seventeen members at 0.4 percent of the total number of Securitate employees (2005, 49). The same statistical information is included in the more recent book edited by Ioanid, *Securitatea si vânzarea evreilor* (The Securitate and the selling of the Jews, 2015, 51).

20. There is very scant information on this association established as "Friends of the United States" in 1925. See American Cultural Center, Bucharest, Romania, 2006, 17–18.

21. In fact Adalbert Przibram, the initiator of the British Library in Timișoara, has written about the night Feld arrested him at his residence in the early hours of May 24, 1950, where Przibram had also gathered and sealed the remaining materials from the library that had been closed in September 1949. In this rare written testimony about our protagonist's activity, the newly minted Securitate Lieutenant Feld, a noncommissioned officer Nemeth, and a sergeant broke into Przibram's house although they had warrants for his arrest and a house search. Przibram (2003) called Feld an opportunist beyond compare, a loyal servant of a regime in which Feld actually did not believe. Przibram was sentenced to two years of reeducation and hard labor at the Danube–Black Sea Canal, a notorious site of labor camps where thousands of political prisoners worked on excavation from 1949 to 1953. The construction of the fifty-nine-mile canal, whose main branch connects the Black Sea port of Constanța with the Danube River, began in 1978 and was opened in 1984. According to David Turnock (1986), the construction of this canal was more involved than the Suez or Panama Canals.

22. Even at the age of eighty-eight, Feld could narrate in great detail events from his childhood when he was harassed and beaten by Romanian kids in Timișoara. He mentioned in particular the Cernescu brothers, who even threatened to kill him.

23. In Getta Neumann's *Destine evreiești la Timișoara* (Jewish destinies in Timișoara, 2014), Tomi Laszlo provides a brief history of the Israelite Lycée, in which he explains that the building had to be evacuated in the beginning

of 1941 to make room for a German army hospital. To continue its activity, the school had to use offices and other rooms and schedule classes both in the morning and in the afternoon after 2:00 p.m. The afternoon series of classes was geared especially toward students born in or before 1925 who were enrolled in the "forced labor squads" (Laszlo 2014, 448).

24. While crossing the border for various black market materials had been an everyday occurrence for some time after the war, a new law was passed (number 4 from January 19, 1948) that modified the Penal Code article 267 and that allowed for harsher punishments for illegal border crossings (Nastasă 2014, 37).

25. In Feld's letter to the author from September 2017, he readily admitted having known about the intention of his uncle to flee Romania. He remembered fondly having often spent Sabbath lunches at his uncle's residence. Feld explained that the photo found on H. Feld was a token of gratitude for his warm hospitality.

26. Liviu Vuc was part of the anti-Communist resistance in Banat, a member of the Romanian fascist organization Legion of the Archangel Michael. See Duica 2003.

27. At least seven of his uncles and aunts, in addition to his father's second wife and their two young children, died in extermination camps (D102, 56–57).

28. As Victor Neumann explains, the situation between Jews who adhered to the new Communist ideology and Zionists was very tense and gave way to mutual accusations and denunciation on both sides (2006, 154–56). See also "Arestarea sioniştilor" (The arrest of the Zionists) in *Raport Final*, which also mentions the waves of arrests and the ensuing trials that took place between 1949 and 1953 and one in 1959 (Comisia Prezidenţială pentru Analiza Dictaturii Comuniste din România 2007, 383–86).

29. According to Victor Neumann, very few Banat Jews were keen on supporting the new regime and "seeking to transform the social structure of the Jews"; the majority tried to leave for Israel or the United States (2006, 157). Ioanid explains that in the aftermath of World War II, some Romanian Jews joined the Communist elite, the party and the military, as well as the Securitate. In 1948, when the Securitate was created, 8.5 percent of its personnel was Jewish, the highest number in terms of minorities but far behind the ethnic Romanian majority at 83.9 percent. His study does not provide any specific statistics for the region of Banat (Ioanid 2005, 49).

30. Ichud was one of the two main Zionist organizations that came to life again in Romania after August 1944. Ichud was the Romanian branch of the Histadruth Haovidim Party, which had its headquarters in Bucharest but had chapters in most every city. After the founding of the state of Israel in 1948, the activity of the Zionist organizations became superfluous, and a violent campaign against the remaining Zionists began in the fall of 1948 that led to many arrests, while the reputation of many Zionist leaders was discredited (Nastasă 2014, 35–39).

31. Horia Sima (1907–93) was the second and last leader of the fascist legionnaire movement Iron Guard in Romania. For more information, see Ioanid 1990.

32. In his letter from September 2017, Feld explained that Moiş intervened on his behalf and facilitated Feld's disciplinary move to Oraşul Stalin. Feld, however, did not know or remember what motives Moiş might have invoked to convince his superiors.

33. Aside from his first aforementioned attempt at a college education in Cluj, a second attempt occurred while in Oraşul Stalin, when he registered to complete a distance-learning law degree, yet this also fell through due to his dismissal from MAI.

34. Officers Suciu (D102, 238), Anghel (D102, 235–36), and an unknown source (D102, 233) refer to Feld's relationship with Molnar. In Feld's 2017 letter to the author, he admitted having helped Molnar.

35. In fact, on October 11, 1971, the Commission for Passport and Visa Problems approved the Feld family's application for emigration but reconsidered its initial approval on October 29, 1971, as it had obtained additional data and as such decided to annul the passports (I 259049, vol. 1, 37).

36. In his letter to the author from September 2017, the historical actor explained that he had never immigrated to Israel. After his several unsuccessful attempts, his brother living in the United States convinced him to apply for emigration to the United States. At the American Embassy in Bucharest, he was then briefed by an FBI officer who was well informed about his activity in the service of the Securitate. Feld did not provide details about this briefing; he just mentioned having explained to the FBI officer that he had joined the Securitate for economic reasons. According to Feld he received his green card at the U.S. Embassy in Bucharest and renounced his Romanian citizenship. During an earlier phone conversation in December 2015, I asked Feld if the FBI was by any chance working with the Securitate given the extent of information they had on a Securitate officer who had worked in counterespionage. He laughed and replied: "You better ask them."

37. Radio Free Europe was a U.S.-sponsored broadcaster for Eastern Bloc countries that the CIA funded until 1972.

38. Feld's career, in fact, spanned a period of eleven years and one week.

References

ARCHIVAL SOURCES

ACNSAS (Arhiva Consiliului Naţional pentru Studierea Arhivelor Securităţii [Archive of the National Council for the Study of the Securitate Archives]). Fond Cadre, file D102.
———. Fond Informativ, file 259048.
———. Fond Informativ, file 259049, vols. 1 and 2.

PUBLISHED SOURCES

American Cultural Center, Bucharest, Romania. 2006. "In Celebration of 125 Years of United States and Romanian Diplomatic Relations." *DISAM Jour-*

nal:15–26. http://www.disam.dsca.mil/pubs/INDEXES/Vol%2028_3
/Bucharest%20romania.pdf.

Banu, Florian. 2001. "Profilul angajatului Securității in anii '50." In CNSAS, *Totalitarism si rezistență, teroare si represiune in România comunistă*, 81–91. Bucharest: CNSAS.

———. n.d. "'Strămoșii' Securității—structuri de poliție politică din România în perioada 23 august 1944–30 august 1948." Accessed December 9, 2017. http://www.cnsas.ro/documente/istoria_comunism/studii_articole /activitati_plan_intern/Precedesorii%20Securitatii.pdf.

Benjamin, Lya. 1993. *Legislația anti-evreiască*. Bucharest: Hasefer.

Brintlinger, Angela. 2008. *Writing a Usable Past: Russian Literary Culture, 1917– 1937*. Evanston IL: Northwestern University Press.

Comisia Prezidențială pentru Analiza Dictaturii Comuniste din România. 2007. *Raport Final*. Edited by Vladimir Tismaneanu, Dorin Dobrincu, and Cristian Vasile. Bucharest: Humanitas.

Duica, Camelia Ivan. 2003. *Din istoria rezistenței anticomuniste din Banat: Organizația dr. Liviu Vuc (1948–1952)*. Galați: Galați University Press.

Eakin, Paul John. 1993. *Touching the World: Reference in Autobiography*. Princeton NJ: Princeton University Press.

Frow, John. 2005. *Genre*. London: Routledge.

Glajar, Valentina. 2016. "'You'll Never Make a Spy out of Me!'—The File Story of 'Fink Susanne.'" In *Secret Police Files from the Eastern Bloc: Between Surveillance and Life Writing*, edited by Valentina Glajar, Alison Lewis, and Corina L. Petrescu, 56–83. Rochester NY: Camden House.

Halfin, Igal. 2003. *Terror in My Soul: Communist Autobiographies on Trial*. Cambridge MA: Harvard University Press.

———. 2011. *Red Autobiographies: Initiating the Bolshevik Self*. Seattle: University of Washington Press.

Ioanid, Radu. 1990. *The Sword of the Archangel*. New York: Columbia University Press.

———. 2005. *The Ransom of the Jews*. Chicago: Ivan R. Dee.

———. 2015. *Securitatea si vânzarea evreilor*. Iași/Bucharest: Polirom.

Jădăneanț, Alexandru. 2015. "The Collapse of Constitutional Legalism: Racial Laws and the Ethno-Cultural Construction of National Identity in Romania during World War II." *Procedia-Social and Behavioral Sciences* 183:40–46.

Laszlo, Tomi. 2014. "Scurt istoric al Liceului Izraelit din Timișoara." In Getta Neumann, *Destine evreiești la Timișoara: Portretul comunității din perioada interbelică pâna azi*, 445–48. Bucharest: Hasefer.

Mozes, Tiberiu. 2014. "Sunt un om de naționalitate evreiască." In Getta Neumann, *Destine evreiești la Timișoara: Portretul comunității din perioada interbelică pâna azi*, 248–70. Bucharest: Hasefer.

Nastasă, Lucian. 2014. "Studiu introductiv." In *Minorități etnoculturale, mărturii documentare: Evreii din România (1945–1965)*, edited by Andreea

Andreescu, Lucian Nastasă, and Andreea Varga, 13–44. Cluj: Ethnocultural Diversity Resource Center.

Neisser, Ulric. 2008. "Memory with a Grain of Salt." In *Transcultural Memory: An Anthology*, edited by Harriet Harvey Wood and A. S. Byatt, 80–88. London: Chatto & Windus.

Neumann, Victor. 2006. *The End of a History: The Jews of Banat from the Beginning to Nowadays*. Bucharest: Bucharest University Press.

Przibram, Adalbert. 2003. *Biblioteca Britanică din Timişoara şi viaţa mea*. Timişoara: Hestia.

Rotman, Liviu. 2003. "Cuvânt înainte: Evreii din Romania—final de istorie." In *Minorităţi etnoculturale, mărturii documentare: Evreii din România (1945–1965)*, edited by Andreea Andreescu, Lucian Nastasă, and Andrea Varga, 7–11. Cluj: Ethnocultural Diversity Resource Center.

Smith, Sidonie. 1998. "Performativity, Autobiographical Practice, Resistance" (1995). In *Women, Autobiography, Theory: A Reader*, edited by Sidonie Smith and Julia Watson, 108–15. Madison: University of Wisconsin Press.

Tismaneanu, Vladimir. 2003. *Stalinism for All Seasons: A Political History of Romanian Communism*. Berkeley: University of California Press.

Totok, William. 2015. "Etnici germani în Securitate: Spicuiri sumare din dosarul colonelului de Securitate Martin Schnellbach (1912–1984)." *România Liberă*, July 3. http://www.romanialibera.ro/aldine/delasarea-secului/etnici-germani-in-securitate-spicuiri-sumare-din-dosarul-colonelului-de-securitate-martin-schnellbach-1912-1984-384367.

Turnock, David. 1986. "The Danube–Black Sea Canal and Its Impact on Southern Romania." *Geojournal* 12 (1): 65–79.

Vultur, Smaranda, ed. 2002. *Memoria salvată: Evreii din Banat, ieri si azi*. Bucharest: Polirom.

2 Man without a Face

The Autobiographical Self-Fashioning of Spymaster Markus Wolf

MARY BETH STEIN

East German espionage was legendary under Markus Wolf, director of the Main Intelligence Directorate (Hauptverwaltung Aufklärung, HVA) in the Ministry for State Security (Ministerium für Staatssicherheit, Mfs) of the German Democratic Republic.[1] For over twenty-five years, his physical identity remained a mystery to Western intelligence agencies. Prior to his 1979 exposure by Werner Stiller, one of highest-ranking HVA officers to defect to the West, Wolf was simply dubbed "the man without a face." This moniker became the title of his 1997 English-language autobiography coauthored with the British journalist Anne McElvoy and subtitled *The Autobiography of Communism's Greatest Spymaster*. A revised and expanded German edition appeared the same year with notable differences under the title *Spionagechef im geheimen Krieg: Erinnerungen* (Spy boss in the secret war: Recollections).

After the fall of the Berlin Wall, the fate of the Mfs and HVA was unclear. Civil rights groups intervened in January 1990 to prevent the destruction of files from many departments. However, the HVA succeeded in destroying (or in some instances trading) nearly all its most sensitive files through late spring of that year.[2] Top priority was given to expunging the dossiers of its full-time employees as well as compromising information about espionage operations that would expose the identity of Stasi agents in the West, known euphemistically in Mfs jargon as "enlighteners" (*Aufklärer*) and "scouts of peace" (*Kundschafter des Frie-*

dens) (Gieseke 2014, 154). Consequently, it is impossible to know how much information about foreign intelligence in general and Wolf's lifework in particular was lost during this time. There can be little doubt, however, that the systematic purge of Stasi files laid the groundwork for later representations of the HVA by Wolf and others that are difficult to corroborate or disprove. What remains of Wolf's thirty-four-year service record, for example, is limited to roughly one hundred pages in three separate files in the archives of the Federal Commissioner for the Records of the State Security Service of the Former German Democratic Republic (GDR), the agency that administers the surviving Stasi files.[3]

The man without a face might have remained the man without a trace were it not for the seemingly insatiable need to tell his life story after emerging from the shadows. Aptly described by David Childs and Richard Popplewell as a "formidable self-publicist" (1996, 113), Wolf was a frequent guest in the German media after 1989, fashioning himself in interviews and television shows as a voice for reform inside the Socialist Unity Party (SED) and as the positive face of the MfS. In addition to the two works discussed in this essay, he also authored or collaborated in three other books about himself and his lifework during his lifetime that bear his name, *In Eigenem Auftrag* (On my own behalf, 1991), *Markus Wolf: "Ich bin kein Spion"* (Markus Wolf: I am not a spy, 1992), and *Die Kunst der Verstellung* (The art of deception, 1998). Other books based on interviews and correspondence have appeared posthumously, including *Markus Wolf: Letzte Gespräche* (Markus Wolf: Last conversations; Schütt 2007) and *Mischa* (A. Wolf 2013).

The following analysis of *Man without a Face* and *Spionagechef im geheimen Krieg* situates the telling of his life story in the turbulent decade following the collapse of the GDR and identifies strategies of narrative self-fashioning that negotiate reader expectations of personal disclosure and honest self-reflection, on the one hand, and the author's need for circumspection, on the other. Applying Philippe Lejeune's notion of the "autobiographical pact" to Wolf's works permits a reading that assumes the author's commitment to telling the truth while recognizing the impossibility of telling the truth about the self or "constituting the self as a complete subject"

Stein

(1989, 131). My approach is not to interrogate truth claims in Wolf's autobiographies but to examine the spymaster's story of himself as a protagonist in the world rather than as a narrative to be verified or falsified. While the paucity of archival sources corroborating or disproving Wolf's truth claims all but necessitates such an approach, this chapter argues that the autobiographical production of high-ranking party officials after German unification offers an important site for critical readings of communist subjectivity in a postsocialist context. Before examining Wolf's presentation of self as unrepentant Communist and successful spymaster on the losing side of the Cold War, however, it will be useful to outline in broad strokes the trajectory of his life, details of which stem from his own writings or published interviews with him unless otherwise indicated.[4]

Wolf's Life Trajectory

The oldest son from playwright Friedrich Wolf's second marriage, Markus Wolf was born in the small town of Hechingen in southwest Germany on January 19, 1923. His brother, Konrad, later renowned film director and president of the East German Academy of Arts, was born two years later. Friedrich Wolf was Jewish, and both he and his wife were members of the German Communist Party; consequently they feared for their lives when Hitler came to power. The Wolf family fled Nazi Germany and arrived in Moscow in 1934, where the eleven-year-old Markus attended the Karl Liebknecht School, a school for the children of German-speaking refugees. He became fluent in Russian, joined the Soviet Young Pioneers, and developed a lifelong appreciation for Russian culture and cuisine.[5] Markus finished school and studied aeronautics at the Moscow Institute for Airplane Engineering from 1940 until 1942. In 1942 he was delegated to the Communist International (Comintern), where he and other youth from Nazi-occupied territories received political training and prepared for the postwar liberation of their homelands. It is here that Markus met his first wife, Emmi Stenzer, daughter of Franz Stenzer, the German Communist Party delegate to the Reichstag who was murdered in Buchenwald in 1933. Between 1943 and 1945, Markus worked as a radio commentator for the German People's Radio (Deutscher Volkssender), the voice of the German Communist Party in the Soviet Union. He married Emmi Stenzer in 1944, returned to Berlin in May 1945, and worked under the pseudonym "Michael Storm" as a commentator and political agitator for the Communist-run Berliner Rundfunk (Berlin Radio) from 1946 until 1949. One of his assignments was to cover the Nazi war crimes trial in Nuremberg. In 1949 Wolf was appointed the first German advisor to the newly created diplomatic mission of the GDR in Moscow. He was recalled to East Berlin in 1951 and assigned to the Institute for Economic Scientific Research, the front for East Germany's nascent intelligence agency. In 1952, at the age of twenty-nine, he was named director. Less than a year later the institute was incorporated into the MfS. Wolf became director of the HVA and deputy to the minister for state security, Erich Mielke. He attained the rank of general and remained the number two man in the MfS until his voluntary retirement at the age of sixty-three in 1986.

It is useful to interrupt this outline of Wolf's life to point out that it was fairly uncommon for Communist functionaries to retire early, because it typically signaled dysfunction within a department or a falling out of favor (Richter and Rösler 1992, 123). While neither appears to factor in Wolf's case, his early retirement became fodder for speculation in the West (Fricke 1987, 231) as well as in the East (Drommer 1998, 116). Wolf writes in his autobiographies that by the early 1980s he had achieved his professional goals and feared he could no longer hide his skepticism regarding "real existing socialism" (1998, 423). He raised the subject of retirement with Mielke in 1983, but was forced to wait another three years before stepping down. For Mielke the timing of his deputy's decision to retire was most inopportune, for it coincided with a serious war scare over the stationing of middle-range missiles in East and West Germany and escalating tensions with the Soviets due to Erich Honecker's dogged pursuit of West German recognition of the GDR. The spymaster had to know how inauspicious the moment was, which makes his early retirement all the more intriguing. The death of Wolf's brother, Konrad, the previous year and the disheartening NATO report obtained by Rainer Rupp, an HVA mole to NATO, on the structural weaknesses of Soviet military and economic power appear to have been significant factors in his decision (M. Wolf

1997, 353–54; 1998, 425–28). The language citing reasons for his retirement provided Wolf with a strategic exit from a position of power and responsibility. Moreover, it allowed Mielke to assure the East German Politburo as well as the Soviets of an orderly transition in the MfS. The resignation letter, dated October 8, 1986, which survived the systematic destruction of Stasi files, mentions the desire to complete his brother's "Troika" project and "the wish to creatively think through and remember the experiences of [his] life and work" (BStU KS60003/90, 59). The plan to write a memoir based on "experiences and insights of the last 35 years working as the head of foreign intelligence" that incorporates "the traditions of our precursors . . . which could be of use in conveying experiences from the struggles of the last fifty years to later generations" appealed to Mielke (BStU KS60003/90, 59) and ensured Wolf's access to the HVA archives for his research. With retirement Wolf received a large, new apartment overlooking the Spree River, a driver, a secretary, and an office in the ministry. In return he agreed to be available in an advisory capacity to Mielke and Wolf's successor, Werner Grossmann (M. Wolf 1997, 358), an extraordinary arrangement that undercuts Wolf's carefully crafted self-image as someone "outside" the system in 1989, when the GDR collapsed.

Wolf had another personal reason for asking to be relieved of his duties that is not cited in the resignation letter. His marriage to his second wife, Christel, was falling apart because of his affair with Andrea Stingl, the woman who would become his third wife. Mielke, whom Wolf characterizes as an "old-fashioned puritan in sexual mores" (M. Wolf 1997, 357), was concerned about avoiding the scandal of divorce and pressured him to "remain married for the sake of appearances" (M. Wolf 1997, 357). He refused. As Wolf's memoirs focus largely on his professional life, it is a significant admission of the entanglement of the personal and professional at this critical juncture when he writes, "With the decision to marry Andrea, I finally supplied [Mielke] the inducement to initiate my departure" (1998, 437). Moreover, the statement gives some credence to Mielke's later claim that Wolf stepped down because of moral transgressions (M. Wolf 1998, 437). The fact is Mielke was even more concerned that a bitter ex-wife might try to blackmail the MfS or could be exploited by Western intelligence agencies intent on damaging the GDR (Colitt 1995, 214). Fearing a security risk, he went so far as to have his deputy's telephone lines tapped (M. Wolf 1997, 358).

Continuing with Wolf's life trajectory, in the first years of retirement Wolf devoted himself to completing Konrad Wolf's manuscript of *Die Troika* (The triumvirate), which was unfinished at the time of his death. The story of three friends growing up in the Soviet Union appeared in early 1989 and became the first East German book to deal with crimes under Stalin. Although Konrad was one of the original troika, Markus benefited from the insinuation that his brother's experiences and views corresponded closely to his own. Indeed, *Die Troika* can be read as Wolf's earliest foray into autobiography, one that transformed the man without a face into a public figure capable of appealing to younger East Germans. In establishing himself as a credible historical witness to terrible repression under Communism, Wolf discovered a successful narrative strategy that he would hone in later memoirs. Around this time he assumed a more public role, through cautious support for Mikhail Gorbachev and *Sputnik*, the German-language magazine from the Soviet Union banned by the SED in the late 1980s (M. Wolf 1998, 441). Buoyed by the positive reception of *Die Troika* and confident that he could successfully pivot from SED insider to a spokesperson for reform, Wolf agreed to speak at the November 4, 1989, mass rally on East Berlin's Alexander Square. He completely misjudged the political climate as well as the extent of his personal appeal and was booed off the stage after identifying himself as a retired general in the MfS and denouncing the scapegoating of the Stasi as the "whipping boys of the nation" (Drommer 1998, 128).[6] The crowd on the Alexander Square was in no mood for lectures from a Stasi officer less than one month after mass arrests and Stasi and police violence against protestors on the fortieth anniversary of the founding the GDR. Years later, in a September 28, 2002, article of *Neues Deutschland*, Wolf would recall: "I felt connected to those who demanded change. But the political climate changed after November 4. In my second book, *On My Own Behalf*, I grapple with feelings of guilt, complicity and responsibility for the things that had happened" (cited in Jung 2007, 57).

East Germany's peaceful revolution forced the SED from power five days after the Alexander Square rally. Mielke's arrest in December was followed by the failure of a bill to pass in the Bundestag that would have granted amnesty to Stasi officers and agents. Wolf realized that he and others would not be able to escape their Stasi past. Fearing imminent arrest he and his wife, Andrea, left on an extended holiday to Austria just a few days before German unification. They moved from place to place "like some German Bonnie and Clyde" (M. Wolf 1997, 365) before fleeing to the Soviet Union with the aid of his KGB contacts. The Soviet Union in the turbulent years of 1990–91 was not the sanctuary where the Wolfs had hoped to find "advice and peace" (M. Wolf 1998, 13). His presence was awkward for the Kremlin and colleagues in the KGB. Direct and indirect appeals asking Gorbachev to raise the possibility of amnesty for Wolf in unification negotiations with German Chancellor Kohl went unanswered (M. Wolf 1997, 365). Wolf feared extradition and realized he could not count on the KGB or the Soviet Union for help. Following the political turmoil after the abortive coup against Gorbachev in August 1991, he and his wife left for Vienna and turned themselves in to the Austrian police after an unsuccessful bid for Austrian asylum. Wolf's lawyer and German prosecutors arranged for an orderly arrest at the German-Austrian border. The spymaster spent much of the 1990s in the public eye, on trial defending himself in courtrooms as well as in the court of public opinion. He lived in Berlin, writing and giving interviews until his death on November 9, 2006, and was buried next to his brother in the Gedenkstätte der Sozialisten (Memorial to the Socialists) in the Berlin city district of Lichtenberg.

Communist Autobiography after 1989

In considering why the "man without a face" would abandon a life-long habitus built around secrecy to write and rewrite the self over the course of a decade, it is important to recall the exigencies of the moment of his writing. The dramatic collapse of the East German state constituted a traumatic rupture for SED party leaders and a significant challenge to their political self-understanding. What followed was a period of existential uncertainty as many faced public condemnation and criminal prosecution. The first to be put on trial, paradoxically, were not SED party elites responsible for abuses of power in the GDR but border guards who had been involved in shootings at the Berlin Wall and along the German-German border. In the most high-profile of the wall trials, General Secretary Erich Honecker and five other high-ranking party members were indicted in 1992 for "indirect complicity" in manslaughter (McAdams 2001, 35). By the time Wolf went on trial for the first time in 1993, German public opinion was sharply divided over the ability of the West German legal system to redress GDR-era injustice. This polarized political context had a profound impact on how high-ranking party officials remembered and narrated Communist experience. Indeed, Wolf spoke for many East Germans, and not just former SED elites, at his own trial when he protested, "Not everything in the forty-year history of the GDR was bad and worthy of erasure, and not everything in the West good and just. This period of historical upheaval cannot be dealt with adequately through the clichés of a 'just state' on the one hand, and an 'unjust state' on the other" (M. Wolf 1997, 379).

The fusion of personal story and political history was a common feature of Communist autobiography in GDR times, and this way of seeing oneself in the world persisted for many after the *Wende* (the period leading up to and including the fall of the Berlin Wall). After 1989 some SED elites turned to life writing as a way of coming to terms with the collapse of the GDR and entering into public debates about the East German past. Life writing became a vehicle for defending oneself against accusation and preserving a usable Communist past. According to historian Martin Sabrow, the belief that the Communist past "could be narrated," that is, had not been discredited by war and genocide, explains the remarkable propensity for Communist autobiography after 1989. In contrast to Nazi party leaders after 1945, former SED elites believed that despite the GDR's spectacular collapse, their lives could be defended as an "upright life lived in error" (Sabrow 2014, 96). The first spate of Communist autobiographies after 1989, as publisher Christoph Links notes, were penned by second-tier officials and published with leftist publishers in the former GDR.

These paved the way for the memoirs by high-ranking party officials who were actually responsible for the policies of the regime
(Links 2007, 226). *Spionagechef im geheimen Krieg* is an example of
the latter that appeared with a formerly West German publisher.

Although Wolf's 1986 resignation letter attests to literary ambi-
tions predating the collapse of the GDR, his prolific autobiographical production after 1989 is inextricably linked to the political and
legal fallout he faced following the collapse of the East German
state. He began work on *Spionagechef im geheimen Krieg* while in
Russian exile for the second time in his life, with the prospect of
criminal prosecution and the criminalization of the HVA weigh-
ing heavily on him. "What followed then was the criminal prosecution, the confrontation with the victor. I felt obligated to convey
not only my own position, but also speak for my colleagues, the
'scouts' [of peace] who were in prison. This had a determining
influence on the content of later books, including my memoir, *Spionagechef im geheimen Krieg*" (cited in Jung 2007, 57)

As the preceding excerpt illustrates, Wolf's autobiographical writing begins first and foremost as a defense for himself as
well as colleagues and agents of the HVA facing prosecution. *Man
without a Face* and *Spionagechef im geheimen Krieg* appeared in
1997 while Wolf was a defendant in the second of two highly publicized trials in Düsseldorf. The 1993 trial for treason, espionage,
and bribery began under intense media scrutiny and concluded
after seven months with a guilty verdict and a six-year sentence.
The Federal Constitutional Court overturned the verdict two
years later, arguing that former East Germans could not be guilty
of treason against the Federal Republic. Wolf was convicted again
in 1997 on charges of kidnapping, bodily injury, and coercion in
the 1950s and 1960s, crimes that occurred in the GDR and were
punishable under East German law. He received a suspended
two-year sentence. As a defendant Wolf denounced the trials as a
farce and an example of *Siegerjustiz* (victor's justice), that is, politically motivated (in)justice exacted by the winners from the losers
of a struggle. His autobiographies continue this line of reasoning,
for example, when declaring that West German courts are primarily interested in "the settling of accounts to ensure that only one

version of history prevails" (M. Wolf 1997, xii). Written for different audiences and with slightly different emphases, the German and English-language autobiographies analyzed in this essay constitute, as I argue, part of Wolf's public relations campaign for personal exoneration and a more positive assessment of East German Communism in the intensely politicized climate of postunification Germany. His memoirs are intended as a counter-history to the prevailing discourse about the end of the Cold War, out of the belief, as he writes in the preface to *Man without a Face*, that "any history worthy of the name cannot be written only by the victors" (1997, xii).

From Spymaster to Master Storyteller

Like most Communist autobiographers before and after 1989, Wolf aligns his life story with the history of the GDR and invokes the antifascist founding myth that was the cornerstone of East Germany's claim of legitimacy (Nothnagle 1999). The rejection of Nazism and political socialization during Soviet exile inform his lifework and give it meaning: "The Second World War was the crucial event in the lives of millions of people, and it was a war that thankfully ended the Third Reich. How could anyone who fought against Hitler's barbarians have considered himself a traitor to Germany? My own contribution, and that of my family, to the fight may have been small, but I am proud of it nonetheless" (M. Wolf 1997, 386). Reprising his defense at the 1993 trial, this statement deftly equates persecution of Communists under the Nazis with the criminalization of SED officials after 1989. For Wolf combatting the revival of fascism justifies his foreign intelligence work during the Cold War. In *Man without a Face* he writes, "Hitler's long shadow was one of the reasons I agreed to the idea of working for a secret service. This was not treason" (1997, 386). Although the HVA continued the GDR's fight against fascism after 1945 "on a less exalted level" than those who resisted Hitler (382), he is proud of his part in "maintaining the status quo in Europe, a status quo that may have been tense and chilly, but which ultimately avoided the unthinkable—but not always improbable— endgame of nuclear war" (1997, 386-87). This line of reasoning echoes East German claims that the Berlin Wall prevented a third world war (Nothnagle 1999, 112) and saved the peace in Europe.

Wolf employs a narrative strategy that burnishes his reputation and that of his "scouts," on the one hand, while normalizing and justifying East German espionage, on the other. The successful spymaster, who built an extensive spy network that infiltrated the inner circles of West German political parties and the upper echelons of industry, the military, and technology in the Federal Republic, depicts the HVA as a "dedicated and elite corps serving an honorable cause" (Dennis 2003, 86). He praises the political idealism and resourcefulness of his scouts and reflects with pride on the work of his top spies, Gabriele Gast in West Germany's Federal Intelligence Service (Bundesnachrichtendienst), Günter Guillaume in the Brandt administration, and Rainer Rupp in NATO's Brussels headquarters. While attributing the success of the HVA to a "strong sense of belonging" (M. Wolf 1997, 228) that he cultivated among his scouts, Wolf acknowledges that it also inadvertently led to the exposure and arrest of Günter Guillaume, when a telegram reading "Congratulations on the Second Man" on the occasion of Guillaume's son's birth caught the attention of West German counterintelligence.

Wolf depicts himself as a compassionate spymaster, personally committed to his agents and concerned about their welfare, when he writes, "I never forgot that behind every case was a human being who had put his trust in us and his life on the line" (1997, 144). He describes the arrest and conviction of Gabriele Gast as a particularly hard blow in "a period rich in personal disappointments and defeats" (1997, 372) and wonders whether espionage is worth the human toll when confronted with the poor health of former moles and agents of his who were forced to testify at his trial. However, when it comes to victims of the HVA's particular methods of psychological manipulation, he has little regret about the "active measures" that damaged political reputations in the West and feels no guilt over seducing, intimidating, or blackmailing people into spying for the GDR.

In justifying East German espionage, Wolf wants readers to believe that the HVA was like other foreign intelligence agencies and better than many. In the preface to *Man without a Face* he acknowledges, "Our sins and mistakes were those of every other intelligence agency" (1997, xi) and asserts that "crimes were committed on both sides in the global struggle" (xii). East German foreign intelligence bore greatest similarity to the Soviet Union's KGB, on which it was modeled and from which its operatives received training in the early years (M. Wolf 1997, 230). The HVA was predicated on the same "chekist" principles and was integrated into the Mfs following a similar arrangement in the Soviet Union. According to Wolf, however, it also operated like intelligence agencies in the West. For example he argues that disinformation campaigns designed to discredit the West through the German People's Radio had parallels in the CIA-backed Radio Free Europe. The HVA appears more professional and scrupulous in Wolf's account than others because he claims to have guarded it against the "operational excesses" (1997, 232) of some Eastern Bloc intelligence agencies that resulted in "wet jobs," a euphemism for "illegal, unauthorized killings in espionage [that] did and still do occur" (1997, 217). While acknowledging that espionage had become a "rough game," Wolf claims to have eschewed the use of nerve toxins and deadly skin poisons developed and disseminated to Eastern Bloc intelligence agencies by the KGB (1997, 236).

As head of foreign espionage, Wolf's primary responsibility was for the operational area of the Federal Republic of Germany, but as Jens Gieseke and Mike Dennis argue, this does not mean the HVA was completely removed from domestic surveillance and political repression in the GDR (Dennis 2003, 170; Gieseke 2014, 155). Nonetheless, that is precisely the impression Wolf creates when he writes, "I considered my own work in foreign intelligence to be a separate and more defensible sphere of activity" (1997, 357). Both the German and the English-language editions gloss over the degree of collaboration between the HVA and other departments in the Mfs. Omitting or downplaying episodes in which the HVA participated in political repression at home allows Wolf to represent himself as he would most like to be known, the indefatigable adversary of the West during the Cold War, who was deeply committed to defending the East German state. He recounts how the HVA recruited West German businessmen and politicians, pressing them into cooperation through extortion, probing them for critical information about West German economic and political policies, and passing this information along to the KGB. He regrets that Guillaume's exposure brought down "the most far-sighted of modern German statesmen, Willy Brandt" (1997, xii) but believes Guillaume was the pretext for rather than the cause of Brandt's downfall (1997, 186). Indeed, he maintains that intelligence verifying Brandt's genuine commitment to *Ostpolitik* contributed to a climate of détente because it reduced KGB and Mfs fears of West Germany. Whether or not this was the case, such an argument has the effect of trivializing the harm done to the West by the HVA without diminishing Wolf's mystique as Communism's successful spymaster.

Wolf is comparatively silent, however, about HVA participation in domestic surveillance and political repression in the GDR. Structural overlap is blamed for information sharing and collaboration between the HVA and other departments of the Mfs. He does not disavow knowledge of the harsh methods of counterintelligence but provides little detail on the exact nature or extent of the HVA's involvement other than to state, "I am not going to claim I had nothing to do with [domestic] repression, but the relatively strict compartmentalization of the ministry meant that my service was explicitly not supposed to engage in internal counterintelligence activities" (1997, 233). Vague denials or tacit admissions of the kind in the preceding quote do little to shed light on the blurred boundaries between defense of the East German state from the incursions of the West and repression of East German citizens who wanted to reform socialism in the GDR or immigrate to the West. Lacking in specificity, they allow Wolf to obfuscate his awareness of, responsibility for, and role in political repression in general.

In addition to drawing a bright line between foreign intelligence and domestic surveillance, Wolf draws sharp contrasts between himself and Erich Mielke. Described by Leslie Colitt as "exact opposites in almost every way" (1995, 63), the HVA chief was cultured, well connected, and came from the ranks of the party intelligentsia, whereas Mielke rose from proletarian street brawler and German Communist Party member in the Third Reich to the upper echelons of power in East Germany as a member of the SED's Central Committee. Wolf depicts his boss as a volatile but shrewd political operator who was envious of his deputy and regarded him as a potential rival. The level of distrust between the two men in Wolf's account strains credulity at times, for example, when Wolf claims he resisted his boss's demand for total control and was able to effectively insulate the HVA's central registration system. Another implausible claim is that Mielke kept the HVA chief out of the loop about plans to build the Berlin Wall in 1961. Even "at the risk of damaging [his] reputation as the man who really knew what was going on in East Germany" (1997, 113), Wolf claims that he first heard the news about the border closing on the radio like everyone else. Jens Gieseke also questions the veracity of this statement, as there was greater overlap in areas of responsibility and more coordination between departments of the MfS than Wolf admits. By recounting their personal differences and moments in their contentious work relationship, Wolf creates the impression that struggles with Mielke contributed to the decision to retire early. His belief that Mielke would have blocked his candidacy for election to the Central Committee and the Politburo (1997, 352) is essentially unprovable, but it allows him to appear as the victim of political intrigue and power struggles within the MfS. His long tenure as head of the HVA is attributed to deep personal connections to the "highest levels of the KGB" (1997, 302), which protected him from Mielke's paranoia and lust for power.

The spymaster had the good fortune to retire before the collapse of East German Communism. This gives him some credibility when assuming a critical stance regarding the GDR past. In his autobiographies he distances himself not only from his boss but also from an SED leadership resistant to reform. He employs the pejorative term "concrete heads" (1997, 354) for the octogenarian SED leaders of a "moribund" (361) regime and recounts trying to battle against Erich Honecker's recalcitrance in a private meeting in which the general secretary vowed he would never allow perestroika and glasnost in the GDR (360). However, Wolf's support for Gorbachev was not as unqualified as he would have readers think. In a March 1989 interview with the West German news agency ARD, Wolf equivocated when asked about the suitability of Perestroika and Glasnost for the GDR, saying, "Here [in the GDR] we must do what we consider to be right and necessary for us" (Drommer 1998, 104). In the same interview, he confined his support for Gorbachev to, "I am cheerful and happy that he is there" (Drommer 1998, 105; Wolf 1997, 361). "There" presumably refers to the Soviet Union. Another possible translation for *das es ihn gibt* might be "that he is alive." Either way the comments reveal a reluctance to fully embrace Gorbachev's reforms and openly break with the policies of the Honecker regime.

In recalling how he was reprimanded for his public support of Gorbachev's perestroika, Wolf casts himself as an uncomfortable outsider at odds with the party he did not abandon while intellectually drawn to dissident groups that did not embrace him. Claiming that some regarded him in the late 1980s as a "reformer inside the party" (M. Wolf 1997, 356), he acknowledges that he and others in the party "waited in vain for a redeemer to emerge as a successor to Honecker from within the system and set a new course" (357). While self-critical admissions like this implicate him in the inertia of a regime incapable of adjusting to new realities, they also illustrate how Wolf attempts to understand his mistakes and his role in maintaining the East German state.

Negotiating Credibility, Asserting Veracity

Although Wolf understands his autobiography to be the "subjective testimony of a time full of contradictions" (1998, 11), he also recognizes the need to establish his credibility as the narrator and protagonist of his life story. He uses statements of purpose and disclaimers in the prefaces to control his image and manage reader expectations. Subtle differences in the German and American editions suggest keen audience awareness and offer insights into how he wants his life story to be read. *Man without a Face*, he writes in the preface, is "not a confessional bid for personal redemption," and its author seeks "neither moral justification nor forgiveness" (1997, xii). Recognizing that readers may question his version of events, he nonetheless remains adamantly unapologetic about his political convictions and his lifework, writing, "I seek no pardon as a representative of the losers" (1997, xii). Similarly defiant in tone, the introduction to *Spionagechef im geheimen Krieg* includes a disclaimer about omissions and limits to his self-disclosure. Citing a moral responsibility toward agents who worked for him, he asks for the reader's indulgence, when he doesn't "name names, exercise restraint in some instances and in others is completely silent" (1998, 10). His caution is understandable because West Germans who worked for the MfS and had not been exposed after unification could still be subject to prosecution under German law. Addressing necessary omissions allows him to appear transparent and to superficially satisfy his end of the autobiographical pact with his German readers, namely, the commitment to truthfulness, without violating his professional and moral obligation to individuals who spied for the GDR.

Both the English-language and the German introductions exhibit concern about what readers will believe or understand. In *Spionagechef im geheimen Krieg*, Wolf begins with an acknowledgment of the high expectations of his readers and that writing such a book is a "gamble" (*Wagnis*) (1998, 9), because touting the success of East German espionage after the spectacular dissolution of the GDR "may appear arrogant" to many (1998, 10). However, he insists on his right "to recount and examine in detail the successes and failures of [his] career" (1997, xii) as well as his hope that "the story of the period as [he] lived it can also be understood on the other side of the Iron Curtain that has disappeared" (10). As a citizen of postunification Germany and a defendant in German courts at the time of his writing, it is hardly surprising that the German edition adopts a more conciliatory tone in explaining the imperatives of East German espionage.

One strategy for establishing narrator credibility evident in Wolf's autobiographies is the anticipation of reader skepticism, for example, when he writes, "One of the occupational hazards for a spymaster is that one usually isn't believed, even when telling the truth" (1998, 274) or when seeking to establish the veracity of his account by providing material proof to substantiate claims about his political views in the form of diary entries in the appendices to the German edition. Indeed no life story can be perceived as credible unless the writer admits to mistakes over the course of his or her life from which lessons can be drawn. Admitting to false thinking and personal failings, Wolf accepts that he must learn to take responsibility "for activities of [his] ministry and those aspects of the system [he] had served and perpetuated, even though they lay outside [his] own experience, knowledge or consent" (1997, 362). At the time of the building of the Berlin Wall in 1961, for example, he was convinced of the necessity of intelligence work and deeply committed to it. Thirteen years later, on the twenty-fifth anniversary of the founding of the GDR, he questions the value of intelligence work in a diary entry. Substantiating his claim that such doubts predated his retirement from the MfS and the collapse of the GDR is the transcribed diary entry in an appendix to the German edition (1998, 497). In a curious oversight, however, this particular entry is not among the facsimiles of handwritten diary entries, leaving the reader to trust he actually held these views in the 1970s.

Many of his admissions of culpability are vague, such as, "I do not claim ignorance of the brutalities of life within our own country" (1997, 236) and "While I did not abet terrorists as such, we certainly did train people in methods that were later abused" (1997, 279). Tacit admissions of this kind beg the question of actual knowledge and complicity. Wolf also employs the first-person plural, whether as the *pluralis majestatis* or a collective "we" in the way East Germans were socialized to think of themselves as part of a whole, for statements of generalized accountability, such as "we erred, we did many things wrong and were too late in recognizing the mistakes and their causes" (1998, 484), and "we didn't realize that the impetus [for reform] had to come from us" (1998, 432). Christoph Jung, Ute Hirsekorn, and Martin Sabrow have identified similar patterns of argumentation in the autobiographies of other former SED officials after 1989. Not all of Wolf's admissions of error are written in the first-person plural; however, the sudden switch from first-person singular to plural in the following example illustrates his tendency to assign guilt or failure to many: "When the long-expected reforms finally came with Mikhail Gorbachev's ascension to power, no one was more enthusiastic for our future than me. But we did not foresee that the change had come too late" (1997, 387). In this passage Wolf, the individual, is enthusiastic about Gorbachev's ideas and uses the first-person singular to align himself with Gorbachev, but Wolf, the party official, is one of many SED elites who failed to see that "glasnost was not going to really solve any of [their] problems" (1997, 387–88). Thinking in terms of "we" and depicting himself as part of a system provide Wolf with legal and moral cover when taking stock of his lifework. He accepts blanket responsibility for his part in a failed system and country that had a "good beginning" in antifascism but fell short of its ideals.

Since the truthful stocktaking of his lifework in East German foreign intelligence necessitates a frank assessment of the GDR and its leaders, he must balance both the positive and the negative sides of the East German history:

> As much as I would prefer to stress its anti-fascist origins, I would never allow myself to pass lightly over the dark side of [GDR] history. I know that there was a great deal wrong with the GDR, including a terrible amount of repression. I am perfectly aware of my own share in the responsibility for this. I was part of the system, and if people attack me (as they often do) as if I had been head of state, as if I had had total control over everything that happened in the GDR, then that is something I will have to bear. (M. Wolf 1997, 387)

A closer examination of this passage reveals a rhetorical strategy of differentiating himself from the SED leadership and casting himself as the victim of unjust criticism. The "as if" statements allow him to downplay his actual importance in the SED state and function to deflect responsibility for political repression in East Germany. Reminding his readers that he was neither head of state nor in a position of (absolute) power shifts culpability to other high-ranking party officials.

In Wolf's autobiographies the SED abuse of power is often depicted as something beyond his knowledge or control. He is a Stasi general who never saw the inside of a Stasi prison but will have to "learn to bear responsibility for activities of [his] ministry and those aspects of the system [he] served and perpetuated, even though they lay outside of [his] own experience, knowledge, or consent" (1997, 362). Use of the passive voice in the following statement allows him to imply that he is the victim of theses abuses: "My own entanglement in the secret side of the Cold War and the experience of the abuse of power done in the name of socialism are deep wounds in my biography" (1998, 474). Words like "entanglement" imply powerlessness, even helplessness, and abuses *done in the name* of socialism is a passive construction that conceals the identity of the decision makers while tacitly justifying excesses that may have occurred as mistakes committed for a "good cause." Admitting to feelings of shame for the misdeeds of the SED or another section of the MfS does not directly discredit him or his lifework.

Expressions of remorse and shame are comparatively few, however, and similarly impersonal in Wolf's autobiographies. A man who compares political conviction to setting oneself on a course and not deviating from it "no matter what terrible things you may see along the way" (1997, 102) is unlikely to express profound regrets about actions done in the name of those beliefs. Moreover, Wolf frequently cites the Cold War in explaining why the ends justify the means. One of the more "personal" examples of an impersonal expression of remorse is when he recites from "Apologies for Being Human," a poem by his father, Friedrich Wolf, at his retirement party in 1986. It is unclear what he is apologetic about; however, the moral transgressions rumored as reason for Wolf's dismissal may have been one reason for reciting this particular poem, the second stanza of which reads: "And if I hated too much and loved too wild, too free. Forgive me for being human, sainthood was not for me" (1997, 359). The quoted text is evidently not impersonal since it is part of his father's oeuvre, but it is odd that Wolf felt it necessary to apologize through the voice of his father on this particular occasion. The quoted stanza, moreover, creates a straw-man apology; he apologizes for ordinary human passions and for not being a saint, as if sainthood were expected of Communists like him or his father.

The uncertainty of his fate at the time of writing the autobiographies might explain why the discourse of victimization occasionally creeps into Wolf's account of his life. Although a well-connected and powerful party member, he appears resigned and lacking agency in the last years of the GDR. Characterizing the Leipzig Monday Demonstrations, which precipitated the peaceful revolution in East Germany, as a "catastrophe" allows him to represent himself and the SED as "victims of historical processes" beyond their control (Zahlmann 2009, 277). On the eve of German unification, Wolf once again felt like a "hostage to historical events" (1998, 13), inviting comparisons between the exile of Communists under the Nazis and the ostracism of East German Communist leaders after 1989. He acknowledges "great bitterness among [their] officers toward the Soviets" (1997, 370), who were disappointed in the Soviet Union for abandoning the HVA in its time of need, but is reticent about his own views regarding East Germany's ally. The arrest and imprisonment of his scouts are also a source of bitterness for Wolf. Victor's justice at the end of the Cold War, according to him, means that "the spies of one state go unpunished . . . whereas those who worked for the other state are sentenced to long prison terms and hefty fines" (1997, 335). He blames "the distorting prism of the highly unsympathetic German media" (1997, 372) for stirring up popular hatred of the Stasi and functionaries of the GDR, "regardless of the positions a particular individual held" (1998, 14), and resents being branded as a symbol of the East German regime when he writes, "My reputation as source of hope, as a supporter of Gorbachev wasn't worth a damn" (1998, 13).

Representing Spycraft: Rumors, Clichés, and Imagery

The "man without a face" was allegedly a fan of spy fiction and flattered by rumors that he was the model for the Soviet spymaster Karla in the novels of John Le Carré (Colitt 1995, 89). Although Le Carré repeatedly refuted the connection and denied intentional parallels between Wolf and the German Jewish character Fiedler in *The Spy Who Came in from the Cold* (1963), the rumors persisted and added to Wolf's mystique. While neither fanning nor refuting rumors about himself, Wolf employs a narrative strategy that alternately invokes and dismisses similarities between the real-world HVA and the fictional world of spies. On the one hand, he distances himself and his lifework from clichéd literary tropes, emphasizing the banality of spy work. Comments such as "vast stretches of this work were very boring" (1997, 110) function to de-romanticize popular impressions of spycraft and explain the unorthodox decision to run a dozen agents himself. Dramatic stories of HVA operations are often prefaced with disclaimers such as, "What then happened, sounds more like a spy thriller than sober reality" (1998, 155).

On the other hand, his account treads familiar territory for readers of spy fiction. His life story makes for fascinating reading and has no shortage of political intrigue, dangerous missions, secret signals, couriers, double agents, and deadly outcomes. Amused when real-world intelligence imitates art, with some of their "madcap schemes and daring ruses" striking him as something of a "spy thriller cliché" (1998, 19), he does not disavow "how rough the game had become" (1997, 236), but writes: "The clichés established by espionage movies and novels notwithstanding, physical violence was the exception, not the rule" (1997, 232). Wolf recalls being "painfully aware" of his own recourse to the clichéd discourse of fictional characters when the CIA attempted to recruit him after 1989. Even though his future was far from certain at this time, he brazenly rejects the offer, suggesting that the weather in Siberia would be just as agreeable to him as the weather in California. He notes wryly the bizarre way in which "real conversations in espionage can sometimes imitate the style of spy novels" (1997, 11).

Tall, handsome, and urbane, Wolf cut a dashing figure and drew obvious comparisons to the most famous character of spy fiction, James Bond. In another example of life imitating art, the real-life spymaster was reputed to be a ladies' man like Bond. He was known to give special personal attention to certain female agents, and both his first and second marriage ended as a result of affairs. He formed a particularly close bond with HVA supermole Gabriele Gast and notes that he gave her "personal attention" because she "needed to feel wanted by him" (1997, 160). Womanizing is a trait the spymaster apparently shared with his father as well, and while acknowledging his mother's pain over her husband's philandering, he is largely silent on the subject of his own dalliances and their toll on his personal life. Leslie Colitt describes in much greater detail, for instance, the messy divorce from his second wife, Christel, whose best friend, Andrea, became the third Mrs. Wolf well after their adulterous affair had become public knowledge.

Anticipating that some readers will expect "something like a James Bond film or espionage thriller" (1998, 9), Wolf writes, "I would be failing to give a truthful picture, however, if I did not reveal in detail some of the more exotic and tragic operations in which my men took part" (1997, 149). Such disclaimers allow him to appear candid while satisfying reader interest in the more colorful and intriguing aspects of espionage. Even when demurring that "not every agent is a born James Bond" (1997, 137), he invokes reader associations with the literary genre: "To outsiders, the world of secret services must sometimes appear absurd, their activities at best a senseless game, at worst immoral" (1997, 384). Rather than romanticize Cold War espionage the way spy novels do, he admits that "people suffered. Life was hard. . . . Crimes were committed by both sides in the global struggle. Like most people in this world, [he felt] remorse" (1997, xii).

The use of Romeo agents, who seduced single West German women in important administrative positions in government and industry, was one of the most sensational and controversial chapters in East German espionage. Striking a rare note of false modesty, Wolf writes, "If I go down in espionage history, it may well be for perfecting the use of sex in spying" (1997, 135) a practice he dates back to biblical times. Protesting that the "link between sex and spying is no invention of mine" (1997, 135), he nonetheless acknowledges that his reputation and some of the more spectacular successes of the HVA can be traced back to the work of his Romeos. The chapter "Spying for Love" both normalizes and romanticizes the deployment of Romeo agents, arguing that other intelligence agencies engaged in similar practices although without as much success, and that it was "natural" for single male agents operating in the Federal Republic to fall in love while on the job. Eager to stress that genuine romantic relationships often resulted, he omits how Romeos were trained and set upon single women to exploit their need for love and draw them into the operational plans of the HVA. Indeed, he is more amused by the caper than remorseful about the deceit perpetrated on one of his "Juliets" (women who aided Romeos and sometimes became spies for the GDR) when he describes the elaborate efforts to create a "Potemkin" wedding ceremony with an HVA officer posing as a priest for a strict Catholic West German woman who felt guilty about living in sin with her Romeo. Rather than lose an asset, Wolf devised a ruse to assuage her guilt and keep the intelligence pouring in. There is little remorse for such deceptions because he was "running an intelligence agency, not a 'lonely-hearts club'" (1997, 165). In the final analysis, whenever Wolf poses the question to himself about HVA methods and dubious outcomes, he concludes that the ends justified the means (1997, 152).

Man without a Face is not a "tell-all" book, as Craig R. Whitney notes in the foreword (M. Wolf 1997, xxv). Neither is *Spionagechef im geheimen Krieg.* The consummate spymaster, while wanting to appear straightforward with his readers, reserves his right to silence. He is cautious in what he reveals and how much he tells. The spy stories he commits to paper are already a matter of public record; the agents he writes about have been exposed, arrested, and prosecuted. Indeed, he admits at one point that he had hoped to write the story of his lifework without mentioning certain agents who are included in the book only because their cover was blown. Wolf is similarly careful in expressions of personal culpability, to avoid opening himself to additional legal problems.

Like other former SED elites, Wolf found himself in an unenviable situation after the East German state collapsed. In writing several memoirs and making numerous public appearances, the man who had spent a lifetime in the shadows threw himself into the limelight and in the crosshairs of contentious debates about the Stasi and the East German past. His autobiographies are marked by the ambiguous space of postunification Germany as he attempts to navigate in the shifting terrains of political discourses. In contrast to other high-ranking officials whose autobiographies have been analyzed by Hirsekorn and Jung, Wolf was neither a Politburo member nor the head of a ministry. He nonetheless wielded considerable power, had access to the inner circles of East German leadership, and enjoyed a privileged lifestyle available to only the highest party officials. His autobiographies, however, tell a different story, one that puts him at odds with his boss and party and, most importantly, not in a position of power when the wall fell. Although politically encumbered by his decades of service, his voluntary retirement three years earlier and his belated, half-hearted engagement for reform allow him to exploit the ambiguity of his status as former power holder and potential change agent in his autobiographies.

Both the German publisher of *Spionagechef im geheimen Krieg* and the American publisher of *Man without a Face* represent the ambiguity and uncertainty of Wolf's situation at the time of publication in fascinating ways. The front covers to both editions visually reinforce his reputation as a man without a face, the spook renowned for being unknown for most of his career. The color palette is dark, and Wolf's face is obscured. The front cover of *Man without a Face* is a medium shot by the East German photographer Sibylle Bergemann of Wolf standing on a dark Berlin street, his head framed by a gun's sight. The bull's-eye is fixed on the pixilated face, rendering it unrecognizable.[7] The gun sight dramatizes the precarious situation of the successful spymaster and performs Wolf's claim—explicitly stated only in the English-language edition—that he was a "wanted man" in unified Germany. The back cover has the same shot as the front—minus the gun sight and with everything *other than* Wolf's face pixilated, as if its protagonist had emerged from the shadows through the process of writing the autobiography. The evolution from faceless spook to visible figure performs one part of Lejeune's "autobiographical pact," the sincere effort of the author to write about his life in a way that makes it understandable to himself and the reader.

The front cover of *Spionagechef im geheimen Krieg* uses what appears to be the same photo. It is a high-contrast close-up headshot of Wolf with half his face obscured in shadow, the other half in light. The last photograph in the German edition is of Wolf in front of the Marx-Engels monument in Berlin in 1993. He stands literally with the founders of Communism. On the opposite page are the words that best summarize how he has defended himself in court and in his autobiographies: "Not far from my apartment in the center of Berlin young people sprayed the words 'We are not guilty' on the Marx-Engels Memorial. They are right. The Cold War is over, a model of socialism that began with great hope, has failed, but I have not lost my ideals" (1998, 488). However, the image on the opposite page undermines his claim of innocence, for his body blocks part of the graffiti so that it actually reads "we guilty." Although almost certainly unintentional, the contradiction between text and image introduces a level of ambiguity for the reader's consideration.

Markus Wolf's life story intersects with and is informed by the political conditions and social forces that defined German and European history in the twentieth century. As a young boy, he fled Nazi Germany with his family for the Soviet Union; he returned to Germany in 1945 to build up East German foreign intelligence and defend the East German state during the Cold War and was put on trial twice as an ex-Stasi general in reunited Germany. His entire professional life coincided with the Cold War, which also informed it: the Soviet-trained political agitator working for the Berliner Rundfunk in postwar Germany; the advisor to East Germany's diplomatic mission in Moscow, whose very person and career embodies the East German ideal of German-Soviet friendship; the Stasi general who cooperated so closely with the KGB that he was considered "Moscow's Man in Europe" (1997, 226); and the supporter of Gorbachev's perestroika in a reform-resistant GDR, disillusioned with intelligence work in later years.

His life writing, by contrast, is entirely the product of a post-GDR era, a radically changed political context from the one that formed the identity of the writing self. Altered social and political circumstances as well as criminal proceedings forced Wolf to reassess the values he lived by and the state he supported. While ultimately reaffirming his political convictions, the trajectory and meaning of his life were profoundly shaped by the time of his writing. Throughout the 1990s he fashioned and refashioned his life story, telling it in multiples venues, to different audiences, and with different emphases. He wrote out of a perceived moral obligation, both personally as well as politically, to defend the GDR, the HVA, and his life from defamation.

An inscription in the copy of *Man without a Face* purchased by the author of this chapter in a used bookstore in Berlin is from the late German television producer Thomas Wilkening to German film director Wolfgang Petersen. It reads: "Dear Wolfgang Petersen, even though this biography of Markus Wolf conceals more than it reveals (so typical of secret service), it is instructive in many regards. In my opinion Wolf certainly offers a highly interesting prototype for a strong filmic character." Wilkening's dedication recognizes two important aspects of Wolf's autobiography that have been argued in this chapter. Wolf's autobiographies, while informative, are strategic in their self-fashioning. They do not reveal too much and are careful to omit information that would be damaging to the spymaster or the agents who worked for him. Discretion is the habitus typical of the secret service, and the HVA chief proves the master of discretion as narrator of his life story. He also presents himself as a strong leading man in his own life story, which has a narrative arc common to many spy thrillers.

Wolf prefers to see his lifework, however, in the tradition of antifascist and Communist heroes like Harro Schulze-Boysen and Richard Sorge, whom he claims as his role models in antifascist agitation and intelligence work. Recalling their martyrdom allows Wolf to compare his lifework with their heroic sacrifice (much as he conflated parts of his own biography with his brother's in *Die Troika*), and to suggest that, like them, he too has been a victim of anti-Communist vilification. In this way both *Man without a Face* and *Spionagechef im geheimen Krieg* contribute to a specific subset of Communist autobiography known in the HVA as the "preservation of tradition" (*Traditionspflege*) (M. Wolf 1997, 227) that is designed to cultivate a strong sense of pride in the history of East German espionage. While acknowledging errors and false thinking that led to the collapse of the East German state, Wolf's autobiographies mount a strong defense for the honor of the HVA and the political conviction and professionalism of his agents. Unrepentant in his political convictions and with undiminished pride in directing the "most successful espionage agency in Europe" (M. Wolf 1997, 375), Wolf makes no apologies for being on the losing side of the Cold War.

Notes

1. Hauptverwaltung Aufklärung has also been translated as the Main Administration for Reconnaissance.

2. The self-dissolution of the HVA had the "tacit approval of the citizens' committees and the Central Round Table" (Gieseke 2014, 177).

3. In German der Bundesbeauftragte für die Unterlagen des Staatssicherheitsdienstes der ehemaligen Deutschen Demokratischen Republik (BStU). The largest of Wolf's files is his personnel file (KS60003/90), which contains *Lebensläufe* (vitae) from 1951 to 1954, performance evaluations, recommendations for promotion, and the conferral of more than twenty honors and medals. Another file (HA IX/11 SV 258/87) contains documentation of the Wolf family's status as victims of Nazi persecution: copies of the 1937 revocation by the Gestapo of their German citizenship, an application to the Verein der Verfolgten des Naziregimes (Association of the Victims of the Nazi Regime, VVN) and their VVN certificate. A third file (MfS-BCD) contains notes on service revolvers issued to Wolf after leaving the MfS.

4. All translations from German-language primary and secondary sources are my own unless otherwise indicated.

5. The title, *Geheimnisse der russischen Küche* (Secrets of the Russian kitchen), underscores the running theme of secrecy in his life.

6. The full text of Wolf's speech is reprinted in *Die Kunst der Verstellung* (The art of deception), including paratextual information on applause and boos.

7. Cover design by Alexander Knowlton.

References

ARCHIVAL SOURCES

BStU (Bundesbeauftragter für die Unterlagen der Staatssicherheitsdienst der ehemaligen Deutschen Demokratischen Republik [Federal Commissioner for the Records of the State Security Service of the Former German Democratic Republic]). Markus Wolf File KS60003/90.

PUBLISHED SOURCES

Childs, David, and Richard Popplewell. 1996. *The Stasi: The East German Intelligence and Secret Security*. New York: New York University Press.

Colitt, Leslie. 1995. *Spymaster: The Real-Life Karla, His Moles and the East German Secret Police*. Reading MA: Addison-Wesley.

Dennis, Mike. 2003. *The Stasi: Myth and Reality*. London: Pearson-Longman.

Drommer, Günther, ed. 1998. *Markus Wolf: Die Kunst der Verstellung*. Berlin: Schwarzkopf & Schwarzkopf.

Fricke, Karl Wilhelm. 1987. "Mitteilungen und Mutmaßungen zu Markus Wolf." *Deutschland Archiv* 3:229–31.

Gieseke, Jens. 2014. *The History of the Stasi: East Germany's Secret Police, 1945–1990.* Translated by David Burnett. New York: Berghahn.

Hirsekorn, Ute. 2010. "Thought Patterns and Explanatory Strategies in the Life Writing of High-Ranking GDR Party Officials after the *Wende.*" In *German Life Writing in the Twentieth Century,* edited by Birgit Dahlke, Dennis Tate, and Roger Woods, 179–95. Rochester NY: Camden House.

Jung, Christoph. 2007. *Geschichte der Verlierer: Historische Selbstreflexion von hochrangingen Mitgliedern der SED nach 1989.* Heidelberg: Universitätsverlag Winter.

Le Carré, John. 1963. *The Spy Who Came in from the Cold.* London: Victor Gollancz & Pan.

Lejeune, Philippe. 1989. *On Autobiography.* Translated by Katherine Leary. Minneapolis: University of Minnesota Press.

Links, Christoph. 2007. "Der Umgang mit ostdeutschen Biographien seit 1989: Erfahrungen eines Verlegers." *BIOS* 20:223–29.

McAdams, A. James. 2001. *Judging the Past in United Germany.* Cambridge: Cambridge University Press.

Nothnagle, Alan. 1999. *Building the East German Myth: Historical Methodology and Youth Propaganda in the German Democratic Republic, 1945–89.* Ann Arbor: University of Michigan Press.

Richter, Peter, and Klaus Rösler. 1992. *Wolfs West-Spione: Ein Insider-Report.* Berlin: Elefanten Press.

Runge, Irene, and Uwe Stelbrink. 1990. *Markus Wolf: "Ich bin kein Spion"; Gespräche mit Markus Wolf.* Berlin: Dietz.

Sabrow, Martin. 2014. *Zeitgeschichte schreiben: Von der Verständigung über die Vergangenheit in der Gegenwart.* Göttingen: Wallstein Verlag.

Schütt, Hans-Dieter. 2007. *Markus Wolf: Letzte Gespräche.* Berlin: Das neue Berlin.

Wolf, Andrea, ed. 2013. *Mischa: Briefe und Texte von Markus Wolf an die Familie, seine Freunde und Weggefährten.* Berlin: Edition Die Möwe.

Wolf, Markus. 1991. *In eigenem Auftrag: Bekenntnisse und Einsichten.* Munich: Schneekluth.

———. 1997. *Man without a Face: The Autobiography of Communism's Greatest Spymaster.* New York: Time Books Random House.

———. 1998. *Spionagechef im geheimen Krieg: Erinnerungen.* 2nd ed. Munich: Econ & List.

Zahlmann, Stefan. 2009. *Autobiographische Verarbeitungen gesellschaftlichen Scheiterns: Die Eliten der amerikanischen Südstaaten nach 1865 und der DDR nach 1989.* Cologne: Böhlau Verlag.

3   The Stasi's Secret War on Books

Uwe Berger and the Cold War Spy as Informant and Book Reviewer

ALISON LEWIS

In the German Democratic Republic (GDR), espionage was integral to the world of books and writing. Throughout the Cold War, the Ministry for State Security (Mfs), or Stasi, policed all aspects of the production and dissemination of literature in the context of culture wars waged against the West and fought out on a domestic stage. A key weapon in the war against homegrown, so-called hostile-negative (*feindlich-negativ*) literature was other writers, reviewers, and editors, many of whom the Stasi recruited as informers. It is no secret that the Stasi enlisted prominent literary figures such as Hermann Kant, the president of the German Writers Guild (Deutscher Schriftstellerverband) (cf. Jones 2011), and members of the unofficial underground, such as Sascha Anderson. But it also conscripted a few influential secret police informants—what the Stasi referred to as "unofficial collaborators" (*inoffizielle Mitarbeiter*, IM)—as peer reviewers of book manuscripts and published books. These informer-reviewers have to date remained faceless.

While they have certainly not been forgotten by the writers who were the targets of their "damning indictment[s]" (Evans 2006, 214), the informers themselves have been quick to run for cover and to erase their Stasi activities from the public record. Some such as poet and novelist Uwe Berger have set up personal websites documenting their life's work that make no mention of working for the Stasi.[1] In the context of such willful forgetting, this chapter attempts to write back into post–Cold War history an important side story in the Stasi's secret war on literature, namely, the untold account of the Stasi informers who were responsible for writing classified book reviews. In the absence of autobiographical testimony from these spies, Cold War "spy stories" of Stasi informers are best told as a "file story" (Glajar 2016, 57), composed primarily from the extensive and telling traces left behind in the Stasi files. I will first explore Berger's personal and professional motivations for working as a Stasi informer and reviewer before demonstrating how these played out in the censorship process. Through a close reading of his evaluations of literature and his Stasi file, I will analyze the salient features of his reviewing in relation to literary aesthetics and politics, features that point to Berger's self-understanding as an aesthetic gatekeeper, on the one hand, and an ideological "policeman," on the other. Finally, from this I will attempt to extrapolate Berger's position and position taking in the literary field over the duration of his association with the Stasi, and to contextualize his Stasi activities against the backdrop of shifts in cultural politics in the GDR. I argue that while continuing to work as a poet, Berger waged his own secret war in his capacity as a Stasi-appointed freelance reviewer. It was a war that he was to lose incrementally and one that did immense harm to those writers and books that came into his purview. He did so, moreover, for reasons that only partially overlapped with the Stasi's.

Censorship in the GDR and the Stasi

After the opening of the Stasi archives in 1992, when many victims of the East German regime gained access to their declassified secret police files, countless Stasi informants among the writing fraternity were exposed and named, including Uwe Berger. Joachim Walther's monumental 1996 study of the Stasi's surveillance of literature detailed Berger's activities for the Stasi both as an informer and as a secret censor of literature (Walther 1996b, 312–13). In 1997 Günter Kunert identified Berger in his memoir *Erwachsenenspiele* as one of three colleagues who spied on him and the source of a damning review of one of his works—a "denunciation masquerading as academic analysis" (Evans 2006, 214), which unequivocally branded him an enemy of the state (Costabile-Heming 2000, 63). Despite the increased attention to informants in recent research on the Stasi (Lewis 2003; Plowman 2003; Jones 2011; Ring 2015, 2016), we know very little about figures such as Berger. We also do not fully understand how the secret book reviews the Stasi commissioned—which will be exemplified here in Berger's story—fitted into the overall censorship process and whether his reviews were effective in blocking publications.

Censorship studies of the GDR have hitherto tended to fall into two categories: either publication histories of censored works or biographical studies of victims of censorship rather than those involved in the censoring. Volker Braun's *Hinze-Kunze-Roman* (Hinze-Kunze novel; Mix 1993) and Christa Wolf's *Nachdenken über Christa T.* (*Quest for Christa T.*; Hilzinger 1999) are examples of the former, and Jurek Becker (Müller 2003, 2006; Joch 2014) and Günter Kunert (Costabile-Heming 1997, 2000, 2002) examples of the latter. In both these strands of research, the Stasi appears in the role of a shadowy minor player, stepping onto the stage as an occasional antagonist rather than as a protagonist in its own right. Yet if we shift perspective for a moment to this antagonist and put the spotlight on the Stasi's involvement in censorship, we discover new perspectives that can serve to enrich accounts of censored works and their authors—what Carol Anne Costabile-Heming has called the "stories behind the stories" (2000, 64). The Stasi was, in addition to its monitoring of writers suspected of being part of a Western-led "inner opposition" (Glaeser 2011, 467) or "political-ideological diversion" (466), a key social "actor" in the censorship process. As Sara Jones has demonstrated in her case study of Hermann Kant—who was a victim of censorship while also being an informant—the Stasi was a constant if not rather opaque presence in the negotiations over censorship, exerting its influence across the entirety of the literary field, from informants working for publishers, informants inside the Writers Guild, and officers who liaised with the Ministry for Culture (Jones 2011, 49–43, 49–71). One of the functions the Stasi assumed was intervening in censorship. In many instances, the Ministry for Culture based its case for banning a work on the foundations laid by so-called expert reviews, written by fellow writers working on consignment for the secret police. With the salvaging of these reviews of literary texts—many of which are now housed in the archives of the Ministry for Culture as well as the Stasi Documents Archive (BStU)—comes the opportunity to read them in connection with the Stasi's declassified personal files on informers. This allows us to join the dots between reviews penned by the same reviewers and to fold these diachronic accounts into the life history of informers as well as the lives of their victims. It enables us therefore to read backward from the literary reviews authored by Berger and to adduce his motivations for willingly participating in secret wars on publishing.

The world of publishing in the GDR was, with few exceptions, highly politicized as was virtually the entire literary field (Parker and Philpotts 2009, 63; Sepp 2016, 242–46). The relationship between power and intellectuals was from the start highly volatile and "precarious," and remained so throughout the forty years of the GDR's existence (Sepp 2016, 252). While all literary fields are at some level suffused by power and/or economics (Bourdieu 1996, 216), in the GDR the production of literature was politically and ideologically driven by the ruling party, the Socialist Unity Party of Germany (Sozialistische Einheitspartei Deutschlands, SED) and its intricate system of controls. Censorship consisted of a "web of interlocking structures" (Costabile-Heming 2000, 55) that was susceptible to political influence at each of the points inside the web. The censorship apparatus, or censorship *dispositif,* was spread across five separate bodies—the publishers, the SED, the Main Directorate for Publishing and Book Trade (Hauptverwaltung Verlage und Buchhandel, HV) in the Ministry for Culture (Ministerium für Kultur), the Office for Copyright (Büro für Urheberrechte), and last, as the fifth censor, the Stasi (Walther 2003, 131). While the HV functioned as the "last instance of power" (Costabile-Heming 2000, 56), the Stasi represented an additional instrument of censorship, an extra rear-guard line of defense that could be mobilized to police works and their authors (Walther 2003, 131; Costabile-Heming 2000, 56). Like the publishers the

Stasi relied heavily on literary experts—mostly writers and some-times university professors—to assess works' suitability for publi-cation. To play its part as the party's "sword and shield," or as Jens Gieseke writes, as "the unconditional bodyguard of the Party lead-ership" (Gieseke 2011, 67), and to provide support for the central-ized control of literary communication, the Stasi commissioned its own reviews.[2] These were provided by its own specialists, whom it recruited in a dual capacity as both experts and informants. The Stasi enlisted various types of informants—ranging from the most common category of "Informer for the Political-Operative Penetration and Securing of the Area of Responsibility" (Inoffi-zieller Mitarbeiter zur politisch-operativen Durchdringung und Sicherung des Verantwortungsbereiches, IMS) (Walther 1996b, 561) to the more specialized category of "Informer for Special Purposes" (Inoffizieller Mitarbeiter für einen besonderen Einsatz, IME) (Walther 1996b, 581; Engelmann et al. 2016, 174), which was an expert informant "for matters beyond a case officer's normal skills" (Schmeidel 2008, 30). It imposed the usual conditions of secrecy and required informants to sign an oath pledging loyalty.

Following Michel Foucault's lead in reconceptualizing power as a dispersed force permeating the social body (1980, 93), schol-ars of literary communication have long argued for reassessing notions of censorship as purely prohibitive and repressive. Beate Müller contends that censorship should no longer be regarded as a "direct form of regulatory intervention" by the state or church (2004, 4). Instead, we should see it, as does Sophia Rosenfeld, as a "constitutive" part of the discourse and communication it pur-ports to control or regulate (2001, 129). Furthermore, we could argue, as does Judith Butler, that censorship is "not merely priv-ative, but formative as well, producing both speech and subjects" (1998, 252). Approaches such as these have encouraged a rethink-ing of censorship as an *intrinsic* part of the assemblage of the insti-tutions that make up the literary field and that control the flow of communication. While analyses of cultural regulation in demo-cratic societies tend to call all kinds of exclusionary mechanisms censorship, many critics still insist on making meaningful distinctions between the rather different forms of controls operating in democratic and totalitarian societies.

Müller, for instance, argues that there are clear differences between the mechanisms that filter communication, such as the market or expert opinion, and the sorts of authoritarian "interventions by a third party" in dictatorships (2004, 11). I would argue, however, that the regulation of literary discourse in Eastern Bloc dictatorships was not *only* located in "third party" interventions subject to direct political control, but that censorship could *also* involve skilled professionals, who provided expert opinion and carried out peer review. These professionals policed ideological as well as aesthetic dimensions of discourse. Most of these experts were commissioned openly by the publishers, but some were deployed covertly behind the scenes by the Stasi. The Stasi's experts conducted reviews of manuscripts that often competed with the publishers' reports in what could evolve into protracted power struggles. Hence, censorship, as well as self-censorship, occurred rarely, as York-Gothart Mix writes, as a "total confrontation" (2013, 498), and was a complex, multilayered affair, negotiated, as Sara Jones points out, via a "maze-like" system of controls, between multiple cultural agents and institutions operating in the literary field (2011, 16). The literary field, especially at the intersection with power, was, as Stephen Parker and Matthew Philpotts have suggested, a "dynamic" rather than a static "site of struggle," "in which agents compete[d] to secure and exchange capital in its various forms" (2009, 5). Censorship, I contend, was but one of the ways in which social agents—writers, publishers, editors, ministerial employees, ministers, members of the Politburo as well as Stasi agents—all vied to secure, exchange, and control the circulation of literary capital. However, far from being a battle merely between the main censors—the Main Directorate for Publishing and Book Trade and writers—censorship could also involve ancillary struggles between other players. As we are beginning to understand better, it could entail power plays between the Stasi and the Ministry for Culture, the Stasi and publishers, as well as tugs-of-war between the Stasi and the Writers Guild, and even between the Stasi's informants and the Stasi itself.

Lewis

The Stasi's Recruitment of Berger: Context and Motivation

The case of Uwe Berger can help illuminate some of these censorship battles fought over the written word. Berger was initially registered in 1969 as an informant involved in "the processing and exposure of persons suspected of hostile activity" (IMV), before being upgraded to an "expert informant" (IME) in 1979.[3] Choosing the undercover name of "Uwe," Berger amassed a thick, multivolume Stasi file of 2,255 leaves. Like many writers the Stasi attempted to enlist, Berger, who was born in 1928 in Eschwege in Hessen, was chosen because of his positive political attitude and his professional standing as a writer. His commissioning officer, Lieutenant Rolf Pönig, wrote in justification of his plan to recruit Berger: "The aforementioned candidate is found to be suitable for political operative counterintelligence work among writers and poets. It is planned to win him over to collaborating with the Mfs and to develop him as an IMV. The candidate is himself a poet and a literary critic and possesses extensive contacts to the circles mentioned below" (AIM 8382/91, vol. I/1, 4). Berger was, it seems, thought to be a good catch for the Stasi, especially in the wake of the crushing of the Prague Spring in Czechoslovakia in 1968. At the time a sizable number of writers in the Writers Guild, of which Berger was a member, had either abstained or absented themselves from the vote on a resolution in support of the suppression of the Czech reform movement (Goldstein 2017, 39). Berger had endorsed the regime and voted for the resolution. He was 100 percent loyal, having been awarded the Johannes R. Becher Medal in 1961 and the Heinrich-Heine Prize in 1968. When Section II (Referat II) in the Mfs's Main Department (Hauptabteilung, HA) XX/7 made the decision to enlist him as an informant on November 25, 1969 (8382/91, vol. I/1, 4), he was employed on a contractual basis by Aufbau to write reviews of literary manuscripts. Prior to this he had worked as an editor for the publisher Volk und Wissen and later for Aufbau from 1949 to 1955 before going freelance.

The immediate occasion for his recruitment was the Stasi's concern to gauge the political climate inside Aufbau. Berger, along with Günther Deicke, was one of the editors of an important new poetry anthology, *Die Lyrik der* DDR (Poetry of the GDR), which Aufbau was in the process of publishing, and which was due to appear in 1970. The collection, which was reissued several times, included some fifty-two poets, one of whom was Berger. As the nation's flagship publishing house, Aufbau was naturally of paramount interest to the regime. Berger was most likely thought to be a valuable source close to the center of power at Aufbau—a center that was seen as vulnerable and unstable. The Stasi had become interested in Günter Caspar, who in 1963 was head of "Zeitgenössische deutsche Literatur" (Department for Contemporary Literature).[4] Caspar had been a member of the Berlin Donnerstagskreis (Thursday circle) of reform socialists and was friends with leading critics of the regime Walter Harich, Wolfgang Janka, and Gustav Just, who were convicted in show trials in 1956 (Walther 1996b, 71, 559). On October 9, 1970, some seven months after Berger's recruitment, Caspar was also approached by the same officers, Rolf Pönig and Peter Gütling, to work as a Stasi informant (Walther 1996b, 558). But unlike Berger Caspar rebuffed the approach, and by confessing to having a peculiar "character trait" that meant he could not keep a secret, he managed to fob the Stasi off (Walther 1996b, 767). The Stasi was probably nonplussed about this refusal, since, as it transpired, it already had a long-standing informant high up in Aufbau in Fritz-Georg Voigt, or IMS/IMF "Kant," who was director of the publishing house from 1966 onward (Walther 1996b, 767).[5]

The Stasi believed at the time that around 60 percent of its informants were prompted by "recognition of society's need" to collaborate with the secret police, as Manfred Hempel found in his PhD dissertation on the "effect of moral factors" on informants completed at the Stasi's university, the Juridical University of the MfS (Juristische Hochschule des MfS) in Potsdam in 1967 (Müller-Enbergs 2008, 107). However, as even Hempel's ideologically biased study revealed, many informants had secondary motives over and above "political-ideological conviction" (Müller-Enbergs 2008, 107). Berger's official motivation was, as his file implies, his positive political-ideological beliefs, but his secondary, ulterior motives remain something of a mystery. At the time he was recruited, Berger was not out of favor with the regime and, as far as we know, was not threatened or coerced to collaborate. There is also no indication that Berger agreed in the short term to further his literary career or because he was having difficulties publishing or indeed passing the censorship authorities. Berger's works had not suffered from any notable delays and were not in any danger of being censored. Indeed, in 1968 Berger received prompt official approval from the Main Directorate for Publishing and Book Trade to publish a volume of poetry (DR 1/2091).

In his self-reporting to his officer, the picture that emerges from Berger's Stasi files is of an extremely combative and manipulative member of the Aufbau team of editors and authors. Berger often appears envious of other writers, anxious that he was not being given enough manuscripts to review, and fearful of being marginalized.[6] On file are numerous references to infighting in the publishing house and to regular squabbles with Caspar. On one occasion on November 5, 1970, Caspar rang Berger to berate him—"You tricked me"—after learning that Berger had phoned the poet Sarah Kirsch and blamed Caspar (and not himself) for writing a negative review of her poetry (UB, vol. II/1, 121). On another occasion a few months later, Caspar lambasted him for writing a bad review of a work that Caspar hoped to publish, declaring: "It was the most 'subjective thing' [Berger] had ever written" (UB, vol. II/1, 196). Berger for his part is captured on file conspiring against Caspar, complaining hypocritically, for example, to Voigt that Caspar was "insincere and scheming" (UB, vol. II/1, 167). In June 1972 there is talk of almost daily disputes between Caspar and Berger over the selection of poems—which he refers to as "the tough, unpleasant, running battles holding up work which are worse than ever" (UB, vol. II/1, 166).

We also find evidence on file that Berger disapproved of the fact that open critics of the regime, such as songwriter and poet Wolf Biermann and poet Reiner Kunze, were flouting censorship processes and copyright laws. He lamented as much to his officer at the outset of his collaboration, expressing hopes that "progressive forces" in the Writers Guild such as himself might be given more support (UB, vol. II/1, 13). As the ex-Stasi officer and infamous defector Werner Stiller admitted in an interview in 2010, resentment among his informants was a prime motivator, and he looked to recruit people who felt disadvantaged or insufficiently recognized by their superiors (Michaelsen 2010, 2). Recruiting those who were bitter was, he confessed, "surprisingly easy" (Michaelsen 2010, 3). If we read between the lines of his Stasi reports, Berger could be interpreted as resenting that he was not receiving proper recognition in the literary community. In collaborating Berger no doubt hoped to gain an advantage that might bolster his standing among his peers, which he felt was weakened by, among other things, the loopholes writers were exploiting by bypassing censorship and publishing in the West.

For a collaboration between the Stasi and its informants to succeed, especially if no grounds for blackmail or coercion existed, there clearly needed to be other factors at work. Very few writers agreed to collaborate for financial gain. Berger was remunerated reasonably well for his reviews, to be sure, and received between 200 and 400 marks for each of his reports, but this cannot be the sole reason for his extraordinarily high level of engagement. Certainly, his hardline ideological views and resentment of his peers meant that he regarded working for the Stasi more as an opportunity than a burden. Reading between the lines of his expansive file and interpreting some of the key events that structure his "file story," it seems fair to say that Berger not only relished undercover work but that he went to extraordinary lengths to keep the Stasi happy.

An alarming instance of Berger's eagerness to please can be found while his wife was dying of cancer between August and October 1970. Throughout her illness Berger was content to hold regular meetings with his case officer, as Pönig testified in his report on August 6, 1970: "This matter is troubling the IM immensely at the moment. Nevertheless, he declared to this staff member that we can approach him with tasks because the work must go on" (UB, vol. II/1, 69). Pönig noted at the next two meetings on September 8 (UB, vol. II/1, 86) and October 4 (UB, vol. II/1, 89) that Berger was unable to leave his flat because his wife was too ill. The best indication, however, of Berger's determination to please the Stasi is the fact that he redoubled his efforts to carry out his Stasi assignments even during his wife's sickest hours. His task at the time was to "firm up the contact to Paul Wiens / determine the causes of the political changes in the behavior of Paul Wiens" (UB, vol. II/1, 56).

As his file reveals, Berger worked proactively on this task, using his wife's sickness as an excuse to phone fellow writer and poet Paul Wiens on August 8, 1970 (UB, vol. II/1, 80). Wiens had been president of the Berlin branch of the Writers Guild from 1961 to 1969 but had come under suspicion after the Prague Spring (7781/83, vol. I/3, 84). Although Wiens had worked for the Stasi from 1962 to 1968, he was seen as such a threat that his telephone was tapped from 1968 to 1971 (Wietersheim 2014, 100). Much was at stake in preventing Wiens from straying too far from the party line. In the days after his wife's death, Berger called Wiens again to try to engineer a visit from him. Wiens duly obliged, whereupon Berger passed off the visit as an espionage success to Pönig: "The atmosphere of the conversation was familiar. On entering Wiens embraced me as an expression of sympathy. Our relationship is— at least in Wiens's opinion—characterized by mutual respect and tolerance (a tolerance that is also based on opposing views). Wiens invited me to return the visit" (UB, vol. II/1, 102). Berger thus exploited the occasion of his own recent bereavement, deploying his own misfortune as a pretext to phone Wiens, anticipating that his wife's death would bring him closer to Wiens, whom he could then milk for intelligence.

Berger's sneaky undercover habitus and rather spiteful disposition come into even sharper focus in relation to his mission to keep Wiens under surveillance. From Berger's accounts for the Stasi, it seems that he denounced Wiens whenever the opportunity arose. For instance he implied that Wiens had no compunctions about expressing approval for Willy Brandt's *Ostpolitik* and watching West German television, something that was frowned on in party circles (UB, vol. II/1, 109). Wiens made no effort to hide his nonconformist, reform-socialist views about cultural politics after a trip to Yugoslavia: "He complained about our cultural politics. We should let people write what they want" (UB, vol. II/1, 100). Reports such as these were designed to mark Wiens as a troublemaker and as someone the regime needed to be vigilant about. Moreover, many of Berger's reports about Wiens are petty and catty and read rather like a schoolboy "telling on" a "naughty" friend to a teacher. On one occasion he relayed the fact that Wiens had told him two political jokes in which "the socialist system of planning and control as well as the GDR was questioned or demeaned" (UB, vol. II/1, 162).

Of the two poets, Wiens had greater access to travel privileges— Berger only traveled to socialist countries, while Wiens was able to visit capitalist countries—and the lesser of the two literary lights may have been envious of his colleague's international life-style.[7] Berger certainly appears to have been in awe of Wiens's chutzpah, which can be seen from a snide comment Berger made to his officer in 1970: "He [Wiens] thinks he'll make an impression if he is a martyr" (UB, vol. II/1, 29). In many respects Berger's surveillance of Wiens thus reads as a kind of clandestine payback designed to cut him down to size. It is not clear whether in 1970 Berger suspected that Wiens had been an informant for the Stasi in the sixties, and indeed, whether later on he knew that Wiens had resumed working for the Stasi, after Wiens was rehabilitated in 1972 (7781/83, vol. I/3, 50-52). It can probably be assumed that over time he gathered that Wiens, like himself, might also be enjoying the protection of the secret police. It is likely that Berger was also aware that the aforementioned director of Aufbau, Voigt, was working for the Stasi. We can deduce this from a throwaway comment made by Voigt, captured on file, that the Stasi had taken objection to a fellow poet's work, whereupon Voigt added: "But I probably should not be telling you this" (UB, vol. II/1, 173). If Berger did suspect Wiens was also a Stasi collaborator, he seems to have resented it, especially since Wiens received more benefits than he did. Interestingly, in 1975 he passed on another colleague's exasperated comment that "she was sick and tired" of Wiens "always" being given preference over her (UB, vol. II/3, 359). One could infer that this was also Berger's view.

Berger's hard work does appear to have at least been acknowledged by the Stasi. After over ten years of collaborating, Wiens, one of Berger's perennial targets, died on April 6, 1982. A few months before his death, Berger's handler, Captain Pönig, convened a special meeting on February 16, 1982, in the presence of Lieutenant-Colonel Brosche. Berger was to be awarded the "Medal for Brotherhood in Arms in Silver" (Medaille für Waffen-brüderschaft in Silber). The report filed on the secret ceremony held in a Stasi safe house underscores just how grateful Berger was for the recognition: "'Uwe' stated he felt very honored by this award, would give everything to fulfill the tasks assigned to him and that the Mfs could always count on him to be a reliable collaborator. Moreover, he expressed his close bonds with and devotion to our party and the Mfs. He described himself as an impartial patriot on the side of the working class and its party" (UB, vol. 6, 210). It is possible that the awarding of the medal was designed to coincide with Berger being groomed to take Wiens's place as a key source inside the Writers Guild.

Berger's Secret Police Reviews of Literature

Berger was one of the Stasi's informers who regularly wrote classified reviews on consignment for the Stasi and was thus a player in the invisible clandestine part of the censorship apparatus. He was in effect one of the "faceless" censors of literature. In his capacity as a Stasi reader, Berger reviewed and, as we shall see, mostly tried to sabotage the publication of works by a string of notable writers: Sarah Kirsch and Paul Wiens (he also spied on both of them, as mentioned above), Rainer Kirsch, Monika Maron, Günter Kunert, Klaus Poche, Erich Loest, Lutz Rathenow, Wolfgang Hilbig, Eva Strittmatter, Franz Fühmann, and Bettina Wegner. From 1969 to 1979, he wrote prepublication reviews of manuscripts for the Stasi. From around 1980 onward, he wrote postpublication reports for the Stasi on works that had already been published, often illegally, in the West.

In his reports that were meant only for the Stasi's eyes, Berger openly vented his displeasure at the "antisocialist" stance of contemporary literature. He was free to do so because he wrote what we now call single-blind peer reviews. Werner Mittenzwei calls manuscript reviews "the most important form of communication" with the censorship office, and in recognition of this fact, the Stasi engineered its own reviews so that it could have a say in this process (2003, 251). However, unlike other reviews, those commissioned by the Stasi were not only single-blind; they were also classified information that was not passed on to the author. Rather than the instrument of "quality control" to eliminate bias that we know from academic peer reviewing (Shatz 2004, 2), the Stasi's assessments served a rather different purpose. These reviewers made no attempt at being impartial or objective but were instead aimed at enforcing a particularly narrow, "socialist realist" style of writing and policing the ideological content of works. Berger saw himself as an aesthetic gatekeeper in his behind-the-scenes reviews, and as a political vigilante who was determined to ensure works with damaging messages or subversive intent did not pass muster. In his rigid view, works could be security risks if they pointed to their author's hostile disposition and attitude vis-à-vis socialism or if they were written in "dangerous" styles—that is, if they drew on modernist, romantic, avant-garde, or expressionist traditions. All these "reactionary" rather than "progressive" literary influences were suspect in Berger's eyes; he saw them as "subjective" (UB, vol. II/1, 110), "decadent," or "nihilistic" (UB, vol. II/1, 38). With such judgments Berger was rehearsing the typical antimodernist arguments from the expressionism debates of the late 1930s, in which the Marxist philosopher Georg Lukács had distinguished a "good" line of "progressive" German literature from classicism to socialist realism from a "reactionary" one that started with romanticism and ended in modernism (Plumpe 1995, 26). Although this dogmatic view of socialist realism was still dominant in the 1950s, by the late 1960s a more accommodating approach to modernism was the order of the day (Parker and Philpotts 2009, 234).

An analysis of the reviews Berger wrote for the Stasi in the period 1970 to 1985 reveals that in his assessments he invariably prioritized politics over aesthetics, although ultimately both were interconnected. With very few exceptions, he overstated the critical nature of the works in question and focused on the putative negative political intentions of their authors.[8] In his very first review of Wiens's poetry, which he handed over on April 23, 1970, Berger adopted an openly dismissive and judgmental tone, which somewhat surprisingly was not immediately to his officer's liking. Pönig (who had by now been promoted to senior lieutenant) criticized it for jumping to political conclusions too quickly. In his report Berger had declared rather categorically: "In [my] opinion the verses of Paul Wiens do not conform to our political standpoint" (UB, vol. 1, 12). Rather like a student of literature who is admonished for not providing enough textual evidence in his essay, Berger was tasked with improving the quality of his reviewing: "He is also going to write an appropriate report which justifies this [his political standpoint] in precise terms by the next meeting" (UB, vol. 1, 12).[9]

An interesting feature of Berger's reports is the fact that he almost never denigrated the quality of his peers' writing. Instead, he targeted writers' hostile political stance or the consequences of the work for socialism or the "counterrevolution." This is no doubt what he thought was expected of him. It came therefore as a surprise to him that his officer disapproved of the cut-and-dried value judgments Berger issued in the above case of Wiens's poetry. But Berger's judgmental reports would in fact have been of limited use to the Stasi, since it needed concrete evidence—in this case hard *textual* evidence—as well as specific details of what *kinds* of nonorthodox or unconventional political views Wiens was espousing. Berger's officer seems to be saying in the aforementioned scolding that he needed intelligence that was more objective in style. Above all the Stasi wanted to be able to form its own opinions about the political dangers of the work in question.

After this dressing down in 1970, a pattern emerges in Berger's reviews whereby he continued to attack the overall political intent of a work but made sure to do so through reference to specific poems or passages. It was but a small concession to make to then admit that the writing was good or the writer talented. Some Stasi reviewers recommended works be published with a few qualifications, wrote considered objective reports that were even worthy of being made public, or that could have been published in journals such as *Sinn und Form*, as one former Stasi officer has revealed (Böthig 1993, 291). Berger by contrast usually offered harsh, unforgiving criticisms with no positives, often ending his reviews by stating that the work in question could not be published.[10] For example in an early review from 1970 of a work by Günter Kunert, with whom he was on friendly terms, Berger attributed its flaws to a sinister intention to harm the republic, saying: "There is every indication that we are not dealing with an artistic failure but rather with a writing style that is consciously directed against socialism, its armed forces and instruments of power, written in a universal slave language the author is hiding behind" (UB, vol. II/1, 35). Later in 1977, a few years before Kunert left for the West, Berger stated in relation to the poetry volume *Unterwegs nach Utopia* (On the path to utopia), which was published by the West German press Hanser, that "objectively" there had been an "artistic decline" in the quality of his writing. This represented a "perversion of his talent," and Berger warned that "a publication . . . must be out of the question" (UB, vol. II/5, 16).

In a postpublication review of a collection of short stories by Erich Loest, *Pistole mit Sechzehn* (Pistol at sixteen), which had been published in the West by Hoffmann and Campe in 1979, Berger claimed he could detect the author's right-wing, profascist, and antisocialist attitudes in all his poems (UB, vol. II/5, 264). Loest, he had to admit, "was an adept writer" who knew how to press emotional buttons in his readers and had access to a broad readership from "the middle-classes, petty bourgeoisie, intellectuals and partially also from workers" (UB, vol. II/5, 268). This, he implied, made him an obvious security risk (UB, vol. II/5, 268).

In a postcensorship review of Klaus Poche's novel *Atemnot* (Short of breath), which had been published by Fischer in the West in 1979, Berger claimed that there were passages which were well written but that it was overall "a poor, indeed a lousy [*mieses*] book that can make no serious claim to quality" (UB, vol. II/5, 118). Even more ominously it was the work of a "pathological psyche" (UB, vol. II/5, 117) made worse by the fact that it was a systematic form of vilification (UB, vol. II/5, 117). Poche, he maintained, was not only the victim of "manipulation" by the GDR's enemies; he was also in thrall to some of the regime's internal opponents (UB, vol. II/5, 117). In his report Berger lists five major objections to the book: it contained attacks on socialist society (UB, vol. II/5,

114), attacks on the party and state functionaries, attacks on Communist ideology, vilification of everyday life in the GDR (UB, vol. II/5, 115), and calls to combat the dictatorship of the proletariat (UB, vol. II/5, 116). He concluded it would be wrong to publish the novel in the East. It represented a danger because it aimed "first to undermine [their] literature," and, second, the author wanted to use it "as an ideological instrument . . . to prepare for the counterrevolution" (UB, vol. 5, 119).

In his assessment of Monika Maron's first novel manuscript, "Josepha," from around the same time (published in the West in 1981 by Fischer under the title *Flugasche* (*Flight of Ashes*), Berger argued that there were similarities between Maron's and Poche's novels "in the attacks and the form" (UB, vol. 5, 192): "It is the same old trick just in a different version and more emotional" (UB, vol. II/5, 192). He conceded that "the manuscript [was] not without talent" (UB, vol. II/5, 192), but it was most certainly written to incite its readers to counterrevolutionary actions: "It is yet another sorry example of poor literature that is written not in order to present a realistic portrayal of life but to express a hostile tendency toward us and to distort reality" (UB, vol. II/5, 193). He was dismissive of what he called "the personal . . . mannerisms of the author" (UB, vol. II/5, 189). The main character displayed psychopathological traits and had a drug addiction manifested in "visions and hallucinations with a counterrevolutionary emphasis" (UB, vol. II/5, 190), which incriminated the author. Berger was at pains to stress that this manuscript, like Poche's, could not be dismissed as an aberration: "It combines intuitive hatred with systematically escalated attacks whose nature and direction point to the controlling hand of enemy agencies" (UB, vol. 5, 190).

In a review of Wolfgang Hilbig's volume of prose from the same period, *Unterm Neumond* (Under the new moon), Berger condemned the poems' form and content, which he saw as belonging to a "late-bourgeois tradition," characterized by a "general feeling of doom and gloom [*Untergangsstimmung*]" and "hostility toward life [*Lebensfeindlichkeit*]" (UB, vol. II/5, 251).[11] Although his report makes no mention of counterrevolutionary tendencies or activity, it was far from benign. Berger extrapolated the author's character and disposition from the texts and, again, imputed a particularly pathological consciousness to the author. The poems betrayed "a virtually pathological sensitivity, a sensitive feel for language with a fundamentally nihilistic outlook on life" (UB, vol. II/5, 252).

In the early eighties, Berger's reviews continued in much the same style, excoriating younger writers, such as Lutz Rathenow, for their anarchic, petit bourgeois tendencies (UB, vol. II/6, 57) or denouncing older writers, such as Franz Fühmann, who displayed a "fascistoid" predilection for absurdist, irrational, and bourgeois traditions (UB, vol. II/6, 112). Fühmann was "more hostile and focused" than Hilbig and was a far more serious threat since he was in danger of joining forces with the "far-right, neo-fascist groups of [the GDR's] enemies" (UB, vol. II/6, 112). In 1981 in relation to the poetry of the underground avant-garde writer and Stasi informant Sascha Anderson, Berger admitted some of it showed talent, but the rest was "trite modernistic drivel cobbled together with a politically hostile intention" (UB, vol. 6, 173). In a brief assessment of the young poet Erwin Thomas, Berger showed some sympathy for the treatment of the theme of loneliness but concluded that the writer was "an endangered talent" (UB, vol. 5, 340).

There is possibly an additional reason why Berger did not simply discredit his peers' talents directly. Publicly, of course, this would be too blatant and would have drawn attention to him as a Stasi spy, but in covert reports that were meant only for Stasi eyes, he could easily have attacked his peers' competencies as writers. But Berger needed to hedge his bets in case some of the writers he disliked proved to be successful or met with approval from other reviewers, and he probably also needed to protect his professional integrity. In other words Berger may have been attempting to shore up the literary side of his expertise against the backdrop of a literary field that was heavily dominated by political concerns. Although Berger's judgments were always dominated by his political views, this was risky especially if cultural politics changed direction, which it did as we shall see below, and hence Berger usually offered opinions on writers' literary merits as well.

There is a curious note on file that sheds further light on the rationale behind Berger's method of admitting writers' talent but condemning their politics. In a handwritten report for the Stasi from January 16, 1976, in which someone in the MfS had underlined two words, Berger relayed an incident when members of the Academy of Arts (Akademie der Künste) walked out in disgust at Erik Neutsch, who had openly criticized a published piece by Volker Braun, stating, "The work was badly written" (UB, vol. 4, 188). Although he was a supporter of Braun, Berger thought "that one should not debate in such a defensive and hypocritical manner" (UB, vol. 4, 188). Hence, we can infer from this that not even a Stasi informant was so defensive as to criticize an established writer's talents.

In another series of reviews, Berger buttressed his judgments with some dubious remarks on gender politics. In fact Berger's reviews of works by women are generally peppered with derogatory, misogynistic, and ageist personal comments. A blatant instance of this is a postpublication review he wrote about a volume of poetry by Bettina Wegner, "Wenn meine Lieder nicht mehr stimmen" (When my songs no longer ring true), which Rowohlt published in 1979. Curiously, his negative impression of the work stemmed not from it being a "direct call to antisocialist, counterrevolutionary action" (UB, vol. 5, 336) but rather from the way the work aimed at producing "a general mood of discontent, disappointment, pique" (UB, vol. 5, 336). Wegner thus serves as a mouthpiece for "all the negative feelings, moods, fears of unstable individuals and groups" (UB, vol. 5, 336). In his review Berger stoops to an all-time professional low when he brands her poetry "tampon poetry" (*Tampon-Lyrik*) (UB, vol. II/5, 336).

In the case of an early review of a volume of poetry by Eva Strittmatter in 1971, Berger sidestepped the issue of whether her works were politically desirable and discredited them instead on the grounds that they appeared to him to be the poetry of a depressed menopausal woman and thus were of no value to anyone: "She frets about loneliness and growing old. . . . Her life is a memory. . . . Everything is shrouded in an eternal sadness. Which readers are these menopausal depressive thoughts supposed to have a liberating effect on? For whom are they supposed to provide support?" (UB, vol. II/1, 251–52). The only redeeming features Berger found in the volume were a few nature poems that he thought salvageable. He recommends keeping these and removing the offensive poems (filling up the volume with others that had already been published) (UB, vol. II/1, 251–52).[12]

Berger's Position in the Literary Field

Read as a corpus, Berger's reviews reveal surprisingly little variation in tone and rhetoric over the course of his secret police career. With their emphasis on "antisocialist" or "counterrevolutionary" tendencies in literature, they mark Berger as positioning himself in that overtly politicized part of the literary field that Parker and Philpotts call the least autonomous and most "heteronomous" end, the end where aesthetics were all but completely overshadowed and controlled by party politics (2009, 18). At the time of his recruitment by the secret police in 1970, Berger had aligned himself with the so-called progressive (i.e., hardline) forces in cultural politics, even stating explicitly in one meeting with his handler that he intended to bolster these forces in the face of rising opposition from writers such as Reiner Kunze (UB, 131/76, vol. II/1, 13). In the wake of the tough stance taken by the GDR regime after 1968, Berger no doubt felt he was on the "right" side of power and also had its backing. But with the "thaw" in the political field that occurred soon after Erich Honecker's rise to power in 1971, and after the head of state's "no taboos" speech at the IV Central Committee Conference in December of that year (Wolle 1998, 239), Berger discovered to his surprise that this was a precarious position to hold. Allying oneself with the dominant party line of the times proved, as we shall see, far from easy, especially when the party line seemed to be shifting or softening. It is hard to say whether this was because Berger was unable to *read* the changed direction of cultural politics after 1971, or whether he read it correctly but simply decided against endorsing the changes. There is nothing in his file to suggest that his officer provided anything in the way of ideological guidance on what the new line on literature should be, and indeed nothing to suggest what the Stasi's line even was. In fact one cannot help thinking that Berger's officer was not interested in spelling out the implications of the thaw and the new, more tolerant thinking on Berger's behalf. Curiously, it almost seems as if the Stasi accepted Berger's rigid position and saw the field of literature as having a certain degree of autonomy or, at the very least, as "having a mind of its own."

By the midseventies, at the height of the more liberal phase of the Honecker era, Berger continued to disapprove of all experimentation in literature and to peddle a position that equated any play with form or style with an unpartisan or even a counterrevolutionary stance. In his view the use of modernist or avant-garde aesthetic styles was sufficient to place a writer in the antisocialist or oppositional camp. In 1973 he noted that attitudes had changed since the sixties and that people no longer believed critical writers were leading the charge of the counterrevolution, concluding that "right-wing, revisionist" views were ascendant in the Writers Guild (UB, vol. II/3, 49). At the end of 1974, he expressed concern to his officer that a new group in the Writers Guild was advocating greater pluralism in literature and the abolition of censorship (UB, vol. II/3, 238). Around this time there were signs that Berger felt writers like him were being marginalized. In 1975, for instance, we find a note on Berger's file stating that there was "a petit bourgeois group of writers in opposition" clustered around Christa Wolf and Franz Fühmann, and Berger was concerned that more writers were aligning themselves with them (UB, vol. II/4, 72).

On another occasion in 1976, when discussing an official literary history published by Volk und Wissen—*Geschichte der Literatur der Deutschen Demokratischen Republik* (History of the literature of the German Democratic Republic)—he complained that some writers like Fühmann and Braun were dealt with in two large paragraphs, while others such as Hermann Kant (who was also a Stasi agent), only had one paragraph each or none of their own. Berger found the attention afforded Biermann, Wolf, Müller, and Braun unwarranted and declared that they were "qualitatively overrated" (UB, vol. II/4, 280). He was particularly outraged that Biermann was included at all (UB, vol. II/4, 278). He asked for an explanation of how Biermann's "emotional lyrical songs" could be criticized politically but still pass muster "artistically" (UB, vol. II/4, 278).

While Biermann's inclusion in an official literary history was no doubt due to a slightly more tolerant approach to criticism—one that in Biermann's case was certainly not to last, as we shall see—to Berger it was dangerous: "Even though Biermann is presented as an enemy of the GDR, in my opinion he still ought not to have been included. There is a danger of violating §106 of the Criminal Code of the GDR" (UB, vol. II/4, 278). It is interesting to note that his argument here is a politico-legal one, namely, that Biermann's works ran the risk of breaking the law. This is a quasi-factual argument that he hoped would trump all others. It reveals that Berger viewed his role in the vetting process so seriously that he thought it appropriate to make legal judgments. It is as if Berger wanted to lend his views extra weight by underpinning them with heavy-hitting legal arguments, and he sensed he was fighting a losing battle. He had made his position on Biermann plain already in 1972 in a report he had written for the Stasi on May 5. He had not minced words, calling Biermann a "blight on GDR literature" (Schandfleck in der DDR Literatur) whom the regime should "remove" (UB, vol. II/2, 134). In a particularly nasty aside to his report, he had recommended: "We [should] just deport BIERMANN to WG [West Germany].... Then BIERMANN would be forced to come to grips with the society whose restoration he was working toward in his literary concoctions targeting the GDR" (UB, vol. II/2, 134).

Berger's position on Biermann was nothing if not consistent. In many ways, though, it was even more extreme than the view of the majority of the Politburo members in the mid-seventies, when the regime kept him under constant surveillance but refrained from following through on its drastic plans. This was all to change abruptly when, on November 16, 1976, in what amounted to the iciest of freezes in cultural politics, the Politburo pounced and put into action a plan that had existed since 1974 to rob Biermann of his citizenship while on an approved concert tour of West Germany (Biermann 2016, 321–22). As Biermann himself has written recently in his autobiography, the regime had various scenarios to deal with him—ranging from an arrest, isolation, causing physical harm in a car accident, criminalization by tempting him with hard drugs, through to arranging extramarital affairs (2016, 235–36)—and one of the more draconian ones, and an alternative to arresting him, was to expel him (234). It is noteworthy that the regime's actions of effectively refusing to allow Biermann back into the country, although harsh and irrevocable, were still milder than Berger's proposal to literally *deport* Biermann.[13]

During the Biermann crisis of late 1976 and early 1977, Berger took an especially intransigent line, and barely concealing his disappointment at the soft option of expelling Biermann rather than arresting him, he told his officer that he had hoped the party would take decisive action to show "negative forces" that there were limits to their liberties (UB, vol. II/4, 339). As a consequence he found himself isolated during the events, playing little or no role of any importance for the regime in the national drama that unfolded. In the words of Biermann, his expatriation "shook the entire country," as twelve prominent figures signed in protest a petition that almost one hundred additional intellectuals endorsed over the following days (2016, 338-39). Among those who signed were writers Berger had no close personal relationship with such as Christa and Gerhard Wolf, Volker Braun, Heiner Müller, and Stephan Hermlin. Among the signatories were also writers he had betrayed in his malicious reviews, such as Sarah Kirsch (who had by now grown suspicious of Berger; UB, vol. II/4, 271), Stefan Heym (whom he spied on; UB, vol. II/2, 15, vol. II/4, 166), and Günter Kunert (with whom he had only a cordial relationship and who no longer trusted him; UB, vol. II/4, 172).[14] Hence, the only opinions he could canvass were of those who were peripheral to the main events. In an account he penned for the Stasi on November 17, 1976, one day after Biermann's expulsion, Berger reported on two responses within his circles. One was from fellow writer and member of the executive of the Writers Guild Peter Edel—who greeted the actions of the SED as a "relief" (UB, vol. II/4, 339)—and the other from Werner Neubert, who endorsed them as "an absolute necessity" (UB, vol. II/4, 339). Neubert's views in particular were already known to the Stasi, since Neubert was a long-standing and loyal informant (IME) for the Stasi (Walther 1996b, 318). Peter Edel's views would soon become readily known to the Stasi, particularly after 1978, when Edel was enlisted as IMS "Thomas" (Walther 1996b, 684, 739).

In the wake of the Biermann affair, Berger no doubt felt quietly justified in taking a tough stance on critical literature and all forms of modernism. The effect of the ensuing freeze was to confirm him in his opinion that it was best to remain true to his by now deeply unpopular, at least in literary circles, "progressive" position. He possibly felt vindicated in doing so by the constant flip-flopping that occurred in cultural politics in the seventies, having witnessed how in 1971 a thaw followed on the heels of the freeze of 1968, and in 1976 a freeze eventually followed the thaw. However, like the regime Berger no doubt underestimated the groundswell of support for Biermann at the time. Moreover, notwithstanding the crackdown on Biermann in 1976 and on the signatories to the protest letter, the regime could not undo the fact that most of the regime's critical but loyal writers—writers such as Wolf, Müller, and Braun—were gaining traction in the East as well as the West. Hence, after the crisis of late 1976, Berger continued to express his concerns about the strength of those factions in the Writers Guild that promoted "negative tendencies," as he had remarked on in 1973 (UB, vol. II/3, 7–9). On April 26, 1977, he met with Caspar from Aufbau, who complained openly to Berger that people wanted to buy books by Wolf, Kirsch, and Kunert, which Aufbau published only in small print runs, and turned their backs on the works they "<u>should</u> buy" ("should" is underlined in his file) (UB, vol. II/4, 421). After this juncture Berger steadfastly continued to defend that part of the literary field that was least independent and most dominated by ideology and party politics, as we have seen with his damning reviews of works by Maron, Poche, and Loest. Even into the eighties, as seen above in his reviews of Rathenow, Fühmann, and Hilbig, he showed little sign of softening in his unrelenting condemnation of anything modernist or slightly critical of socialist society. In the post-Biermann period toward the end of the seventies, Berger's reviewing was briefly in demand as the Stasi regrouped and intensified its efforts to bring the Writers Guild and publishers under control. Berger's postpublication reviews of works were sought after mainly so that the Stasi could assess how much of a security risk their authors presented.

Yet Berger could not have been oblivious to the fact that he was fighting a losing battle in his efforts to stem the tide of liberalization among his peers. For instance early on Berger lost his "running battle" with Caspar over Sarah Kirsch's work when Aufbau eventually published those poems Berger had traduced in his "subjective" review.[15] Although there is no mention of this fact on file, there is mention that he had called Kirsch upon hearing that Paul Wiens was about to write a review of her poetry, even hypocritically offering to communicate with Aufbau on her behalf (UB, vol. II/2, 148). His negative views of Hilbig were overridden when Reclam Leipzig released an edited collection of poetry and prose in *Stimme, Stimme* (Voice, voice) in 1983 (Cooke 2000, 55).

Berger made no secret of his disappointment over losing some of these battles, and in 1982 he wrote a position paper on the situation in the Writers Guild, in which he spoke about "a strong sense of dissatisfaction" and "a certain polarization of forces" among its members (UB, vol. II/5, 215). On the one hand, there were loyalists like him "who until now always went on the offensive to represent the interests of the party in complex political situations and political-ideological confrontations" and who felt insufficiently supported in their work (UB, vol. II/5, 215). On the other hand, there were authors of dubious ideological credentials such as Hermlin, Fühmann, and Wolf, who at the time were opportunistically enjoying the support of the party leadership because they were strategically useful in the "struggle for peace" (UB, vol. II/5, 215). These writers were being surrounded by "an indeterminate number of quiet sympathizers, who were aggrieved, that is, vacillating politically-ideologically" (UB, vol. II/5, 216).

Perhaps the clearest signal that Berger was hopelessly entrenched in his hardline position came at the end of 1981 during Cold War tensions over the nuclear arms race and the peace movement. Unexpectedly for many the regime lent its support to a joint initiative of Stephan Hermlin and the Academy of the Arts called "Berlin Encounter" that allowed writers, scientists, and journalists from the East and the West to meet freely in East Berlin for peace talks. Even though the initiative had the blessing of Erich Honecker and the Stasi (Braun 2007, 340–51), Berger is reported in an "Information on reactions from writers' circles to a contribution . . . by the Minister for Culture, Com. Hans-Joachim HOFF-MANN" (UB, vol. II/5, 232) soon after in February 1982 to have been "angered" by the event, seeing in it "an insidious defamation of writer comrades, who ha[d] hitherto challenged in good faith those political-ideological negative forces in the Writers Guild" (UB, vol. II/5, 232–33).

By the early eighties, Berger had been overtaken on the left by virtually everyone, including the Minister for Culture, Honecker, and even some in the Stasi. This did not stop him from continuing to brand writers such as Wolf and Hermlin "negative forces" and even to disapprove of the new trends in reconciliation in politics and culture. Hence, it seems that Berger's savage reviewing techniques eventually became too tiresome and predictable, even for the Stasi. Although we find no explicit criticism of Berger's method of reviewing on file, we do find other indications that the Stasi was becoming irate with him. In 1983 Berger's officer was displeased with his judgmental style of reporting. On December 7 Pönig wrote: "With IM the topic of reporting must be dealt with thoroughly at the next meeting. Facts must be compiled in more extensive and concrete fashion. Value judgments should be avoided!" (UB, vol. II/6, 325). Indeed, Berger's tendentious and biased reviews had always posed challenges for the Stasi, which clearly preferred a more objective mode of reporting and reviewing, a fact that seems to have been lost on Berger.

Berger's file continued to remain open until the end of the regime, although the last volume is empty. There are no extant reports from 1985 onward.[16] If Berger had by this time lost influence with Aufbau as well as the Stasi, he nonetheless left a damaging legacy. Of all the prepublication works Berger reviewed, only a few works that came across his table—the one mentioned above by Sarah Kirsch, which Aufbau commissioned, two volumes by Eva Strittmatter, and another one by Hilbig—obtained a green light to be published in the GDR. To add insult to injury, subsequent reviewers of Kirsch's poetry were overwhelmingly positive, which made it easy for the Main Directorate for Publishing and Book Trade to issue two volumes with publication permits, for *Zaubersprüche* (Magic spells) in 1973 (DR 1/2102a, 73) and for

Rückenwind (Tailwind) in 1976 (DR 1/2110a, 217). It seems ironic that the author of these positive reports was Pönig's other Stasi agent, Paul Wiens. Of the critical postpublication reports Berger wrote (once the works had been released in West Germany), the Office for Copyright gave the green light to publish a few of these works in East German editions. For instance Aufbau released Kunert's *Unterwegs nach Utopia* in 1980 and his *Die befleckte Empfängnis* (The maculate conception) in 1988 (Costabile-Heming 2000, 64). Berger's verdict on Maron's first novel was eventually overturned internally in 1987, but the Ministry for Culture never actually issued a publication authorization.[17]

Possibly even more damaging than the delays or ensuing bans on works were the harmful effects of Berger's collusion with the Stasi on the repression writers suffered. Of those authors whose works he assessed, many were to leave the GDR permanently: Sarah Kirsch in 1977, Günter Kunert and Klaus Poche in 1979, Bettina Wegner in 1983, and Wolfgang Hilbig in 1985. Others such as Monika Maron were issued a series of temporary exit visas from 1983 to 1988. While a multitude of factors influenced their decision to go into exile, and some were presented with little choice, Berger's damning indictments of their works certainly played a role. They helped to cement the regime's verdict that these intellectuals were dangerous examples of "political-ideological diversion." For instance Berger's unfavorable assessment of her first novel was to plague Maron and haunt her Stasi file, as a series of Stasi officers and ministers continued to refer back to her initial transgression in writing a work that, thanks to Berger, was seen to depict a "hostile image of a 'gray-on-gray socialism'" right up until 1987.[18]

Over the duration of his collaboration, Berger waged an insidious secret war on behalf of the Stasi against dissident and critical-loyal writers while in part pursuing his own private vendettas against his colleagues, albeit in the name of curbing modernist tendencies in literature. Berger's main motives for his reviewing work seem to have involved the promise of power and influence that working for the Stasi afforded him, however elusive this proved to be. He was possibly propelled to continue his work by the secret reserves of capital he was able to accrue through participating in the Stasi's impressive secret surveillance society. If we think of individual players in the cultural arena such as Berger as being "symbolic bankers" seeking to secure capital for themselves and for their organizations, as Parker and Philpotts argue in relation to editors-in-chief of prestigious journals such as *Sinn und Form* (2009, 8), it is possible that Berger saw his reviewing work as an opportunity to "bank" symbolic capital for himself. This was albeit secret capital, but capital nevertheless that still held currency in what many officers and some informants saw as a type of secret order or secret society (Gieseke 2000, 144). Apart from this his secret reviews of literature provided him with a chance to work off personal grievances and resentments.

In addition to these motivations, it would appear from reading his file that Berger was driven by an inexplicable need to ingratiate himself with power, and that secret meetings and the spiteful clandestine reports he wrote were a welcome and necessary part of a double life he rather enjoyed leading. There is a striking textual passage in his file that would support this reading. One day early in 1979, Christian Schlosser, an editor of Aufbau, left his address book at Berger's house by mistake (UB, vol. II/5, 138–53). Berger seized on the opportunity and diligently transcribed all sixteen pages of names and addresses by hand and presented them to his officer at his next meeting. This begs the question why he would bother since there is no evidence that he was asked to do so or that Schlosser was even under suspicion. This is a patent breach of someone's privacy for no obvious political gain other than possibly Berger's delight in providing a premium surveillance service for his handler and one that was as comprehensive as possible. Tellingly, there is no evidence that Pönig praised him for his excessive vigilantism.

There is a further reason why Berger was particularly susceptible to recruitment by the secret police. Reading between the lines of his dutiful but damaging reviews and recognizing his anxieties at other writers receiving recognition at his expense, we could conclude that he feared he could not compete on a level playing field with others if he did not have special links to the levers of power. It is true that Berger never had any difficulties in gaining a publishing permit, so he never experienced firsthand the sorts of delays that most writers did. However, it does seem that Berger craved more attention than he was being afforded, especially in reviews of anthologies in the West, where he was often dismissed as "too emphatic" (UB, vol. II/4, 87) or played off against writers of the caliber of Biermann, Kirsch, and Wiens (UB, vol. II/4, 87). He hoped to compensate for a lack of talent and recognition by wielding an excess of power via the Stasi. Envy, resentment, and careerism were, as Joachim Walther remarks, often the hidden drivers for many informants who felt they were not getting sufficient attention or their just deserts (1996b, 519). A good example of this was the writer Dieter Noll, who had written a successful first novel, *Die Abenteuer des Werner Holt* (The adventures of Werner Holt), but became resentful of others when he failed to replicate this success. What Walther claims for Noll could equally be said of Berger: "There are numerous complaints from party-loyalist writers about how the state leaders did not sufficiently acknowledge their own works and promoted the allegedly less 'class-conscious' poets. The slighter one's own body of work, the greater the resentment" (1996a, 228).

After unification Berger's fears of becoming irrelevant were no doubt exacerbated, as writers he had spied on discovered evidence of his betrayal in their Stasi files. Kunert in particular was galled to learn that Berger, whom he had thought was a friend, had been shadowing him at the Stasi's behest. Berger's defamatory depiction of *Unterwegs nach Utopia* as the work of a hateful, pessimistic enemy of socialism could easily had resulted in his arrest, if he had not had the good fortune to emigrate to the West (cf. Costabile-Heming 2000, 63).

For Berger being an informant arguably provided him with a patriotic sense of belonging, albeit to what he increasingly came to see as an *endangered* secret society. Indeed, his secret service work nurtured a sense of belonging to a secret *surveillance* society made up of likeminded "progressive forces" (i.e., hardliners) that as time went on felt themselves under siege both from the West and from liberal forces within Communism itself. As Georg Simmel has argued, in secret societies secrets bind those who are initiated into them in inexplicable but compelling ways, according to the motto that "what is withheld from the many appears to have a special value" (1906, 464). Informers like Berger thus became part of what amounted to a closed secret fraternity in the GDR, based on the belief that initiates possessed and shared in an exclusive form of secret knowledge that others did not have. Working for the Stasi afforded Berger a means of subtly distinguishing himself from his peers through, as Simmel writes, an "accentuated feeling of personal possession" (464), thereby offering the "possibility of a second world alongside of the obvious world" (462).

Belonging to the Stasi permitted Berger to tap into further reserves of capital over and above those he could access through public channels such as affiliation with the Writers Guild or the party. Part of the attraction of the Stasi might have been that he could draw on secret reserves of symbolic capital and power, from which he derived additional prestige and status as well as a sense of self-worth he felt was owed him. Although he might have hoped he could cash in on these clandestine reserves of capital and convert them into more visible forms of acclaim, it seems that he saw rewards in simply being associated with the MfS. He ultimately believed that recognition in the GDR (and not in the West) was sufficient for him to survive, not realizing that, as Parker and Philpotts put it, "literary capital validated in the GDR was a worthless currency if it . . . could not be exchanged in the hard currency of the international field" (2009, 7). In the end it was probably just as much the ritualized nature of his secret Stasi business that sustained him as it was the presence of any tangible rewards or benefits. In light of this, it seems rather ironic that as a "true believer" he found himself marginalized in literary circles and even within the ranks of Stasi informers such as Wiens, for the very reasons the Stasi had sought him out in the first place. Rather than providing protection, the secret society of Stasi initiates left him dangerously out on a limb, and by the time the winds of change of perestroika and glasnost had swept across the country, Berger appears to have been swept aside and was all but forgotten as a writer. Unification subsequently did nothing to rehabilitate him as a poet, particularly after he had been exposed as a Stasi collaborator. Unperturbed by these allegations, however, he continued to write and publish until his death in 2014, albeit with far smaller publishers than Aufbau, and tried to cleanse his public vitae from the blemish of Stasi collaboration. By refusing to participate in all forms of *Vergangenheitsbewältigung* (mastering the past) and reconciliation, Berger forewent an important opportunity to include his perspective in the account of the Cold War spy story presented here. Thus the story of Berger's deeply aggressive secret war on contemporary literature, which he waged both on behalf of the Stasi and for his own personal reasons, must be captured as a "file story," excavated and constructed from the masses of banal and incriminating intelligence the Stasi harvested in his file and the files of his victims. As his case demonstrates, even though the Stasi mobilized writers as literary experts to combat dissent covertly from within literary circles, the system of single-blind peer review that weaponized Berger was at best a very blunt instrument of control and at worst a hindrance in the fierce cultural wars the regime fought and eventually lost in 1989 against freedom of speech.

Notes

1. See the well-maintained personal website of the author, http://www.uwe -berger.net.

2. Unless otherwise noted all translations are mine.

3. The IMV category existed from 1968 to 1979, when it was renamed IMB, "Unofficial Collaborator in Counterintelligence with Enemy Contacts, Namely, with Direct Involvement in the Processing of Persons Suspected of Hostile Activity" (Inoffizieller Mitarbeiter der Abwehr mit Feindverbindungen bzw. zur unmittelbaren Bearbeitung imVerdacht der Feindlichkeit stehender Personen; Engelmann et al. 2016, 173).

4. Berger first task was to provide a report on the anthology as well as on Caspar himself.

5. The category of IMF was similar to that of IMV and was defined as "Unofficial Collaborator in Internal Counterintelligence with Hostile Contacts to the Area of Operation" (Inoffizieller Mitarbeiter der inneren Abwehr mit Feindverbindungen zum Operationsgebiet; Engelmann et al. 2016, 173).

6. For instance, he complained in a file note that he was not being given manuscripts to review; he also complained that his "objective" and "consistent/logical" (*konsequenter*) viewpoint was no longer being tolerated (UB 131/76, vol. II/1, 200).

7. We read in Berger's file that he traveled to Siberia in 1978 (UB, vol. II/5, 107), whereas Paul Wiens is repeatedly mentioned in Berger's file as traveling to destinations such as France, Italy, or Switzerland (UB, vol. II/2, 151).

8. One exception was a review he wrote of a story by Katja Lange. He contended that the work was only an indirect attack on the state but that its aesthetic quality was poor (UB, vol. II/5, 125). Berger thus seemed intent on ensuring that, like most of the works he reviewed, it was not published in the GDR.

9. Notwithstanding the Stasi's irritation with his intelligence, Berger continued to be dismissive of the more established and decorated poet Wiens. Appraising Wiens's poetry cycle *Weltbilder* (Images of the world) in a review for which he was paid 200 marks, Berger remarked that the poems were "anarchic" and not worthy of being published in a student newspaper (UB, vol. II/1, 44).

10. Carol Anne Costabile-Heming writes in connection with Gunter Kunert that other Stasi reviewers, such as Werner Neubert, were frequently critical but did not always argue against issuing an authorization to print. See Costabile-Heming 2000, 60.

11. *Unterm Neumond* was published by Fischer (Frankfurt a.M.) in 1982.

12. Curiously, Berger seems to have changed his view on Eva Strittmatter's poetry, and in a review of her next volume for the Stasi in 1974, he mentions that the "literary quality was significant" and recommends issuing permission to publish, stating he could detect "no hostile intentions of the author" (UB, vol. II/3, 189–92).

13. Biermann writes that he misinterpreted the permission to travel to the West as a sign of a more favorable "historical wind" blowing from the Politburo (2016, 323). He even went as far as to hope his trip might be the beginnings of a new Prague Spring stemming from the new Eurocommunism movement (324) and dismissed any thoughts that it might be a trap and he might not be allowed back in.

14. Berger was tasked with spying on Kunert as well as writing reviews of his poetry. By 1975 Kunert no longer seemed to trust him, which shines through one of Berger's reports on a meeting with Kunert when Kunert declined Berger's offer to be included in a poetry anthology and disagreed with him on most things, such as the lack of freedom of speech and the dire state of the Writers Guild (UB, vol. II/4, 172).

15. Berger had succeeded in delaying the publication by Aufbau of Kirsch's poems until 1973, when Aufbau decided to proceed with publishing *Zaubersprüche*. It was later released in 1977 by Langewiesche-Brandt (Ebenhausen near Munich).

16. Berger's file was never officially closed, and it is unclear why one volume is empty. The last entry in volume 6 is a meeting report from December 18, 1985, in which he talked about his West contacts. His brother, Peter, was living in Wilhelmshaven in the West, and this information was being sent off for evaluation on December 27, 1985 (UB, vol. II/6, 432). A further reason why the Stasi may have ceased issuing Berger assignments is because he was elected into the Presidium of the Cultural League (Kulturbund) in 1982, serving as its

vice president from 1982 to 1989. Since the Cultural League was closely linked to the SED, it is possible that it was not thought fit that a high-ranking functionary of the Cultural League also be an informant. Joachim Walther also gives the proven period of his collaborating as 1969 to 1986 and even "presumably to 1989" (1996b, 647).

17. In the archives of the Ministry for Culture there is a positive review of the book on file from September 25, 1987, which recommended it be published, but it wasn't (DR 1/16.910.1–6).

18. The publication history of *Flugasche* was repeatedly invoked whenever Maron tried to apply for an extension to her visa in the years 1983–86; see in particular the last volume of her five-volume Stasi file: BStU MfS AOP 6784/89, vol. 5 and vol. 7, 5–6.

References

ARCHIVAL SOURCES

BA (Bundesarchiv [Federal Archive]) DR 1/2091.

BStU (Bundesbeauftragter für die Unterlagen der Staatssicherheitsdienst der ehemaligen Deutschen Demokratischen Republik [Federal Commissioner for the Records of the State Security Service of the Former German Democratic Republic]) MfS (Ministerium für Staatssicherheit [Ministry for State Security]) Personnel file AIM (archivierter IM-Vorgang [archived Informant-File]) file 8382/91, 2 vols. [Cited as AIM.]

BStU MfS A (Working file) file 131/76, 6 vols. [Cited as UB.]

BStU MfS AIM 7781/83, 8 vols.

BStU MfS AOP (archivierter operativer Vorgang [archived operative procedure]) 6784/89, 5 vols.

PUBLISHED SOURCES

Biermann, Wolf. 2016. *Warte nicht auf bessre Zeiten*. Berlin: Propyläen.

Böthig, Peter. 1993. "Gedächtnisprotokoll mit Herrn K." In *MachtSpiele: Literatur und Staatssicherheit*, edited by Klaus Michael and Peter Böthig, 288–95. Leipzig: Reclam.

Bourdieu, Pierre. 1996. *The Rules of Art: Genesis and Structure of the Literary Field*. Translated by Susan Emanuel. Stanford CA: Stanford University Press.

Braun, Matthias. 2007. *Kulturinsel und Machtinstrument: Die Akademie der Künste, die Partei und die Staatssicherheit*. Göttingen: Vandenhoeck & Ruprecht.

Butler, Judith. 1998. "Ruled Out: Vocabularies of the Censor." In *Censorship and Silencing: Practices of Cultural Regulation*, edited by Robert C. Post, Issues & Debates 4, 247–59. Los Angeles: Getty Research Institute.

Cooke, Paul. 2000. *Speaking the Taboo: A Study of the Work of Wolfgang Hilbig*. Amsterdam: Rodopi.

Costabile-Heming, Carol Anne. 1997. "Censorship and Review Processes: The Case of Günter Kunert." In *What Remains? East German Culture and the Postwar Public*, edited by Marc Silberman, Research Report, 552–63. Washington DC: American Institute for Contemporary German Studies.

———. 2000. "'Rezensur': A Case Study of Censorship and Programmatic Reception in the GDR." *Monatshefte* 92 (1): 53–67.

———. 2002. "Offizielle und inoffizielle Zensurverfahren in der DDR: Der Fall Günter Kunert." *Literatur für Leser* 25 (1): 33–46.

Engelmann, Roger, Bernd Florath, Helge Heidemeyer, Daniela Münkel, Arno Polzin, and Walter Süß, eds. 2016. *Das MfS-Lexikon: Begriffe, Personen und Strukturen der Staatssicherheit der DDR*. Berlin: Links.

Evans, Owen. 2006. *Mapping the Contours of Oppression: Subjectivity, Truth and Fiction in Recent German Autobiographical Treatments of Totalitarianism*. Amsterdam: Rodopi.

Foucault, Michel. 1980. *Power/Knowledge: Selected Interviews and Other Writings 1972–1977*. Edited by Colin Gordon. New York: Pantheon Books.

Gieseke, Jens. 2000. *Die hauptamtlichen Mitarbeiter der Staatssicherheit: Personalstruktur und Lebenswelt 1950–1989/90*. Berlin: Links.

———. 2011. *The History of the Stasi: East Germany's Secret Police, 1945–1990*. Translated by David Burnett. New York: Berghahn.

Glaeser, Andreas. 2011. *Political Epistemics: The Secret Police, the Opposition, and the End of East German Socialism*. Chicago: University of Chicago Press.

Glajar, Valentina. 2016. "'You'll Never Make a Spy out of Me': The File Story of 'Fink Susanne.'" In *Secret Police Files from the Eastern Bloc: Between Surveillance and Life Writing*, edited by Valentina Glajar, Alison Lewis, and Corina L. Petrescu, 56–83. Rochester NY: Camden House.

Goldstein, Thomas W. 2017. *Writing in Red: The East German Writers Union and the Role of Literary Intellectuals*. Rochester NY: Camden House.

Hilzinger, Sonja. 1999. *Christa Wolf's Nachdenken über Christa T.* Neuwied: Luchterhand.

Joch, Markus. 2014. "Dort die Genossen, hier die Quote? Jurek Becker zu Zensur in Ost und West." In *Kunstfreiheit und Zensur in der Bundesrepublik (1949–2009)*, edited by York-Gothart Mix, 150–64. Berlin: De Gruyter.

Jones, Sara. 2011. *Complicity, Censorship and Criticism: Negotiating Space in the GDR Literary Sphere*. Berlin: De Gruyter.

Lewis, Alison. 2003. *Die Kunst des Verrats: Der Prenzlauer Berg und die Staatssicherheit*. Würzburg: Königshausen & Neumann.

Michaelsen, Sven. 2010. "Sechs Ehefrauen—Fünf Pleiten—Vier Staaten—Drei Geheimdienste—Zwei verlassene Kinder—ein Leben." *Die Welt*, December 5, 1–10. https://www.welt.de/print/wams/kultur/article11400827/Sechs-Ehefrauen-Fuenf-Pleiten-Vier-Staaten-Drei-Geheimdienste-Zwei-verlassene-Kinder-Ein-Leben.html.

Mittenzwei, Werner. 2003. *Die Intellektuellen: Literatur und Politik in Ostdeutschland 1945–2000*. Berlin: Aufbau.

Mix, York-Gothart, ed. 1993. *Ein "Oberkunze darf nicht vorkommen": Materialien zur Publikationsgeschichte und Zensur des Hinze-Kunze-Romans von Volker Braun*. Wiesbaden: Otto Harrassowitz.

———. 2013. "Zensur." In *Handbuch Literaturwissenschaft*, edited by Thomas Anz, vol. 1, *Gegenstände und Grundbegriffe*, 492–500. Stuttgart: Metzler.

Müller, Beate. 2003. "Hinter verschlossenen Türen auf der Bühne deutsch-deutscher Öffentlichkeit: Publikationsgeschichten über Jurek Becker's *Schlaflose Tage*." In *Zensur im modernen deutschen Kulturraum*, edited by Beate Müller, 195–214. Tübingen: Niemeyer.

———. 2004. "Censorship and Cultural Regulation: Mapping the Territory." In *Censorship and Cultural Regulation in the Modern Age*, edited by Beate Müller, 1–32. Amsterdam: Rodopi.

———. 2006. *Stasi—Zensur—Machtdiskurse*. Tübingen: Max Niemeyer.

Müller-Enberg, Helmut. 2008. *Inoffizielle Mitarbeiter des Ministeriums für Staatssicherheit*. Part 3, *Statistiken*. Berlin: Links.

Parker, Stephen, and Matthew Philpotts. 2009. *Sinn und Form: The Anatomy of a Literary Journal*. Berlin: De Gruyter.

Plowman, Andrew. 2003. "Escaping the Autobiographical Trap? Monika Maron, the Stasi and *Pawels Briefe*." In *Writers and the Politics of Culture: Dealing with the Stasi*, edited by Paul Cooke and Andrew Plowman, New Perspectives in German Studies, 227–42. New York: Palgrave Macmillan.

Plumpe, Gerhard. 1995. *Epochen moderner Literatur: Ein systemtheoretischer Entwurf*. Opladen: Westdeutscher Verlag.

Ring, Annie. 2015. *After the Stasi: Collaboration and the Struggle for Sovereign Subjectivity in the Writing of German Unification*. London: Bloomsbury Academic.

———. 2016. "Collaboration as Collapse in the Life Writing and Stasi Shadow-Documents of Monika Maron and Christa Wolf." In *Secret Police Files from the Eastern Bloc: Between Surveillance and Life Writing*, edited by Valentina Glajar, Alison Lewis, and Corina L. Petrescu, 115–36. Rochester NY: Camden House.

Rosenfeld, Sophia. 2001. "Writing the History of Censorship in the Age of Enlightenment." In *Post-Modernism and the Enlightenment: New Perspectives in French Intellectual History*, edited by Daniel Gordon, 117–45. New Haven CT: Yale University Press.

Schmeidel, John Christian. 2008. *The Stasi: Shield and Sword of the Party*. London: Routledge.

Sepp, Arvi. 2016. "Profession and Ideology: Cultural Institutions and the Formation of Literary Circles in the Soviet Occupied Territory and the Early GDR." In *Precarious Alliances: Cultures of Participation in Print and Other Media*, edited by Martin Butler, Albrecht Hausmann, and Anton Kirchhofer, 241–56. Bielefeld: Transcript.

Shatz, David. 2004. *Peer Review: A Critical Inquiry*. Lanham MD: Rowman & Littlefield.

Simmel, Georg. 1906. "The Sociology of Secrecy and of Secret Societies." *American Journal of Sociology* 11 (4): 441–98.

Walther, Joachim. 1996a. "Im stinkenden Untergrund." *Der Spiegel*, September 23, 224–33.

———. 1996b. *Sicherungsbereich Literatur: Schriftsteller und Staatssicherheit in der Deutschen Demokratischen Republik*. Berlin: Links.

———. 2003. "Der fünfte Zensor: Das MfS als die letzte Instanz." In *Zensur im modernen deutschen Kulturraum*, edited by Beate Müller, 131–48. Tübingen: Niemeyer.

Wietersheim, Annegret von. 2014. *"Aber—ist mein liebster laut": Ambivalenzen in Biographie und lyrischem Werl von Paul Wiens*. Heidelberg: Universitätsverlag Winter.

Wolle, Stefan. 1998. *Die heile Welt der Diktatur: Alltag und Herrschaft in der DDR 1971–1989*. Berlin: Links, 1998.

Targets

4 Of Sources and Files

The Making of the Securitate Target Ana Novac

CORINA L. PETRESCU

Files produced by the secret police forces of former Eastern Bloc countries are complex documents, not completely reliable and yet not fully untrustworthy either—or as the British historian Timothy Garton Ash has remarked, "There is a truth that can be found [in a secret police file]. Not a single, absolute Truth with a capital T but still a real and important one" (2002, 282). As historical documents—texts anchored in a time and place and resulting from specific circumstances—files in general "supplement or rework 'reality'" and are never "mere sources that divulge facts about 'reality'" (LaCapra 1985, 11). In thinking with Paul Ricoeur, secret police files prefigure meaning—that is to say, they provide a network of everyday life occurrences and their interpretation through the eyes of the people and institutions that produce them, which call forth narrative and make storytelling possible (1984, 54–64). They bear the quality of "as yet untold stories . . . that constitute . . . the living imbrication from which [a] told story emerges" (75–76), as they amass documents verified by the various people who wrote, commented, approved, or reviewed the information therein. This leaves researchers who turn their attention to them regardless of their field of expertise in need of organizing, analyzing, and making sense of this information, which can only come about through critical engagement with the material at hand and its proper contextualization. After all, as Cornelia Vismann has shown, "when files are opened to reveal their contents, they are not simply read. Files are *processed*" (2008, xi). Thus researchers configure meaning through emplotment: they sow the information in the files into a story with characters, events, and settings that depicts a time and place. Emplotment has a mediating function, as it renders these elements meaningful in the context of a larger whole, and by so doing it creates a unity that has a narrative and temporal structure that endows the constitutive elements with an explanatory role. This allows any reader of the researchers' story to follow and refigure it in the act of reading, by extracting it from an abstract, hypothetical time and integrating it into a lived, real one. The reader can bring to light uneffected links between circumstances, agents, actors, or motives by drawing connections between the researchers' story and a reader's own knowledge of events that have occurred since and given the story another angle. In this sense and returning once more to Ricoeur, the reader enters the world of the narrative and completes the story, which becomes a "joint work of the [researchers'] text and [the] reader" (1984, 76).

According to Valentina Glajar, a productive method for literary scholars to process and configure files is to unearth the "file story" encapsulated in each file (2016, 57). She defines the term as "a multilayered and polyphonic biographical act" that combines the pieces of information offered by the files with the gaps equally present in them. This collage is "precarious" and "capricious" as "any overlooked or missing detail [in a file] has the potential of disturbing or rearranging the life fragments" captured between the covers of the file (this volume, 31). In my analysis of Securitate files, I build on Glajar's work and suggest that file stories unveil an identity of the surveilled that the secret police have constructed, which is that of a "target" (*obiectiv*).[1] Consequently, when configuring a file story from the porous material in a file, one can primarily unveil a surveilled person's *target identity*—the distinguishing traits of character and behavioral patterns that stirred the Securitate's interest and motivated the person's shadowing. As it reflects a secret police's take on the surveilled at a given time and in a specific context, this target identity does not necessarily correspond to reality nor does it have to. Ultimately, it serves the secret police's intention vis-à-vis an individual deemed suspicious, which is to police and discipline her or him. The closest expression of a surveilled's own views comes in her or his filed intercepted correspondence, even though the voice behind the letters can be equivocated by self-censorship or code talk, if the person has suspected surveillance. When the surveilled's own voice comes to life in wiretapped conversations, it is also distorted and feeds into the individual's target identity. No recordings of wiretaps have been found in the archives of the former Securitate, so only transcripts of conversations are available. Whether penned verbatim or in summary, they are mediated through the Securitate employees who transcribed or summarized them for their superiors. The employee's voice thus blurs the surveilled's by determining which aspects of the conversations to stress.

Indispensable to the construction of a target identity are the informative notes and reports that sources produced for their case officers. During Romania's years of Communism, "source" was a general term designating "a person . . . through which [the Securitate] could collect information" irrespective of her or his specific capacity in the hierarchy of the secret police's informative services, which included the support person, the agent, the collaborator, the informant, the resident, and the party member (Albu 2008, 13).[2] The materials that sources provided expressed not only what they knew or learned about the individual under surveillance but also their sentiments about the person on whom they spied. Depending on their attitudes toward the surveilled, the reports could seem harmless or hurtful, apologetic or damning, but in any case, they were a breach of trust and a betrayal.

In this chapter I examine how two Securitate sources, "Magda" and "Karl Fischer," helped shape the target identity of playwright and novelist Ana Novac (1924–2010).[3] Their informative notes are included in Novac's own surveillance file I 264513 (February 28 to November 29, 1963) and in the file of her former husband, Paul Schuster (I 184937, vol. 1, September 1961 to January 1963).[4] What emerges from them is not the complex personality of a female playwright and Shoah survivor but an objectified Securitate target. Both sources portray Novac as a subversive element and an enemy of the state, a deviant with a bourgeois lifestyle, and an open and vocal critic of Romania's Communist regime. She is said to have ties to foreigners who helped her smuggle her work out of Romania and, eventually, emigrate herself. To anchor the file story into Novac's existence prior to her surveillance, I reconstruct her life story—in the absence of an "Ana Novac Nachlass" anywhere—based on Novac's own statements in the preface to her first publication in a Western country in 1967, on research in the Paul Schuster Nachlass in Munich, and on Novac's last two interviews before her death in 2010.[5] Also, to explain Novac's fall from grace with the Communist regime, without which her file story is incomprehensible, I re-create that context based on articles published about Novac in the magazine *Teatrul* (The theater) between 1956 and 1958. This was the main theater publication at the time and articulated the official discourse of the Romanian state with respect to dramatic art.

Ana Novac's Life Story

Ana Novac was the pen name of Zimra Harsányi, now a forgotten writer, who lived in Romania until 1963, when she immigrated to Budapest, then West Berlin, finally arriving in Paris in 1965. In Romania she wrote socialist realist plays in her mother tongue, Hungarian, which were also translated into Romanian and Yiddish and performed to great acclaim. In France Novac wrote mostly autobiographical plays and novels in French and Romanian; the latter she then translated into French either by herself or with the help of friends such as the writer, translator, and Russian Studies scholar Luba Jurgenson. Even though she had longed to live in Paris, life in the French capital seems to have disappointed her badly: in one of her last interviews for a German newspaper she declared, "French became my homeland but never France" (Das Französische ist meine Heimat geworden, das Land nie; Herwig 2009). She voiced her disillusionment also when she declared that Auschwitz had proven a disaster for her literary work, since it had turned her into a "survivor" (*Überlebende*) and thus had denied her the status of a "living being" (*Lebende*) and implicitly a life, no matter where she dwelled (Novac quoted in Hoch 2009).

Novac's life story is worth knowing because it showcases the tragic fate of an East European Jew during the twentieth century, when first nationalism and fascism and later Communism uprooted and almost decimated the Jewish community in Transylvania.

Born into a low-middle class Jewish family in Northern Transylvania in 1924, Zimra Harsányi was by law a Romanian citizen, but her family followed the traditional way of Transylvanian Jewry, which was "Hungarian by mother tongue and culture" (Tibori Szabó 2004).[6] In view of Transylvania's complex history, this was a common situation. Until the demise of the Austro-Hungarian monarchy in 1918, this province had belonged to the Kingdom of Hungary, where Jews had been emancipated in 1867, and as a result, in the 1890 census 63.7 percent of the Jewish population was recorded as ethnic Hungarian by mother tongue, 33 percent as German, and 3.3 percent as other (Silber 2017). After World War I Transylvania became part of the Romanian kingdom and remained a Romanian territory until 1940, when, per the Second Vienna Dictate, the province's northern part was returned to Hungary. Between May 16 and June 27, 1944, the Hungarian government of Regent Miklós Horthy had Northern Transylvanian Jews deported to Auschwitz (Shoah Resource Center 2017), and although on separate transports Novac and her family were among them. Only she survived, and after May 6, 1945, when the Soviet army freed Kratzau, the concentration camp to which she had been transferred (Novac 1967, 183), she returned to Northern Transylvania, which was again a part of the Romanian kingdom (Novac 1967, 5). She brought along a diary she had kept over the course of her year of imprisonment.[7] By her own statements, Novac spent the next two years in the Jewish hospital in Cluj and in 1950 moved to Bucharest, where she lived until 1963, when she immigrated to Hungary by entering a *marriage de complaisance* with a Hungarian national (Novac 1965, 5–7).[8] Of her previous three marriages, two had long-term consequences: her second husband was the mathematician Liviu Solomon, whom she divorced in 1956, but with whom she maintained contact her entire life.[9] On June 21, 1958, she married the German Romanian writer Paul Schuster. Even though this relationship also ended in divorce in 1960, Novac and Schuster continued a close relationship until Schuster's death in 2004.[10] In the early 1950s in Bucharest, Zimra Harsányi became the writer Ana Novac and joined the Communist Party, as she sympathized with its ideals.[11]

By the mid-1950s Ana Novac was a promising playwright. Theater houses across the country performing in Romanian, Hungarian, and Yiddish successfully staged her plays since they were in line with the requirements of socialist realism.[12] For example, *Familia Kovacs* (The Kovacs family) depicts the fate of an upper-middle-class ethnic-Hungarian family in Northern Transylvania between 1941 and 1943. Caught up in their bourgeois lifestyle, the parents do not notice the dangers of fascism until it is too late, and their own son joins the Nazis. Under the influence of a young Communist named Andras, the family's daughter, Eva, overcomes her lighthearted and apolitical disposition and joins the antifascist struggle, because, as she explains, "When you listen [to the Communists] everything gains a different color, even the air brightens up. You feel like a better, stronger person; in any case, you would want to fight, to write, to speak, to do great, unusual things, as if happiness were only up to you and you only had to want it" (Novák 1955, 72). At the end of the fourth act, the father loses his mind, unable to process his social downfall, the son commits suicide as the German defeat at Stalingrad draws nearer, while the mother, the daughter, and her now-husband Andras are active members of the Communist underground. Thus the superior Communist cause triumphs over both fascism and bourgeois liberalism. Novac's next play, *Preludiu* (Prelude), is equally embedded in socialist realism. In a provincial town, the Communists establish a theater school to train actors who can perform in accordance with the new principles of the so-called peoples' democracy. They recruit new actors among people from various walks of life (workers, a former ballerina, a teacher, the descendent of a bourgeois family) and retrain old theater people (a diva and a theater director) to embrace their ideals. The play's central theme is "we built socialism" (Novák 1955, 7 and 21), and it illustrates it by focusing on the trials and tribulations that transform a group of individuals into a collective between 1946 and 1949. In 1957 Novac received the State Prize, Third Class, for these two plays, which brought her not only official recognition and fame but also a substantial monetary reward of 15,000 lei.[13]

Novac's next work completely changed her life: On December 24, 1957, the play *Ce fel de om ești tu?* (What kind of a person are you?) opened in Bucharest at the Municipal Theater, where Lucia Sturdza-Bulandra, the grande dame of the Romanian stage at the time, was manager (Institutul Național al Patrimoniului n.d.).[14] Shortly after the premier, Lucia Sturdza-Bulandra mentioned the play favorably in an article (1957, 17), while other critics praised it for its "partisan zeal" and "ideological pathos," proclaiming it "an admirable drama," even if a "failed" one, due to "confused formulations."[15] Yet in March 1958, in a review published anonymously under the title "Așa arată oare o piesă de actualitate?" (Is this what a topical play looks like?) in the party journal *Scînteia* (The spark), its author reproached the playwright with having wrongly constructed her characters, whose problems she considered from "profoundly erroneous perspectives." This led to a "false conception" of the play, which "absurdly oppose[d] the preoccupation and the efforts for the construction of the socialist economy to the concern for the improvement of the life conditions of the working people" and "grave ideological deficiency." Other publications followed suit, and the play metamorphosed into "a work infused by a negative spirit, written from false ideological positions" ("Consfătuirea" 1958, 5), and Novac was admonished for not admitting her ideological deviation and performing self-criticism (Mira 1958, 50). It did not help that she defended her work in an article in the cultural publication *Tribuna* (The tribune) by invoking the autonomy of art and a writer's right to artistic freedom.[16] Consequently, she was excluded from the party in 1958 and the Writers Union in 1960 and was blacklisted, that is, while she was not officially banned from publishing or her plays from being performed, her works were neither printed nor staged ever again in Communist Romania.[17]

One would expect the Securitate to pay attention to such a high-profile artist gone astray, and it did, even though not at the height of Novac's conflict with the cultural authorities in 1958. Indeed, the first surveillance file under the name "Novac, Ana" is only from 1960, and according to the decision to close it on November 25, 1960, Novac had been included in the file "Uniunea Scriitorilor" (Writers Union) by mistake (I 405789, 15). It is source "Magda's" informative note from January 9, 1959, included in Schuster's file (I 184937, vol. 1, 187–89) that brought Novac into the Securitate's spotlight. "Magda" is a very elusive character in Novac's file story. In a document from March 26, 1963, outlining her responsibilities vis-à-vis Schuster, she referred to herself as "H. P." (I 184937 vol. 1, 111), and in a report from December 21, 1965, she indicated that she was the granddaughter of Michael Albert (I 211829, vol. 1, 93), a nineteenth-century Transylvanian Saxon writer and pedagogue (Theil 2013). Aside from this no other information about her is available. The reasons for her collaboration with the Securitate are not apparent from the files at hand, yet her habitus as an informant suggests that she might have been a vigilante.[18] When she first wrote about Novac in January 1959, the playwright was a mere collateral target, as the Securitate was primarily interested in Schuster's activities in Romania and his ties to the German Romanian émigrés in the Federal Republic of Germany. "Magda's" main objective in producing intelligence about Novac appears to have been to show the Securitate Novac's true colors. She titled her first informative note dedicated to Novac "The writer Ana Novac, an enemy of our regime" (I 184937, vol. 1, 186), when it was not customary for notes to have titles, and wrote, "This is the true face of the writer Ana Novak" in the note's concluding paragraph (189). While accusing her of the worst crime against the Romanian state at the time when she labeled Novac "an enemy of [the] regime," she also dutifully brought to the Securitate's attention that Novac was working on her Auschwitz diary (187). She indicated that she had met Novac at the end of 1958, while working as Schuster's dactylographer in her house. She described Novac as a woman in her thirties, slender, pale, with a fashionable short haircut, who did not wear makeup, walked around the house in pajamas and a robe, and worked on her diary mostly in bed. Such a routine hardly conformed to the expectations of a Communist state vis-à-vis its subjects, and "Magda's" information put Novac in danger by presenting her as a deviant with a bourgeois lifestyle. Furthermore, "Magda" emphasized that Novac was congenial and smart but also an open and vocal critic of Romania's political regime. She even went so far on one occasion as to call the East Germans "jackasses" (*dobitoci*) and criticize them for having fallen prey to the same proletarian zeal as the Romanians (188). According to "Magda," Novac reproached the Romanian regime "disdainfully" for keeping people in chains and ordering them what to think (187). She was very proud of her lack of inhibition in expressing criticism and confided in "Magda" "with great satisfaction" that she had been excluded from the party (188). As if to validate her claims about Novac, "Magda" maintained that Novac had taken a liking to her from the start and talked to her freely, as though they had known each other for years. During one of their frank conversations, Novac supposedly declared that Anne Frank's diary was "a trifle" (*un fleac*) and hers was a serious work, which was why she was working on it at the time (188). It is noteworthy that "Magda" initiated her reporting on Novac; she was even unsure whether the information would be of interest to her case officer as exemplified by her direct questions: "Does any [of this] interest you? Can I be of help in any matter?" toward the end of her informative note (189). She seems to have volunteered her services to the secret police after being faced with Novac's ungratefulness vis-à-vis the Romanian regime: while Novac complained about her "miserable life," the regime afforded her a ten-day writing retreat in the mountain resort of Sinaia, in which Novac partook happily (189). It comes as no surprise that "Magda's" case officer, Lieutenant Major Aneta Roşianu, instructed her to deepen her relationship with Novac and keep informing on her, which "Magda" did diligently.

"Magda's" subsequent informative notes leave no doubt about her rejection of Novac in terms of lifestyle and personality. On

January 14, 1959, she reported on what she perceived to be tensions between Schuster and Novac, who, per "Magda," thought herself to be "considerably superior" to her husband, whom she denigrated in front of "Magda" as an adventurous and undisciplined person (I 184937, vol. 1, 186). "Magda" portrayed Novac as a dissatisfied, nagging wife who nonetheless spent ten days in Sinaia working on her own writing, while her presumably irresponsible husband had to procure firewood for their house in Bucharest in order to be able to work there himself (186). The comparison between the two clearly favored Schuster even before "Magda" wrote: "Paul Schuster is a very kind man and he works with great enthusiasm, but he is constantly despised by his own wife, Ana Novak" (186). The juxtaposition passes judgment on Novac for her alleged disdain for a husband who, "Magda" suggested, was a dedicated homemaker. "Magda" cemented her portrayal of Novac as a parasite who took advantage of Schuster in the next available note she penned on September 17, 1962 (I 184937, vol. 1, 149–51).[19] She informed her case officer that Schuster had approached her to type up Novac's Auschwitz diary even though at that point Schuster and Novac were divorced and Schuster had remarried (149). Novac had tried to publish the diary in Romania, but it had been rejected, which left her only with the option to smuggle it out of Romania and find a publisher abroad. To this end, without his wife's knowledge, Schuster helped Novac by editing and translating the diary into German (150). He is said to have considered it "a unique manuscript" and "an extremely valuable document" that "w[ould] bring great success" (149).

Schuster's concern for Novac and her spinelessness are further emphasized in "Magda's" next informative note from October 25, 1962, in which she related her attempts to get Schuster to talk about his progress on Novac's diary (I 184937, vol. 1, 144–45). Claiming that he had not made the desired progress as he had translated only two-thirds of the diary by that time, Schuster also confessed to the source that he was apprehensive for Novac's safety should her diary be smuggled out of Romania while she still lived there (144). Consequently, he wanted to wait until she had left the country, which, "Magda" asserted, he believed she would do with help from abroad (144). Again, in her writing "Magda" placed Novac outside the norms of socialist society, by bestowing on her a form of behavior incongruous with the state's expectations, when she reported that Novac was unemployed yet received monthly financial support from her last two husbands, who paid her 300 lei each. Compared to the net average salary of 880 lei (Ministerul Muncii și Justiției Sociale n.d., year 1962), Novac seems to have enjoyed a modestly comfortable income (600 lei) without participating herself in the country's workforce.

Source "Karl Fischer" has a stronger presence in Novac's file story, as he authored or provided his case officers with the information for nineteen informative notes, which cover the time span August 1961–October 1963.[20] He was himself a writer and during those years the editor of the German-language newspaper *Neuer Weg* (New way).[21] His reasons for spying on her are not apparent from his notes or reports, but his prolificacy left few aspects of her life untouched. He wrote about her tireless efforts to survive as a writer, about her troubled love life and frail health, about her complicated plans to find a way out of Romania, and about her Auschwitz diary. He provided details that flesh out Novac's image that "Magda" had drawn of her. He informed about her frustration with the cultural authorities who had rejected two new plays she had written (I 264513, 102), documenting Novac's persistence to have her works performed in Romania in spite of being blacklisted. He claimed that in a conversation with him, Novac rationalized from the state's point of view her exclusion from the Writers Union and the subsequent impossibility to publish by admitting her inability to compromise, since she was "an enemy of any absolutist system" (I 264513, 87). On November 21, 1962, he mentioned for the first time the two aspects that became the focus of his reporting on Novac: her desire to emigrate and her Auschwitz diary (I 264513, 84–85).

While Schuster had alluded to "Magda" that Novac was exploring the possibility to emigrate with help from abroad, "Karl Fischer," who enjoyed Novac's trust, provided specific details about her plan: she wanted to marry a Hungarian national and relocate with him to Hungary (I 264513, 85). The source maintained that even though Novac had accepted a job as a pediatric medical consultant in a small town, which paid 500 lei per month and allowed her to live "like a tzar" (85), she had made up her mind to leave Romania because she needed to feel free to travel and move around, as this had become her obsession since Auschwitz (84–85).[22] Novac's goal-oriented matrimonial plans, while surely not uncommon even in Communist Romania, positioned her outside the proclaimed official moral norms of mainstream society and added promiscuity to her target identity. "Karl Fischer's" note enhanced this aspect of her constructed personality even more when he indicated that Novac had confided in him that she was willing to abandon her emigration plans should she be able to rekindle her relationship with Schuster (85). Considering that Schuster was married to Edith Gross at the time, Novac's desire attested to her deviant sexual propensity.

"Karl Fischer" brought further evidence of Novac's questionable character in his note from January 4, 1963, when he claimed to reproduce the disapproving observations of Novac's friend Magda Stroe, who had told him that "she did not know anymore what this woman [i.e., Novac] wanted. She [did] not get along with basic work discipline preferring a life without employment so as to work when she felt like it [and have] endless conversations until midnight, etc." (I 264513, 77). This bohemian outlook on life was, so Stroe per "Karl Fischer," further aggravated by Novac's desire to be different from others and to stand out (78). This individualistic, selfish disposition, however, had to give way as Novac had "to finally learn some truths and rules of society, stop living on other people's backs, and find out on her own that if you do not work, you do not eat" (78). "Karl Fischer's" note thus strengthened Novac's depraved reputation, which source "Magda" had helped establish. At the latest by January 28, 1962, when the source noted that Novac had taken vacation time followed by an unpaid leave of absence for an unspecified duration because she did not like either her work or her workplace, her standing as a parasite seems buttressed. In the same note, the source indicated that Novac was getting her papers ready for a *marriage de complaisance* with a fifty-year-old Hungarian because she continued to feel "confined in her creative mission" (76) in Romania. "Karl Fischer" also revealed to the Securitate that Novac shrewdly used not her well-known literary alias but her given name in those papers to avoid any difficulties with the Romanian authorities (76).

If the Securitate needed more proof of Novac's debauched character, "Karl Fischer" produced it on May 8, 1963, when he included in his note Novac's alleged description of her fourth husband: he was a sixty-year-old Hungarian national, a serious man and party activist, whom she did not love (I 264513, 65). Yet she was so desperate to leave Romania that for a passport, she was "willing to sell [her]self piece by piece" (65). She hoped her future husband did not love her either as that would only have complicated things. Consiliul de Stat (State Council) had approved their union, and she assumed that things had gone so fast because her trick had worked, and the authorities had not identified her under her given name, Zimra Harsányi. A comment in "Mențiuni" (Remarks) indicates that the authorities had indeed not connected Harsányi with Novac (I 264513, 68), despite "Karl Fischer's" warning from January 1963. Furthermore, "Karl Fischer's" note from May 8, 1963, also intimated that Novac did not hold Hungarians in high esteem despite her cultural background and marriage to a Hungarian. To the contrary she ostensibly described them as "chauvinistic, mean, savage, a kind of mixture between Prussians and Mongols" (66). Yet life in Hungary was considerably better than in Romania since people enjoyed more freedom and could travel freely to Western countries, which was her ultimate goal. Novac's willingness to marry advantageously and even to live among a people she despised further revealed her egotistical nature and incriminated her with the Securitate. "Karl Fischer's" note also added yet another dimension to Novac's description as a parasite, when he maintained that in the West she planned to live off the reparation money to which she was entitled as an Auschwitz survivor and descendent of victims of National Socialism—purportedly Novac counted on $8,000 for herself and her deceased parents and sister (67).[23] Thus Novac appeared willing and ready to profit even from her own family's tragedy.

The extent of this tragedy from her own point of view Novac

had recorded in her Auschwitz diary, to which "Karl Fischer" also dedicated his attention. Already in November 1962, he described the diary as "partly written in the camp and later edited" and claimed that Novac was having it translated into French for publication abroad, after having tried and failed to have it published in Romania (I 264513, 84). She was convinced that the publisher had rejected the work because of her controversial relation with Romania's political regime, not due to lack of quality (84). This information supplements "Magda's" from September 17 and October 25, 1962, that Paul Schuster was working on a German translation of the diary and investigating options for the diary to be smuggled outside Romania. A year later, on March 13, 1963, "Karl Fischer" specified that, while Novac had written the diary in Auschwitz at the age of nineteen, she estimated that she would never again write anything as good as that (I 264513, 73). After having read a quarter of it, he described it as "a well-written work, with novel images, depicting the tormented life of the inmates in the camp from Auschwitz. The author [was] filled with natural (and well described) hatred against the ss beasts and boundless feelings of revolt against acts of injustice and the permanent terror" (73). Yet he also criticized it, claiming, "This revolt [was] however the spontaneously human reaction of the helpless, of the inmates who ha[d] lost not only their hope but also their dignity, their drive to fight. One d[id] not learn anything about the numerous inmates, who, although at times discouraged, fought with determination; one d[id] not feel the presence of the Communists" (73). This take on Novac's writing could suggest a reason for her failure to publish the diary in Romania: she would have had to alter it to fit the expectations of the regime, which meant somehow subordinate her survival to the Communist cause and present it as an ideological rather than an existential struggle. And she was not prepared to do so, as her critique of the regime's infringement on artistic freedom as reported by both "Magda" and "Karl Fischer" proposed. Interestingly, at the time of "Karl Fischer's" note, Novac's diary was already outside Romania, namely, in her future home country by choice, Hungary. According to a source named "Kovacs Peter," a Hungarian journalist identified as Adam

Raffy had smuggled it into Hungary before October 1, 1962, when "Kovacs Peter" had informed his case officer about it (I 264513, 90-92). This event had also surprised the Securitate, which although warned about Novac's intentions by both "Magda" and "Karl Fischer" had failed to prevent it from happening.[24] Novac's surveillance seems to have been poorly coordinated, or at least poorly carried out, since the various Securitate departments and offices involved in her shadowing did not connect the dots correctly or in time with respect both to the smuggling of her dairy in 1962 and, as already mentioned, to her application to marry a foreign national in 1963.[25]

Novac's diary makes a last appearance in an informative note by "Karl Fischer" in August 1963 (I 264513, 25-27).[26] In it he pointed out that the diary was already in France, where an unnamed publisher had read it in Romanian and had shown great interest in it. However, since Novac did not have a French translation of it yet, she held back its publication (26). Also, while still waiting for her permission to leave Romania and join her husband in Hungary, she did not want to risk being arrested because her diary had been published in France (26).

With this Novac's file story concludes as inexplicably as it had begun when source "Magda" took an interest in Novac although she was only expected to focus on Schuster. Its conclusion is typical for the narrative endings that files impose on people's lives. The narrative arc of her file story, though, tells us how precarious life was in Communist Romania in the late 1950s and early 1960s, when a bad review in the party's journal was enough to destroy a writer's career, and one's reference in the informative note of a curious source could transform one into a target. Once Novac succeeded in having her diary smuggled out of Romania for publication abroad, the Securitate had a solid reason to act against her, and both Novac's life and file story might have ended differently had she not thwarted the Securitate's "plot" by deceiving the secret police and leaving the country.

Through the informative notes of sources "Magda" and "Karl Fischer," who reported on her between 1959 and 1963, the target Ana Novac emerges as an enemy of the state. The two sources described her as erratic and capricious, as well as moody and constantly dissatisfied with her life in Romania. She was a parasite who did not lead a regular life in which she worked for an income but rather relied on her former husbands to support her. "Magda" and "Karl Fischer" also ascribed to her a preference for a bourgeois—even bohemian—lifestyle, in which the mores and social norms of the Communist state played no role. She emerges as a promiscuous woman, impelled by an adventurous spirit, which also drove her to leave Romania. Her decision to emigrate was thus not the result of the regime's oppressive nature and inability to deal with criticism but a natural consequence of her carefree and thrill-seeking disposition. Consequently, the target Ana Novac was an ethnically unbound, psychologically volatile, and socially deviant cosmopolitan wanderer. Yet on October 11, 1963, a "Notă sinteză" (Synthesis note) concluded, "It does not follow that HARSANYI ZIMRA carries out a nationalistic activity organized against [Romania's] socialist state. Some acts of discontent are of material nature, and others stem from her adventurous spirit, which possesses her to leave the country, something she has done already" (I 264513, 237). With this her file was closed, and the two sources concluded their activities involving her, at a time when Novac, under the name Zimra Mikó, had already departed from Romania on September 20, 1963 (244).

As a target Novac acquired a new identity, one that the Securitate configured based on its sources' informative notes and reports and classified according to stock types of enemies of the state. She fit the type of the critical, bourgeois intellectual. Yet as an ethnically Jewish, culturally Hungarian Romanian citizen, Novac also eluded a linear configuration, which led the Securitate to oscillate between labeling her a Jew, a Hungarian, or a Romanian.[27] This hybridity coupled with Novac's critique of the regime enhanced the threat she could pose to the Romanian state. It is thus surprising that Novac escaped from Romania and was able to do so legally. Was it professional negligence on the part of the Securitate officers charged with her surveillance, considering that "Magda's" and "Karl Fischer's" notes incriminated her? Did the Securitate simply loose interest in her? Her file story ends anticlimactically without providing answers to these questions or any indications that Novac had escaped the Securitate's gaze completely or for good. Another file harboring another file story set in a different time (1981–86) and place (Paris, France) speaks not only to Novac's ongoing criticism of Romania's Communist regime but also to the Securitate's persistence in pursuing its targets even across time and space.

Notes

1. "Target—person, group of people, or institution under surveillance by the Securitate" (Obiectiv—persoană, grup de persoane sau instituție în supraveghearea informativă a Securității). See CNSAS n.d. Unless otherwise noted all translations are mine.

2. After the fall of Communism and particularly after Law 293/2008 was passed, "source" maintained its general meaning but in a different sense. Article 3, Paragraph b of the law stipulates that a collaborator is someone who "has supplied information regardless of its form, such as written notes and reports, verbal communications written down by employees of the Securitate, through which actions or attitudes were denounced that were hostile to the totalitarian Communist regime *and* aimed at limiting fundamental human rights and liberties" (in Monitorul Oficial al României [Official Monitor of Romania], part 1, no. 800 from November 28, 2008, emphasis added). The law also establishes that the two conditions must be fulfilled simultaneously and cumulatively. If none of the conditions are met, CNSAS issues a certificate of noncollaboration (Adeverință). If only one condition is met, CNSAS issues the same certificate of noncollaboration but with an addendum explaining which of the two conditions were met and in what context. Given the complex implications of the term "collaborator," talking about "sources" has become much more productive and also safer for a researcher.

3. The name also appears spelled as Novak or Novák, which follows the Hungarian spelling. In the files the changes in spelling are aleatory. Novac published her two plays—*Familia Kovacs* (The Kovacs family, 1955) and *Preludiu* (Prelude, 1956)—in Romania also under the name Novák. Both publications indicate on their front pages that the works were translations from the Hungarian yet without mentioning the translator's name.

4. The Securitate had two more surveillance files on Novac: one that covered the period March–November 1960 (ACNSAS I 405789) and another for the period September 1981–March 1986 (ACNSAS SIE 45862). Since neither includes reports by "Magda" or "Karl Fischer," they are not of interest for this analysis. Paul Schuster (1930–2004) was a German Romanian writer. For more details on him and the Securitate's interest in him, see Sienerth 2009.

5. I base my conclusion regarding the absence of an "Ana Novac Nachlass" on email correspondence (September 19, 2017, September 20, 2017, and Sep-

tember 6, 2018, respectively) between this author and Cécile Lauvergeon from the Mémorial de la Shoah, which holds only the original of her Auschwitz diary; Elisa Martos from the Institut Mémoires de l'Édition Contemporaine (IMEC), which has no records of her; and Adriana Vasilescu, niece of Novac's second husband, Liviu Solomon. I am reconstructing Novac's life story based on the following texts: "Lesenslauf statt eines Vorworts" (Curriculum vitae instead of a foreword) in *Die schönen Tage meiner Jugend* . . . (1967); Hoch 2009; and Herwig 2009; correspondence with Stéphanie Danneberg, researcher at the Institut für deutsche Kultur und Geschichte Südosteuropas an der Ludwig-Maximilians-Universität München (IKGS Munich) in charge of cataloging the Paul Schuster Nachlass (April–July 2017); and correspondence with Vasilescu (September 2018).

6. Novac always claimed to have been born in 1929, which would have made her fourteen when she was in Auschwitz; see, for example, the 1982 French edition of her diary titled *J'avais quatorze ans a Auschwitz*. However, all documents from the archives of the Securitate list 1924 as her year of birth. Hence, I am using this year in my analysis. For a convincing explanation of why some Shoah survivors chose to alter particular aspects of their lives prior to or during the Shoah, see Hájková 2014.

7. Novac published her diary several times over the course of her life not just in different languages but also in more or less edited versions. The first edition appeared in Hungarian in 1966 as Harsányi Zimra, *A téboly hétköznapjai: Egy diáklány naplójából* (Daily life of madness: From the diary of a schoolgirl). Subsequent editions appeared under her pen name Ana Novac with a German translation by Barbara Frischmuth as the first in a language with a wide readership: *Die schönen Tage meiner Jugend* (1967). According to Kata Bohus (2017), Hungary's Kádár regime had no problem publishing memorialistic accounts about the Shoah as long as they portrayed Jews as one group among others of victims and described the social conflict of the 1940s as a confrontation between fascist and antifascist forces. Novac's diary could be co-opted to conform to these tenets.

8. Except for her first married name, Nirvai, which appears in Novac's Securitate file from the 1980s, I have been unable to learn anything about this aspect of Novac's life ("Hotarîre de deschidere-închidere" [Decision to open-close (a file)], September 6, 1981, in ACNSAS SIE 45862, 1). Had she been married prior to her deportation and had her husband perished in the Shoah alongside Novac's parents? Had she been married between her liberation from the camp and her arrival in Romania? I do not know. The cultural studies scholar Louise O. Vasvári, who researches Novac's life and work as a Shoah survivor, could not answer any of these questions either. She explained to me, though, that it was not uncommon for female survivors to marry as soon as they recovered physically from their traumatic experiences in the camps, either to regain a sense of "normalcy" as soon as possible or as a means to an end: immigration to somewhere far from Europe (email exchange with this author, September 7, 2017).

9. Liviu Solomon was born in Romania in 1927 and in 1971 defected to France, where he taught mathematics at the Université de Poitiers until his death in 2013. Between 1945 and 1948, he studied mathematics at the University of Bucharest. He continued his studies by pursuing a doctoral degree in Moscow at the Institute for Mechanics of the Academy of Sciences of the Soviet Union between 1950 and 1953. Upon his return to Bucharest, he became associate professor of mathematics at the local university. In this capacity he attended a conference in France in 1971 from where he refused to return to Romania (email exchange from May 12, 2017, and September 6, 2018, respectively, with Danneberg and Vasilescu).

10. Information based on email correspondence with Danneberg from April 18, 2017.

11. According to source "Karl Fischer," Petru Dumitriu (1924–2002), who was a regime-friendly author till he escaped Romania in 1960, suggested to Harsányi that she use Ana Novac as her pen name (informative note from May 8, 1963, ACNSAS I 264513, 66).

12. For example, *Familia Kovacs* was performed in Romanian in Timişoara and Bucharest, in Hungarian in Sf. Gheorghe, and in Yiddish in Bucharest (see *Teatrul*, April 1956, 76–78; June 1956, 13; September 1957, 21; and December 1957, 21).

13. "Însemnări" 1957, 91. For purposes of comparison, according to Ministerul Muncii şi Justiţiei Sociale (Ministry for Work and Social Justice) the net average salary in 1957 was 619 lei, which equates Novac's prize to twenty-four times the average income in the country. For details on the different categories of the State Prizes and the selection criteria, see Vasile 2011, 107–12.

14. Teatrul Municipal (Municipal Theater) is today Teatrul Lucia Sturdza-Bulandra. According to Mirela Ringheanu, librarian at the Library of the Romanian Academy of Arts and Sciences in Bucharest, the play was never published (email exchange with the author from June 29, 2017).

15. These positive reviews belong to critics Vicu Mîndra and Radu Popescu and are quoted in Florin Tornea's extensive analysis of the shortcoming of literary criticism in Romania at the time. Tornea (1958) rebukes them and admonishes their authors for their lack of vigilance in evaluating Novac's work.

16. "To name everything you believe in or condemn, everything you hope for and dream about, here, now, is too great of a pleasure, [it is] a passion beyond prudence and calculations, it is according to me the very rationale of a writer's existence" (A spune tot ce crezi sau condamni, tot ce speri şi visezi, aici, acum, e o plăcere prea mare, o pasiune deasupra prudenţei şi a calculelor, e după mine însăşi raţiunea existenţei pentru un scriitor) (Novac 1958, 11).

17. Regarding her exclusion from the party and the Writers Union, see "Stefan Dragomirescu's" informative note from July 21, 1958, in ACNSAS I 405789, 14. Curiously, Novac's exclusion does not appear in the records kept by the party about its excluded members either under the letter H or N (ANIC). Novac's file from the Writers Union indicates her membership dates as June

1956 until April 1962 (AUSR). See also "Hotărîre" (Decision) from November 25, 1960, in ACNSAS I 405789, 15, where she is said to still be a member of the Writers Union but not of the party. The information about her blacklisting comes from Vasilescu (September 6, 2018). According to historian Cristian Vasile, writers never received a formal letter prohibiting them from publishing when they fell from grace with the regime; the interdiction was implied in their new status as outsiders to the cultural apparatus. Hence, there is also no written evidence of Novac's publishing ban (personal communication between Vasile and this author, May 2017).

18. My use of the term "habitus" follows Alison Lewis's definition of the "habitus of collaborators" as a "set of dispositions, structured by external forces (class, income, milieu, and even generation)" that shaped an informant's behaviors and actions (2016, 30).

19. The note is also included in Novac's file, ACNSAS I 264513, 49-50.

20. The exact dates are August 22, 1961; May 17, 1962; October 19, 1962; November 21, 1962; December 15, 1962; January 4 and 28, 1963; March 13, 1963; April 19, 1963; May 8, 15, and 29, 1963; June 12 and 19, 1963; August 3, 10, and 16, 1963; September 9, 1963; and October 16, 1963, in ACNSAS I 264513.

21. "Karl Fischer's" case officer, Lieutenant Major Ioan Wagner, who typed up the note, mentioned the source's real name here and in the note from May 17. For privacy reasons that name cannot be revealed.

22. In his note from January 4, 1963, "Karl Fischer" indicated that Novac's job was in Păclişa, Hunedoara County (ACNSAS I 264513, 77). The note from December 15, 1962, had erroneously indicated Păltiniş, which is in Sibiu County, as her location (ACNSAS I 264513, 82).

23. Novac had a brother, not a sister, who died during the Shoah

24. In Romania the attempt to smuggle something across the border bore serious consequences. For details, see Vasile 2011, 153-85.

25. At the time under scrutiny in this chapter, three directorates of the Securitate were involved in Novac's surveillance: Direcţia a II-a (Second Directorate), the counter-espionage service; Direcţia a III-a (Third Directorate), which was the internal information service; and Direcţia a VII-a (Seventh Directorate) in charge of shadowing and investigations. People at the national and regional offices worked on her case for each directorate, which would not make it hard for details to fall between the cracks.

26. "Karl Fischer's" other informative notes listed at the beginning of this article but not analyzed here contain details about Novac's intimate life or medical history, which cannot be disclosed due to privacy concerns.

27. "Hotărîre de deschidere a dosarului de verificare" (Decision to open a verification file) from February 28, 1963, in ACNSAS I 264513, 1-3; "Cerere de verificare la cartotecă" (Request to verify at the register) from October 18, 1961, in ACNSAS I 264513, 108-9; Writing from the Seventh to the Third Directorate of the Ministry of the Interior, from November 26, 1962, in ACNSAS I 264513, 105-6.

References

ARCHIVAL SOURCES

ACNSAS (Arhiva Consiliului Naţional pentru Studierea Arhivelor Securităţii [Archive of the National Council for the Study of the Securitate Archives]). Fond Informativ, file I 184937, vols. 1 and 2.
———. Fond Informativ, file I 211829, vol. 1.
———. Fond Informativ, file I 264513.
———. Fond Informativ, file I 405789.
———. SIE 45862.
ANIC (Arhivele Naţionale Istorice Centrale [Central National Historical Archives]), Biroul Arhive Contemporane (Office for Contemporary Archives). Fond Comitetul Central al Partidului Comunist Român—Colegiul Central de Partid (Fond Central Committee of the Romanian Communist Party—Central College of the Party), Inventar (Inventory), letters D–L and M–O.
AUSR (Arhiva Uniunii Scriitorilor din România [Archive of the Romanian Writers Union]), file 903 (Novac Ana).

PUBLISHED SOURCES

Albu, Mihai. 2008. *Informatorul: Studiu asupra colaborării cu Securitatea.* Iaşi: Polirom.
"Aşa arată oare o piesă de actualitate?" 1958. *Scînteia,* March 16.
Bohus, Kata. 2017. "Anne and Eva: Two Diaries, Two Holocaust Memories in Communist Hungary." *European Network of Remembrance and Solidarity,* April 20. http://www.enrs.eu/en/articles/1743-anne-and-eva-two-diaries -two-holocaust-memories-in-communist-hungary.
CNSAS (Consiliul Naţional pentru Studierea Arhivelor Securităţii [National Council for the Study of the Securitate Archives]). n.d. *Index de termeni şi abrevieri cu utilizare frecventă în documentele Securităţii.* Accessed September 4, 2016. http://www.cnsas.ro/documente/arhiva/Dictionar%20termeni.pdf.
"Consfătuirea oamenilor de teatru." 1958. *Teatrul,* July, 3–12.
Garton Ash, Timothy. 2002. "Trials, Purges and History Lessons: Treating a Difficult Past in Post-communist Europe." In *Memory and Power in Postwar Europe: Studies in the Presence of the Past,* edited by Jan-Werner Müller, 265–82. Cambridge: Cambridge University Press.
Glajar, Valentina. 2016. "'You'll Never Make a Spy out of Me!'—The File Story of 'Fink Susanne.'" In *Secret Police Files from the Eastern Bloc: Between Surveillance and Life Writing,* edited by Valentina Glajar, Alison Lewis, and Corina L. Petrescu, 56–83. Rochester NY: Camden House.
Hájková, Anna. 2014. "Israeli Historian Otto Dov Kulka Tells Auschwitz Story of a Czech Family That Never Existed." *Tablet,* October 30. http://www .tabletmag.com/jewish-arts-and-culture/books/186462/otto-dov-kulka.
Herwig, Malte. 2009. "Das Buch Auschwitz." *Die Zeit,* February 19. http:// www.zeit.de/2009/09/Auschwitz-09.

Hoch, Jenny. 2009. "KZ-Überlebende Ana Novac: Horror ist, wenn man trotzdem lacht." *Spiegel*, May 23. http://www.spiegel.de/kultur/literatur/kz-ueberlebende -ana-novac-horror-ist-wenn-man-trotzdem-lacht-a-620789.html.

"Însemnări—Premii de Stat." 1957. *Teatrul*, May, 91.

Institutul Național al Patrimoniului (National Institute of the Patrimony). n.d. "Premiere." Accessed March 31, 2017. http://www.cimec.ro/scripts /TeatreNou/prem_detaliu_pag.asp?sq=CE+FEL+DE+OM+E%C5%9ETI +TU&sq3=C.

LaCapra, Dominick. 1985. *History and Criticism*. Ithaca NY: Cornell University Press.

"Lege 293/2008." 2008. Monitorul Oficial al României, part 1, no. 800, from November 28.

Lewis, Alison. 2016. "The Secret Lives and Files of Stasi Collaborators: Reading Secret Police Files for Identity and Habitus." In *Secret Police Files from the Eastern Block between Surveillance and Life Writing*, edited by Valentina Glajar, Alison Lewis, and Corina L. Petrescu, 27–55. Rochester NY: Camden House.

Ministerul Muncii și Justiției Sociale (Ministry for Work and Social Justice). n.d. "Salariul mediu anual 1938–1990." Accessed June 13, 2017. http:// www.mmuncii.ro/pub/imagemanager/images/file/Statistica/Statistici %20lunare/s38-90.pdf.

Mira, Iosif. 1958. "De ce dibuiri și echivocuri? Intrebări pe marginea unei anchete a revistei 'Tribuna.'" *Teatrul*, August, 48–51.

Novac, Ana. 1958. "Ancheta 'Teatrul azi.'" *Tribuna*, June 14.

———. 1967. *Die schönen Tage meiner Jugend*. Reinbeck bei Hamburg: Rowohlt.

———. 1982. *J'avais quatorze ans a Auschwitz*. Paris: Presses de la Renaissance.

Novák, Ana. 1955. *Familia Kovacs*. Bucharest: Editura de stat pentru literatură și artă.

———. 1956. *Preludiu*. Bucharest: Editura de stat pentru literatură și artă.

Ricoeur, Paul. 1984. "Time and Narrative: Threefold *Mimesis*." In *Time and Narrative*, translated by Kathleen McLaughlin and David Pellauer, 1:52– 87. Chicago: University of Chicago Press.

Shoah Resource Center. 2017. "Transylvania." http://www.yadvashem.org /odot_pdf/Microsoft%20Word%20-%205884.pdf.

Sienerth, Stefan. 2009. "Der siebenbürgisch-deutsche Schriftsteller Paul Schuster im Visier des rumänischen Geheimdienstes 'Securitate.'" *Spiegelungen: Zeitschrift für deutsche Kultur und Geschichte Südosteuropas* 4 (58): 16–39.

Silber, Michael K. 2017. "Hungary before 1918." http://www.yivoencyclopedia .org/article.aspx/Hungary/Hungary_before_1918.

Sturdza-Bulandra, Lucia. 1957. "Un bogat și valoros bilanț." *Teatrul*, December, 16–18.

Theil, Hermann. 2013. "Michael Albert ruht im Sachsenheim-Garten." *Siebenbürgische Zeitung*, May 15. https://www.siebenbuerger.de/zeitung/artikel /kultur/13344-michael-albert-ruht-im-sachsenheim.html.

Tibori Szabó, Zoltán. 2004. "Transylvanian Jewry during the Postwar Period, 1945–1948." *East European Perspectives* 6 (18–19) (October). http://www .rferl.org/a/1342466.html and http://www.rferl.org/a/1342467.html.

Tornea, Florin. 1958. "Probleme și sarcini ale criticii noastre dramatice." *Teatrul*, September, 9–17.

Vasile, Cristian. 2011. *Politicile culturale comuniste în timpul regimului Gheorghiu-Dej*. Bucharest: Humanitas.

Vismann, Cornelia. 2008. *Files: Law and Media Technology*. Palo Alto CA: Stanford University Press.

5 Soviet Narratives of Subversion and Redemption during the Second Cold War and Beyond

The Case of Father Dmitrii Dudko

JULIE FEDOR

On June 20, 1980, following the evening news, Soviet Central Tele-vision screened a remarkable "telerepentance" by the famous nonconformist Orthodox priest Father Dmitrii Dudko. Six months earlier he had been arrested by the KGB on suspicion of anti-Soviet activities; now, dressed not in his priest's robes but in an ill-fitting civilian suit, he proceeded to address the Soviet people with a con-fession, in which he declared himself guilty of anti-Soviet activ-ities, condemned such activities, and pledged to give them up. This episode, remembered by many former Soviet citizens as an emblematic moment, occurred in the wake of the Soviet invasion of Afghanistan and in the lead-up to the 1980 Moscow Olympics, during what is sometimes called the "Second Cold War" of the early 1980s.[1] The Second Cold War has received little attention from scholars of Cold War culture and propaganda, yet this was a period marked by important changes in the superpower relation-ship and in the discursive construction of their ideological struggle. It was a period in which the notion of human rights, now elevated to a prominent position in global politics, became securitized, and both sides fought to control the way in which Soviet dissidents were depicted on the world stage.[2] Were dissidents who passed information on human rights violations in the USSR to Western correspondents heroes, or were they traitors? Was this heroic resis-tance or duplicitous and base espionage and subversion?

The Dudko episode, which was carefully stage-managed by the

KGB, offers insights into the Soviet attempt to challenge the heroic image of the dissident and to reclaim the moral high ground by recasting the figure of the dissident as the puppet of Western special services. The case thus illuminates Soviet Cold War culture and ideology, which has generally been less widely studied than its U.S. variants to date. On the whole we know more about Western Cold War culture than we do about its Eastern counterparts. Numerous studies have been done in recent decades, for example, on Hollywood and propaganda or on the CIA's cultural interventions and psychological warfare strategies (see, for example, Hixson 1998; Shaw 2001; Rosenberg 1993). By contrast the study of the KGB side of the struggle is in its infancy and has been further hampered by the fact that declassification of the Russian state security archives has been moving in a reverse direction since the mid-1990s. The situation is different in some of the former Soviet republics, notably the Baltic states and more recently Ukraine, and scholars are beginning to take advantage of the greater openness of the archival regimes in these countries (see, for example, Cohn 2017). Meanwhile, great strides have been made when it comes to advancing our knowledge of state security operations and discourses in Poland, East Germany, Czechoslovakia, Hungary, and Romania in particular (see, for example, Szwagrzyk 2005; Graczyk 2007; Piotrowski 2006; Piotrowski 2008; Glajar, Lewis, and Petrescu 2016). Yet scholars working in the security archives in these countries still face the challenge that was identified by historians at a 2005 Warsaw international conference on this topic, namely, the task of developing scholarly tools for "translating" the archival and other materials produced by the Soviet secret police and the filials it created through the socialist bloc (see further Fedor 2011; Glajar, Lewis, and Petrescu 2016, 1–23).

Those KGB documents that have come to light, mostly through the efforts of scholars and activists who were granted access during the short-lived thaw of the Gorbachev and early Yeltsin eras, have only confirmed the urgency of the need for such interpretive tools. Historian of the Cold War Vojtech Mastny commented in the mid-1990s that "perhaps the greatest surprise to have come out of the Russian archives is that there was no surprise: the thinking of the insiders conformed substantially to what Moscow was publicly saying. Some of the most secret documents could have been published in *Pravda* without anybody's noticing. There was no double bookkeeping" (1996, 9). The human rights activist Ludmilla Alexeyeva was also struck by this after reading declassified KGB documents: "They sounded exactly like the newspaper articles they used to denounce us. . . . We always thought that among themselves, Soviet officials used plain language about what we were trying to do. Who would have guessed that they talked about us in private in the same way they did in public" (Rubinstein and Gribanov 2005, 3).

Others have claimed that it is possible to identify a distinctive style associated with the Soviet state security apparatus. The writer Vasilii Aksenov, analyzing another dissident recantation that was evidently ghostwritten by KGB officers, comments that the KGB "didn't make much of an effort to camouflage themselves; every phrase is marked by their special style" ("V beskonechnom ob"iatii" 2011).[3] The question of the specificity of this style and its relationship to content is one that is ripe for historical and literary interpretation, and it is especially well suited to an interdisciplinary approach.[4] The boundaries between history, politics, fiction, and theater are particularly blurred when it comes to the history of Cold War espionage and intelligence.[5]

Paul Fussell famously argued that many of the key metaphors, modes, and habits of imagination of modernity could be traced back to the seminal twentieth-century experience of World War 1 (Fussell 1975, 75–77). A similar claim could be made for the Cold War and the "secret world" of espionage and counterintelligence to which it gave rise. This was in many ways a deeply theatrical (and indeed, cinematic) world, with its props and its clichés; the poisoned umbrellas, newspapers, and flowers in buttonholes; the passwords, codenames, and anonymous encounters in exotic locations; the glamour, the paranoia, and the brutality. Sir Richard Dearlove, the former head of MI6 and now master of Pembroke College, Cambridge, has argued that the Soviet side played the leading role in shaping the trappings and practices of this world. The Soviet security apparatus is also important from a broader historical perspective. Anne Applebaum (2012) has recently made the case for viewing the process of setting up clones of the Soviet state security apparatus in the East European satellite states as central to the installation and survival of the postwar regimes in the region; yet, again, our knowledge of the history of the functioning, development, and culture of the Soviet state security apparatus remains very patchy.

At one level this chapter engages with the ongoing task of examining the worldview of the chekist—to use the Russian term designating staff of the Soviet and now the post-Soviet Russian security apparatus.[6] Exploring the categories and filters through which the chekist perceived, described, and classified Soviet citizens and their actions can advance our understanding of the distinctive moral universe in which the KGB operated and over which it sought to hold sway. In this chapter I approach this topic from the perspective of the chekist's victim, via an examination of a rich body of autobiographical writings produced by Dudko throughout the decades following his arrest and recantation. For the remainder of his life, Dudko returned again and again to the pivotal moment of his encounter with the Soviet state security apparatus in 1980, reflecting on it in a range of different texts, which offer insights into the workings and categories of Cold War chekist discourse, in this case, as refracted through the life-writing of a former dissident turned loyal supporter of Soviet power. I focus in particular on repentance, a key but understudied trope in the Soviet state security discourse, and one that was central in the framing of Dudko's case, both in Dudko's autobiographical writings and in the accounts produced by his contemporaries.[7] The writer and Gulag survivor Varlam Shalamov highlighted the importance of what he called a "repulsive [Soviet] tradition of 'repentance' and 'confessions'" (Makarov 2016). The Dudko case marks an important milestone in this tradition, but one that has been understudied to date.

In the second half of the chapter, I explore the post-Soviet life of this Soviet Cold War story. I show how, more recently, Russian nationalists have adapted and used Dudko's story to underpin ideological projects aimed at renarrating Cold War history in the service of an authoritarian vision of Russian history and identity, in which the only rightful position that a loyal Russian could take during the Soviet era was that of obedience to the KGB as the defender of Russia's interests in the struggle against the West. In these post-Soviet texts, Soviet Cold War categories of subversion, loyalty, repentance, and redemption are revived and reconstituted, and the Cold War itself is recast as a mere episode in an epic, eternal spiritual struggle between Russia and the West. Conveniently for the Putin regime with its strong KGB roots, this narrative also allows the figure of the Soviet chekist to be reclaimed—improbable as this might seem—as a sacred custodian of Russian spirituality.

Historical Background

At the time of his arrest in January 1980, Dmitrii Dudko was one of the leading lights of the Russian Orthodox religious renaissance of the 1960s and 1970s. Born in 1922 and imprisoned in the gulag during the late Stalin era, he was one of several nonconformist Orthodox priests who rose to prominence and attracted a large following from the late 1960s (Shkarovskii 2010, 277) via his writings published in samizdat, and his sermons and interviews broadcast to the USSR via Western radio "voices" such as Voice of America. He was also the spiritual father of many of those who converted to the Orthodox faith during this period and who would go on to become leaders of the religious and other human rights-based dissident movements, such as Zoia Krakhmal'nikova (Iliushenko 2009) and Lev Timofeev (*News.ru* 2005).

Dudko's growing popularity and standing, and especially the attention he was attracting abroad, was a source of alarm for the KGB, and a long campaign of chekist surveillance and harassment was duly conducted against Dudko with the aim of silencing him.[8] Finally, in early 1980 the KGB took him into custody, as part of the wave of crackdowns on religious and other dissidents that took place in the wake of the Soviet invasion of Afghanistan and in the lead-up to the 1980 Moscow Olympics. Dudko's appearance on Soviet television came just a few weeks before the games opened on July 19. It followed Andrei Sakharov's banishment into exile in Gorky in January 1980 and the arrests of other religious dissidents such as Viktor Kapitanchuk, secretary of the Christian Committee for the Defence of Rights of Believers, who was arrested on March 12, 1980, and pressured into making a public recantation the following October ("Sud" 1980).[9] According to Aleksei Smirnov, director of the Moscow Research Center for Human Rights, rumors circulated in the Soviet prison system in 1980 that the KGB was aiming to "cleanse" the country of all dissidents by 1983 (Levi n.d.).[10]

Dudko's television appearance was an uncanny fulfillment of Khrushchev's 1960 pledge that "the last Soviet *pop*" (a derogatory colloquial term for priest) would be shown on Soviet television in 1980, as a kind of last surviving specimen of a species that was about to become extinct (Vigilianskii 2001). It made a deep impression on those who saw it, since Dudko had been so important symbolically as "a moral counterweight to the supine and passive Patriarch Pimen of Moscow" (Dunlop 1983, 190). It is striking just how often the intense experience of watching Dudko on TV is recounted in detail in the dissident memoir literature. For Dudko's followers, many of whom learned of his recantation from behind bars or barbed wire, this was a huge blow, in some cases experienced as nothing less than a personal tragedy (Levi n.d.; Kevorkova 2004; Pomerants 1984; Nikol'skii n.d.). Some viewers speculated that Dudko might have made this television performance under the influence of psychotropic drugs, presumably administered by his KGB handlers (Aver'ianov [1998] 2004). For Leonid Borodin Dudko's television appearance represents "the most resounding of the KGB's victories" during this period (Borodin 2003).

The shock was surely intensified by the fact that Dudko was one of an increasing number who raised their voices precisely against the secret police's effective enslavement of the church through the recruitment and deployment of secret informers. In a 1975 samizdat text, for example, Dudko quoted one KGB officer as summarizing the Brezhnev regime's strategy when it came to the Orthodox Church: "We don't persecute [*gonim*] [the church] these days; that was before. Before we demanded that people renounce their faith, but now we don't demand it. Just so long as they collaborate with us. The church is ours now. And we can

Fedor

arrange everything for you. If you want—you'll be a bishop. Whoever you like, just help us" (Dudko 2004). In the 1960s and 1970s, this was a key issue mobilizing religious dissent—again, as Dudko put it in 1976, because of widespread rumors that priests at the time were all just chekists in disguise (*pereodetye chekisty*) (Dudko 2004). Opposition to the KGB's infiltration of the church had broken out into open protest in the mid-1960s with a series of famous petitions issued by nonconformist priests (Shkarovskii 2010, 273).

Contrary to the charges leveled against him, Dudko did not in fact generally raise political issues in his sermons (Shkarovskii 2010, 277). But he was a vocal proponent of the need for the church to take a strong moral stance on two issues in particular: the KGB's current infiltration of the church (which he lamented as a catastrophe that was destroying the church) (Shkarovskii 2010, 277; Dudko 2004); and the need for the church to repent and honor the memory of those priests who had been murdered by the Soviet state in the early decades of Soviet power. His position on the latter issue, that of the so-called new martyrs, is no longer controversial and has become firmly established as the hegemonic position within the Russian Orthodox Church now (see further Fedor 2014). The first of these two issues, that of the church's complicated and ambiguous relations with the secret police during the late Soviet period, remains something of a "blank spot" in the church's history. The issue of the presence of KGB informers at the very top of the church hierarchy exploded in the media in the wake of the failed August 1991 coup, after a parliamentary commission investigating the coup uncovered KGB documents confirming the extent of the KGB's penetration of the church hierarchy. While this issue had already been raised in samizdat and later in press articles published during the late Gorbachev period, this was the first time that the claims had been supported by documentary evidence from the KGB archives (Fedor 2011, 171n98).[11] The church did set up an internal commission to investigate this issue, but its work more or less fizzled out. It apparently met only once and did not do any real work (Komarov 2002, 1).

Dudko's televised capitulation to the state in 1980 made such a powerful impact that his name became virtually a synonym for submission to the KGB, such that more than half a decade later it was possible to talk of being "dudko-ized" by the KGB. In 1986, for example, the prominent nonconformist priest Father Aleksandr Men', at a time when he was under intense pressure from the KGB to make some kind of public recantation of his views, reportedly said, "They [the KGB] want to 'dudko-ize' me" (Bychkov 1992).[12] Dudko had become an emblematic figure symbolizing the Soviet state's power to break its opponents and to manipulate them into orchestrated public displays of penitence and also a symbol of the weakness of the Orthodox Church.

This KGB operation was clearly also intended to destroy Dudko's reputation, and in this sense it was successful, at least in the short term. The period immediately following his recantation and subsequent release was among the most difficult in his life, as his former parishioners and other supporters turned away from him in large numbers. This experience caused Dudko a great deal of pain, and he would later describe this period as much more difficult than his time in prison (Smyk 1990).

Dudko's Confession

The day after Dudko's television appearance on June 20, 1980, a full written version of his recantation was published in the newspaper *Izvestiia* (Dudko 1980). The text was prefaced by a brief, unsigned official summary, stating that the investigation had established that Dudko had "maintained a criminal link with representatives of foreign anti-Soviet organizations, [and] passed to them slanderous materials demeaning the [Soviet] state and social system, [materials] which were widely used in conducting hostile activities against the USSR. Dudko himself ha[d] confessed his guilt, condemned his anti-Soviet activities, and pledged to renounce them henceforth" (preamble to Dudko 1980). This preamble was followed by a lengthy personal statement by Dudko. This took the form of a confession, in which he also traced the process of reflection that had led him to see his errors. Dudko wrote:

> At first, I denied my guilt and declared that I had never acted against the Soviet regime, but was rather waging a struggle against godless-

ness as a priest. Later, I understood that I had been arrested not for my faith in God but for a crime. Even before my arrest I had doubts about the rightness of my actions, which, of course, had not only a religious meaning. Reflections have helped me to reach what I am now sure are the correct conclusions. I understand what harm I have brought to my country and my church. And at the same time I recognize, despite my conflict with the law, how long and patiently the Soviet regime has treated me, has had mercy on me, has made concessions to me, has tried repeatedly to guide me onto the true path. (Dudko 1980)

The text of Dudko's statement was surely at least partly scripted by Dudko's investigator—later, as we shall see, Dudko would write gratefully about having been gifted a typewriter by his KGB investigator—but it also seems to have been important that Dudko should physically produce and sign off on the text himself. This long and rather rambling text is mostly written in the first person, but at times it shifts to the second person. We can read it as an example of what Cristina Vatulescu has called the "ventriloquized confession" (2010, 39) typical of the Soviet secret police file, whereby the suspect was "coopted in the penning of a life story whose definitive version the file aimed to record," his or her voice ultimately "blend[ing] . . . with the language of the secret police" (40-41, 44). Indeed, according to Viktor Sokirko, a dissident who was also caught up in the same wave of arrests in January 1980, many dissidents objected precisely to the fact that Dudko had "agreed to speak in the TV statement and in print 'in their language.'"[13]

In his written confession, Dudko attempted to reconcile his calling as a priest with loyalty to the Soviet atheist state. He recounted his arrival at the realization that the aims pursued by the church and the state in fact had much in common: both struggled against "drunkenness, hooliganism, moral corruption, [and fought for] the strengthening of the family, and thereby also of society" (Dudko 1980). He also described the shame he felt over his past oppositional activities: "In my reflections I went ever further and further; I recalled what I had written and published abroad. The content of my books and articles aroused particular distress. It was awkward for me to recall those anti-Soviet expressions, the slander that was in them. I blushed, I became distressed, I felt guilt. Can't you see [he wrote, slipping into the second person as he does from time to time in the text] that for all your good intentions . . . you turned out to be spitefully minded? And so, repent!" (Dudko 1980).

"Telerepentance" as Late Soviet Genre

Not only Dudko himself but also both Soviet officials and Soviet dissidents, religious or otherwise, tended to use religious language to depict Dudko's capitulation to the KGB, describing it as an act of repentance (*raskaianie, pokaianie*) or apostasy (*otstupnichestvo*).[14] The preoccupation with this religious concept might seem unexpected for a society living under a militant atheist state, but as many scholars have argued, Soviet ideology borrowed widely from Christian discourse and practices (see, for example, Brooks 2001). As I have argued elsewhere, the figure of the chekist featured in Soviet official discourse as a kind of spiritual shepherd replacing the priest, and the notion of caring for those who had "strayed from the path" was an important part of the official rationale of the KGB's notorious antidissident Fifth Directorate, created by KGB chief Yurii Andropov in 1967 with the aim of countering the increasingly active dissident movement (Fedor 2011, 54; Sokolov 1997). The notion of repentance was also central to the ethos of Soviet dissent (Boobbyer 2005), and later repentance would also become an important catchword of the Gorbachev-era prodemocracy movement, lending its name, for example, to the taboo-breaking film about the trauma of the Stalinist past, Tengiz Abuladze's *Repentance*.[15] This motif was especially powerful because it resonated with the traditional focus in Russian thought on issues related to morality and spirituality and the centrality of the idea of moral purification in the Russian democratic movement (Lukin 2000, 61; Averintsev 2001). It also reflected a traditional Soviet chekist preoccupation. As Igal Halfin puts it in his discussion of early Soviet trials for subversion, "the object of investigation was the soul of the accused, its moral inclination" (2007, 1).

Dudko's was not the first such telerepentance that the KGB had staged. A number of prominent dissidents were forced to perform in this way on Soviet television in the 1970s.[16] Reportedly this practice was the brainchild of General Colonel Filip Bobkov, the former head of the KGB's antidissident Fifth Directorate (Sokolov 1997). According to Aleksei Smirnov, the KGB was "skilled at using the press and television to create a big noise around each repentance" (Levi n.d.). Smirnov recounted one such case in which the prisoner in question, Aleksandr Bolonkin, was reportedly still wearing his prison-camp trousers and footwear under the desk, having been hurriedly dressed in "civilian" wear only on the top half of his body visible during the TV performance (Levi n.d.).

The most famous of these cases was that of human rights activists Petr Yakir and Viktor Krasin, whose recantation at a televised press conference in 1973 dealt a massive blow to the Soviet human rights movement and attracted attention worldwide (Barbakadze n.d., http://antology.igrunov.ru/authors/yakir/).[17] The issue of how to respond to this case and, in particular, what attitude should be taken to Yakir and Krasin brought about a damaging split in the Soviet human rights movement. The human rights activist Sergei Kovalev has recounted, for example, the criticism he faced from other dissidents over his call to refrain from harsh condemnation of Yakir and Krasin (Svetova 2013).

At least some of these performances were reportedly made under pressure of threats; in some cases the protagonists were told that they would be executed if they refused or that their families would be harmed.[18] Sometimes they also involved deals whereby a lighter sentence was offered in exchange for a public display of loyalty and for testifying against fellow dissidents.[19] While there are documented cases in which such testimony led to additional arrests and convictions, some dissidents have argued that the latter aim was secondary. According to prominent former dissident Aleksandr Podrabinek, writing on the basis of his own experience of numerous encounters with the secret police, "for the KGB the public repentance of dissidents was much more important than their testimony against their friends" (2014).

Other former dissidents, too, have asserted that these chekistchoreographed performances of repentance were designed above all else as public displays of Soviet state power and its triumph over the individual will. The famous Soviet dissident Vladimir Bukovskii, for example, who had dealings with chekists at close quarters for decades, has commented that the KGB "wanted from people only one thing: repentance" (Novodvorskaia 2012). Showing the state's ability to break the will of leading dissident heroes was a highly effective way of undermining the dissidents' moral authority and credibility; the spectacle of a former hero now cowed and in shackles made for powerful propaganda. The journalist Yevgeniia Al'bats recalls that each dissident telerepentance would be followed by a propaganda campaign whose key message was "'look, even those who only yesterday were pouring filth over the achievements of the great Soviet power, even they have now come to their senses'" (2001). It would appear that some chekists also derived personal satisfaction from these shows of the secret police's strength. Aleksandr Ogorodnikov, a former follower of Dudko who was serving a prison-camp sentence at the time of Dudko's telerepentance, has noted of his chekist overseers in the camp: "[They] even wanted to take me to a television so as to show me: look, there's your dissident" (Nikol'skii n.d.).[20]

It seems likely that Dudko's performance was also designed to convey a different message to external, Western and global audiences. Vitalii Aver'ianov reads the episode as follows: "What [the Soviet regime] needed from father Dimitrii . . . was that he recognize that freedom of conscience was inviolate in the Soviet Union" ([1998] 2004). In other words Dudko's statement was called on to support the Soviet Union's image on the world stage as a progressive state that had enshrined civil liberties in its constitution. At first glance these two messages might seem mutually exclusive—but not from the perspective of Soviet citizens, skilled in the arts of reading the Aesopian language of Soviet official-speak. On the contrary, from this perspective the fact that Dudko was now mouthing the false slogans of the Soviet state was inherent to the main message of this public relations stunt: anybody could be broken in the end.

Dudko's public confession also reproduced chekist categories of subversion, redefining his own past activities in these terms.

He recounted his realization that he was a mere puppet of Western masters: "My activities . . . were incited and later essentially directed from abroad. Slanderous materials received from me by the *New York Times* correspondent C[hristopher] Wren, American professor A[rcadi] R. Nebolsine, archbishop of Brussels and Belgium Vasilii and other foreign citizens were used in hostile propaganda against our state. If previously too I was no fan of foreign places [*zagranitsa*, lit. that which is 'beyond the border'], then now I am convinced that foreigners interfering in our internal affairs bring us nothing but harm" (Dudko 1980). A key moment in this conversion narrative hinges on Dudko's revelation that there could be no true understanding or friendship with people in "the West." In an emotional passage, he appeals to his readers to give up any naive dreams of solidarity with activists in Western countries:

> Do you really think that in the West they'll understand us better than we understand ourselves? . . .
>
> God has decreed that you live not just anywhere, but here, in the Soviet Union. . . . It is no accident that you live here. And you need not to be away with your head in the clouds, dreaming, but to be present here, doing work that is useful for everyone. . . .
>
> Do you think they [people in the West] need you? People who left [the USSR for the West] and have been disillusioned with the way of life there have already been writing to you, [warning you that] the West is chasing sensations, it's amusing itself with you, once it's had its fill of amusement it will abandon you—even now they've started closing ranks against you there. So whom are you serving? Do you understand now? (Dudko 1980)

The peculiar emotional tenor of this passage, suggesting a complicated and intense set of feelings towards "the West," captures another dimension of the Soviet Cold War experience. The sense of disillusionment, sadness, even unrequited love that Dudko's confession conveys is reminiscent of the Soviet Cold War fantasy image of the West described by Svetlana Boym (1994, 23–24). Here, however, this wistfulness is transformed into bitterness and a distinctive kind of performative and stylized righteous anger characteristic of Soviet Cold War discourse.

Renarrating Repentance and Subversion in the Post-Soviet Period

I will now examine a curious body of autobiographical writings produced by Dmitrii Dudko throughout the remainder of his life until his death in 2004. In these texts Dudko not only wrote and rewrote his own life story, but he also participated in a broader project characteristic of a strand of radical nationalism in post-Soviet Russia aimed at retrospectively sacralizing the Soviet state and its security agencies in particular. According to this view, the Soviet state was only superficially godless, and the visible surface of the chekist campaign against dissent in fact masked a deeper reality and a deeper truth. In this vision of the Soviet past, the true Russian patriot and martyr was not the dissident resisting Soviet state power, but he who had been willing to risk public disgrace by collaborating with the Soviet security organs and thus supporting Russia's interests in the Cold War struggle. The figure of the chekist, in turn, features in this account as the unjustly maligned and misunderstood sacred custodian of Russian statehood.

In his post-Soviet incarnation, Dudko became a celebrated figure in the radical nationalist circles of the so-called spiritual opposition to the Yeltsin regime from the early 1990s. According to Gleb Yakunin, the ex-prisoner of conscience and nonconformist priest, the extreme nationalist milieu offered Dudko a kind of refuge in the aftermath of his public disgrace (*Portal-credo* 2004). Dudko became the confessor for the ultranationalist newspaper *Zavtra* (Tomorrow). He used the newspaper and other organs of the right-wing nationalist press, such as the journal *Nash sovremennik* (Our contemporary), as a forum for his distinctive and indeed often quite idiosyncratic meditations on his encounter with the Soviet security apparatus and the meaning of the Soviet period for Russian history more broadly. Aleksandr Prokhanov, *Zavtra*'s editor in chief, has in turn cited Dudko's association with his newspaper as evidence that the emerging statist ideology aimed at creating a new synthesis out of the "great white monarchist idea and the red, soviet imperial idea" had gained a "spiritual" core to complement and underpin its intellectual components (Prokhanov 2010). Dudko's works have also been mentioned by former high-ranking chekist memoirists, such as Nikolai Golushko, former head of the Ukrainian KGB between 1987 and 1991 (among other high-ranking posts), who has cited Dudko as vindication of the KGB's approach to the religious issue (Golushko 2012, 204).

In his writings Dudko produced what amounts to an elaborate and prolonged public apologia for his capitulation to the KGB. One of his former followers, Aleksandr Ogorodnikov, has reflected that "later, after coming out of imprisonment, he [Dudko] effectively devoted all his creative activity [*tvorchestvo*] to justifying this, so as somehow to justify himself, why he had done this, how this had come about" (Nikol'skii n.d.). In these writings Dudko was concerned not only with justifying his actions in 1980 but also with sharing the privileged knowledge, the insights into Russia's fate, that he believed he had acquired through this experience.

From the mid-1990s, various patriotic commentators and ideologues exploited these writings, frequently making quite extravagant claims for the significance of Dudko's submission to the Soviet state security apparatus. Orthodox philosopher and patriotic ideologue Vitalii Aver'ianov describes this episode as "one of the most symbolic pages of [Russians'] shared history," and as an example on which future generations would judge the twentieth century and the meaning of the events of that century (Aver'ianov [1998] 2004), and the writer Vladimir Smyk, a former follower of Dudko, has asserted that Dudko's personal drama, his public disgrace, and the insights it brought him are emblematic of the history of Russia itself (1996).

Post-Soviet Russian patriotic press commentators often celebrate Dudko precisely and explicitly for his capitulation to the KGB in 1980. This act of submission, they claim, far from being a manifestation of weakness or a source of shame, was in fact an act of rare courage, moral fortitude, and prescience. Thus one such newspaper article on the subject was titled "Ne padenie—triumf" (Not a fall—a triumph; Smyk 1996), while another claimed that Dudko's chief moral feat lay in the fact that he had "embarked upon collaboration with the [security] organs" (*Zavtra* article, cited Borodin 2003).

Dudko's post-Soviet writings prompted renewed debates in the

Russian press over the moral admissibility of collaborating with the KGB and the correct relations that should obtain between society and the state security apparatus more broadly. These debates took place against a background of several scandals and legal suits launched by public figures accused of having acted as collaborators in the Soviet period. In one particularly odd case, the KGB defector Oleg Kalugin, who was being sued after "outing" an ex-informer, attempted to defend himself against slander charges by citing KGB documents listing the positive characteristics that agents must possess, with a view to demonstrating that there was nothing shameful about informing for the KGB.[21] Meanwhile, some Russian nationalist writers attempted to transform Dudko's story into the cornerstone of a new ethical justification for collaboration with the Soviet security organs, whereby chekists and collaborators alike feature as the true unrecognized saints and martyrs of Russian history.

Of the numerous published works in which Dudko reflected on his 1980 public recantation, it was his 1996 book on the subject, *Propoved' cherez pozor* (Sermon through shame) that touched a nerve and generated the most media commentary. A recurring motif in the debates that followed the publication of this book was the notion that Dudko's submission contained hidden layers of meaning—a lesson that could not be grasped rationally or fully absorbed at the time, yet whose presence had nevertheless been sensed at some deeper, intuitive level. Vitalii Aver'ianov asserted that for many Soviet people the memory of Dudko's public repentance in 1980 had lingered ever since, leaving "a vague sense of something else that had not been made sense of completely, not cleared up completely, not absorbed into consciousness. This story had not been understood, but it had stuck in many people's memories" ([1998] 2004). Sergei Baburin, writing in *Zavtra* in 1997, couched the topic in similar terms, speculating that the Russian people had yet to become fully "conscious" of Dudko, as "a spiritual phenomenon of [their] life [and] as a very important criterion of the Russian national spirit" (*Zavtra* 1997b).

In these and other examples, the commentary is often obtuse when it comes to elaborating on the content and message of Dudko's lesson. But the chief thrust of this lesson would appear to be twofold: first, the role played by the Soviet secret police in Russian history should be radically reassessed in a positive light; and second, there must be a reckoning of the profound culpability of the Soviet dissidents for the Soviet collapse and other catastrophes befalling Russia in the 1990s. Both of these themes are treated at some length in Dudko's writings.

The Chekist as Guardian Angel

Central to Dudko's writings is the motif of the chekist as a kind of disguised guardian angel. Dudko focused especially on the nature of his relationship with his chekist investigator.[22] Over the years Dudko set forth these relations in a series of parables relating scenes and dialogues from his interrogation and imprisonment (see esp. Dudko 2001). Here we can situate Dudko within the Soviet tradition identified by Eric Naiman and Anne Nesbet (1995, 53, 56), whereby the trope of the interrogation provided not just "an arena for the demonstration both of personal integrity and historical 'truth'" but also "the metaphysical occasion for a grander, metaphorical investigation of history."[23]

Dudko's writings are also an idiosyncratic example of the Soviet confessional autobiographical genre. In his reminiscences Dudko charted a highly distinctive radical transformation of self—one that is engendered precisely by his intimate and intense encounter with his KGB investigator. In many respects the text resembles a conversion narrative recording the path to spiritual rebirth and transformation into a new person. But what is striking about Dudko's epiphany is that it comes about precisely through his contact with chekists, his communion with them. Chekists were the agents or catalysts of Dudko's spiritual growth. In some mysterious way, Soviet chekists, despite their external superficial appearance as agents of an atheist state and as persecutors of believers, actually functioned as the vehicles of God's will, as disguised manifestations of virtue.

Dudko first mentioned his bond with his chekist captors during his television address in 1980, when he said: "My investigator and I have a single patronymic: Sergeevich. [Does this not point to the fact that we are in fact brothers?] My investigator and I, it turns out, are brothers?" (2001, 222). In later writings he described the process whereby he had become imbued with love for his investigator during his stay in prison (Smyk 1990; Dudko 2001, 218–23). This deep identification with the chekist is a consistent feature of Dudko's writings, to the point where, indeed, we might even think of this as a case of Stockholm syndrome.[24] At one point, for example, Dudko imagined his interrogator as the physical embodiment of Dudko's own conscience (2001, 218–19). More conventionally in his written press statement issued the day after his television appearance, Dudko (1980) further described how in prison he had finally arrived at the realization that despite his crimes, the Soviet state had shown great patience and mercy, making concessions for him and making repeated attempts to steer him onto the true path before being forced to resort to arresting him.

Dudko elaborated on his encounter with his investigator in greater depth in texts produced the year after his arrest. By Dudko's own account, it was in fact his KGB investigator who encouraged Dudko to write up his reflections on his encounter with the KGB, even providing him with a typewriter and a kind of writer's retreat in order to do so (Dudko 2001, 223). The result was a text in which Dudko outlined what was to become a key motif of his writings: the notion of the "Christlike" attributes of the chekist.

Dudko drew a direct link between the Passion of Christ and the martyrdom of the chekist—the sacrifices that the chekist makes, his suffering at the hands of those who slander him and turn away from him. He painted a picture of the chekist as gentle, as tender toward the weak (Dudko 2001, 223–24), and he suggested that the chekist will be rewarded for his meekness and humility and may be the first to enter the kingdom of Heaven (Pomerants 1994, 211).[25] Dudko's chekist will be rewarded for his sufferings and the contempt and hostility he has endured; he calls upon the "haters" to recall that Christ was also hated and to look within themselves, to ask themselves whether they might not be Pharisees (Pomerants 1994, 211).

More broadly Dudko also made a case for viewing the entire Soviet state as a kind of crypto-Christian enterprise, only nominally "godless." He emphasized, for example, the fact that the chekists whom he met in prison secretly observed Christian rites.

His investigator and his wife and children had all been baptized, and his investigator accepted Dudko's blessing (Dudko 2001, 219). Dudko further stated, "[The chekists] even asked forgiveness for having arrested me. And they accept[ed] my blessing" (1999, 3). Here, then, this becomes a two-way relationship, where close contact between the church and the Soviet state transforms and purifies both parties. One 2009 article on Dudko says: "People were drawn to him. The most diverse people, even his persecutors. Even the investigators who put him in prison later, at the end of life, would come to him and repent; they asked forgiveness; they turned to faith and to God" (*Literaturnaia Rossiia* 2009).

Dudko would further continue this theme of retrospective sanctification and extend it to various Russian World War II heroes, arguing that even if they were technically atheists, they had been baptized through their blood sacrifice and should be classified and canonized as Christian martyrs (Prokhanov 2010). Dudko also spoke in favor of what he called the "spiritual rehabilitation" of Stalin, who he also claimed was a secret believer and a secret champion of the church, citing various apparently fictitious archival documents in support of this thesis (see, for example, "Polveka bez vozhdia" 2003 and Kurliandskii 2007). Dudko described the caritative traits of the chekists in terms reminiscent of saints' lives. He noted, for example, a "very meek and cautious" chekist who brought Dudko timber to fix his house after he had been released and went to live in the countryside (2001, 223). This example then spread to other local chekists who also began to help others in the village (224). Dudko's chekists are instinctively and naturally Christian. They live for others; they care for their prisoners spontaneously and selflessly.

For Dudko many of his investigator's words and questions took the form of enigmas whose meaning had only become clear with time. Dudko recalls, for example, how the chekist said to him: "You don't know what a friend I am to you"—words that Dudko understood only years later (Dudko 2001, 218). Here again, Dudko's encounter with his interrogator is a trial, a test arranged by God, intentionally obscure and allusive. The clues to the meaning of this divine test are contained partly in small, spontaneous acts of mercy and kindness shown to him by his chekist interrogator (Dudko 2001, 218). In one fanciful passage, Dudko imagines that after he dies and goes to heaven, the first to rush to meet him will be his investigator, who will continue to help him even beyond the grave: "He will grab my hand and say: 'It's hard for you to walk, let me help you'" (218–19).

In an interview posted in 2006 on the official website of the key body responsible for relations between the Orthodox Church and the military and law enforcement agencies, the Moscow Patriarchate's Synodal Section for Mutual Cooperation with the Armed Forces and Law Enforcement Institutions, Dudko said: "The chekists beat us, beat us sincerely, without mercy, but at the same time, these were . . . our people [*svoi liudi*], who had simply strayed on life's path" (Murzin 2006). He returned to this theme of chekist state repression as a kind of vehicle of national salvation elsewhere, writing: "I was arrested three times, twice condemned, they exhausted me with constant searches. But now I thank God sincerely for this. The chekists were our saviors. They beat us and thus they saved us" (quoted in Murzin 2006). Because of their shared suffering, he declared, "the chekists and the Russians will be the first to enter the Kingdom of Heaven, the first to lay down a path for mankind" (quoted in Pomerants 1994, 211).

In one 2002 article, Dudko presented his friendship with his KGB investigator as a kind of riddle or paradox and a jumping-point for reflecting on the Russian national identity:

> I want to ask you, readers, what is a Russian person? Do you know?
>
> We used to live among Russian people; nowadays in Russia we live among foreigners. But after all a Russian person—both chekist and *zek* [a Soviet shorthand term for "prisoner"]—these are one and the same Russian people; it's only foreigners who tell us that chekists cannot be Russians; they're hell-spawn, they say, and when I say that I had two friends: a chekist-investigator and a political activist, whom the chekists were persecuting . . . foreign-minded people, even Russian people, perhaps, will say: how can this be combined? (quoted in Divnich 2002)[26]

For Dudko, then, the unique, seemingly illogical potential for a loving friendship between chekist and *zek*, between prison guard and prisoner, constitutes an essential marker of Russianness. Prison guard and prisoner are joined in a kind of sacred pairing, locked into a joint martyrdom, whereby both are purified through their suffering and their compassion for each other.

This anomaly or paradox of the love between the chekist and his prisoner is also something that we find in the Soviet tradition. The notion of a vital affinity between chekist and prisoner and the trope of the chekist's sorrowful love for and intense empathy with his prisoner were present in early Soviet representations of the Cheka. This was encapsulated in one of the famous aphorisms attributed to the founder of the Cheka, Feliks Dzerzhinsky: "He is not a chekist whose heart does not engorge with blood and contract with pity at the sight of a man imprisoned in a prison cell" (Semenov 1977, 34). In another example, on the fifth anniversary of the Cheka, Dzerzhinsky proclaimed: "Those of you who have become callous, whose heart cannot relate sympathetically and considerately toward those undergoing imprisonment, [should] leave this institution. Here more than anywhere else, one must have a kind heart, sensitive to the sufferings of others" (Sobolev et al. 1999, 178). Mikhail Geller has argued that this new Soviet code of morality with its glorification of the figure of the chekist represents a radical departure from the prerevolutionary traditions of Russian literature in which the perspective of the humiliated and the wretched was valued above all. For the first time in the history of Russian culture, Geller writes, it was the prison guard, not the prisoner, who had become the hero (Geller [Heller] 1996, 288). It was Dudko's own past as a prisoner of the camps in the late Stalinist period that gave him the moral standing and credibility to pronounce on these issues. The fact that Dudko was not only a strong statist but also a former prisoner was often held up in the patriotic press as giving him a special right to speak (see, for example, Prokhanov 2010; on Dudko's term in the camps, see Shkarovskii 2010, 277).

When Dudko died in 2004, his obituary in *Nezavisimaia gazeta* (The independent gazette) was titled: "He was a hero of faith and a repentant dissident." This phrase "repentant dissident" became a key label applied to Dudko, who is often said to have been the first of a wave of "repentant dissidents." As one *Zavtra* journalist put it, "Dmitrii Dudko was, perhaps, the first of those who had thrown down a challenge [to the Soviet—G.S.] regime who understood [that] . . . in fighting with the KGB, CPSU, with the state Soviet machine—they were fighting with Russia" (*Zavtra* 2009). This trope of the epiphany of the former dissident who comes to understand the harm that he has inflicted on his nation is encapsulated in the catchphrase "We were aiming at Communism, but we hit Russia"—a formulation usually attributed to the writer Aleksandr Zinov'ev and used frequently in texts criticizing the dissidents of the Soviet era.[27] Smyk's 1996 text reflecting on the Dudko case is a typical example of the genre: "Many former dissidents—the best of them—after seeing the fruits of perestroika and reforms: a ruined great power and a dying, destitute nation carried out a reevaluation of their activities. . . . In this sense, f. Dmitrii's repentance was prophetic. He was the first to leave the ranks of the dissidents, so as, in the tragic denouement that Russia is undergoing at the end of the second millennium, to be in the same rank as her defenders."

We might read this nationalist trope of the "repentant dissident" as representing an attempt to reappropriate and redefine the concept of "repentance." Democratic activists in the late Soviet period had used the term as a rallying cry for a radical confrontation with and critical evaluation of the Soviet past, including the history of relations between the Orthodox Church and the security apparatus. For Smyk (2002) such activists had led both Dudko and Russia itself "down the path of shame, spitting on [Russia's] past, arrogantly demanding repentance of the Russian people." Smyk draws a connection between Dudko's path of shame or disgrace and Russia's, and rejects the democratic dissident emphasis on repentance: "After all," Smyk writes, "Russia too was led down the path of shame, spitting [*opleyvaia*] on her past, arrogantly demanding repentance of the Russian people." In such texts post-Soviet Russian nationalists have set out to reclaim the notion of "repentance" and to turn its moral force against those who had resisted the Soviet regime. This move in turn enables rehabilitation of the figure of the chekist, whose persecution of the Soviet dissident movement is thus reconstituted as a noble struggle in defense of the nation.

In 2001, a year into former chekist Vladimir Putin's first term as president of the Russian Federation, Dudko looked back on the negative attitudes to the KGB that prevailed in the late Soviet period: "I remember when I was released and I wrote that the chekists had conversed with me as friends, people laughed at me" (2001, 219). By the time he wrote this sentence, the rising currency of the modern-day security apparatus seemed to vindicate his position. The rise of Putin had meant that many patriots moved out of opposition and began to align themselves with the Putin regime, or at least to offer it cautious support and qualified loyalty. This shift also appears to have been connected to a tendency within religious nationalist circles toward venerating the special services as defenders of the Russian spirit (see Tabak 2004).

There is a certain amount of ideological convergence between Dudko's writings on the history of the chekist campaign against the dissident movement and contemporary official mainstream discourse in Russia, especially when it comes to public statements made over the past decade by ex-chekists on the subject of the history of the KGB's infiltration of the Orthodox Church. For example, in 2003 Georgii Poltavchenko, former KGB officer and now governor of St. Petersburg, then Putin's plenipotentiary in the Central Federal District, commented that during the Soviet era, priests collaborated with the KGB out of patriotic considerations, as opposed to Judas, who "worked not in the interests of his own government" (Kevorkova 2003). Viktor Cherkesov, a famous KGB "dissident hunter" in Leningrad in the 1970s and 1980s, has also reflected publicly on the topic of "repentant dissidents." In a programmatic 2004 article in the tabloid newspaper *Komsomol'skaia pravda* (Komsomol [Communist Youth] truth), Cherkesov describes the journey of the writer Aleksandr Zinov'ev: "One day, Aleksandr Zinov'ev, a prominent figure in Soviet and post-Soviet political literature, saw the light. And he squeezed out of himself the tragic confession: 'We were aiming at Communism, but we hit Russia.'" Now, in the post-Soviet period, former dissidents had realized that they were in fact nothing but the puppets of "an alien . . . hand. . . . A hand for whom ideological conflict is a screen, a pretext for settling not ideological accounts but other ones. [Accounts that are] in some sense eternal, fundamental, definitive" (Cherkesov 2004). In the context of this new narrative, Dudko's public recantation of his dissident views in 1980 is a sign of his prescience. Thus the writer Mikhail Lobanov observes that while Dudko's television confession had caused Dudko a "deep emotional trauma" at the time, "there was also something providential in this"—subsequent events had demonstrated that Dudko had been right to take the path that he did (2002, 108). In particular "his break with dissidents even before so-called 'perestroika' was providential," Lobanov claimed (quoted in Prokhanov 2010).

Orthodox philosopher and nationalist ideologue Vitalii Aver'ianov reflects on the Dudko story at length in a passage that is sufficiently rich to warrant quoting in full. Aver'ianov sees the lesson of Dudko's experiences with the chekists as follows:

> Father Dmitrii's wisdom after his arrest was expressed in the fact that he sensed the course of history. In his contact with the investigator chekists, with high leadership, which acknowledged that the state was not correct in everything with regard to the church, he sensed that in life everything is much more complex than it seems to political dissidents. Much had changed over the decades of Soviet power; much was changing and would still change. The historicism of what was occurring, the three-dimensional meaning of events, was revealed. The face of the Russian *narod* was revealed, of Russian statehood, which had not been erased definitively over 70 years but in a paradoxical way was beginning to show through from underneath the crimson mask of "totalitarianism." The Russia *narod* had proved to be much more living and expansive in its possibilities for assimilating alien and imposed laws than those who despaired had thought. The Russian *narod* proved capable of swallowing the seemingly fatal poison of Marxism and atheism without taking it into its spiritual system. Most important of all—the Russian *narod* had taken these 70 years precisely as a great divine test [*popushchenie*] and despite everything had continued the age-old process of manufacturing its own *narodnyi* character, its own national spirit. It had survived. (Aver'ianov [1998] 2004)

In this passage Aver'ianov makes explicit the role of the chekists in bringing about Dudko's enlightenment. It was precisely his contact with them that enlarged Dudko's perspective on the Soviet regime and on Soviet history more broadly, as compared to the black-and-white view of political dissidents. According to this reading of the Soviet past, it is now clear that Soviet ideology had been grafted onto the Russian spirit only superficially. The Russian spirit proved to have mysterious reserves of strength; ultimately it rejected the alien transplant and preserved its own integrity. This notion is encapsulated in Aver'ianov's text in the image of the true face of Russian statehood, showing through from under the "crimson mask" of totalitarianism. This image, suggesting a pale and angelic Russian countenance shining mysteriously through a ruddy and crude veneer, is a curious inversion of the Soviet trope of "unmasking" the enemy.[28] It is also reminiscent of National-Bolshevik ideas about the superficially repellent, bloody, and brutal face of the early Soviet regime as concealing the new face of a great Russia.[29] This true face had miraculously survived the Soviet period, and according to Aver'ianov, it had been revealed to Dudko through his ordeal in the early 1980s. Again, the figure of the chekist plays a crucial role in this account, functioning as a vehicle for an authentic Russian essence that had survived and outlived Soviet totalitarianism. The chekist sprang from Russian soil and acted as custodian of Russian statehood, ensuring its survival throughout the Soviet period.

Aver'ianov's account, like many others in this genre, offers a consolatory message: as a nation Russians have survived the Soviet catastrophe. At the same time, we might also read Aver'ianov's text as an attempt to reclaim the Soviet past—to find a way to recognize oneself in the bloody history of the twentieth century and to find a way to contemplate this past with equanimity. Perhaps one reason why such accounts tend to fall back on elements of the Soviet mythology of the Cheka is that this mythology shared the same basic drive to make bloodshed comprehensible and bearable.

Tracking the Soviet Cold War spy story of Dmitrii Dudko across the post-Soviet transition, we see how the stuff of Soviet chekist discourse is being used today to spin a set of new, national spy stories, as the legacy of Russia's Soviet experience continues to unfold in unexpected ways. At one level the case of Dmitrii Dudko is a story about ideological instrumentalization and exploitation. Dudko was used twice over: first by the KGB, as a tool in the Soviet Cold War struggle, and then once again by the ideologues of the emerging ultranationalist discourse of the post-Soviet era who turned to Dudko's case in their search for a spiritual core for their vision of Russia's past and future. This story is also part of an ongoing process of forging new historical narratives about the Soviet past, aimed at synthesizing and reconciling the Soviet period with the wider stream of Russian history and creating a historical pedigree for the current chekist-led Putin regime. The renarration of Dudko's submission to the KGB as an act of heroism dovetails with a broader drive to weave the Soviet past, and the history of the Soviet secret police in particular, into a seamless unbroken national narrative of Russian history. In this narrative the figure of the chekist plays a crucial role, bridging the gulf between the Soviet and the Russian eras and anchoring new visions of the Russian national identity.

Notes

Research for this chapter was supported under the Australian Research Council's Discovery Early Career Research Awards (DECRA) funding scheme (project DE150100838). The views expressed herein are those of the author and are not necessarily those of the Australian Research Council. I would like to thank the volume editors for their thoughtful comments on an earlier version of the text. I am also grateful to Rustam Alexander for his speedy and efficient assistance in locating some misplaced references for the chapter.

1. Carole K. Fink writes that the Second Cold War "arose . . . when the new U.S. administration took the offensive—ideologically and strategically—against the Soviet Union. Unlike his immediate predecessors, who had viewed the USSR as a permanent presence in international affairs and an unavoidable if difficult partner, Reagan viewed the Soviet Union as an incorrigible adversary that he was determined to vanquish" (2013, 204).

2. On the use and significance of human rights issues in U.S.-Soviet relations on the global stage during this period, see Peterson 2011.

3. All translations from the Russian cited in this chapter are my own unless otherwise stated.

4. There is a growing body of scholarship in this area; see especially Cristina Vatulescu 2010 and István Rév 2005.

5. See further Glajar, Lewis, and Petrescu 2016, 9–17. The Russian scholar Mikhail Geller has even claimed that there is a sense in which "the history of spy literature is the most precise history of the twentieth century"; see Geller [Heller] 2000, 318.

6. The term "chekist" is derived from the title of the original Soviet security and intelligence apparatus, the Cheka, created in December 1917. This term has remained in use ever since to designate employees of the Soviet and now the post-Soviet Russian security apparatus. The term has a distinctive set of meanings that is not adequately captured by the available English-language equivalents, as I argue in Fedor 2011, 2–6.

7. For a fascinating history of the trope of repentance in the early Soviet and Stalinist periods, see Halfin 2007.

8. On Dudko's biography and significance, see further Dunlop 1983, 49–51, 190–95; Ellis 1986; Borodin 2003; Kevorkova 2004; and *Nezavisimaia gazeta* 2004.

9. Prior to Sakharov's banishment, in late 1977 another prominent dissident, Petr Grigorenko, had been stripped of his Soviet citizenship. Dudko presided over Grigorenko's marriage shortly before Grigorenko left for the United States to undergo medical treatment.

10. Smirnov did not explain the significance of the year 1983 as a deadline for the completion of this operation.

11. On KGB-church relations, see further Ellis 1996, 133–38.

12. Aleksandr Men' was eventually murdered with an ax on September 9, 1990, under circumstances that remain unclear.

13. In a sympathetic personal letter to Dudko in 1982, Sokirko wrote, "The fact that many 'dissident-minded' people choose not to speak a language in common with the authorities and to turn their backs on you is entirely understandable and inevitable; one must regard this without anger, even though it is impossible to regard it without pain" (Sokirko 1982).

14. See, for example, the entry on Dudko in Barbakadze n.d., http://antology.igrunov.ru/authors/Dudko/.

15. The film was completed in 1984 but only released to a mass audience during glasnost; see further Davies 1989, 8, and Shlapentokh and Shlapentokh 1993, 228. The need for repentance was also a key theme, for example, of the TV debate between dissident Vladimir Bukovskii and new KGB chief Vadim Bakatin in September 1991 (Bukovskii 1996, 45).

16. Another prominent example was that of the Georgian dissident Zviad Gamsakhurdiia, whose public recantation took place in 1978, on which see Chevtaeva 2012.

17. The dissident Petr Grigorenko later said that the spectacle of Yakir's repentance had a "strongly oppressive effect" on him (Reif 2009).

18. For example, Petr Yakir and Viktor Krasin both stated that they were threatened with the death penalty in the event that they refused to publicly

recant; Yakir's interrogators also told him that his daughter would be arrested if he did not cooperate (Zubarev and Kuzovkin 2017).

19. The case of Gleb Pavlovskii is a notorious example. For Pavlovskii's own account, see Morev 2014.

20. Ogorodnikov has also noted that Dudko's recantation led to a drying up of Western support for Russian religious dissidents, since "people in the West decided that if such pillars as father Dimitrii Dudko were being broken, then what could one expect of [his younger followers]" (Nikol'skii n.d.).

21. Incidentally, while chekists tended to shout most loudly about the dangers of unleashing witch hunts against ex-collaborators, they were also the ones stoking the fires, especially when it came to pointing the finger at ex-informers and spreading disinformation. In 1997, for example, the former KGB general Aleksandr Korzhakov "outed" TV current affairs anchorman Yevgenii Kiselev as an ex-informer, apparently in revenge for Kiselev's negative media coverage (see Gerasimov 1997).

22. According to Andrew and Mitrokhin (1999, 647), Dudko's investigator was Vladimir Sorokin; according to Yakunin, his investigator was Podkopaev, and he was decorated after breaking Dudko. *Portal-credo* interview available at Krotov site, http://krotov.info/spravki/persons/20person/1922dudk.html.

23. More recently Vatulescu (2010) has also written on this subject in her study of interrogations in Soviet literature and on literary works stimulated by encounters with the secret police.

24. My thanks to Alison Lewis for pointing this out.

25. These qualities of meekness and humility make the chekist the direct opposite of the figure of the dissident, whose chief sin is pride.

26. For additional commentary on Dudko's writings about the figure of the chekist, see a personal letter sent to Dudko in 1982 by Viktor Sokirko, in which the author comments that many dissidents broke with Dudko because "they did not wish to listen to the truth, difficult for them to face, that chekists are also human beings, and that the real cause of being released from prison was not so much 'weakness' as the beginning of a conversation in prison about understanding and compromise [. . .] I consider that you did the right thing when you did not renounce a human relationship with the prison guards, you tried to understand them, to converse with them, to inspire them to do good, you accepted help from them and managed to reach an agreement on leaving prison and [being granted] normal conditions of life and work after prison" (Sokirko 1982).

27. The phrase is sometimes also attributed to Vladimir Maksimov. *Zavtra* claims that Zinov'ev and Maksimov coined the phrase together in a conversation first printed on the pages of *Zavtra*; see, for example, *Zavtra* 1997a and Bondarenko 2000.

28. On this trope, see Fitzpatrick 2005.

29. On which see Dobroliubov 2007. On post-Soviet Russian nationalist reinterpretations of the Soviet project as an "emanation of the Russian spirit," see further Verkhovskii 2007.

References

Al'bats, Yevgeniia. 2001. "Kto s miachom k nam prishel." *Novaia gazeta*, May 21.

Andrew, Christopher, and Vasilii Mitrokhin. 1999. *The Mitrokhin Archive: The KGB in Europe and the West*. London: Allen Lane, Penguin Press.

Applebaum, Anne. 2012. *Iron Curtain: The Crushing of Eastern Europe*. London: Penguin Books.

Aver'ianov, Vitalii. (1998) 2004. "Putem yurodstva: Pamiati protoiereia Dimitriia Dudko." *Pravoslavnoe literaturnoe obozrenie*. Republished in *Russkaia narodnaia liniia*, July 1. http://ruskline.ru/monitoring_smi/2004/07/01/putem_yurodstva/.

Averintsev, Sergei. 2001. "Preodolenie totalitarizma kak problema: Popytka orientatsii." *Russkii zhurnal*, May 17.

Barbakadze, Mark, ed. n.d. *Antologiia samizdata*. Accessed October 10, 2018. http://antology.igrunov.ru/.

Bondarenko, Vladimir. 2000. "Yest' upoenie v boiu." *Zavtra*, December 12.

Boobbyer, Philip. 2005. *Conscience, Dissent and Reform in Soviet Russia*. London: Routledge.

Borodin, Leonid. 2003. "Bez vybora: Avtobiograficheskoe povestvovanie." *Moskva*, no. 8.

Boym, Svetlana. 1994. *Common Places: Mythologies of Everyday Life in Russia*. Cambridge MA: Harvard University Press.

Brooks, Jeffrey. 2001. *Thank You, Comrade Stalin! Soviet Public Culture from Revolution to Cold War*. Princeton NJ: Princeton University Press.

Bukovskii, Vladimir. 1996. *Moskovskii protsess*. Moscow: Russkaia mysl' and MIK.

Bychkov, Sergei. 1992. "Khronika neraskrytogo ubiistva Aleksandra Menia." *Moskovskii komsomolets*, July 31.

Cherkesov, Viktor. 2004. "Moda na KGB?" *Komsomol'skaia pravda*, December 29.

Chevtaeva, Irina. 2012. "Leonid Razvozzhaev soobshchil pravozashchitnikam, chto yego 'yavku s povinnoi' sledovateli zapisali na video." *Novoe vremia*, October 29.

Cohn, Edward D. 2017. "Coercion, Reeducation, and the Prophylactic Chat: *Profilaktika* and the KGB's Struggle with Political Unrest in Lithuania, 1953–64." *Russian Review* 76 (April): 272–93.

Davies, R. W. 1989. *Soviet History in the Gorbachev Revolution*. London: Macmillan.

Divnich, Yevgenii. 2002. "Pochemu ya prekratil bor'bu protiv Sovetskoi vlasti (k 85-letiiu Oktiabr'skoi Sotsialisticheskoi revoliutsii)." *Nash sovremennik* 11. https://www.litmir.me/br/?b=135093&p=30.

Dobroliubov, Yaroslav. 2007. "Budushchee sistemy." *Spetsnaz Rossii*, no. 12 (December). http://www.specnaz.ru/articles/135/1/674.htm.

Dudko, Dmitrii. 1980. "'Zapad ishchet sensatsii . . .' Zaiavlenie sviashchennika D. Dudko." *Izvestiia*, no. 144 (June 21).

———. 1999. "Prichina vsemu—zolotoi telets." *Rus' derzhavnaia* 1:3.

———. 2001. "Poema o moem sledovatele." *Nash sovremennik* 4:218–25.

———. 2004. *Na skreshchenii dorog: Vyiavlenie iskusnykh; V ternie i pri doroge.* Moscow: Izdatel'stvo Sretenskogo monastyria.

Dunlop, John B. 1983. *The Faces of Contemporary Russian Nationalism.* Princeton NJ: Princeton University Press.

Ellis, Jane. 1986. *The Russian Orthodox Church: A Contemporary History.* Bloomington: Indiana University Press.

———. 1996. *The Russian Orthodox Church: Triumphalism and Defensiveness.* Houndmills, UK: Macmillan.

Fedor, Julie. 2011. *Russia and the Cult of State Security: The Chekist Tradition, from Lenin to Putin.* London: Routledge.

———. 2014. "Setting the Soviet Past in Stone: The Iconography of the New Martyrs of the Russian Orthodox Church." *Australian Slavonic and East European Studies* 28 (1–2): 121–53.

Fink, Carole K. 2013. *Cold War: An International History.* Boulder CO: Westview Press.

Fitzpatrick, Sheila. 2005. *Tear Off the Masks! Identity and Imposture in Twentieth-Century Russia.* Princeton NJ: Princeton University Press.

Fussell, Paul. 1975. *The Great War and Modern Memory.* Oxford: Oxford University Press.

Geller [Heller], Mikhail. 1996. *Kontsentrasionnyi mir i sovetskaia literatura.* Moscow: MIK.

———. 2000. "Shpion, kotoryi prishel v teplo." In *Vmesto memuarov: Pamiati M. Ya. Gellera*, edited by L. Geller and N. Zelenko. Moscow: MIK.

Gerasimov, Aleksei. 1997. "Aleksandr Korzhakova khotiat posadit'." *Kommersant*, no. 113 (July 18).

Glajar, Valentina, Alison Lewis, and Corina L. Petrescu, eds. 2016. *Secret Police Files from the Eastern Bloc: Between Surveillance and Life Writing.* Rochester NY: Camden House.

Golushko, N. M. 2012. *V spetssluzhbakh trekh gosudarstv.* Moscow: Kuchkovo pole.

Graczyk, Roman. 2007. *Tropem SB: Jak czytać teczki.* Cracow: Znak.

Halfin, Igal. 2007. *Intimate Enemies: Demonizing the Bolshevik Opposition, 1918–1928.* Pittsburgh: University of Pittsburgh Press.

Hixson, Walter L. 1998. *Parting the Curtain: Propaganda, Culture, and the Cold War, 1945–1961.* London: Macmillan.

Iliushenko, Vladimir. 2009. "Geroi dukhovnogo soprotivleniia." *Novaia Yevropa* 4. Tiur'ma i volia, website of the Center for Assistance to Reform of Criminal Justice. http://old.prison.org/personal/krahmalnikova.shtml.

Kevorkova, Nadezhda. 2003. "Iuda 'rabotal' ne v interesakh svoei strany." *Contra Mundi: Ofitsial'nyi sait zhurnalista Nadezhdy Kevorkovoi*, March 2. http://kevorkova.com/iuda-rabotal-ne-v-interesax-svoej-strany/.

———. 2004. "Pastyr' ovets pravoslavnykh: Umer otets Dmitrii Dudko." *Russkii zhurnal*, June 29.

Komarov, Yevgenii. 2002. "FSB podtianula RTs: K svoemu 'piaru.'" *Novye izvestiia*, no. 41 (March 12).

Kurliandskii, Igor'. 2007. "Protokoly tserkovnykh mudretsov: K istorii mni-mogo povorota Stalina k religii i Pravoslavnoi Tserkvi v 1930-e gody." *Politicheskii zhurnal* 32 (175) (November 26). http://www.interfax-religion.ru/?act=print&div=7403.

Levi, Vladimir. n.d. "Tsena lzhi." Accessed October 2, 2018. http://levi.ru/article.php?id_catalog=52&id_position=220.

Literaturnaia Rossiia. 2009. "Dela ottsov—znak dlia synovei." October 16.

Lobanov, Mikhail. 2002. "Na peredovoi (Opyt dukhovnoi avtobiografii)." *Nash sovremennik* 3:97–130.

Lukin, Alexander. 2000. *The Political Culture of the Russian "Democrats."* Oxford: Oxford University Press.

Makarov, Aleksei. 2016. "'Sud idet po vsemu miru.'" *Novoe vremia*, February 8.

Mastny, Vojtech. 1996. *Soviet Insecurity: The Stalin Years*. Oxford: Oxford University Press.

Morev, Gleb. 2014. "Gleb Pavlovskii: 'Ideia zaniat'sia politikoi dialoga s Butyrkoi byla plokhaia.'" *Colta*, December 5. https://www.colta.ru/articles/dissidents/5609.

Murzin, Yevgenii. 2006. "'Eto bylo vremia schast'ia . . .'" *Mir vsem*, May 29. http://www.kapellan.biz/content/view/76/310/.

Naiman, Eric, and Anne Nesbet. 1995. "Documentary Discipline: Three Interrogations of Stanislav Govorukhin." In *Soviet Hieroglyphics: Visual Culture in Late Twentieth-Century Russia*, edited by Nancy Condee, 52–67. Bloomington: Indiana University Press.

News.ru. 2005. "Predstaviteli moskovskoi intelligentsia proveli vstrechu v podderzhku organizatorov vystavki 'Ostorozhno, religiia!'" March 17. http://www.newsru.com/religy/17mar2005/vorsicht.html.

Nezavisimaia gazeta. 2004. "On byl geroem very i raskaiavshimsia dissidentom." June 30. http://www.ng.ru/events/2004-06-30/9_dudko.html.

Nikol'skii, Valerii. n.d. "Mnenie." *Portal-credo*. Accessed July 1, 2017. http://www.portal-credo.ru/site/?act=authority&id=225.

Novodvorskaia, Valeriia. 2012. "Tiur'ma vysokoi izoliatsii." *New Times*, October 29, 35–36.

Peterson, Christian. 2011. *Globalizing Human Rights: Private Citizens, the Soviet Union and the West*. London: Routledge.

Piotrowski, Paweł, ed. 2006. *Aparat bezpieczeństwa v Polsce: Kadra kierownicza*. Vol. 2, *1956–1975*. Warsaw: Institut Pamięci Narodowej.

———, ed. 2008. *Aparat bezpieczeństwa v Polsce: Kadra kierownicza*. Vol. 3, *1975–1990*. Warsaw: Institut Pamięci Narodowej.

Podrabinek, Aleksandr. 2014. *Dissidenty*. Moscow: AST. http://www.urantia-s.com/library/podrabinek/dissidenty/25.

"Polveka bez vozhdia." 2003. *Rodina*, February 17.

Pomerants, Grigorii. 1984. "Akafist poshlosti." *Sintaksis* 12:4–54.

———. 1994. "Akafist poshlosti." *Russkoe bogatstvo* 2 (6): 208–53. http://imwerden.de/pdf/russkoe_bogatstvo_6_1994_pomerants_ocr.pdf.

Portal-credo. 2004. "Mnenie: 'My s ottsom Dimitriem Dudko ne tol'ko zhili po sosedstvu, no i v Lefortovskoi tiur'me okazalis' riadom',—byvshii uznik sovesti O. GLEB YAKUNIN." July 1. http://www.portal-credo.ru/site/index.php?act=news&id=23776.

Prokhanov, Aleksandr. 2010. "Svetlyi nash batiushka . . ." *Zavtra*, February 24. http://zavtra.ru/blogs/2010-02-2441.

Reif, Igor'. 2009. "Kazhdyi prozrevaet v odinochku." *Vestnik Yevropy*, June 15.

Rév, István. 2005. *Retroactive Justice: Prehistory of Post-Communism*. Palo Alto CA: Stanford University Press.

Rosenberg, Emily S. 1993. "Commentary: The Cold War and the Discourse of National Security." *Diplomatic History* 17 (2) (Spring): 277–84.

Rubinstein, Joshua, and Alexander Gribanov, eds. 2005. *The KGB File of Andrei Sakharov*. New Haven CT: Yale University Press.

Semenov, Yu. 1977. "Parol' ne nuzhen." In *Led i plamen': Dokumental'no—khudozhestvennyi sbornik*, edited by V. Dudko, 35–46. Vladivostok: Dal'nevostochnoe knizhnoe izdatel'stvo.

Shaw, Tony. 2001. *British Cinema and the Cold War: The State, Propaganda and Consensus*. London: I. B. Tauris.

Shkarovskii, Mikhail B. 2010. *Russkaia Pravoslavnaia Tserkov' v XX veke*. Moscow: Veche, Lepta.

Shlapentokh, Dmitry, and Vladimir Shlapentokh. 1993. *Soviet Cinematography, 1918–1991: Ideological Conflict and Social Reality*. New York: A. de Gruyter.

Shurygin, Vladislav. 1998. "Istochnik." *Zavtra*, November 10.

Smyk, Vladimir. 1990. "Kak syn pravoslavnoi tserkvi i otechestva." *Literaturnaia Rossiia*, January 19.

———. 1996. "Ne padenie-triumf." *Zavtra*, April 30.

———. 2002. "Smirennaia proza Dmitriia Dudko." *Literaturnaia Rossiia*, September 6.

Sobolev, V. A. et al., eds. 1999. *Lubianka, 2: Iz istorii otechestvennoi istoriografii*. Moscow: Izdatel'stvo ob"edineniia "Mosgorarkhiv," AO "Moskovskie uchebniki i kartolitografiia."

Sokirko, Viktor. 1982. "Pis'mo sviashchenniku O. Dmitriiu Dudko." May 15. www.sokirko.info/ideology/vokrugpoiskov/5.3.htm.

Sokolov, Maksim. 1997. "Chertverovatel'naia vlast'." *Ekspert*, December 8.

Strigin, Yevgenii. 2004. *KGB byl, yest' i budet: Ot KGB SSSR do MBRF (1991–1993)*. Moscow: Eksmo, 384–85.

"Sud nad Viktorom Kapitanchukom." 1980. *Vesti iz SSSR*, no. 19 (October 15). https://vestiizsssr.wordpress.com/2016/12/06/sud-nad-victorom-kapitanchukom-1980-19-3/.

Svetova, Zoia. 2013. "Anatomiia soprotivleniia i predatel'stva." *Novoe vremia*, September 23. https://newtimes.ru/articles/detail/71249/.

Szwagrzyk, Krzysztof, ed. 2005. *Aparat bezpieczeństwa v Polsce: Kadra kierownicza*. Vol. 1, *1944–1956*. Warsaw: Institut Pamięci Narodowej.

Tabak, Yurii. 2004. "Prezident Rossii v zerkale mifologicheskogo soznaniia radi-kal'nykh natsionalisticheki-religioznykh grupp." *SOVA Informatsionno-analiticheskii tsentr*, January 18. http://www.sova-center.ru/racism-xenophobia /publications/antisemitism/articles-reports/2004/01/d1632/#12.

Vatulescu, Cristina. 2010. *Police Aesthetics: Film, Literature and the Secret Police in Soviet Times*. Stanford CA: Stanford University Press.

"V beskonechnom ob"iatii: Perepiska Belly Akhmadulinoi i Borisa Messer-era s Vasiliem i Maiei Aksenovymi." 2011. *Oktiabr'*, October 10. http:// magazines.russ.ru/october/2011/10/ob2.html.

Verkhovskii, Aleksandr. 2007. "Ideinaia evoliutsiia russkogo natsionalizma: 1990-e i 2000-e gody." *Polit.ru*, December 28. http://polit.ru/article/2007 /12/28/verhovsky/.

Vigilianskii, Vladimir. 2001. "Novoe issledovanie po starym retseptam." *Novyi mir*, no. 4. http://magazines.russ.ru/novyi_mi/2001/4/wigl.html.

Volkova, Yelena. 2014. "Religiia i magiia iskusstva: Ot khudozhestvennoi agiog-rafii—k protestnoi aktsii." In *Montazh i demontazh sekuliarnogo mira*, edited by Aleksei Malashenko and Sergei Filatov, 203–53. Moscow: ROSSPEN.

Zavtra. 1997a. "Il'ia Glazunov: 'Menia spas narod.'" September 2.

——. 1997b. Untitled text. February 18. http://zavtra.ru/blogs/1997-02-186about.

——. 2009. "Apostrof." September 23.

Zubarev, Dmitrii, and Gennadii Kuzovkin. 2017. "Yakir, Petr Ionovich." In *Entsik-lopediia Krugosvet: Universal'naia nauchno-populiarnaia onlain-entsiklopediia*. http://www.krugosvet.ru/enc/istoriya/YAKIR_PETR_IONOVICH.html.

Secret East/West Operations

6 Espionage and Intimacy
West Berlin Turkish Men in the Stasi's Eyes

JENNIFER A. MILLER

In a May 1967 Ministry for State Security (Ministerium für Staatssicherheit, Stasi or MfS) memo on the psychology of border
crossers and policing them, an official notes that a crosser's "position" is "predominantly determined by the societal system of the
crosser's homeland" and by the political relationship between
his homeland and the GDR ("Zollverwaltung der Deutschen
Demokratischen Republik: Informationsmaterial über die Kon-
trollpsychologie in grenzüberschreitenden Reiseverkehr," BStU
67/846, vol. 3, 21). Yet it also notes that the Stasi should distin-
guish all travelers as individuals who cannot be grouped together
in a "homogenous mass that is only roughly divided into the categories of West German, Foreigner, Retired Person, and so forth"
(67/846, vol. 3, 21).[1] West Berlin–residing Turkish guest workers escaped easy categorization. After all which societal system
applied to them—that of West Berlin or of Turkey? In 1979, years
after regular Berlin-Berlin border crossings had become common,
a Stasi operative justified the need for broad-reaching surveillance of "Turks" crossing from West to East Berlin. He explained,
"Monthly, around 8,000 Turks arrive in the capital of the GDR . . .
who have a multitude of contacts of an unexplained character to
GDR citizens" (HA II 29668, 7). Interestingly, in contrast to their
usual level of detail, the Stasi files used the term Turk without
qualification, not always specifying whether the Turkish nationals were participating in the official guest-worker program or liv-

ing in West Germany for other reasons, such as to study at West German universities.

The MfS's Main Department II (Hauptabteilung II), tasked with surveillance of the economic and military sectors, took over this vital espionage mission to protect citizens from "criminal and subversive dealings against the GDR or the socialist community," including drug smuggling, and in general to look for solutions to the ill-defined "Turkish Problem" (HA II 29668, 7). Fear of infiltration by right- and left-wing Turkish extremist organizations motivated the Stasi to act and emphasized the need to discover plans and intentions in advance (HA II 29668, 7). The GDR deemed it a matter of national importance "to secure via official and unofficial sources . . . an operational view of the Turkish concentration in [East Berlin]" (HA II 29668, 7). The Stasi report does not just focus on transgressors and "subversive dealings" but also demonstrates a more general concern over the growing Turkish concentration in East Berlin.

However, this operational outline was a poor fit for the reality at hand. A great many Turkish nationals crossed from West to East Berlin regularly, with ease, and for years, maintaining mostly intimate, cross-border relationships from the 1960s through the 1980s. These border crossers presented an interesting paradox. West Berlin society deemed them suspicious as foreign and "Eastern"—a cultural and ethnic distinction that created social outsiders. At the same time, the Stasi found them suspect because they not only came from West Berlin but also, in the eyes of the Stasi, embodied Western capitalist culture and as such offered a figurative and literal escape route to the West. Guest workers' experiences in and perspectives of East Berlin complicate the divided city's story, as many of them saw the East German state as a space to explore and enjoy greater social autonomy and acceptance among Germans, especially in contrast to feelings of social isolation in the West.

The 1979 Stasi report explicitly states that operatives were to observe Turkish men between the ages of twenty and thirty-five years. The Stasi's files about these border-crossing Turkish nationals are almost all about foreign men meeting with East German women, adding a loaded gender dynamic. Considering the dubious nature of intimacy and privacy in a police state, scholars have since pointed out that the women of East Germany were uniquely positioned to understand how the state worked not just because of their participation in traditional gender roles at home but also often due to their intimate relationships (Merkel 2001). Various power dynamics charged these cross-border encounters politically with asymmetries of wealth, allegiance, access, and freedom of movement. The Stasi considered these men dangerous not just as foreigners but also as men with an ability to infiltrate a hard-to-police intimate space. Furthermore, as a group the men discussed in the Stasi files are necessarily a skewed sample—they had violated a regulation or engaged in suspicious behavior that had warranted the Stasi's attention in the first place. Most of the Turkish nationals who ended up in the Stasi files missed the midnight deadline to cross back into West Berlin or were caught with illegal goods, involved in political organizations considered dubious, or suspected of assisting with the illegal departure of an East German citizen to the West. In short they were distrusted as rule breakers, and not necessarily singled out by their nationality, ethnicity, or religion.

This is a story of paradoxes—of suspicion and acceptance, love and manipulation, and transgression and compliance—that reveals unknown aspects of Cold War espionage, focusing on West Berlin–residing Turkish men and their own involvement with the Stasi. For decades a large population of West Berlin-residing Turkish nationals built social lives, business deals, intimate relationships, and transnational families across divided Berlin. The unusual cases provide a novel window through which to view the Berlin border, its crossing, and its definition and present a little-known Cold War spy story. Traditionally, economic and political histories have dominated the narratives of divided Berlin and the Cold War writ large (Bruce 2014, 47–58). The particular history of guest workers in Berlin tells a new narrative of divided Berlin, specifically one about how porous its borders were. This perspective reveals points of contact between foreign nationals and East Germans, the East German state's opinion of the guest-worker program in West Germany, and, significantly, moments of integration and acceptance. Various personal interactions reveal different and moving allegiances, sometimes based on attraction and other times on exploitation. This study presents West Berlin–residing Turkish nationals from multiple vantages, each with its own bias: the recollections of border crossers, the concerned Stasi, and East German women whom the border crossers courted and sometimes married. Drawing on the Stasi's documentation of Turkish citizens in East Germany and using the files held in the Stasi Archives (BStU), this work considers the Stasi's point of view in identifying "suspects" among guest workers in its jurisdiction. This police surveillance folds guest workers into the larger narrative of the East German state's gaze.

After a brief look at the larger historical context, this chapter explores guest workers' roles in divided Berlin through three themes: lovers, border crossers, and transgressors. These lovers' stories provide access to the private, intimate realm—a sphere with which historians of totalitarian states have long been fascinated (Richthofen 2009, 11). The idea of "Eigensinn," or "self-will," has dominated discussions of how individuals negotiated, in distinct and idiosyncratic ways, the dictatorship at the grassroots level (Lüdtke 1994; Lindenberger 1999). Johannes Huinink has highlighted "individual spaces for action," in which GDR citizens negotiated personal dealings in ways that demonstrated their ability to exploit situations and behave tactically, and not just accept dictates and conditions. He points out that they always had "the potential to shape things themselves" (Huinink 1995, 38, quoted in Richthofen 2009, 15).

Cross-border encounters in East Berlin, whether fly-by-night or long term, offered welcoming embraces and even, ironically, more privacy than could be found in West Germany, the Turkish guest workers' true "host country." These men found a sense of home across the border, under the watchful eyes of the Stasi. Some couples went to great lengths to form relationships that defied borders and showed an alternative social organization to the state. Other lovers' motivations were more elusive, and answers to the following questions remain speculation: Were these trysts part of East Germans' plans of escape or of exploiting access to Western goods? Did these cross-border lovers seek sexual outlets they could visit and leave at their own discretion or long-term partners? Not everyone crossed the border for love. Indeed, the border crossers reflected a unique and often bizarre social and cultural cross-border world. They offered multiple vantage points on relationships between foreign nationals and East Germans (including the Stasi officials tasked with tracking them)—all of which add a new dimension to our understanding of both the guest-worker program and Cold War narratives. These untold stories provide a fuller and, at times, paradoxical picture that demonstrates that the closed border was indeed crossed, that Turkish nationals and Germans socialized, and that these relationships threatened the GDR as well as pat concepts of what constituted the "West" and the "East."

The final theme, transgressors, delves into a deeper level of human psychology: the complicity of collaborators, including Stasi-recruited Turkish nationals. In truth transgression is a theme woven throughout this chapter, as it is implied in myriad borders that are crossed—politically, culturally, bodily, and linguistically. Just crossing the inner-Berlin border was a transgression in the most literal sense. The search for fun, some freedom, and sexual and domestic comforts was another type of transgression, especially in light of the restrictions on private life that West German employers imposed in their workers' dormitories (Eryılmaz and Jamin 1998; Miller 2018). However, there is also a larger level of transgression at work here, one more akin to betrayal, in the overt breaking of laws, flouting of regulations, and cooperation and formal collaboration with East German authorities to report on one's countrymen. Betrayal, complicity, and coercion combine to some degree in transgression and collaboration. While not operating with total free will, collaborators were, at some level, both choosing and manipulating their collusion with the state. Questions of whether love is true and why people betray also dovetail with ideas of nationality and belonging. In short these border crossers were constantly renegotiating their statuses. They were both Eastern and Western. They were insiders in private relationships with East Germans, in economic relationships as West Germans' employees, and as workers in West German companies. At the same time, they were outsiders as foreign nationals and—as collaborators—insiders within the Stasi, which tracked their compatriots, placing them outside their national community.

Historical Context

The border between West and East Germany, with Berlin as its symbol, defined the Cold War locally and internationally. When the two German states were founded in 1949, the contestation over who could be representative of "Germans" also began, adding a political classification to the blood-based one. The Federal Republic asserted that only it, with its freely elected government, could legitimately represent Germans. Indeed, under the Hallstein Doctrine (1955–70), the West German government could not, it argued, even recognize the GDR as a state (Hertle 2011, 30). When other states entered into diplomatic relations with the GDR, the Federal Republic reacted with countermeasures, breaking off diplomatic ties with such states and politically isolating the GDR. East Germany, in turn, also expressed the desire to unite all Germans, but only under the flag of socialism. However, the socialist state began to lose its population as it lost its appeal.

Once the socialist planned economy proved to be inefficient, partly because of the heavy burdens the Soviets placed on it, many East German residents fled for financial, political, and family reasons. *Republikflucht* (fleeing the republic), as the East German state referred to those immigrating to the West, caused the population drain that prompted, on the one hand, the Berlin Wall's construction in 1961 and, on the other, the expansion of the West German guest-worker program to West Berlin to replace the missing workers from the East (Mushaben 2008, 46–47; Göktürk, Gramling, and Kaes 2007, 9; Mandel 2008, 6). The question of who and where the "real Germans" were—before and after the wall's construction— was eerily prescient of the post–Cold War debates about German citizenship for guest workers and their descendants.

On August 13, 1961, the East German authorities constructed the Berlin Wall to stem the out-migration of their citizens. In the sixteen years before the wall's construction, 3.5 million people had fled East Germany (Hertle 2011, 32). The West, however, considered this out-migration representative of people voting with their feet. Previously, West Berliners had also regularly traveled to East Berlin; in fact, until August 1961, about 80 percent of West Berliners had visited East Berlin at least once a month (Alisch 2000, 34). The inner-German border had an undeniable appeal for West Germans in general, and by the end of the 1950s, it had become a well-established tourist attraction, where visitors would hike, picnic, and take photos (Eckert 2001, 245–46). From the very first instance, the GDR saw "border tourism" as a provocation and an attempt at propaganda for the "better Germany" by the Federal Republic (245–46).

Like much of postwar Europe, East Germany also imported foreign workers to assuage its industrial labor shortage. Beginning in 1966 with a treaty with Poland, the GDR signed treaties through the 1980s with Hungary, Algeria, Cuba, Mozambique, Vietnam, Mongolia, and China, offering occupational training or employment for foreign "contract workers" (Milewski 2010, 8). These workers were relegated to unappealing shift work and low-skilled jobs, and the states involved further exploited the workers to relieve trade debts and improve production without investment. For example, according to the bilateral "Treaty of Friendship and Cooperation," Mozambique received East German agricultural machinery, trucks, and training for its workers, and the GDR obtained grain, coal, and several thousand contract workers (Dennis and LaPorte 2011, 90). By the mid-1970s the focus on occupational training had waned, and the state increasingly viewed the workers in terms of their economic utility. East Germany limited contract to three to five years, workers primarily lived in company-owned hostels or community housing, and the government strongly discouraged contacts between these so-called Third World citizens and its own (Milewski 2010, 8). Contract workers lived throughout the GDR but were heavily concentrated in East Berlin and in the southern industrial cities of Chemnitz, Dresden, Leipzig, and Halle (Dennis and LaPorte 2011, 89). East Germany's foreign nationals lived mostly in isolation from mainstream society, creating a monocultural society (Kurthen, Bergmann, and Erb 1997, 144–45).

Historians have long noted xenophobia's prevalence in East Germany, which exploded into blatant violence after reunification in the 1990s (Kurthen et al. 1997). During the lifespan of the GDR, "socialist friendship among peoples" was the official party line, but acceptance of others was not always the norm (Kurthen, Bergmann, and Erb 1997, 144). The media were also forbidden to report on the numbers of foreign workers living in the GDR while at the same time encouraged to scorn West Germany's guest-worker program as capitalist exploitation (Milewski 2010, 8). According to a sociological study of antisemitism and xenophobia in East Germany, in the 1980s—when actual conditions and government propaganda differed the most—public opinion on "friendly socialist countries" soured while sympathy for "imperialist enemies" grew (Kurthen, Bergmann, and Erb 1997, 144). On August 2, 1975 the Socialist Unity Party's (SED) most important organ, its official newspaper, *Neues Deutschland* (New Germany), reported on West Germany's guest-worker program two years after its official end with the double intention of exposing the exploitation of workers in the West and of pointing out the responsibility that receiving countries had to give them fair job options, job training, language training, humane living conditions, and much more ("Wirtschaftliche und soziale Aspekte der Wanderarbeit," ZAIG 11129). Indeed, Turkish guest workers with West Berlin residence permits skated the line between constituting "imperialist enemies" with their consumer goods and belonging to the exploited working class.

In addition to political and social constraints, the Berlin Wall was a serious and dangerous border: between 1961 and 1989 at least 136 people were killed there (Hertle 2011, 124). This is the Berlin Wall story that is commonly told—the daring escape attempts from the East, the shoot-to-kill order, the tragic family divisions, and the state's escalating surveillance and countermeasures. Less well known, however, is that the borders were also less dramatically crossed, often daily. Indeed, the border was porous. After August 13, 1961, a series of treaties and agreements regulated the border, starting in 1963 with a border-pass agreement between the West Berlin Senate and the GDR that allowed Christmas and New Year's visits (Gieseke 2006, 108–17). That year 730,000 people put up with the long processing period and registered 1.2 million visits to East Berlin between December 19, 1963, and January 5, 1964 (Hertle 2011, 100). The agreement continued until 1966, when negotiations broke down and the Christmas visits ended. The 1970 Four Powers Agreement and the subsequent Transit Agreement between the Federal Republic and the GDR were significant for their regulation of border crossings, visa requirements, and exchange rates (Gieseke 2006, 108–17).

The Soviet Union, however, was not thrilled to see the two German states growing closer. The Soviet Communist Party's general secretary, Leonid Brezhnev, responded to the GDR's general secretary, Erich Honecker, directly in July 1970: "Erich, let me tell you quite frankly, never forget this: the GDR cannot exist without us, without the Soviet Union, its power and strength. Without us there would be no GDR. . . . There must not be any process of rapprochement between the FRG and the GDR" (Hertle 2011, 135). Nevertheless, both German states acted in their own interests and agreed at the start of 1970 on pacts to ease travel; to open new border crossings; and to improve road, rail, postal, and telephone connections between the two countries (Hertle 2011, 134). After years of division, starting on October 3, 1972, the GDR allowed West Berliners to visit multiple times a year for up to thirty days for "humanitarian, family, religious, cultural or tourism" reasons, resulting in 44 million trips before 1989 (134).

East Germany also stood to gain financially from its relaxed border controls. It collected transit, postal, and visa fees in addition to the exchange of currency required of visitors (*Zwangsumtausch*) to the GDR—all paid in the hard foreign currency that Eastern Bloc countries desperately needed to operate in the world market.[2] Starting in 1973 Honecker allowed West German visitors into the GDR with this mandatory currency exchange and allowed West Germans to transfer funds to East German relatives. This hard currency could then be spent in *Intershops*, or the government-run stores that sold select goods for Western currency (Zatlin 2007a). Between 1975 and 1979, border-crossing income had increased from almost 600 million DM to 1.56 billion DM, and it remained at this level for the following years (Hertle 2011, 136).

Guest workers, estimated to form almost 10 percent of the West Berlin population, were uniquely positioned within the divided city. On the one hand, because they were guest workers, their employment permits required that they have West German residency permits, and these allowed them to live in West Berlin. On the other hand, because they were foreign nationals, their passports allowed them into East Berlin with greater ease than West Berliners—as long as they crossed the border as foreign tourists and returned by midnight when their same-day visas expired (Henrich 1983). In 1977 the count of border crossers by street and by train, including West Germans, West Berliners, and foreigners, was 18,084,000 (Delius and Lapp 1999, 177). As a result guest workers and other foreign nationals who did not have the same historical ties and political motivations as West Germans also became part of the everyday landscape in East Berlin.

Significantly, East Germans often considered Turkish nationals as Western, not just because of their ready access to consumer goods but also because of their Western lifestyles. At the same time, many West Germans considered them as inassimilable "Easterners." This East-West confusion mirrored ambiguity about the Turkish republic itself: a NATO member and U.S. ally but deemed by many to be at the heart of the "Orient," with all the trappings of Orientalism. Yet this small case study, featuring seemingly trivial social interactions—between Turkish men and East German women—reveals layers of meaning that recast traditional narratives of restrictive Cold War Berlin and guest-worker experiences.[3] For this group the Berlin Wall was easy to traverse, and East Germans seem to have been more welcoming to foreigners than extant literature has allowed us to believe.

Despite both the relaxation of the border regulations and the political and financial gains of border crossing, East Germany remained deeply concerned with ideological infiltration from the West in the form of packages, media, uncensored news, private messages, and contact with Westerners themselves. The Stasi, known as the "Shield and Sword" of the SED, took its mission very seriously. After détente with West Germany, it expanded its surveillance system considerably with the number of Stasi employees doubling to eighty thousand between 1970 and 1980 (Delius and Lapp 1999, 177). In 1972, in the midst of the "humanitarian" treaties, Honecker actually ordered new land mines installed at the inner-German border (Hertle 2011, 136).

It is not surprising that border crossing and the ensuing international relationships sparked suspicion among East German authorities. After all the East German state is well known for its close watch of its citizens. When the Berlin Wall fell in 1989, the Stasi employed 91,015 full-time employees and 173,000 informants, or roughly one in fifty East Germans between the ages of eighteen and eighty (Bruce 2014, 48). In short it was a highly policed state. Indeed, the GDR took foreign visitors' potential to corrupt and influence its population so earnestly that it set up an Arbeitsgruppe Ausländer (Working Group on Foreigners), specifically for foreigners who resided in West Berlin. The Stasi, like many in West Germany, found guest workers in its territory marginal yet threatening. For many guest workers living in West Berlin, in sharp contrast to the countless negotiations, transnational bureaucracy, treaties, and visa applications that had preceded their residence in the city, Berlin's own border proved easier to cross. Monthly, thousands of guest workers moved between West and East Berlin for their social lives—to go dancing, to eat out, and, for the largely male population, to meet women.

Lovers

The theme of lovers explores the various types of intimate relationships between male Turkish guest workers from West Berlin and East German women. Though the literature reveals that cross-border relationships were much more varied, the Stasi files on guest workers assumed that it was primarily heterosexual Turkish men who represented the guest-worker population arriving from West Berlin. A diversity of relationships developed, with the potential grounds for these romantic trysts including attraction, adventure, manipulation, and for the East Germans access to the West, including escaping to the West permanently. Stasi operatives followed border-crossing guest workers with both great interest and much concern, especially the ensuing romantic and sexual relationships with their citizens. Their fears were broad based, ranging from concern that these men would negatively influence their citizens (especially their morality) and induce them into illegal activities to anxiety that they would assist citizens in leaving the GDR. More often than not, the Stasi considered foreign border crossers suspect because their intimate relationships with East German women could result in marriage and emigration out of East Berlin, a topic of perhaps the greatest concern for the Stasi.

Emigration through marriage thus put a figurative hole in the border and the officially coined *eheähnliche Verhältnisse*, or "marriage-like relationships," between Turkish men and East Berlin women continued to preoccupy East German officials for decades. Concern over and the regulation of sex between those deemed to be "threatening outsiders" and "one's own women" are age-old tropes and were equally true for both West and East Germany, but they still bear examination in this context. Communist prudishness was also nothing new. Despite the official rhetoric of socialist feminism that purported equality among the sexes as a counter to bourgeois, Western gender roles, the East German state, like the Soviet Union before it (and also similar to West Germany), actually took a repressive and conservative view of the body, sex, and relationships: abortions, though legal in the first trimester, were difficult to obtain; prostitution and adultery were socially condemned; homosexuality was banned; and the state promoted the traditional nuclear family (McLellan 2011). According to historian Josie McLellan, promiscuity and erotica counted as Western vices: "During the early Cold War, [the East German state] portrayed pinups, stripteases, and prostitution as typical of an Americanized, profit-oriented West German sexuality, contrasting them with the healthy sexuality of the East based in marriage and childbearing" (2011, 51).

In the eyes of the Stasi, political infiltration through the private realm was a real concern. Regardless of any moral code, intimate relationships can challenge belief systems successfully. According to one operative's report, "often marriage-like relationships . . . between Turks living in West Berlin and female citizens of the

GDR [arose]," which could lead to some of these female citizens being "pulled into the potential circles of the unlawful candidates for leaving the GDR" (HA II 22858, 335). By marrying a foreigner, an East German woman could apply for emigration (*Ausreiseant-rag*) from the GDR. The operative above noted in the report that in 1980, seventy female citizens had applied to emigrate specifically through marriage with Turkish citizens (335). Highlighting the ubiquity of the problem, an East Berlin customs officer who routinely searched Turks crossing the border apparently found Turkish men in possession of "hundreds of contact addresses and telephone numbers of GDR female citizens per year" (335). The Stasi recognized, just as many East German women must have, that these foreign men provided a way out of the GDR for them.

Not all relationships were of convenience or for personal gain, however. In fact love-based relationships flourished, as evidenced by private photos of couples together. One man was reported to have attempted to go as far as to take up permanent residence in East Berlin because, according to the Stasi operative, he had developed an "intense love relationship" with his East German girlfriend; the file also included pictures of them on picnics and in bed together (HA II 27442, 314). In another case, a foreign man decided to divorce his West Berlin wife to marry an East Berlin woman instead (HA II 27962, 116). One East Berlin woman applied to marry a Turkish guest worker residing in West Berlin whom she had dated and from whom she had received financial support for twelve years since 1967 (ZKG 286, 40). The woman's daughter considered the Turkish man a father figure as he had been in her life consistently since she had been six years old. The mother wished to marry and move with her fiancé to Turkey, but the GDR denied her request (ZKG 286, 40). Despite the border they had built a life and a family together. Significantly, these reports reveal an unmistakably high level of contact between the two groups that allowed relationships to develop over years despite the border.

On the whole Stasi officials found the relationships between foreign men and East German women to be dubious and continued to comment on whether these relationships were "real" and on what types of contact they were based, often noting the promiscuity of the people involved. Those relationships deemed "real" were often couples who had been together for one or two years, seeing each other once or twice a week—or communicating through daily telephone contact. One woman had a "close relationship" with a "Turkish citizen from West Berlin" who, at the time of the report, arrived every Friday and stayed through Sunday for a year, sending her daughter to stay with her grandparents each time (HA II 28084, 29). In another case an officer noted, "Because the Turk arrives almost daily from West Berlin, one can assume that it is a case of a steady relationship" (ZKG 286, 10). In a more common case, a woman appealed to the state to let her immigrate to Turkey with her West Berlin–living fiancé, but the Volkspolizei (People's Police, VP) refused her request because of doubts about the relationship's authenticity; they explained that she had "steadily changing relationships with men" (ZKG 286, 20). The VP's impressions of her relationships' genuineness had a major impact on her life.

The Stasi's suspicion of the nature of these relationships was not unfounded. The case of two people, "Mesut" and "Corinna," shows the slippery politics of cross-border relationships.[4] "Mesut" met "Corinna," an East German dancer, when her troupe was on tour in Turkey in 1954 (HA XX 18529, 26). In love with her, "Mesut" moved to Germany as a student in 1958 and studied in Bavaria (HA XX 18529, 10). In 1963 he began to petition the East German state for permission to marry "Corinna" and have her join him in the West (HA XX 18529, 10). He wrote moving letters, pleading to be with his fiancée, writing that their "destiny and future together hang in the balance" (HA XX 18529, 10). He appealed to the state's sense of morality, writing, "Surely it cannot be in the interest of a state to get involved in the deeply personal affairs of its citizens" (HA XX 18529, 10), which ironically was a statement that the Stasi noted. "Mesut" also appealed to the state's international reputation: "In my homeland, in which each citizen is entitled to every freedom, the GDR's negative stance toward its own citizens will not be understood. It is of upmost importance to not hinder the positive image of the GDR to my fellow citizens" (HA XX 18529, 11). In the letter explaining the denial of his request, the East German authorities made two points: first, that Turkey did not recognize the state of East Germany and, second, that without state representation in Turkey, his future wife would have no political protection there (HA XX 18529, 13). The geopolitics of the Turkish Republic's refusal to recognize East Germany is played out in this one man's request to be with his love.

In the meantime his fiancée became pregnant with their child (leaving one to infer that they still had regular contact with each other), and she also lost her job, which implies that the East German state was punishing her for her wish to leave. Once again "Mesut" appealed to the international reputation of the East German state, writing, "The attraction of the socialist societal form on us developing countries is a certain factor" (HA XX 18529, 14). He also took an emotional tone, saying it did not make sense to give his bride false hope (HA XX 18529, 13). "Mesut" petitioned for help in the West German state as well, writing to the Bundesnotaufnahmeverfahren (Federal Emergency Department, BNV) for assistance. The BNV assisted refugees and those fleeing the East German state and did so based on a law from August 22, 1950, that stated that "Germans from other lands" who were in states of emergency would be accepted in the Federal Republic (HA XX 18529, 25). In 1967 the agency wrote back that what "Mesut" was asking for was extremely difficult to achieve (HA XX 18529, 18). Indeed, it noted, only those considered unable to work and the elderly were granted the right to leave the GDR (HA XX 18529, 17). After the construction of the Berlin Wall, leaving the GDR was nearly impossible.

"Corinna" applied for and was granted a travel visa to Turkey supposedly to search for her fiancé there, though she never traveled to Turkey. It is odd that the state would grant this visa in the first place, demonstrating a curious labyrinth of both bureaucracy and reasoning. "Corinna" apparently somehow traveled to Vienna and then to Munich, legally, and on June 28, 1967, she obtained a residence permit for the family in Kreuzberg, West Berlin (HA XX 18529, 26). It took almost five years of wrangling for the couple to come together in West Berlin.

However, this story is no fairy tale. A statement in the file notes that someone overheard "Corinna" saying that once she was in the West, she would leave "Mesut" (HA XX 18529, 28). She had apparently fallen in love with a man she had met in a Pankow hospital in 1966, all the while waiting for permission to move to West Berlin with "Mesut" (HA XX 18529, 28). The witness also explained that "Corinna" and her family had ostensibly been economically exploiting "Mesut" for years (HA XX 18529, 28). Was he naive? Was "Corinna" trying to improve her image with her family by not admitting to being in love with this foreign man? In any case the couple began a messy divorce, in which custody of the son and possession of a Turkish rug were hotly debated. The Stasi concluded, however, that "Mesut" was the suspicious one, for having helped an East German citizen leave the country. It did not comment on "Corinna's" apparent exploitation of "Mesut."

The lines between intimacy and betrayal were often blurred. A Turkish man who worked unofficially for the Stasi, "Murat," reported on an East German woman whose address men crossing into East Berlin regularly gave as a destination on the entry visa for years until 1988 (HA II 27002, 1). When the Stasi questioned her about her relationships with foreign men, she curtly replied that she "just couldn't sleep with white men" (HA II 27002, 1). The Stasi reports indicate that she had a well-cared-for appearance and dressed primarily in Western clothing, obtained either from Intershop or from her "Western friends"—whom the Stasi identified primarily as "Arabs" who drove Mercedes (HA II 27002, 2). These border crossers' status as foreign, as "Eastern," and as cultural others apparently also played a role in how the Stasi perceived them. In short even men who had not broken any rules were dubious because of their intimate relationships, which were not necessarily illegal but nonetheless had great potential power to subvert the East German state.

Many East German women engaged in relationships with Turkish nationals also seized opportunities for personal gain. A case in point is a January 3, 1989, report from IM (*inoffizielle Mitarbeiterin*) "Ina," who noted that a woman who had contact with "Arabs" had filed for an exit visa to leave East Germany for West Berlin (HA II 27081, 4). Starting in the mid-1980s, East German citizens exploited the 1975 Helsinki Accords, which guaranteed freedom of movement. "Ina" reported that the woman in question had had extensive contact with "Turks and other foreigners," frequently meeting them in the popular Café Moskau on Karl-Marx Boulevard or the famous disco Lindencorso on Unter den Linden (HA II 27081, 5). The woman was suspected of prostitution and of taking advantage of her job at a travel agency on Alexander Square to provide customs declarations forms illegally. An earlier report notes that she was extremely interested in securing West German marks and would often use intimate relationships to do so. The Stasi watched her entire family, especially her parents, as a result of her actions but found that they had the correct political leanings (HA II 27081, 5). Since she lived with her parents, having men over was awkward. In the summer months, her parents would stay at their weekend cottage, which allowed her to have male visitors at home. This was a case not of romance but of financial transactions.

Border Crossers

Unlike their lives in West Berlin, which were dominated by low status at work, poor living arrangements in company dormitories, and a general suspicion and dislike of foreigners on the part of many West Berliners, East Berlin provided a place for these men to socialize freely. One Turkish man residing in West Berlin, Cahit, who eventually married his East Berlin girlfriend, noted in a 1995 interview: "We had heard that in the East there were a lot of women, and there really were. So the Turks were always there. We were young, so naturally it was normal that men needed women" (DOMiD "Cahit" 1995).[5] Cahit recalled: "The Western [West German] women didn't really want to have much to do with the Turkish men" (DOMiD "Cahit" 1995). Cahit's point about social exclusion in the West was genuine. For example, an archived photo of the front window of a Gelsenkirchen disco, taken in 1974, shows a handwritten sign that reads, *"Für Ausländer Zutritt VERBOTEN"* (Entry for foreigners is FORBIDDEN) (Eryılmaz and Jamin 1998, 310).[6] The sign's capitalization makes for an aggressive tone, and the sign itself is reminiscent of prewar signs forbidding the entry of Jews. Informal discrimination against guest workers in West Germany included refusal to rent to foreigners and exclusion from bars and clubs, and it escalated in the 1970s as German unemployment rose for the first time in the postwar era (Castles and Miller 2003, 215).

In contrast multiple files mention Turkish men eagerly crossing to dance for the evening with East Berlin women and girlfriends at Lindencorso or Café Moskau (HA II 28079, 10; 27962, 13; 27962, 50). The Stasi was less enthusiastic about the meetings, and it began to track and investigate the East Berlin women who met with foreign men. It was common for foreign crossers to provide a contact name and address, and often East Berlin women served this purpose, which placed many of them under suspicion with the Stasi—so much so that it often had notes in its files about these women's suitability for "unofficial collaboration" with the Stasi (HA II 27962, 42; 27962, 77). Considering that historians now report that men dominated the Stasi informant network (between 80 and 90 percent), accessing potential female informants was noteworthy (Gieseke 2001, 113). One woman was reported to have "frequently changing [foreign] male acquaintances," who would go home with her, have small parties there, and spend the night (HA II 27962, 28). Three different couples in her building were informing on her and her interactions with these foreign men (HA II 27962, 28). They reported, for example, that a man from West Berlin visited with his Mercedes and renovated her whole apartment, apparently bringing his own tools and materials (HA II 27962, 28). The woman later became engaged to a Bulgarian man, and when the Stasi questioned her about why Turkish men had given her address when they entered the GDR, she (dubiously) replied that a former female friend must have passed it on. Furthermore, she was pleased that the Stasi questioned her about it privately so that her fiancé would not learn about the Turkish men (HA II 27962, 49). Apparently, she had worked as a secretary for the Stasi and became alarmed when her relationship with a Turkish man had become known, so she implored him to provide various other addresses when he crossed the border; her file noted three different addresses. The report on her concludes with the point that she is "feminine and attractive" and a good potential candidate for "unofficial collaboration" with the Stasi (HA II 27962, 49). Her assignment would be to work at Café Moskau. It appears that her associations with the West Berlin Turkish men resulted in her (possibly coerced) decision to work for the Stasi. It is unclear what appeal the foreign men, especially the Turks, had for her—entertainment or material concerns. However, it is clear that her associations affected her standing with her neighbors and her state.

Turkish nationals went to East Berlin for myriad reasons: exploration, adventure, and perhaps a feeling of greater social freedom. After the guest-worker program officially ended in 1973, very little changed in the Stasi's tracking of Turkish nationals in the GDR. Indeed, the files continue through 1989. Regardless of the reasons stated in 1979, such as suspicions of drug smuggling, illicit political activities, and the sale of illegal passports, it seems that the Stasi deemed many of the men they tracked risky solely because of their contact with East German women. For example, the Stasi traced a Turkish man from Varto, in eastern Anatolia, for his encounters with four different East German women in 1979, as noted in a report titled "Summary of a Turkish Citizen Who Has Contact with Multiple GDR female Citizens" (HA II 29778, 7–8). The man apparently was reported on in the name of "political filtering activities," a Stasi term for surveillance at the border train stations. Even under the guise of political suspicion, the contact with East German women always made it to the fore of the reports. When asked about the differences between East and West Berlin, a Turkish man noted that the widespread xenophobia common in West Berlin was not prevalent in East Berlin (HA II 28209, 9). He was not just trying to appease an East German friend; his answer was most likely sincere, since he followed with negative comments on the East German state, saying that it was not, in his opinion, "the real socialism" (HA II 28209, 9). According to a report three years later, this same Turkish national planned to marry his East German girlfriend and hoped to move to East Berlin to live with her. He reasoned that he did not think that "as a Turk" he had good employment chances in West Berlin, expanding his comfort level in the East to the economic sphere (HA II 28209, 50).

Reinforcing his East-West comparison, the same man also commented that former East Berliners who had moved to West Berlin were having difficulties socially and felt "as discriminated against as did the Turks" (HA II 28209, 50). The report concluded with the foreign man apparently saying that in the East he had enjoyed "hospitality toward foreigners," even "as a Turk" (HA II 28209, 50). Indeed, an undercover agent noted in his report that this man had "known no form of xenophobia in the GDR," and with an odd undertone, the writer also deemed him to be "intelligent" and "trustworthy," with "clean" and "orderly" clothing (HA II 28209, 50). In other words it was a point of pride for the Stasi that these foreign workers, whom the West German state exploited economically, apparently found more social inclusion and economic freedom in East Berlin.

The Stasi tracked another Turkish national ostensibly for his participation in an extreme right-wing political group, the ultranationalist Gray Wolves (Bozkurtlar), yet his file concentrates mostly on his loose relationships with various East Berlin women (HA VIII 3506, 146). The officers noted that he had been involved in the "terrorist group" in West Berlin as well as in Turkey, and as a result a detail was assigned to him from October 22, 1985, through January 30, 1986. However, files on his activities in East Berlin mainly report that he was out for a good time, not engaged in political organizing. The man under suspicion, known in the file as "Number 279594" and also as the *Objekt* (target) lived with his wife in West Berlin, where he worked for the Ford Company (HA VIII 3506, 155). He was a thin man of around twenty to twenty-five years, with an olive complexion, dark hair, a mustache, and "straight and separated" eyebrows (HA VIII 3506, 155). The operative deemed his German to be "broken . . . foreign-speak" (HA VIII 3506, 155). During his frequent evenings out in East Berlin, he was in the company of women, including a woman given the cover name "Tunte" (HA VIII 3506, 155). "Tunte" was between eighteen and twenty-three years old, thin, blond, and blue-eyed, with full lips, a bit of a sunken chin that almost formed a double chin, and thin plucked eyebrows lined with black pencil (HA VIII 3506, 155).

A typical evening out for "Number 279594," as reported by the Stasi, occurred on November 22, 1985, when he acted more like a womanizer than a political radical (HA VIII 3506, 155). The Stasi tracked his every move, minute by minute, once he entered East Berlin at exactly 5:24 p.m. At exactly 6:01 p.m., "Number 279594" greeted "Tunte" with a hug and went home with her. He was wearing a black leather jacket, black-gray speckled pants, and loafers. About ninety minutes later they emerged from her home, with "Tunte" having changed her clothes from black pants to red pants and a black Adidas jacket. They first stopped at Café Moskau before continuing on to Lindencorso. The informant reports that the target no longer showed any interest in "Tunte" once they arrived in Lindencorso. He sought out "other female companionship," leaving "Tunte" at a table so that he could pick up women at the bar and then dance with them instead (HA VIII 3506, 155). Around 11:55 p.m., apparently "other foreigners" who were the target's acquaintances pointed out the late hour—it was quickly approaching the midnight deadline—and they all left at 12:01 a.m. for the Friedrich Street border crossing, entering it at exactly 12:08 a.m. (HA VIII 3506, 155). More than a month later, this Turkish man had a similar evening out, arriving in East Berlin at 7:27 p.m. and then hanging out at Lindencorso to drink champagne with other "foreign men" while "openly searching for female companionship" (HA VIII 3506, 159). The report's clinical tone adds an air of judgment to the target's free-spirited evening, leaving readers to wonder whether this man was really followed for his political activities or for his philandering.

These border crossings are significant from different vantage points: to East Berliners, these visitors not only were novel but also served as a conduit for hard-to-obtain goods. In contrast to most narratives of ethnic Turkish guest workers—which feature uneducated, Anatolian or rural, and devotedly Muslim men—these border crossers were constructed as "Westerners," not just with their West Berlin residence permits but also through their ready access to Western material goods and promiscuity. In many cases the

Stasi primarily worried that these Turkish nationals served as representatives of West Berlin, of Western consumerism and political ideologies, and of the Turkish Republic's alliance with the Western Bloc. Indeed, the history of material culture and consumerism in the Eastern Bloc is vast and draws on a wide range of sources; most socialist countries recognized both the spiritual alienation money creates and how poor material conditions contributed to their own demise (Bren and Neuburger 2012).

The categories in this chapter all involve a level of transgression—literally and figuratively—but this final section focuses specifically on the point of view of the state and its deep suspicion of foreign nationals who entered its territory and broke its rules. In many of the cases against Turkish men, the GDR invoked moral codes. Morality was indeed a Cold War weapon. The East German struggle to define not only new legal codes but also new social ones made morality a part of the revolutionary rebuilding of society (Poiger 2000; Evans 2003, 2005; Field 2007). According to Jennifer Evans decency mattered; "in East Germany, the struggle to define new social and legal maxims turned on the place that morality was to have in the revolutionary rebuilding of society" (2010, 554). For a case in point, in 1983 a Turkish man, Mr. Halil, who had come to West Germany to work at the Ford factory, was arrested in East Berlin for carrying a pornographic film and a pornographic keychain in the lining of his coat (HA II 27962, 57). Halil said in his defense that a friend had given them to him two weeks prior, and that he had carried them in his coat ever since, having apparently forgotten that they were there. While plausible Halil's explanation is not very believable; it is more likely that he was smuggling the pornographic goods into East Berlin to sell them for a profit and that he had been doing so once a week for thirteen years, from 1970 to 1983 (HA II 27962, 57). This case prompts the question of which aspect bothered the state more: the unwholesome nature of pornography or the underground economy. Despite its official morality, the East German state often used sex to sell its own ideas, most famously in its monthly *Das Magazin* (McLellan 2011, 49–65). *Das Magazin* specialized in racy stories and articles and was authorized to publish a nude photo in every issue, being

East Germany's official source of publicly available pornography (McLellan 2011, 49–65). Maintaining the state monopoly on pornography was not easy, but keeping up the pretense of state morality remained a priority.

Another form of transgression was Turkish nationals who worked with the Stasi, challenging the view that they were only the Stasi's targets. The relationships between the Stasi and the West Berlin–residing guest workers defied simple definitions. It is noteworthy as well that much of this information was gathered with the help of Turkish IMs reporting on their countrymen, calling into question loyalties on many levels. Many guest workers also sought to profit from their unique position as border crossers. In a few cases, marriages between Turkish guest workers and East Berlin women reportedly occurred for money. Reports in the files note Turkish men charging between 10,000 and 12,000 marks (and in one case up to 30,000 DM) to facilitate the smuggling of people out of East and into West Berlin through marriage (HA I 15176). In one case a border guard reported with exasperation that a Turkish man had been trying to befriend him and strike up a conversation with him whenever he crossed, wanting to know his address and offering him a pair of "real oriental slippers" from his homeland. It is hard to tell whether the Turkish man sought to befriend the border guard for a possible future benefit or simply out of cultural differences about appropriate familiarity. In another case extensive photographs demonstrated how a Turkish man rebuilt the inside of his car to hide a woman behind the dashboard and console; they were discovered and arrested in December 1973 (HA VI 441, 2-11). Another couple was discovered and arrested in 1979, and in 1987 an attempt to smuggle a man and a child out in the trunk of a Ford was also thwarted (HA I 15176, 1; HA VI 919, 14).

Foreign men also spoke informally with Stasi officials. Historian Gary Bruce (2008) has written that informal contacts, those the Stasi operatives sought for information but with whom they did not formalize the relationship into IMs, were integral to Stasi work (2008, 93–94). For example, Turkish *Kontaktpersonen* (contact persons, KP) were common in the files, as was the case with "Panther," who reported on another West Berlin–residing Turk who had bragged to him about dating the tall, blonde daughter of a manager of the border crossing at Friedrich Street and therefore presumably knew when the "strictest" controls would be (the Stasi found the report dubious) (HA II 24068, 3–4). The fact that there were cases of guest workers functioning in a wide variety of roles for the Stasi, whether as informal contact persons or as official IMs, implies that the East German state viewed these men as useful, necessary, and competent.

According to Bruce today the archived Stasi files are organized into four categories of people, and these categories shed light on the various ways people worked with the Stasi. The archives avoid the loaded terms *Opfer* and *Täter* ("victim" and "perpetrator") (HA II 2406893–94). As a result, the first category is the "affected," known in German as *Betroffene* to avoid the tricky term of *Opfer* (victim). The "affected" category refers to those monitored, arrested, or controlled in some way and is the category containing much of the information on the border crossers in this chapter. However, the people in this category do not tell the whole story. The second group is "third party," individuals on whom there was specific information in the Stasi files although they were not the targets of specific information-gathering operations. The third group is the "collaborators," which included both official and unofficial collaborators; and, the fourth group is "advantaged persons" whom the Stasi supported with material or career gain (93–94). Reliable figures on the numbers of IMs who were foreign nationals do not exist, but some information can be gleaned from the records. According to historian Jens Gieseke, in 1988, for example, there were 1,553 West German citizens working as IMs. Gieseke reports that non-German foreign nationals served in even smaller numbers, despite the fact that from the mid-1970s onward the total number of IMs remained between 170,000 and 180,000 (2005, 198–202).

Informants played such a large role in the everyday dealings of the Stasi that some historians have even debated whether the GDR could count as a "participatory dictatorship" (Fulbrook 2005). Motivations for working as an IM were often linked to fear and having been arrested, as in the case of Hidir Çiçek, who had come to West Germany from Istanbul in 1968 to work as a mechanic.

Even in an internal Stasi poll (with potential bias), up to 45 percent of IMs reported that "pressure and fear had played a role in their being recruited" (Fulbrook 2005, 203). Indeed, many of the Turkish guest workers who became unofficial coworkers of the Stasi did so after having been arrested and "turned," though scholars remain divided on the relative roles consent and coercion played (Müller-Enbergs, 2007; Bruce 2014, 52). The recruitment and roles of Turkish contact persons and unofficial workers were diverse; in August 1980 one West Berlin–living Turk sought to help the Stasi because he thought it might aid his attempt to marry his East Berlin girlfriend, for example (HA II 28872, 3).

The Stasi typically tasked the Turkish IMs with reporting on other Turks who had contacts and relationships with East Berliners. They were to investigate whether people were planning on leaving the GDR. Hidir Çiçek, who had come to West Germany from Istanbul in 1968 to work as a mechanic, became an IM after his arrest. Çiçek had often visited the East Berlin cafés Sofia and Pressecafe, where he got to know a woman from Königs Wusterhausen (AIM, file 8196/78, vol. 1, 23). After missing the midnight deadline for the third time, he was banned from entering the GDR with an *Einreisesperre* (entry ban). As a rule the East German authorities fined and banned Turkish nationals who missed the midnight deadline, including those who did so because of intoxication (in one case for being both drunk and barefoot) (HA II 28084, 5); those who spent the night illegally; and those who tried to smuggle unauthorized goods across the border (often scarves, perfume, and tobacco) (HA II 28084, 35). Desperate to return to East Berlin, Çiçek borrowed a friend's passport and forged the friend's name on the currency exchange form. His plan failed; he was arrested and sentenced to fourteen months in jail (AIM 8196/78, vol. 1, vol. VII/2, 149).

During his incarceration Çiçek reported on illegal drug smuggling, the transport of an East Berlin woman out of the GDR over the Czech border, the selling of Turkish passports, and his "close relationship" with the woman from Königs Wusterhausen (AIM 8196/78, vol. VII/2, 26). The files contain no information on his treatment in jail or his motivations for providing these details. He spoke with the officials in German, as they noted that he understood German and spoke "broken German" (AIM 8196/78, vol. VII/2, 74). At the time of his release to West Berlin, on November 23, 1971, Ciçek had agreed to work as an IM under the code name "Tanju Abisch" (AIM 8196/78, vol. VII/2, 62). Ciçek apparently "wished to protect the GDR from harm" and wanted to "support the Stasi" in its mission (AIM 8196/78, vol. VII/2, 62). The same memo also noted that he would have to be surveilled to see whether he could be trusted and counted on to provide truthful evidence (AIM 8196/78, vol. VII/2, 62). During his tenure as an IM, he continued to live in West Berlin and was to report on ethnic Turks and other foreigners living there, especially those who started relationships with East Berlin women. In a 1971 report, a Stasi operative noted that the GDR required "high quality unofficial work" to protect its borders because its opposition had a "global strategy" to "infiltrate the socialist states and undermine them from within" (AIM 8196/78, vol. VII/2, 62). In particular Ciçek was to work to thwart "attacks on the border" that originated in West Berlin and to draw on his contacts in West Berlin to learn of anyone seeking to help an East Berliner leave. On July 9, 1972, the *Berliner Zeitung* (an East Berlin paper) reported that Ciçek's place of employment in West Berlin planned to shut its plant by the end of the year—information that the Stasi included in his file, implying that he had little to compel him to stay in West Berlin (AIM 8196/78, vol. VII/2, 114).

It is hard to tell why Ciçek initially risked arrest by trying to cross the border with a borrowed passport and what his true motivations for becoming an informant were: Was he so determined to get back to his East German girlfriend? Was he really dissatisfied enough with the capitalist systems in his life to turn to espionage work? Did the prospect of unemployment frighten him? Did he feel so threatened by his imprisonment in East Germany that he felt he had no alternative? We can only guess at definitive conclusions, but we can assume that Ciçek and many more like him had become quotidian parts of the suspicious, permeable border landscape of the divided city.

Other Turkish men flouted or tried to skirt the border laws of the East German state, often resulting in their arrest. If emigration through marriage was not possible, some Turkish nationals attempted to sneak their girlfriends out of the GDR illegally (HA II 27838, 2). "Georg," a contact person, reported that a Turkish national, who was no longer allowed into the GDR because of previously overstaying a visa, planned to smuggle out his East German girlfriend, her three children, and an unknown acquaintance (plus the acquaintance's wife and two children) who had lost his job because of applying to leave the GDR (HA II 27838, 3). The extraordinary plan was to build a balloon to fly everyone out, and an East German citizen had implored "Georg" to bring books from West Berlin on how to construct such a balloon (HA II 27838, 3). It was of immediate significance to find out more about these acquaintances who had grand plans of escape, so a separate IM, "Mehmet," who was noted as being Turkish Kurdish, was assigned to the case (HA II 27838, 28,29).

The family who had hoped to escape via a balloon is a significant case for multiple reasons. They were already under suspicion in 1982 for their involvement in illegal trade union organizing at work in East Berlin and, especially, for their connections with the famous and historically significant Polish trade union Solidarity just across the border (HA II 27838, 16). The Stasi was also suspicious of the family because of their connections with "imperialist countries" seen in their application to leave the GDR. Last, the Stasi watched the family due to the fact that their daughter's boyfriend was a West Berlin–residing Turk. Indeed, the files note that the family's "contact with foreigners" should be closely monitored. Significantly, three different Turkish nationals— the boyfriend in West Berlin and the informants "Georg" and "Mehmet"—were working on different sides of the Iron Curtain in n historically significant moment of rising dissent. Their seemingly personal histories overlapped with the larger themes of the Cold War—dissent, deception, and political maneuvers.

The relative ease with which West Berlin–residing Turkish nationals could maintain relationships with East Germans was fraught with political implications and irony. The surprising conclusion that this chapter's stories suggest is that—despite the Stasi's attention and the distrust they faced in West German society—these men were able to satisfy the most ordinary of human desires for connection, personal gain, and fulfillment and to operate in the two societies in a remarkably diverse and contradictory range of ways. Unexpectedly, even though they lived on the margins of West Berlin and West German society, these men represented Western consumer culture for East Berliners; despite their limitations of language, employment status, and social standing, they epitomized the successes of Western capitalism. It is also ironic that behind the Iron Curtain they gained increased social liberty, demonstrated with their successes with East German women.

Writ large these examples highlight unique but important actions of minorities in Europe, show how integration can occur, and comment on Cold War interactions between the two Germanys. Border crossers both exemplify and complicate the Cold War climate—one of division, suspicion, and espionage. These stories also highlight constructions of gender in this period: Were East Berlin women informants? What role did controlling their morality and sex lives play in state decisions? Did they risk their standing with the state and with their families for relationships with foreign men? Were their relationships with foreign men a form of escapism or protest? Could their view of the state and their opinion of its ideas be gauged from their choices in their personal lives?

Many Turkish nationals who traveled to East Berlin invested in new lives and families there that spanned decades. In the Stasi files, they were, for the most part, a monolithic group of "foreigners" whose status was not decided by work visas, the guest-worker program, applications, or relationships with West Germans in any way. The workers in these peculiar cases had no intention of leaving when the program officially ended in 1973 or of having merely a temporary stay in Germany—West or East. Their personal relationships complement policy documents on immigration, citizenship, and labor laws in important ways by providing a view from the margins that changes our understanding of Cold War history as a whole. Private relationships between Turkish citizens living in West Berlin and East German citizens continued well into the 1980s, demonstrating a participation and investment in a life—a personal one—in Germany.

Notes

1. Unless otherwise noted all translations are mine.

2. Communist countries had large debts to the World Bank, the IMF, and private bankers for hard currency with which to purchase consumer goods they needed and that their citizens would buy. Historian Tony Judt notes that by its last years the GDR admitted to spending over 60 per cent of its annual income on interest on Western loans (2005, 582).

3. Important early work empathetically exposed guest workers' miserable conditions, though such depictions have also effaced complex human experiences. See, among others, Berger and Mohr 1975; Steinen 1985; Gunter Wallraff 1985; Fassbinder 1974; Aladağ 2010. For important studies on xenophobia in East Germany, see Zatlin 2007b.

4. I have chosen these two pseudonyms to ease reading this couple's narrative. In the files their names are completely redacted.

5. Cahit was one of several men whom the Documentation Center and Museum of Migration to Germany interviewed and whose interview is now housed in their archives in Cologne, Germany. DOMiD Interview 15, Berlin, August 30, 1995.

6. Photo by Manfred Vollmer, Essen in Eryılmaz and Jamin 1998, 310.

References

ARCHIVAL SOURCES

BStU (Bundesbeauftragter für die Unterlagen des Staatssicherheitsdienstes der ehemaligen Deutschen Demokratischen Republik [Federal Commissioner for the Records of the State Security Service of the Former German Democratic Republic]), Archive der Zentralstelle (Central Archive). 67/846.
——. mfs, AIM, file 8196/78 1/1.
——. mfs, AIM, file 8196/78 1/2.
——. mfs, AIM, file 8196/78 1/3.
——. mfs, AS 9/73.
——. mfs, GH, file 73/78.
——. mfs, HA I, file 15176.
——. mfs, HA II, files 22858; 24068; 27002; 27081; 27084; 27442; 27575; 27836; 27837; 27838; 27962; 28079; 28084; 28209; 28872; 29717; 29668; 29778; 40416.
——. mfs, HA VI, files 441; 919.
——. mfs, HA VIII, file 3506.
——. mfs, HA XX, files 10221; 18529.
——. mfs, Sekr. Mittig: 63.
——. mfs, Sekr. Neiber: 225.
——. mfs, ZAIG, file 11129.
——. mfs, ZKG, file 286.
——. mfs, ZKG, file 11540.

Aladağ, Feo, dir. 2010. *Die Fremde*. Feature film. ARTE, Independent Artists Filmproduktion, RBB, WDR.

Alisch, Steffen. 2000. "Berlin-Berlin: Die Verhandlungen zwischen Beauftragten des Berliner Senats und Vertretern der DDR-Regierung zu Reise- und humanitären Fragen: 1961–1972." FU Berlin, Arbeitspapiere des Forschungsverbundes SED-Staat, 3:34.

Berger, John, and Jenn Mohr. 1975. *A Seventh Man: Migrant Workers in Europe*. New York: Viking.

Bren, Paula, and Mary Neuburger, eds. 2012. *Communism Unwrapped: Consumption in Cold War Eastern Europe*. Oxford: Oxford University Press.

Bruce, Gary. 2008. "Access to Secret Police Files, Justice, and Vetting in East Germany since 1989." *German Politics and Society* 26 (1): 82–111.

———. 2014. "Participatory Repression? Reflections on Popular Involvement with the *Stasi*." *Bulletin of the German Historical Institute* 59:47–58.

Castles, Stephen, and Mark Miller. 2003. *The Age of Migration: International Population Movements in the Modern World*. 3rd ed. New York: Guilford Press.

Delius, Friedrich Christian, and Peter Joachim Lapp. 1999. *Transit Westberlin: Erlebnisse im Zwischenraum*. Berlin: Links.

Dennis, Mike, and Norman LaPorte. 2011. *State and Minorities in Communist East Germany*. New York: Berghahn.

Eckert, Astrid M. 2001. "Zaun-Gäste: Die innerdeutsche Grenze als Touristenattraktion." In *Grenzziehungen, Grenzerfahrungen, Grenzüberschreitungen: Die innerdeutsche Grenze, 1945–1990*, edited by Thomas Schwark, Detlef Schmeichen-Ackermann, and Carl-Hans Hauptmeyer, 243–51. Darmstadt: Wissenschaftliche Buchgesellschaft.

Eryılmaz, Aytaç, and Mathilde Jamin, eds. 1998. *Fremd Heimat—Yaban, Sılan olur: Eine Geschichte die Einwanderung aus der Türkei—Türkiye'den Almanya'ya Göçün Tarihi*. Essen: Klartext.

Evans, Jennifer V. 2003. "*Bahnhof* Boys: Policing Male Prostitution in Post-Nazi Berlin." *Journal of the History of Sexuality* 12 (4): 605–36.

———. 2005. "The Moral State: Men, Mining, and Masculinity in the Early GDR." *German History* 23 (3): 355–70.

———. 2010. "Decriminalization, Seduction, and 'Unnatural Desire' in East Germany." *Feminist Studies* 36 (3): 553–77.

Fassbinder, Rainer Werner, dir. 1974. *Angst essen Seele auf*. Feature film. Munich: Tango-Film.

Field, Deborah A. 2007. *Private Life and Communist Morality in Khrushchev's Russia*. New York: Peter Lang.

Fulbrook, Mary. 2005. *The People's State: East German Society from Honecker to Hitler*. New Haven CT: Yale University Press.

Gieseke, Jens. 2001. *Der Mielke-Konzern: Die Geschichte der Stasi*. Stuttgart: Deutsche Verlags-Anstalt.

———. 2005. "German Democratic Republic." In *A Handbook of the Communist Security Apparatus in East Central Europe, 1944–1989*, edited by Krysztof Persak and Lukasz Kaminski, 198–202. Warsaw: Institute of National Remembrance.

———. 2006. *The GDR State Security: Shield and Sword of the Party*. Translated by Mary Carlene Forszt. Berlin: BStU.

Göktürk, Deniz, David Gramling, and Anton Kaes. 2007. *Germany in Transit: Nation and Migration, 1955–2005*. Berkeley: University of California Press.

Henrich, Wolfgang. 1983. *Wehrdienstgesetz und Grenzgesetz der DDR: Dokumentation und Analyse*. Bonn: Urheber.

Hertle, Hans-Hermann. 2011. *The Berlin Wall Story: Biography of a Monument*. Berlin: Links.

Huinink, Johannes. 1995. "Individuum und Gesellschaft in der DDR—Theoretische Ausgangspunkte einer Rekonstruktion der DDR-Gesellschaft in den Lebensläufen ihrer Bürgers." In *Kollektiv und Eigensinn: Lebensläufe in der DDR und Danach*, edited by Johannes Huinink, Karl Ulrich Meyer, Martin Diewald, and Heike Solga, 25–44. Berlin: Akademie Verlag.

Judt, Tony. 2005. *Postwar: A History of Europe since 1945*. New York: Penguin.

Kurthen, Herman, Werner Bergmann, and Rainer Erb, eds. 1997. *Antisemitism and Xenophobia in Germany after Unification*. New York: Oxford University Press.

Lindenberger, Thomas. 1999. *Herrschaft und Eigen-Sinn in der Diktatur: Studien zur Gesellschaftsgeschichte der DDR*. Cologne: Böhlau.

Lüdtke, Alf. 1994. *Alltagskultur, Subjektivität und Geschichte: Zur Theorie und Praxis von Alltagsgeschichte*. Münster: Westfälisches Dampfboot.

Mandel, Ruth. 2008. *Cosmopolitan Anxieties: Turkish Challenges to Citizenship and Belonging in Germany*. Durham NC: Duke University Press.

McLellan, Josie. 2011. "'Even under Socialism, We Don't Want to Do without Love': East German Erotica." *Bulletin of the German Historical Institute* S7:49–65.

Merkel, Ina. 2001. "Sex and Gender in the Divided Germany: Approaches to History from a Cultural Point of View." In *The Divided Past: Rewriting Post-War German History*, edited by Christoph Klessmann, 91–104. New York: Oxford University Press.

Milewski, Nadja. 2010. *Fertility of Immigrants: A Two-Generational Approach in Germany*. Heidelberg: Springer.

Miller, Jennifer A. 2018. *Turkish Guest Workers in Germany: Hidden Lives and Contested Borders*. Toronto: Toronto University Press.

Müller-Enbergs, Helmut. 2007. *Inoffizielle Mitarbeiter des Ministeriums für Staatssicherheit*. Part 3, *Statistiken*. Berlin: Links.

Mushaben, Joyce Marie. 2008. *The Changing Faces of Citizenship: Integration and Mobilization among Ethnic Minorities in Germany*. New York: Berghahn Books.

Poiger, Uta G. 2000. *Jazz, Rock, and Rebels: Cold War Politics and American Culture in a Divided Germany*. Berkeley: University of California Press.

Richthofen, Esther von. 2009. *Bringing Culture to the Masses: Control, Compromise, and Participation in the* GDR. New York: Berghahn.

Steinen, Inga. 1985. *Leben zwischen zwei Welten*. Köln: Kiepenheuer & Witsch.

Wallraft, Günter. 1985. *Ganz Unten*. Köln: Kiepenheuer & Witsch.

Zatlin, Jonathan, R. 2007a. *The Currency of Socialism: Money and Political Culture in East Germany*. Cambridge: Cambridge University Press & GHI.

———. 2007b. "Scarcity and Resentment: Economic Sources of Xenophobia in the GDR, 1971-1989." *Central European History* 40:683-720.

7 Fleeing to the West

The 1978 Airplane Hijacking from Gdansk to West Berlin

AXEL HILDEBRANDT

In August 1978 two East German citizens, Hans Detlef Alexander Tiede and Ingrid Ruske, together with Ruske's young daughter, Sabine, planned to escape to the West by taking a ferry from Poland to West Germany with forged West German passports. They were assisted by Horst Fischer, Ruske's West German partner, who attempted to deliver these travel documents to Poland. As the Stasi (the East German secret service) had learned about the escape plan well in advance, officers arrested Fischer on the East German–Polish border, and an East German court later convicted him. In order to prevent their arrest, the East Germans Tiede and Ruske changed their plan and instead of taking a ferry, they hijacked a Polish plane heading to East Berlin, forcing the pilot to land in West Berlin. Upon their arrival U.S. Military Police arrested them at the Tempelhof airport, but they received a lenient sentence handed down by an American judge who took over the trial proceedings.

This Cold War story involving both an illegal escape and a hijacking was the subject of intense media reporting, and speculation, on both sides of the wall at the time. In the ensuing twenty-five years, our understanding of what was surely one of the more spectacular spy stories of the era has been enriched by various versions of the events: eyewitness accounts, most notably by the presiding judge at the trial, the declassified Stasi files, and more recently a fictional television film *Westflug—Entführung aus Liebe* (Flying west—

hijacking out of love; Jauch 2010) and a novel *Tupolew 134* (2004) by Antje Rávic Strubel. All these sources contribute unique and varied perspectives on the incident. When read comparatively, their various accounts provide a rich, multiperspectival description of the incident. They can, moreover, aid our appreciation of what these different sources—rather than mere sources they are narratives in their own right—can tell us about the past and how they do so. For instance a key source about the hijacking are the personal memories of the presiding American federal judge Herbert J. Stern, who wrote about it in his memoir *Judgment in Berlin* (1984). Published five years after the trial, Stern's book provides an eyewitness, legal perspective that forms an interesting complement to the many journalistic accounts of the incident. It presents, moreover, a personal, non-German perspective on the event that is framed by Cold War ideologies of the eighties. Far less well known are the various accounts captured in the Stasi archives (BStU). The Stasi files are one of the most detailed sources of information about the hijacking and offer a comprehensive but ideologically charged backstory to the event. They document the hijackers' backgrounds, the occurrences prior to the hijacking, the course of action during the hostage taking and hijacking of the Polish airliner, and the Stasi's investigations and findings after the fact.[1] The files on each of the individuals involved (among other things) offer specific insights into the different participating agencies and individuals: the hijackers, Ingrid Ruske's West German boyfriend Horst Fischer, the airplane crew, and the passengers. The files also document the results of the Stasi's surveillance and investigations starting with Tiede's denied application to leave East Berlin for the West in December 1976 (AOP 9816/82, vol. 3, 159) and ending with a general amnesty that included Ruske in November 1987 (HDAT/IR 3263/88, vol. 11, 525).

Of the two fictional accounts, the most interesting for the present study is Strubel's *Tupolew 134*.[2] Strubel's novel departs from the historical narrative and fictionalizes this spy story, thereby connecting the historical events with discourses about memory, truth, and the effects of politics on disenfranchised East German citizens. As I will show in this chapter, Strubel's fictional protagonists and their recollections contribute to a multilayered literary discussion of this incident that also engages with the varying interpretations of this event in Cold War history.

In what follows I discuss one instance of each type of account of the event—the Stasi archival sources, eyewitness memory in Stern's *Judgment in Berlin*, and Strubel's postunification fictional interpretation. The first two of these belong to "factual" or referential types of texts, and the third is an example of historical fiction. In my analysis of the Stasi files, I read them as hybrid narrative forms that "appear to straddle the divide between fact and fiction" (Lewis, Glajar, and Petrescu 2016, 9). The files were a "finely calibrated" "technology of power" (Lewis 2003, 388) compiled by the Stasi to police the population. They contain detailed "hostile biographies" (Lewis 2003, 383) about citizens suspected of illegal activity, which we can use to compose "file stories" (Glajar 2016, 57). In reading memory sources, I follow Aleida Assmann in treating personal memories as complex interactions between individual and collective frames of experience (Assmann and Frevert 1999, 50). In accordance with Dorrit Cohn's distinction between referential genres and historical fiction (1999, 121, 153), I finally examine why a fictional account such as Strubel's novel is not bound to an accurate representation of events and deviates from facts to provide an alternative, fictional history.

The Planning and Flight as Reported in the Stasi Files

The Stasi began to collect information on Ruske and Fischer in December 1976 and continued with its investigation for several years after the flight of Ruske and Tiede took place. The sustained Stasi surveillance appears to have been an attempt to discover whether friends and family members were implicated in the planning or to ascertain the views on the event of all people involved. The collected information stems from different Stasi divisions, such as Hauptabteilung VI (border traffic), IX (investigation), XIX (traffic), and PS (personal protection). Some of the files include reports by informants (*inoffizielle Mitarbeiter*, IMs) and contact persons (*Kontaktpersonen*, KPs) whose motivations are not always clear. According to their accounts, the Stasi case officers

(*Führungsoffiziere*) had to demonstrate that the surveilled subjects were planning to commit a crime, which in this case was *Republikflucht*, or "ungesetzlicher Grenzübertritt," paragraph 213 of the Criminal Code (StGB). The Stasi files contain much duplication of information, which was the inevitable result of the Stasi's method of continuously adding intelligence to the file in order to gain a comprehensive picture of the people involved in the hijacking and their activities. For that purpose the Stasi compiled an expansive profile of the hijackers. The surveillance report "Fähre" (Ferry) contains information on all persons involved, other compilations include sizable files on Hans Detlef Alexander Tiede, interrogation reports and court documents pertaining to Horst Fischer, and collections of newspaper reports from East and West Germany.

As the Stasi files detail thoroughly, Ingrid Ruske was born in Berlin in 1944 and grew up in East Germany, where she went to school. She did not attend university and worked as a waitress in restaurants and bars for most of her life. In December 1976 she met the West German engineer Horst Fischer in East Berlin in Café Moskau, where she was working at the time (AOP 9816/82, vol. 1, 216). Fischer worked occasionally in the GDR and, despite being married, began a relationship with Ruske. After some time and more seriously in 1978, they began concocting a plan for Ruske and her eight-year-old daughter, Sabine, to flee to the West. They considered hiding in the trunk of a car or in the cargo area of a truck to escape across the border, but Ruske rejected these plans as too dangerous. She feared that in the probable case that East German border guards found and arrested her, she would have likely spent years in prison before being bought free by the West German government. Her daughter would have had to live in a foster home, and Ruske could probably have lost custody of her child.

Ruske and Fischer assumed correctly that the Stasi was surveilling them—which was cause for extra caution—but they were not aware of the full extent of knowledge the Stasi had about their relationship. According to their files, the Stasi already knew about the relationship and flight plans in April 1977, over a year before Ruske actually attempted to leave East Germany (AOP 9816/82, vol. 1, 216-42). Although the documents show that the Stasi had collected sufficient information to arrest Fischer and Ruske, at that time the Stasi officers decided not to arrest them, presumably preferring to catch them in the act and thus ensure a harsher sentence.

The most realistic and apparently least dangerous plan was for Ruske and her daughter to travel to Poland and take a ferry from Gdansk to Travemünde in West Germany. For that purpose the two needed West German travel documents. Horst Fischer asked a female acquaintance in West Berlin, whose appearance resembled Ruske's, to apply for temporary ID documents and submit Ruske's passport pictures instead of her own. She agreed and Fischer paid her 300 DM for her help (HF 21217/80, vol. 1, 391).

Furthermore, Ruske and Fischer decided to reveal their plans to a friend of Ruske's because they needed someone to travel to Poland first in order to assess the risk at the border. This coconspirator was Hans Detlef Alexander Tiede, who was Ruske's coworker and also wanted to escape to the West. Tiede had applied several times to leave East Germany to be able to see his child, who lived with his divorced Polish wife in West Berlin, but the GDR authorities had either rejected or ignored his applications. In order to get travel documents for Tiede, Fischer stole a passport out of the desk of a West German colleague whose physical appearance somewhat resembled Tiede's (HF 21217/80, vol. 1, 231–35). Tiede was supposed to attempt an East German–Polish border crossing with this document before Ruske and her daughter followed to find out whether he would raise any suspicions (AOP 9816/82, vol. 2, 201). An important part of the plan was to learn how to forge the Polish entrance stamp in the passport to prevent complications when leaving Poland by ferry. To that end Fischer went to Hamburg to buy rubber materials to make a stamp, and later, when he took the train to Poland, he hid them in the sole of his shoe (AOP 9816/82, vol. 2, 126–32). He also inquired which ink color the border guards used and purchased numerous felt pens to emulate the color as closely as possible. These preparations, which are all documented in the Stasi files, underscore how meticulous their plans were and how closely the Stasi monitored their every move using informants and contact persons in East Germany. Fischer was therefore in danger of being arrested if Ruske, her daughter,

Sabine, and Tiede went ahead with the escape (AOP 9816/82, vol. 1, 31–35). As the Stasi files document, these risks were real, and even Ruske's and Tiede's family members, who remained in East Germany and were not part of the planning, faced serious consequences. Ruske's brother, for example, was not able to find employment in the GDR due to his sister's flight to the West (AOP 9816/82, vol. 1, 312–17).

According to the Stasi files, Fischer planned to take the Paris-Leningrad express train from West Berlin to Gdansk and was supposed to meet Ruske, her daughter, and Tiede at the train station in Gdansk. However, Fischer never arrived at the meeting place because the Stasi had arrested him upon his arrival at the East German–Polish border (AOP 9816/82, vol. 2, 74). The Stasi found the ferry tickets from Gdansk to Travemünde, the forged travel documents, felt pens, and rubber material for making stamps that Fischer had hidden in the sole of his shoe. Besides these items the Stasi also collected documents for Ruske's poodle that Fischer had obtained from a West Berlin veterinarian and carried with him (HF 21217/80, vol. 1, 290, 389–405). Although not all the information the Stasi received from informants and contact persons was accurate, it was sufficient for the border authorities to arrest Fischer. There was, however, one crucial piece of misinformation, which was the incorrectly reported date of the attempted flight, which might have contributed to the failure to arrest Ruske and Tiede (AOP 9816/82, vol.1, 31–32).

Since Fischer did not arrive at their meeting place in Gdansk, Ruske and Tiede correctly presumed that something had gone wrong and feared the Stasi would arrest them as soon as they returned to East Germany. However, they were not aware that the Stasi and the Polish secret service, Ministerstwo Spraw Wewnętrznych (MSW), had been cooperating the entire time and that the Poles had monitored their activities in Gdansk (AP 9648/80, 7). It is remarkable that the Polish authorities did not arrest them, for by planning to flee to West Germany, they had already violated paragraph 213 (3) of the January 12, 1968, GDR Criminal Code (StGB). The Polish authorities likely assumed that after Fischer's arrest there was no alternative for them except to return to East

Germany, where the Stasi awaited them. Before Fischer's arrest the Stasi officers alerted their Polish counterparts that the four people were planning to take a ferry to escape to the West, which explains the Stasi's code name for the entire operation as "Fähre" (Ferry). Yet the Stasi did not know from which town they wanted to depart, and it entrusted the Polish secret service with their arrest before they could board a ferry in Gdansk. Since Ruske and Tiede had met a Swedish woman who was in possession of a Polish consular passport at an unspecified place in Poland, the Polish secret service also suspected that they might try to take a ferry to Sweden or Finland (AP 9648/80, 10).

Ruske and Tiede abandoned the idea of taking a ferry to West Germany and considered flying instead. To avoid attracting suspicion, Ruske had bought round-trip airline tickets from East Berlin to Gdansk for her daughter and herself. The return flight was on August 30, 1978, the planned date for the hijacking. Upon arrival in Poland, Ruske and Tiede decided to sell several personal items to have enough money to buy a ticket for Tiede as well, which enabled him to take the same return flight to East Berlin. Additionally, they were able to purchase a pistol at a market in Poland, even though hijacking a plane was not part of the original plan. After the hijacking this pistol was in the possession of the American prosecution as evidence in West Berlin, which is why the Stasi never had the opportunity to see the weapon, and the East German investigators later speculated whether it was a gas pistol or perhaps a toy gun (HA XIX 4985, 7). Stern, however, clarifies in his memoir that it was an eighty-year-old "Mondial" starter pistol, which had been used in the past at sports events but from a distance apparently looked real (1984, 282).

On the day of the hijacking, Ruske's daughter carried the pistol in her luggage, and the Polish security officer, recognizing that it was not a real weapon, let her take it on board the airplane in her carry-on item. Even at this late point, the Polish secret service did not arrest the three at the Gdansk airport, most likely assuming that getting off the plane in Berlin-Schönefeld was the only option and their East German counterparts could arrest them there. This proved to be a serious misperception. After takeoff Tiede drank some alcohol and then took the starter pistol and walked toward the cockpit. He yanked one of the flight attendants by her hair and threatened to shoot her if the pilots refused to land at Tempelhof airport in West Berlin. According to Stasi records, the pilot and the navigation officer attempted to get a better look at the weapon. Later, during their interrogation, the pilot and the navigating officer claimed that in order not to further escalate the tense situation, they abandoned the initial plan to disarm the hijacker Tiede although he was acting aggressively and refused to leave the cockpit. When the flight mechanic tried to get close to Tiede, he made threatening gestures and claimed that he would shoot the flight attendant. Hence the members of the crew did not attempt to disarm him again (HDAT/IR 3263/88, vol. 10, 80–87, 95–99).[3]

The Stasi files contain the complete transcript of the conversation between the commanding officer of the airplane, Ryszard Lukomski, and the East German air-traffic controllers (HA VI 1574, 88–89). Lukomski informed the air-traffic controllers that Tiede was unwilling to negotiate, had threatened to shoot a flight attendant, and demanded that they land at Tempelhof. East German authorities at first tried to buy time, but Lukomski underscored the urgency of the situation by saying: "My terrorist does not want to wait" (HA VI 1574, 89).[4] At this point the East German air-traffic controllers permitted the airplane captain to contact their Western counterparts to negotiate a landing in West Berlin, which was eventually granted. The plane was allowed to enter West Berlin air space and to land in Tempelhof, where U.S. military personnel ordered Tiede to give up the pistol, which he did, before they arrested him. Neither the hijackers nor the police used violence, which stands in stark contrast to the hijacking of a Lufthansa plane by Palestinians a year earlier and might partially explain the relatively lenient sentence in this case.

The U.S. Military Police then asked all other passengers to leave the plane and strongly encouraged all East German citizens on the plane to consider staying permanently in the West. For Cold War propaganda purposes, the Americans were very keen on persuading the East German passengers to stay in the West. In fact they did not allow the passengers to return right away but instead took them on a long sightseeing bus tour through West Berlin to show them how attractive living in the West would be (AP 9648/80, 29). This attempt to introduce them to the West was superfluous, however, since most East Germans were able to access illicitly West German TV and radio stations and were already familiar with life on the other side of the wall. Despite the Americans' efforts, only six out of sixty-two passengers decided to stay in West Berlin, and the East German government later tried actively to persuade the six to return. For this purpose the Stasi questioned their neighbors and coworkers to determine what might motivate them to come back to East Germany. The Stasi even permitted one woman's father to travel to West Berlin to convince his daughter to return (see Laske 2008).

After the sightseeing tour, the passengers willing to return to the GDR arrived by bus at the Schönefeld airport, where East German officials were expecting them. Upon their arrival in East Berlin, reporters interviewed and photographed the passengers. The Stasi then questioned and released them after all passengers provided handwritten reports with their recollections of the hijacking. Some passengers identified how near or far they had sat in relation to the pilot's cabin; their position on the plane explains discrepancies and omissions in their descriptions, particularly those who sat farther back and did not notice much of the hijacking. However, some passengers who were closer to the cockpit provided comprehensive accounts of Tiede's actions (HDAT 3263/88, vol. 10, 120–27).

Diplomacy and Tiede's and Ruske's Trial in West Berlin

The hijacking of this Polish airplane by East Germans caused major diplomatic and judicial problems in the West. This was in part because it occurred one year after the so-called German Autumn of 1977, when four Palestinians hijacked the airliner *Landshut* on its way from Palma de Mallorca to Frankfurt/Main. The hijackers wanted to force the government of Chancellor Helmut Schmidt to release leading Red Army Faction (RAF) members who were incarcerated in Stammheim prison. These hijackers used real pistols, hand grenades, and explosives and even shot the pilot in Mogadishu, Somalia, before West German GSG 9 special forces freed the hostages and killed three of the four hijackers.

After the *Landshut* hijacking, both Eastern and Western Bloc countries signed a treaty that stipulated that hijackers be returned to their native countries and prosecuted harshly to deter future attempts. Countries that failed to comply with this treaty would be excluded from the international flight system. Thus the governments of the GDR and Poland, and the Soviet ambassador to the GDR, Piotr Abrassimov, demanded in 1978 that Tiede and Ruske along with her daughter be extradited to East Germany (AP 9648/80, 32). Chancellor Schmidt faced a quandary. On the one hand, he could ill afford not to adhere to the treaty and not send Tiede and Ruske back to the East, especially since his government claimed to be taking a tough stand on terrorism. On the other hand, West Germany had a long track record of accepting East German refugees, or *Übersiedler*, and under different circumstances it would have welcomed Tiede and Ruske with open arms. To circumvent this dilemma, the West German government asked the United States to take the lead in dealing with the hijackers because the Americans were technically still an occupying force. The U.S. Department of State agreed to take over the proceedings by installing a U.S. court in West Berlin. Such a court had not existed before this hijacking, and the West German government agreed to pay all costs of the trial, even though the Americans would be prosecuting East Germans (Stern 1984, 31).

The American judge Herbert J. Stern addresses the historic context of the hijacking and trial in his memoir, although his is not the only account of the trial, since the Stasi gathered information about it as well, some through the West German media but also by gathering court documents that illustrate the complicated situation. In this context the confrontation between East and West Germany extended to the GDR's Eastern allies as well. As mentioned above, the East German and Polish secret service agencies had cooperated to observe Tiede and Ruske and to arrest Fischer. During the West Berlin trial, according to Stern, it transpired that Polish state officials attempted to influence the statements of the Polish airplane crew to achieve a more severe sentence for Tiede (1984, 273–

75). Stern, however, claimed that throughout the trial, it became evident that there had been no real danger to passengers and crew, despite the fact that Polish government officials had instructed the airplane personnel to overstate the threat (1984, 259). According to the West German defense lawyers, Tiede had shown the crew pictures of his children, had a smoke with them, and engaged in casual conversations in Polish (Stern 1984, 266–79).

Stern, who had come to West Berlin from Newark, New Jersey, describes the trial thoroughly in his book *Judgment in Berlin*. His memoir adds a distinct American legal perspective to the events. As specified in court documents, the prosecution accused the defendant Tiede of severe crimes, including the hijacking of an aircraft, taking of hostages, deprivation of liberty, physical mis-treatment of another, and carrying of a pistol without a license.[5] These charges were serious and comparable, as mentioned above, to those of the *Landshut* hijacking one year earlier. The U.S. Department of State and Walter J. Stoessel Jr., the U.S. ambas-sador to West Germany, attempted to put pressure on the newly appointed Stern, demanding a harsh sentence to comply with the new international treaty to punish airplane hijackers severely. This reaction was partially a response to demands from Poland and the GDR through their proxy, the Soviet Union (Stern 1984, 190). Stern, for his part, was concerned about what he consid-ered undue influence from the U.S. Department of State. Accord-ing to him such demands would have deprived the defendants of any basic judicial rights due to the special status of the Amer-icans as an occupying force in their sector of Berlin after World War II (1984, 44). To prevent a potentially unjust trial, Stern came up with a highly unconventional solution: he decided to install an U.S.-style jury that consisted of West Berlin citizens, even though Germany had abolished the jury system in 1924 (Moritz 1987, 28).[6] Instead of following the German model with a judge, a prosecu-tor, and a defender, at this trial not only did a jury of West Berlin citizens decide the case, but the accused East German Tiede also had a West German and an American defense lawyer (Stern 1984, 119). The hijacker Tiede furthermore hoped to be able to stay in the West and possibly also expected to become famous for his actions. After the trial according to conversations Tiede had with his mother, whose phone was tapped by the Stasi, he had tried to sell the story rights to the media (AOP 9816/82, vol. 5, 131–38).

The outcome of the trial provoked controversy in both East and West. Ruske did not face serious charges because she had not been directly involved in the hijacking. She and her daughter had stayed in their seats in the airplane during the incident, and neither had carried any real weapons. Ruske had also not threatened the crew or other passengers and was also not offered a public defender after leaving the airplane. This Cold War story culminated in her acquittal and a very light sentence of nine months for Tiede, for having taken hostages only. Because Tiede had been required to stay at the airport throughout the nine-month-long trial, which counted as time served, he was permitted to leave the airport immediately after his sentence was passed (Stern 1984, 370). Typically, the minimum sentence for hijacking an airplane was three years. For this reason both the East German and the Polish television and print media reacted harshly. Reporters described Tiede's sentence as too lenient and Ruske's acquittal as a provocation to the GDR, declaring the U.S. court to be an accomplice of the hijackers (HA IX 3910, 110).

The Stasi diligently collected West German newspaper articles about the trial (HA IX 3910, 100). West German publications that were sympathetic to the East German perspective, such as *Wahrheit*, the newspaper of the Sozialistische Einheitspartei Westberlins (Socialist Unity Party of West Berlin), followed the eastern Communist line of argumentation. Those newspapers and magazines that were not allied with East Germany focused mainly on the fact that it was a highly unusual procedure for the court and an attempt to prevent a case that could set a precedent for prosecuting potential future hijackings (HA IX 3910, 101–2, 105).

In East Germany plans for an official reaction to the trial began shortly before the sentencing, which makes it likely that the authorities were prepared for the verdict and not particularly surprised by it (ZAIG 11454, 367–69). In retaliation for the lenient sentence, the East German media released private details about Tiede and Ruske. For example the GDR media described Tiede as an "antisocial alcoholic" and Ruske as "promiscuous" and also supplied other sordid details about their personal lives in East Germany (HA IX 3910, 110). In the West the press focused on attempting to prevent this case from setting a legal precedent for future hijackings that might lead to lenient sentences. It is quite apparent that Cold War propaganda played a role on both sides, both in the Stasi files and in the West and East German media. The Stasi's collection of articles about the case includes, for example, one published in the West German *Berliner Morgenpost* on May 31, 1979, that had appeared right next to short articles about alleged child labor and food shortages in East Germany, which exemplifies the Cold War tensions that existed at the time (HA IX 3910, 105). This compilation of articles emphasizes the differing interpretations of this Cold War event by the media in general, and this particular incident became part of the larger confrontation between the East and the West that was fought not only in court.

Fischer's Tale in East Berlin

The legal and political responses of the East to the outcome of the Ruske and Tiede trials came just one day after the end of the trial against Tiede in West Berlin. Fischer, Ruske's West German boyfriend, was sentenced to eight years in prison in East Germany for participating in organized crime and forging official travel documents (AOP 9816/82, vol. 2, 453). This harsh sentence was apparently a direct response to the lenient outcome of the trial in West Berlin. However, Fischer only served about one year in prison before he was pardoned and allowed to return to West Berlin. There is no evidence in Fischer's Stasi file or in media reports about his case revealing whether the West German government, as it had done in many cases, paid to have him released before the end of his sentence or if other considerations played a role (HF 21217/80, vol. 7, 184).

Before Fischer's trial started, he was interrogated for several months, and he asked repeatedly to see employees of the West German consulate because his health was declining rapidly in jail (HF 21217/80, vol. 7, 45). Yet the influence of the West German government and diplomats on his case before and during the trial was marginal at best because they were not in regular contact with Fischer (HF 21217/80, vol. 6, f4). The Stasi files demonstrate not only the lack of support from the West German government but also the secret service's concrete interrogation plan that included questions to ask Fischer and anticipated potential responses. Apparently, the strategy of the Stasi to repeatedly ask the same questions worked to some extent because Fischer revealed after several interrogations the names of people who had not been involved in the planning of Ruske's and Tiede's flight but were acquaintances the Stasi was not aware of before (HF 21217/80, vol. 2, 555–56). The Stasi was also interested in Fischer's political activities and connections after it learned that he had been a member of the Christian Democratic Union (CDU) and active at the local level in the 1970s, even though, according to his statements, he had not played a significant role in it and was no longer an active member (AOP 9816/82, 224).

Although numerous interrogations revealed the entire escape plan of his friends, it appears as if Fischer tried to avoid pulling unrelated people into the plot. He mentioned almost exclusively people who were already in the West, such as Tiede and Ruske, and just few of their friends of whom the Stasi was not already aware. Stasi officers tried to catch Fischer's attempts to reveal as little as possible by asking him repeatedly to clarify or complete his previous statements at the beginning of several interrogations. Apparently, the officers tried to learn more about some people or events in order to fill existing gaps and thereby solidify their knowledge of the events preceding the hijacking. Whenever the officers suspected that Fischer was concealing information, they told him during the interrogations that they did not believe his statements or asked the exact same question on subsequent days, expecting Fischer to contradict himself (HF 21217/80, vol. 1, 271–74).

Because Fischer had been arrested before the hijacking took place and had no access to media reports while in jail, he had no concrete knowledge about the hijacking of the Polish airliner. When the Stasi questioned him about it, he stated that he would have never agreed to it had he known about Tiede's plans. The Stasi files contain a personal statement by Fischer to this effect, in which he also wrote that he considered the hijacking an act of terrorism and an appalling crime, stating that he could never live with "such a person who could have committed such a crime," obviously referring to Ruske (HF 21217/80, vol. 1, 566). The files do not reveal whether Fischer was coerced into writing this statement, but one might assume that he hoped for a more lenient sentence by doing so.

As stated above Fischer's trial in East Berlin began right after Ruske's and Tiede's trial ended in West Berlin in 1979, and the West German government asked for permission to have observers in the courtroom (HF 21217/80, vol. 6, 4). Fischer's defense lawyer was the well-known East German Wolfgang Vogel, who was also under contract with the West German government and defended thousands of East Germans who were incarcerated in the GDR. Vogel secured their release, and West Germany paid the East German government for allowing them to move to the West (Wölbern 2014, 130). After Fischer was sentenced to eight years in prison, Vogel appealed the verdict (HF 21217/80, vol. 6, 69–72), but the court denied the request (HF 21217/80, vol. 6, 78). Fischer wrote to the West German consulate stating that he hoped for an appeal in cassation because he considered his trial a perversion of the course of justice and his sentence a deterrent rather than a fair punishment (HF 21217/80, vol. 7, 45). This letter never reached the West German consulate. It remained instead in Fischer's Stasi file, including a note from a Stasi officer declaring that the content of the letter was hostile toward East Germany and that the accusation about the trial was not justified because, as per this note, unjust trials did not exist in the GDR (HF 21217/80, vol. 7, 42). Fischer was pardoned on September 17, 1980, and allowed to return to West Germany on October 2, 1980 (HF 21217/80, vol. 7, 184). Contrary to the statement that he had written in jail rejecting Ruske for her criminal actions, after his release Fischer moved into an apartment with Ruske in West Berlin and married her soon thereafter.

Despite Ruske's exculpation in West Berlin, the East German prosecution continued to investigate her until she was granted amnesty on November 4, 1987 (IR 3263/88, vol. 11, 525). The Stasi also surveilled Ruske while she lived in West Berlin and even obtained a sketch of her apartment to gain a more complete understanding of her living situation (AOP 9816/82, vol. 1, 273). In East Berlin the Stasi tapped her family's phone to get more information on Ruske. The wiretapped phone conversations allowed the Stasi to learn about Ruske's living conditions in the West and her opinions about East Germany. One transcription points out, for example, that Ruske called the GDR "the largest ghetto." Ruske also stressed that she would never return, regardless of how bad her life in the West might become (AOP 9816/82, vol. 4, 307).

In 2010 Ruske, who still lives in the western part of Berlin, gave an interview to the magazine *Der Spiegel* in which she sounded dispassionate. Ruske declared that her former life in East Berlin had been happier than her life in the West; this is presumably partially due to the fact that she had left her family and friends behind. Whether Ruske really had been more content in East Berlin and held this opinion the entire time she lived in the West is doubtful. Not only did she go through with her plan to leave the East, but in conversations after the flight, as mentioned above, she called the GDR a "ghetto" to which she would never consider returning.

Strubel's Literary Adaptation of the Hijacking of LOT 165

In her novel *Tupolew 134*, Strubel contributes to the narratives of this hijacking by introducing the investigation of a fictitious journalist who attempts to reconstruct the events decades later. Her novel is a hybrid escape and spy story that presents a complex tale of an illegal attempt to leave East Germany and the subsequent surveillance of the Stasi to prevent the escape. It offers a literary perspective on the East German society, based on a selection of historical and memory sources. The narrative revolves around the question of how the airplane hijacking can illuminate the larger picture of life in East Germany in the 1970s and how Strubel's portrayal of East and West German history over a time span of three decades fits into Cold War history.

Strubel consulted various media sources, as the news media reported widely on the hijacking and trial, in both East and West Germany after the event. For example the novel begins with a quote from a *Spiegel* article published on May 21, 1979.[7] Strubel also drew on eyewitnesses' recollections of the event, most notably that of Stern. In fact Strubel has stated that she first learned about the airplane hijacking of Polish Airlines flight LOT 165 through Stern's book.[8] Strubel relied on Stern's memoir for information about the planning, hijacking, and trial, all of which serve as points of departure in her attempt to highlight the interaction between historic events and the (un)reliability of memory.

The female protagonist Katja Siems, who resembles Ingrid Ruske, works in a large truck factory in Ludwigsfelde, south of Berlin, where she gets to know the West German engineer Hans Meerkopf, the literary equivalent of Horst Fischer, who has business dealings with a branch of his company in East Germany. Unlike Ruske Siems does not have a daughter, but like Ruske she begins a relationship with Meerkopf, which leads her to consider fleeing to the West to be with him. As in the real case, Meerkopf does not arrive at their arranged meeting point in Poland to deliver the West German travel documents. Lutz Schaper, who represents Tiede, and Siems presume that he has most likely been taken into custody by the East German or Polish authorities. While the Stasi is informed about their plan, readers do not learn whether the Stasi learned about the flight attempt on its own through informants or if acquaintances might have known the plan and betrayed the coconspirators to the secret service. In the novel Strubel suggests that Siems's friend Verona may have denounced Meerkopf to the East German secret service because she knew that the Stasi was spying on Siems. It is also likely that Siems's companion, Schaper, might have reported Meerkopf to the East German authorities (2004, 30–32). These insinuations demonstrate real and persistent suspicions and mistrust toward friends, family members, and colleagues in East German society. Although surveillance was expected in Strubel's novel, it does not play a central role. The author chooses to focus instead on the monotonous life in East Germany at the time of the escape and the protagonists' recollections many years later.

As in the actual hijacking, Schaper and Siems follow through on their amateurish plan to hijack a Polish airplane and use an eighty-year-old blank-cartridge pistol. But in the novel, the flight attendants and the pilot instruct Schaper on how to successfully hijack the plane so that the crew can land at the West Berlin airport Tempelhof instead of at Schönefeld in East Berlin (Strubel 2004, 141–47). The hijacking is not described as a particularly dramatic act, emphasizing the notion that Schaper was not a violent and aggressive person, which resonates to some degree with Judge Stern's recollections in his memoir—a source that, as mentioned above, Strubel had consulted.

In contrast to the bureaucratic account of the Stasi files, the novel introduces each chapter with one of the spatial levels "*oben*" (up), designating events taking place in 2003, "*unten*" (down), describing the period of the flight 1978–79 and "*ganz unten*" (far down), depicting the time prior to 1978, as well as the term *Schacht* (manhole, pit) which connects the three other levels and depicted memories. Strubel also introduces a narrative frame projected twenty-five years after the escape took place. This narrative voice tries to bring to light the seemingly historically impenetrable situation by means of the conversations with the young journalist who tries to reconstruct the occurrences around the hijacking after German unification. Strubel's novel exemplifies that history and memory are an open and ongoing process and that fiction writers do not have to offer historical accuracy in terms of time, place, and character. By the form of narration she uses, Strubel emphasizes that memories are not necessarily linear, and the novel cannot provide a complete description of the events. Strubel's narrative style provides overlapping versions of the hijacking event but does not favor any of the protagonists' recollections. This rather fragmented depiction resembles the production of collective memories that are often shaped by the news media to discuss and alter personal and collective memories (Erll 2005, 251).

Strubel emphasizes early in her text how unreliable personal memories are when Siems meets with a young journalist in 2003 who is unfamiliar with living conditions in the GDR and who had wanted to write about the hijacking twenty-five years earlier. Siems invites the journalist to consider different versions of past events in the course of their conversations and encourages her to switch seamlessly between them at any time. Siems reminds the journalist to trust neither Siems's memories nor those of other eyewitnesses with whom she intends to speak. Not only does she consider their memories unreliable, but she also asserts that the protagonists themselves still do not completely understand what happened: "They go up and down and very far down and up, and on each floor stand those who don't know where to go. They stare from all three levels of time. They guard memory. The future is a root that springs from memory. You should not trust me. You might feel betrayed in your pursuit of truth / Truth" (Strubel 2004, 12–13). The novel does not reveal an absolute truth but rather expresses the complicated relationship between history and memory. The author downplays the value of truth demonstratively in her fictional work and favors ambiguous forms of cultural memories (Assmann and Frevert 1999, 50).

Metahistorical texts question the linearity of history and show the construction of memory, identity, and history through the literary structure itself (Nünning 1999, 28–29). By using this self-reflexive structure in *Tupolew 134*, which calls into question the retroactive construction of meaning, Strubel is able to show multiple perspectives on the events, both temporal and spatial. As her text focuses on before, during, and after the hijacking of LOT 165 and the spatial levels mentioned above, it allows for various interpretations of the events that question the official GDR version of this hijacking. On the other hand, readers might also question the intentions of the fictional West German who offers Siems a means to a less restricted existence, although Siems concisely and rather dispassionately expresses her views on life in East Germany: "I don't enjoy living like this anymore" (Strubel 2004, 36, 85). The protagonist's statement seems to express general resentment, rather than grievances referring to political suppression or lack of freedom to travel, as one would expect in a novel on the GDR.[9]

By avoiding overly strong binary differences between East and West, Strubel shows a new and creative way to write about the German past (Norman 2012, 69). As her text does not favor Siems's perspective over those of other characters, Strubel goes beyond Paul Cooke's notion of "writing back," which describes the way many East German authors purportedly respond to the West German majority discourse by insisting on a distinct East German identity after German unification (2005, 14). The author does not simply deny differences between East and West German society; instead, she emphasizes that even if people share similar experiences, one cannot presume that they will share the same interpretation of past events, as is the case of the hijacking event. It is therefore difficult to determine why some past occurrences become part of this collective memory and other, equally important events do not (Kansteiner 2002, 192). Strubel's novel addresses the East and West German justice systems and the recording and processing of memories from the 1970s to the present by underscoring the "constructedness" of history and presenting the formation of and relationship between collective and cultural memory. This turns out to be an effective and creative approach to dealing with and writing about the German past as well as to critiquing discourses on the formation of memories on a personal and societal level that does not rely on Stasi archival files.

The Stasi files describing the hijacking of LOT 165, Stern's memoir, and Strubel's novel allow detailed multifaceted insights into the life of East German citizens, as well as the oppressive surveillance they had to endure during the Cold War. All these accounts of the escape and hijacking story illustrate the degree of difficulty and danger East Germans faced when trying to emigrate to the West—whether through legal or illegal means. The Stasi files and media reports included in this discussion of German history as background for the novel *Tupolew 134* underscore how easily people could be branded as disloyal and treated as potential enemies of the state if they attempted to leave. The state perceived opinions that differed from the official doctrine as opposition to the government, as they betrayed the ideals of a socialist society that one was expected to consider more just than any other existing system. There was but little space for public debate or difference of opinion. The opportunities for freedom of speech and travel significantly decreased after the Berlin Wall was built in 1961. Furthermore, the presence of the Stasi emphasized the mistrust of the East German government toward its citizens. In the case of Ruske, Fischer, and Tiede, the Stasi collected an immense amount of data, processed it, and had it readily available should the opportunity arise. Yet looking back at all those resources employed in the scrutiny of this event and of East German citizens in general, the Stasi appears to be part of the failure of an oppressive regime that could not fulfill the needs of its own citizens. Instead of allowing open debate and the freedom to travel, the East German government established an extensive surveillance system to create intimidation and suspicion. The constant concern that the Stasi might spy on individuals' everyday activities undermined the coherence of East German society. This partially explains why the Stasi became a prominent target for East German citizens who demonstrated against the government and its institutions in the fall of 1989, and it is remarkable that the formerly powerful Stasi was disbanded without significant resistance within a few months in early 1990.

Notes

1. This chapter is part of a larger study on the surveillance the Stasi conducted on this airplane hijacking.

2. For other depictions of this event, see also Leo Penn's feature film *Judgment in Berlin* (1988).

3. The commanding officer Lukomski stated after the hijacking: "After crossing the border, the flight mechanic approached me to inform me that we had a hijacker on board who held the stewardess at gunpoint and demanded to land in West Berlin. The hijacker threatened that if this demand were not met, he would shoot the stewardess. After receiving this information, I gave the flight mechanic a sign with my hand to move because he blocked my view of the kitchen area and then I saw Ewa Przybysz sitting on the floor. Above her stood a man who had grabbed her hair with one hand; in the other hand I noticed a metal object that was pointed at her head.... In this situation I made a hand gesture that he should come to the cockpit in order to see what kind of weapon the hijacker had and [I] also considered disarming him, but he shook his head to let me know that he would not move" (HDAT/IR 3263/88, vol. 10, 82–83). All translations from German to English are mine.

4. Later, during the interrogation, Lukomski no longer used the term "terrorist" and described Tiede as a hijacker.

5. Complete copies of Tiede's and Ruske's American arrest warrants and complaints for violation are included in the Stasi files (HA IX 3910, 37–39).

6. Stern later mentioned that it would have been ironic if a Jewish American judge like himself, whose family had been forced to flee Germany in the 1930s, had treated defendants more than thirty years after the end of World War II not unlike the Nazi judicial system did during the Third Reich (1984, 95–96). On the thirtieth anniversary of the hijacking in 2008, *Deutsche Welle* inter-

viewed Stern about his recollections and role in the trial. During this interview he expressed his strong discontent with the circumstances of the trial and compared the defendants' situation to that of prisoners in Guantanamo after September 11, 2001 (Fong 2008).

7. See, for example, "Hören und sehen" 1979.

8. The author revealed this information during a discussion I had with her at the Women in German Conference in Shawnee, Pennsylvania, October 27, 2012.

9. Strubel stated in an interview that Siems's desire to leave East Germany in the novel is less motivated by a lack of freedom but rather is due to her monotonous experience of everyday life there (Strubel in Lorenzen 2005).

References

ARCHIVAL SOURCES

BStU, MfS, AOP 9816/82, 5 vols. (Referenced as AOP.)

BStU, MfS, AP 9648/80. (Referenced as AP.)

BStU, MfS, AU 3263/88, 11 vols. (Referenced as HDAT/IR.)

BStU, MfS, AU 21217/80, 7 vols. (Referenced as HF.)

BStU, MfS, HA VI 1574. (Referenced as HA VI.)

BStU, MfS, HA IX 3910. (Referenced as HA IX.)

BStU, MfS, HA XIX 4985. (Referenced as HA XIX.)

BStU, MfS, ZAIG 2859. (Referenced as ZAIG.)

PUBLISHED SOURCES

Assmann, Aleida, and Ute Frevert. 1999. *Geschichtsvergessenheit—Geschichtsversessenheit: Vom Umgang mit deutschen Vergangenheiten nach 1945*. Stuttgart: Deutsche Verlags-Anstalt.

Cohn, Dorrit. 1999. *The Distinction of Fiction*. Baltimore: Johns Hopkins University Press.

Cooke, Paul. 2005. *Representing East Germany since Unification: From Colonization to Nostalgia*. Oxford: Berg.

Erll, Astrid. 2005. "Literatur als Medium des kollektiven Gedächtnisses." In *Gedächtniskonzepte der Literaturwissenschaft: Theoretische Grundlegung und Anwendungsperspektiven*, edited by Ansgar Nünning and Astrid Erll, 249–76. Berlin: Walter de Gruyter.

Fong, Diana. 2008. "U.S. Judge: Berlin Plane Hijack Trial Had Parallels to Guantanamo." Interview with Herbert J. Stern, *Deutsche Welle*, August 30. http://www.dw.com/en/us-judge-berlin-plane-hijack-trial-had-parallels-to-guantanamo/a-3587971.

Glajar, Valentina. 2016. "'You'll Never Make a Spy Out of Me': The File Story of 'Fink Susanne.'" In *Secret Police Files from the Eastern Bloc: Between Surveillance and Life Writing*, edited by Valentina Glajar, Alison Lewis, and Corina L. Petrescu, 56–83. Rochester NY: Camden House, 2016.

"Hören und sehen." 1979. *Der Spiegel*, May 21, 124–26.

Jauch, Thomas, dir. 2010. *Westflug—Entführung aus Liebe*. Television film. H&V Entertainment GmbH.

Kansteiner, Wulf. 2002. "Finding Meaning in Memory: A Methodological Critique of Collective Memory Studies." *History and Theory* 41 (May): 179-97.

Laske, Karsten. 2008. "Ausflug nach drüben." *Freitag*, August 8. https://www .freitag.de/autoren/der-freitag/ausflug-nach-druben.

Lewis, Alison. 2003. "Reading and Writing the Stasi File: On the Uses and Abuses of the File as (Auto)Biography." *German Life and Letters* 56 (4): 377-97.

Lewis, Alison, Valentina Glajar, and Corina L. Petrescu. 2016. Introduction to *Secret Police Files from the Eastern Bloc: Between Surveillance and Life Writing*, edited by Valentina Glajar, Alison Lewis, and Corina L. Petrescu, 1-25. Rochester NY: Camden House.

Lorenzen, Max. 2005. "Wahrheit lässt sich nun mal nicht beweisen: Nur die Lügen lassen sich nachweisen." Interview with Antje Rávic Strubel, *Marburger Forum: Beiträge zur geistigen Situation der Gegenwart*, no. 1. http://www.philosophia-online.de/mafo/heft2005-1/Strubel.htm.

Moritz, Klaus. 1987. *Das französische Arbeitsgericht*. Berlin: Duncker & Humblot.

Norman, Beret. 2012. "Strubel's Ambiguities of Identity." *Women in German Yearbook* 28:65-80.

Nünning, Ansgar. 1999. "Beyond the Great Story: Der postmoderne historische Roman als Medium revisionistischer Geschichtsdarstellung, kultureller Erinnerung und metahistorischer Reflexion." *Anglia* 117 (1): 15-48.

Penn, Leo, dir. 1988. *Judgment in Berlin*. Feature film. New Line Cinema.

Stern, Herbert J. 1984. *Judgment in Berlin*. New York: Universe Books.

Strubel, Antje Rávic. 2004. *Tupolew 134*. Munich: C. H. Beck.

Wölbern, Jan Philipp. 2014. *Der Häftlingsfreikauf aus der DDR 1962/63–1989: Zwischen Menschenhandel und humanitären Aktionen*. Göttingen: Vandenhoeck & Ruprecht.

IV

Spies on Screen

8 Espionage and the Cold War in DEFA Films

Double Agents in *For Eyes Only* and *Chiffriert an Chef—Ausfall Nr. 5*

CAROL ANNE COSTABILE-HEMING

The Cold War is typically defined as the political power struggle between the two nuclear superpowers, the Soviet Union and the United States, from the end of World War II until the fall of the Berlin Wall in 1989. Both countries sought to gain territory and hence influence over other nations and convert those nations to their own political ideology, be it communist or capitalist. One of the most hotly contested territories was the geographic epicenter of Europe, the crossroads dividing the Warsaw Pact countries from the NATO nations, East and West Germany. Following the founding of the Federal Republic of Germany (FRG) and the German Democratic Republic (GDR) in May and October 1949, respectively, the two countries formed the border of the Iron Curtain. It should come as no surprise then that security agencies such as the CIA, the KGB, the West German Bundesnachrichtendienst (BND, Federal Intelligence Service), and the East German Ministerium für Staatssicherheit (Mfs or Stasi, Ministry for State Security) found divided Germany to be fertile ground for surveillance and (counter)intelligence activities. Given their geopolitical role, the two nations and most especially divided Berlin also became natural settings for films about the Cold War, an appeal that has continued, as the success of Stephen Spielberg's 2015 blockbuster film, *Bridge of Spies*, confirms. It is therefore also not surprising that espionage had high cinematic currency, given the dense concentration of spies in divided Berlin; the CIA for instance had some 8,000 agents stationed in Dahlem, a number that doubled following the June 17, 1953, uprising in the GDR (Schweitzer 2015, 250). Though official information regarding the number of Soviet KGB officers is not readily available, one source indicates that there were some 350 staff officers in Karlshorst between 1947 and 1962 ("Berlin Operations" 2015).

In this chapter I focus on the spy film genre in the GDR, analyzing the representation of double agents in two East German films, *For Eyes Only—streng geheim* (Veiczi 1963) and *Chiffriert an Chef—Ausfall Nr. 5* (Coded message for the boss; Dziuba 1979). Produced by the state-owned film studio, the Deutsche Film-Aktiengesellschaft (DEFA), both films depict the period shortly before the construction of the Berlin Wall in 1961, a time of heightened tensions between East and West, one in which agents and double agents played a pivotal role. Using stereotypical portrayals of Western military and intelligence officials and drawing on state-supported propaganda, both films present the West, in particular the United States, as a threat to the security of the GDR. By publicizing and politicizing this threat via feature films, the ruling Socialist Unity Party (SED) in the GDR presented its populace with believable justifications for the construction of the Berlin Wall. Despite the fifteen years that separate the films' premieres, both films stake out the construction of the Berlin Wall as a significant milestone in protecting the East German capital not just as a barrier against the influence of Western provocateurs but also as a pivotal tool in protecting the GDR from invasion by Western powers.

For Eyes Only premiered on July 19, 1963, in the East Berlin Kosmos theater.[1] Directed by János Veiczi (1924–87) and a product of the "Solidarity" artistic production group at DEFA, it was the most popular of DEFA's spy films. The main character, Hansen, is an agent employed by the Stasi to infiltrate the U.S. Military Intelligence Division (MID) in West Germany. While the Americans believe he is a defector, he actually is tasked by the GDR with stealing classified military intelligence documents from the United States that point to a NATO plot to invade the GDR. Set in July 1961, the film is loosely based on the theft of U.S. military documents by the Stasi agent Horst Hesse in 1956 (Böhm 2016).[2]

Directed by Helmut Dziuba, *Chiffriert an Chef—Ausfall Nr. 5* premiered on November 11, 1979, and is often compared to *For Eyes Only*.[3] The main character, electronic engineering student Wolf Brandin, is recruited by the CIA specifically to decode messages from the GDR and the Soviets. He notifies the Stasi, and his interrogator and later supervisor, Werner, convinced of his loyalty to the GDR, encourages him to accept the CIA's offer, thus marking the beginning of his life as a double agent. In the end Brandin double-crosses the CIA, preventing the West from learning about the East's plans to build the Berlin Wall.[4]

During the Cold War, both the East and the West used feature films as a medium especially suited to transmitting specific (and stereotypical) images of both allies and enemies. The images that the films conveyed corresponded closely to widely held beliefs among the viewers. The state intentionally created belief systems, which feature films were then supposed to support and help maintain. According to historian Bernd Stöver, "Enemy portrayals in films are especially effective when they are compatible with established belief systems, corroborate and expand on existing information transmitted in other media, and simultaneously deliver 'proof' of 'truth'" (2006, 50).[5] Espionage films in particular play a unique role in substantiating these belief systems, for they operate within the simple binary of good versus evil and prey on audience emotions with themes of loyalty, betrayal, patriotism, and xenophobia.[6] Sabine Hake describes the Cold War cinematic topography as one of "demarcation, exclusion, and containment" (2005, 159). The United States' position during the Cold War focused on a policy of liberation—the goal was to free the Eastern Bloc countries from the control of the Soviet Union. The GDR's leaders viewed this liberation policy as a constant threat to the GDR, and Cold War DEFA films played on these fears (Stöver 2006, 51).[7] By combining facts and truth with the characteristics of feature films, these Cold War–era films gained a documentary air, resulting in a high level of believability among viewers that the events were real or at least plausible. To think of it in Hake's terms, the GDR espionage films were tasked with clearly marking the rival, while working to exclude and contain the enemy.[8] Moreover, like James Bond films, these films take contemporary concerns into account, which makes their fictional world more believable (Begg 2016, 33). To this end characterization is key: the East German spies' successes are portrayed as victories that, at least temporarily, appear to resolve political conflicts. Moreover, the reliance on exaggerated stereotypes typecasts the Western characters as unscrupulous and immoral, playing to widely held misperceptions of West Germans as Nazis and U.S. military forces as warmongers. In contrast Stasi agents and the East German double agents appear as morally upright citizens whose espionage activity supports the GDR fledgling state. In both films the double agents successfully foil the West's attempts to invade the GDR, and the agents are rewarded for their efforts with the restoration of a routine family life. One can argue that much like James Bond films, these feature films portray a "nationalist fantasy," whereby the sovereignty of the East German nation and its superior intelligence system are brought to the forefront.[9] My analysis shows that *For Eyes Only* purposefully calls attention to a perceived real threat to the GDR from the West. *Chiffriert an Chef* looks back at the late 1950s and early 1960s, reminding viewers that threats from the West were deterred by the building of the Wall. In both instances the dramatization of these threats captivates audiences by appealing to their sense of fear, further rationalizing the importance and effectiveness of the Berlin Wall. Because the film appeared just two years after its construction, audiences watching *For Eyes Only* could leave the theater feeling secure that the wall would protect them, even though it is never directly mentioned. Premiering some eighteen years after the construction of the wall, *Chiffriert an Chef* touts the wall as a success by looking back at the threats that were commonplace in the late 1950s and early 1960s. The film thus reminds audiences of the wall's ability to prevent attacks, which in turn, means that audiences remain willing to accept its existence. It was intended to serve as propagandistic support for Leonid Brezhnev's recently announced peace initiative (Habel 2017, 135). The film focuses intently on character development, where Brandin is depicted not as a superhero but as an ordinary citizen willing to assume responsibility and protect his society.[10] More than just nostalgia, the portrayal of Brandin's agent handler as benevolent depicts the Stasi in a positive light, deflecting the resentment of the people toward the Stasi, which had become further heightened following the expatriation of the controversial and dissident singer-songwriter Wolf Biermann in 1976.

The agenda of East German espionage films was firmly rooted in the very mission of film in East German society. When DEFA was founded, Sergei Tulpanov, the director of the Propaganda Administration for the Soviet Military Administration in the Soviet Occupied Zone, emphasized the important role the film studio was to play in the creation of a new socialist society: "The DEFA film studio has to tackle important tasks. . . . Film as mass art must be a sharp and powerful weapon against reaction and for the deeply developing democracy, against war and militarism and for peace and amity among peoples of the world" (Schittly 2002, 27). Initially, in the immediate postwar years until 1949, DEFA films focused on a single enemy: the Nazi as criminal (Mückenberger 1993, 49). By 1950 the approach broadened to include the Western Allies as villains. Kurt Maetzig's *Der Rat der Götter* (Council of the gods, 1950), based on material from the Nuremberg trials, was the first DEFA film to feature "crass and negative portrayals" of Americans, a trend that continued for many years thereafter (Mückenberger 1993, 51). According to Hake anti-American portrayals were common in "contemporary dramas that focus[ed] on the reorganization of public and private life, the changing relationship between work and leisure, the emergence of new forms of association and community, and the gradual transformation of cultural tastes and preferences in accordance with an emerging socialist culture" (2005, 150). The SED tightly controlled film and print media, underscoring the media's role in legitimizing the messages that the government transmitted. Especially in the beginning, film and other media "were supposed to convince, in other words, explain the approved political direction of the time, deliver educated arguments to convince the masses, but also clearly define the enemy" (Stöver 2006, 52). The creation and perpetuation of the enemy image of the West was of primary importance and served as the central theme of the political propaganda depicted in early feature films.

Not surprisingly the Stasi was involved in every aspect of film production in the GDR (Schittly 2002, 295). Dagmar Schittly describes the Stasi's influence as "massive": "On the one hand, in direct decision making and thus preparing the party's cultural policy and, on the other, using unofficial operatives, who took care of the flow of information and also interfered and helped determine procedures" (2002, 306). As a result very few productions dared to portray the Stasi on screen; for those films that did contain depictions of its agents, the Stasi worked together with DEFA openly in order to provide advice. Indeed, in the case of *For Eyes Only*, the Stasi's press office sent a booklet titled "Flight through the Night: A Factual Report about the Mysterious Disappearance of Two Safes from the American Secret Service," which related the story of Horst Hesse's double-crossing of the United States (Scholz 2008). The best-known portrayal of the Stasi was the television series *Das unsichtbare Visier* (The invisible gun sight), which ran from 1973 until 1979.[11] It was created by DEFA to counter the underground popularity of James Bond (Rogers 2015). The show's success is often attributed to the main character, Werner Bredebusch, played by Armin Müller-Stahl until December 1976, when Müller-Stahl fell out of favor for signing the petition against Wolf Biermann's expatriation.[12] The best-known filmic portrayals of the Stasi, Heiner Carow's *Verfehlung* (Transgression, 1991) and Frank Beyer's *Der Verdacht* (The suspicion, 1991), were not made until after the fall of the wall and the end of the GDR and represent some of the last films by DEFA, which was dissolved in 1992 (Brockmann 2010, 232). Most portrayals of the Stasi in film and television focused exclusively on foreign espionage, a tactic designed to reinforce among the populace the need for an espionage organization (Löser 2016). The focus on foreign threats represents a one-sided portrayal of the Stasi, for that perspective ignores the Stasi's extensive surveillance of its own citizens, most egregiously following the expatriation of Biermann.[13] Reading *Chiffriert an Chef* in the context of the aftermath of this November 1976 decision, however, can be fruitful for understanding the perceptual divide that existed between ordinary citizens and the state security apparatus.

Commonly referred to as the GDR's most famous spy movie (Berghahn 2005, 41), *For Eyes Only* is loosely based on real events from 1956, when the Stasi sent Horst Hesse and Hans Wax, the "real" double agents, to infiltrate U.S. military installations, and they succeeded in stealing safes from the U.S. Military Intelligence Division in Würzburg in what was known as Aktion Schlag (Action Strike).[14] The safes contained classified documents, the personnel files of 137 U.S. spies stationed in the GDR (Scherer 2006, 224). Because of this information, the East Germans were able to arrest the Western agents, who were viewed as a danger to the country's stability (Mittmann 2002, 81). The East exploited the success of this mission as a means to document the domestic strength of the MFS and to promote the agency's value to the general public (Mittmann 2002, 81). The East German state viewed the capture of the agents as a major step toward thwarting the West's liberation attempts.

For Eyes Only was produced six years after the Hesse incident. Thus, its debut occurred at a highly critical period of the Cold War, following the construction of the Berlin Wall, and a year after the Cuban missile crisis, an event that was fresh in the minds of GDR audiences, particularly because in October 1962, the SED initiated a nationwide propaganda campaign against the United States and its attempted overthrow of Fidel Castro (Weiß 2006, 170). This was a time that Peter Ulrich Weiß describes as one "in which the production of enemy stereotypes was running at full speed" (170). The film particularly appeals to cultural functionaries for the way it exposes weaknesses within Western intelligence services. The Stasi spy Hansen is a hero who is willing to work for the good of socialist society, forsaking personal risk and even abandoning his son in the GDR. Though seemingly nondescript, he appears to have almost superhuman strength, a character like any other action figure. Rather than remaining true to the life story of Horst Hesse, Hansen's charge derives from the belief that there is a Western plot to overthrow the GDR. Due to the heightened tensions at this point in the Cold War, this feature film corroborated the idea that the West had sinister plans with regard to its Cold War rival. Thus the plot of the film reminded people of the need for vigilance with regard to the enemy in general and specifically in relation to the recent construction of the wall.

The believability of the film in part has to do with the very controlled way in which East Germany marketed the dangers of Western efforts to overthrow or liberate the GDR. Using scare tactics such as reminders that the Cold War could turn "hot" at any moment, the Stasi managed to keep the dangers from the West constantly in the minds of GDR citizens. This was an active strategy designed, among other things, to create support for the construction of the Berlin Wall among the citizenry, at least psychologically, a logical objective given the context at the time. The film's production relies on the use of factual material and authentic documents, which contribute to the film's documentary feel (Stöver 2006, 65). Situated within the highly charged context of the Cold War, media accounts leading up to the film's release reported on various plots by the West to overthrow the East German government, accompanied by witness testimony from former spies in the West who defected to the East (Stöver 2006, 63). As Stöver explains, *For Eyes Only* functions in the propaganda campaign as conclusive "proof" that the GDR narrowly avoided an attack in August 1961 (2006, 76). Even the film's opening credits allude to the factual basis of the plot: "The action of the film is fictional—similarities to actual events and living persons are intentional" (Veiczi 1963). Secret service advisors were on hand during filming to certify that the film conveyed a positive image of the agency. These advisers were able to influence the relationship between reality and fiction in the film, promoting fiction in order to make it believable.[15] Further adding to the believability of the film, the dialogues among the actors portraying Americans were filmed in English and subsequently dubbed with voice overs in German (Stöver 2006, 70).[16]

The film has been described mistakenly as the GDR's answer to James Bond, primarily because it premiered six months after the West German debut of the first James Bond film.[17] However, James Bond films were not available for viewing in the GDR, and the film had been already in production before *Dr. No* was released. DEFA dramaturge Dieter Wolf, who worked on the film, states that there is no evidence documenting a connection between the two films (Scholz 2008), and he emphasizes that the GDR actually was very proud of the fact that it had created a different type of spy hero (Wolf 2013). According to the Federal Agency for Civic Education (Bundeszentrale für politische Bildung n.d.), the film was a popular success: within three months more than one million GDR citizens had seen it. It was screened throughout Eastern Europe,

Costabile-Heming

especially in Poland and Romania (Stöver 2006, 62). It was also a political success; because it made the external threat to the GDR believable to audiences, the film contributed to a "consolidation of the SED state in the 1960s" (Stöver 2006, 59).

The opening sequences of the film immediately draw the audience into the milieu of espionage and counterespionage as concerns about a mole in the U.S. Military Intelligence Division, led by Major Collins, are intercut with scenes of the Stasi discussing strategies to steal documents from the Americans that outline plans for an invasion of the GDR. The film begins with shots of Hansen in the woods near the German-German border and then cuts to his immediate supervisor Collins's office, where he informs him that two West German spies have been captured. Collins is concerned about the sudden disappearance of seven Western agents in fourteen days as they attempt to gain access to GDR telegraph offices. Hansen remains cool, though Collins is visibly alarmed, for he has been fooled by a double agent before. Before he departs for a meeting in Frankfurt, the camera pans his office and zooms in on a large safe without revealing its contents. While others are suspicious of Hansen (he is the only employee from the East and the only one without a Nazi background), Collins had handpicked him and is therefore confident in his loyalty. As a clear sign of his trust, Collins places Hansen in charge of Concordia Import-Export, the cover name for the MID office in Würzburg, while he travels to Frankfurt for a meeting at military headquarters. That meeting reveals that the plans for E-Day, the West's invasion of the GDR, are ready to be distributed. The camera closes in on the cover of a file, labeled "for eyes only," thus the film's English title is a wordplay on the security level of the plans. As the meeting concludes, Collins's superiors question him about the captured agents and the possibility of a mole in his office. While Collins denies the likelihood of a security breach, the commanding officer instructs Colonel Rock to investigate.

It is not until Hansen travels to West Berlin with Collins that viewers become privy to his real name (Lorenz) and his role as an agent for the Stasi. Hansen slips out of his West German hotel room and crosses the border into East Berlin, evading the West German agents that Collins has instructed to watch him, despite

Collins's supposed trust. He delivers information about MID to his Stasi superior, who then takes him to a high school swim meet, where Hansen is able to watch his son, Manfred, from a distance. Hansen's son believes that he has fled the GDR illegally. Though Hansen is clearly pained at not being able to speak to his son, he willingly sacrifices his personal life for the safety of his country. This characterization posits Hansen as a hero figure who loves his family, his home, and his homeland and is willing to accept personal sacrifice in order to protect what he holds most dear. As a character he is quite flat—loyalty to the state comes at all costs, even abandoning his son. During this visit to East Berlin, Hansen is tasked with stealing the plans for the E-Day invasion.

The East-West dichotomy is prominently personified in stark characterizations. Whereas Hansen is portrayed as a clean-cut, moral, and upstanding model citizen, his Western counterparts, particularly the Americans, are portrayed in common stereotypes as corrupt and immoral "gangsters" (Grob 1991, 185). Collins is unscrupulous, buying precious artworks to sell on the black market, engaging in extramarital affairs, and falsifying payments to undercover agents. The MID doctor is a drunkard who mistreats women. Conversely, Hansen's Stasi commander is portrayed as fatherly, treating his agents more like sons than subordinate operatives.[18]

Colonel Rock suspects Hansen is the MID mole, and only a loyalty test can convince him otherwise. When an East German worker, Wilhelm Hartmann, is captured in Nuremberg for making propagandistic speeches to groups of workers, Hansen is tasked with his interrogation. This is a pivotal scene in the film, for Collins knows that Hansen and Hartmann were acquainted before Hansen's defection. When MID agent Schuck is unable to coerce a confession from Hartmann, headquarters orders Hansen to Nuremberg to conduct the interrogation. After listening to the recorded interrogation, Rock becomes increasingly suspicious of Hansen. Though others think Hansen is trustworthy, Rock points out that Hansen is the only German at MID who is not "from the Gestapo, the security service, or at least the SS" (Veiczi 1963). In order to put the issue to rest, Rock decides to have all MID employees undergo a lie detector test.[19] The interrogation, supervised by the MID doc-

Costabile-Heming

tor and conducted personally by Rock, takes place in a basement, which as Weiß suggests, is eerily reminiscent of a Gestapo interrogation (2006, 164). He argues further that the American characters are so plastic that they are completely interchangeable, for the film is not about "the portrayal of a specific enemy but rather the depiction of a preconceived image" (Weiß 2006, 164). The camera work in this scene is composed of a series of rapid close shots alternating between Rock and Hansen. Hansen remains calm, despite the psychological strain he experiences under Rock's rapid-fire questioning. Rock, on the other hand, sweats profusely, embodying the physical characteristics that one expects not from an interrogator but rather from the one being questioned.

During the interrogation Hansen's own safe is searched. Agents discover photographs of MID agent Schuck and an unknown woman, later identified as Madame Adelheid, an agent for the West German Gehlen organization, the precursor to the West German Federal Intelligence Service. As it turns out, Schuck is a double agent working for Gehlen and tasked with obtaining copies of the MID's plans. When Rock learns the woman's identity, he and Collins return to the MID office, where they find Schuck in the process of copying documents. Rock and the doctor drive Schuck to the woods and turn him over to Madame Adelheid; Schuck is shot and his body disposed of in the Wannsee lake. Schuck's discovery diverts attention away from Hansen, for all believe that the mole has been found and eliminated. The following weekend Hansen again is left alone at the Würzburg headquarters. He loads a safe into the car and heads for the German-German border. In a spectacular showdown with West German border patrols, which shoot out his tires and his windshield, Hansen crashes through the border and transports the secret documents safely across. The East Germans publish the documents, thus foiling the West's plans to invade the GDR. Given Hansen's upstanding character and loyalty to the GDR, it is no surprise that his mission is successful. Indeed, because of the documented success of Hesse's earlier escapade made public in the documentary portrait, *Disco Film 5* (Hedwig 1975), the feature film seems to draw on a factual basis, making it believable. Unlike a James Bond film, which closes with the hero in bed with a woman, *For Eyes Only* stresses family values. In the closing sequence, Hansen's Stasi superior drops him off at his son's school, where the two are reunited. This happy ending with family points to a type of domestication of espionage, something not typical of Western spy films and a theme that is repeated in *Chiffriert an Chef.*

This final scene underscores the Stasi characters as positive, moral, and clean living. Hansen exudes puritan qualities that prevent him from succumbing to Western extravagances. He remains true to his principles (Grob 1991, 185). The portrayals of the West are convincing, even though no filming took place there, and despite the temptations offered in the West, life in the East is both honest and staid. The primary objective of the film was to support the belief widely held by East German leaders that the West had been planning to invade the GDR. Indeed, the original sketch was intended to warn GDR citizens about the tactics of Western agents, in the hope that they would report any unusual situations to the proper authorities. Thus because of the widespread belief in the threat from the West, the film's narrative plants the seed in viewers that vigilance was essential and that, among other things, the construction of the Berlin Wall was necessary to protect the citizenry. This film's message follows a more alarmist narrative than what we typically find in the discourse about the construction of the wall that focuses on the bleeding of the population or protecting the citizens of East Berlin from the attractions of capitalism. Indeed, as Stöver suggests *For Eyes Only* "was also the precisely calibrated, political endpoint of a chain of evidence against Western liberation policies that the GDR had been developing since 1958. Above all, the purpose of the film was once and for all to justify, in the eyes of the East German citizens, the construction of a wall that would cut off the GDR" (2006, 2).

By portraying the West's liberation policy as a very real threat, the film also sought to project an overall positive image of the Stasi: "The Ministry [for State Security] saw an opportunity to optimally represent its operations to the public and to polish its public images. *For Eyes Only* thus also became an advertising vehicle for the MfS" (Stöver 2013, 6). The positive character traits that Hansen exhibits were designed to project the nature of the Stasi's work as based on humanistic tenets (Stöver 2006, 71); his personal sacrifices were portrayed as necessary for the continued existence of the socialist state. After its release the film was heralded for its realistic portrayals. Moreover, the film along with the cast and crew received awards including the Merit Medal of the National People's Army in silver for Harry Thürk, author of the screenplay, and for the actors Alfred Müller (Hansen) and Helmut Schreiber (Collins). Thürk received his medal personally from Stasi chief Erich Mielke. While the positive reception in the East may come as no surprise, even Western media praised the film as a DEFA achievement, with the *Frankfurter Rundschau* declaring it the most attractive example of a DEFA film for that year (Stöver 2006, 75).

Like *For Eyes Only*, *Chiffriert an Chef* immediately immerses the viewer in the world of foreign espionage. The opening sequences show video and still images of the main character, Wolf Brandin, and his family spanning the period from June 1959 through April 1960. A non-diegetic narrator comments on these surveillance images of "Number 5" for an unnamed boss. The audience quickly learns that the CIA is aware that Brandin, an electronics student in the GDR, works with classified information, and the CIA agent, Dr. Baum, is tasked with contacting him. This sets a series of events in motion, about which Brandin seems very naive. His status as a university student prohibits travel to the West, but this does not prevent him from traveling to West Berlin to visit his aunt Caroline, who regularly procures a medicinal salve for his father, her brother. During that visit Brandin encounters a man named Wagner, who pays him for answering banal questions about life in the GDR such as the price of butter and the availability of razor blades. Wagner informs Brandin that he is willing to pay him for such information and gives him a slip of paper with an address where they are to meet. This is Brandin's first contact with a Western agent, and he does not fully realize that it is an attempt to recruit him for the West.

Brandin reports the encounter to the Stasi. This important information occurs offscreen, and viewers only understand it based on the conversation between Brandin and Werner, the Stasi agent who remains his contact throughout the assignment. Werner interrogates Brandin about his visit to the West, whether he has discussed his report to the Stasi with anyone, and about his motives. When Werner is satisfied that Brandin has answered honestly, the interrogation ends, and Werner's tone and demeanor change from a gruff and distanced interrogator to a convivial and sympathetic mentor. He proposes that they speak to each other with the informal *du* and makes tea for them.

Werner encourages Brandin to meet with Wagner. Brandin agrees, and Wagner leads him to the West Berlin aquarium, where CIA agent Baum awaits him. Baum uses coercion tactics to convince Brandin to cooperate with the CIA, including showing him pictures of himself in the West along with a recording of a conversation. He even tries to ply Brandin with alcohol and women, though the East German shows little interest. Baum informs him: "We appreciate talent and expertise" and promises Brandin an American passport if he performs well (Dziuba 1979). He then undergoes rigorous training with Baum, who instructs him in discharging a weapon, using martial-arts techniques, and decoding encrypted messages. He also learns how to tap into communications lines. Through regular meetings with Werner, Brandin keeps the Stasi informed of his activities. These meetings are essential, for it is through his fatherly demeanor that Werner is able to encourage Brandin to continue his covert activities. Living a double life takes a toll on Brandin, as he neglects his thesis, his wife, Renate, and his daughter. Whereas Renate suspects that he is having an affair, she has no idea of the real reason for his petulance and exhaustion. In a sign of benevolence, Werner discloses Brandin's secret life to Renate after the death of Brandin's father.

Over time the CIA agent Baum becomes a sympathetic figure, who displays great concern for Brandin's well-being. He devises an emergency means of communication to connect with Brandin that he classifies as "private." As tensions between the two German states intensify, Baum's boss wants information at all costs, and using the emergency communication route communicated to Brandin earlier, Baum schedules a meeting at the Olympic Stadium. There Baum informs him: "The meeting is solely my responsibility. We are here privately" (Dziuba 1979). He informs Brandin of

West Germany's plan to reprivatize the East and to cancel trade agreements. He further tells Brandin that headquarters is extremely pleased with his performance thus far. Believing in his loyalty, Baum instructs Brandin to tap into the underwater communications cable. Because Brandin has informed Werner of the West's plans every step of the way, the East is ready with a ruse. The East intentionally transmits an unencoded message, followed immediately by the encoded one. This enables the West to decipher the code. The West falsely believes that circumstances in East Berlin are calm, and that there is no reason to worry about the increased troop movements that have been observed. However, the opposite is true: the GDR has closed the border between East and West Berlin. The construction of the Berlin Wall thus comes as a total surprise to the West. The film's closing sequence shows Brandin and Renate in their apartment, where she says: "Now we can live like everyone else here" (Dziuba 1979). Following the successful completion of his mission, Brandin can look forward to a peaceful family life.

The film draws heavily on the political context of the early 1960s, incorporating television and radio broadcasts that reflect the heightened tensions of the time. These broadcasts serve to remind viewers of the very real threats that the GDR faced then. Brandin sees a broadcast of Khrushchev's speech warning that peace is in danger. Similarly, a radio report from April 1960 draws attention to the importance of the upcoming Paris Summit, which was convened to discuss the situation of divided Germany, the possibility of arms control, and the relaxation of tensions between the United States and the Soviet Union. A report a few months later reveals details about the trial of Gary Francis Powers, a U.S. pilot captured by the Soviet Union while spying. Likewise video footage of the atomic bomb attack on Hiroshima, shown to commemorate the fifteenth anniversary of the bombing, underscores the fragility of peace. These all serve as reminders not just that threats to the GDR were real but also that it is necessary to maintain high levels of vigilance and security with regard to enemies of the state. Thus audience members can revel in the fact that the Berlin Wall has protected them from such threats in the ensuing eighteen years and that it will continue to do so.

In *Chiffriert an Chef*, the stereotyping of Western agents is not as crass as in *For Eyes Only*. The CIA agent Dr. Baum is a philologist trained in German. While he initially is portrayed as arrogant about his intelligence, to which his superior responds, "Being too clever is not good" (Dziuba 1979), his character softens over time. He is straightforward with Brandin about the dangers of the mission, and as he watches from the Western shore as Brandin attempts to tap into the communications cable, he appears genuinely concerned for his well-being. Baum's superior, on the other hand, is portrayed as more callous, focusing on the mission rather than the human cost. This is depicted most egregiously in a scene where he dines on an extravagant meal of fish, while imploring Baum to put Brandin to use.

Because the film takes place primarily in the East, it is also logical that it focuses more on Brandin and his relationships. It emphasizes a positive and sanitized image of the Stasi evoked by Werner's compassion and benevolence, which stands in stark contrast to the more calculated nature of the Western spies. Approximately the same age as Brandin's father, Werner assumes a caretaker role in his life. When Brandin's double life begins to take a toll on his personal life, Werner, as the only one who knows what is really going on, makes him tea, offers him a place to take a nap, and consoles him when his father dies. Werner, as emblematic for the Stasi, is never portrayed in a negative light. In his interactions with Brandin, he always presents a cool head. Conversely in the West, Brandin is actively schooled in espionage including armed hand-to-hand combat. Such contrasts position the East as a defender of peace, whereas the West is portrayed as actively seeking violent conflict.

It is not surprising that comparisons of *For Eyes Only* and *Chiffriert an Chef* can be made since the two films have multiple plot elements in common. In both films the double agents (Hansen and Brandin) are positive figures who engage in espionage activities to protect their way of life in the GDR. Though both of their private lives suffer as a result of their leading a double life, their experiences are temporary and portrayed as a necessary evil. While Hansen was already employed at MID, *Chiffriert an Chef* explores the CIA's covert recruitment of Brandin. The characterization of Western agents draws on stereotypes of unscrupulousness, womanizing, a razor focus on violence and war, and questionable Nazi backgrounds, whereas the Stasi agents are sympathetic and patriotic figures who exhibit a fatherly compassion for their agents. In both films the main characters are subjected to lie detector tests in the West as a means to determine their loyalty. These tests are both physically and psychologically grueling. In the East by contrast, loyalty is a given. Even in the case of Brandin, his initial interrogation with Werner occurs in Werner's apartment without the need for machinery. The lie detector tests underscore the suspicious nature of the Western espionage agencies and the lengths to which they will go to determine loyalty. Such extremes contrast openly with the more benevolent treatment that the Stasi handlers portray.[20] Ultimately, both Hansen and Brandin betray their Western handlers, which permits the reconciliation of the agents with their families. Moreover, there is a cinematic connection in Alfred Müller; the actor who plays Hansen makes a cameo appearance as Werner's superior.

These films are unapologetic about their positive portrayals of the Stasi. Hansen and Brandin participate willingly in the "spy games," and the Stasi is represented as a necessary tool in the fight to maintain the GDR's preferred socialist way of life, as an alternative to the imperialist and fascist West. Moreover, they depict the Stasi exclusively as an essential component of national security, with its view fixated totally on threats from the outside. In other words these films do not reveal any of the intrigue that we have come to expect from the shadow world of unofficial operatives, as presented in high-grossing films such as *The Lives of Others* (Henckel von Donnersmarck 2006).[21] Because these films also served to portray the Stasi in a positive light, viewers are presented with reconnaissance not as something that violates the private sphere but rather as something that is necessary to defend their way of life. The Stasi stepped up its domestic surveillance following the suppression of the Prague Spring uprising and continued to increase it throughout the 1970s. Thus the emphasis on foreign espionage in *Chiffriert an Chef* deflects the negative perception of

Stasi scrutiny as an invasion of the private sphere by redirecting the image to the Stasi as a necessary reinforcement of state security. By refocusing audience attention on the early 1960s and away from the upheaval of the late 1970s that occurred following the expatriation of Biermann, the director Dziuba is able to recast the Stasi as a key component in protecting GDR citizens from external threats. Moreover, the conclusion of *Chiffriert an Chef* alludes to the fact that Brandin's affiliation with the Stasi was a temporary task, and upon completion he and his family will return to their normal lives. Again, this message deflects the idea that the Stasi is all pervasive and omnipresent. The film arouses the viewers' empathy precisely because the focus is on protecting the GDR from the foreign enemy and reminding the audience that external threats are still real (Dueck 2016, 427). Indeed, it is significant that both films portray the threat as coming from the United States, not the Federal Republic, a clear sign that imperialism was to be associated with the Western allies, who exerted considerable influence over the Federal Republic.

Unlike actual Stasi spies such as Heinz Barwich, neither Hansen nor Brandin spied to defect but instead to help the GDR.[22] In both of these DEFA films, the Stasi agents do not conform to the surreptitious images that we have become accustomed to in Western spy films. Indeed, the Stasi was actively involved in the character portrayals in *For Eyes Only*. Dramaturge Dieter Wolf explains for instance that the Stasi objected to the initial characterization of the Stasi colonel and two colleagues at the headquarters in East Berlin. Whereas director Veiczi cast the actors to emphasize their proletarian nature, the Stasi wanted them to exude "a stronger intellectual aura" (Wolf 2013), in essence characterizing the agents occupied with Western espionage as the elite among agents, similar to Bond. As a result this sequence had to be reshot, even though the set had been dismantled. Wolf states that this type of change "was very unusual and was meant to strengthen how the representatives of the Stasi appeared in comparison to the opposing side" (Wolf 2013). Thus the Stasi was keen on crafting the particular image of a patriotic hero, one who focuses on family values, unlike the sex—and glamour—obsessed Bond figure. Whereas the depiction of an external threat in *For Eyes Only* derived from a carefully orchestrated marketing campaign designed to convince the GDR populace that a threat from the West was imminent, the situation in 1979 was much different. Though the wall's stability assuaged fears of invasion, new threats emerged from internal dissidence. Moreover, the signing of the Helsinki Final Act in 1975 opened the GDR to international scrutiny regarding human rights violations. The return to threats from the 1960s in *Chiffriert an Chef* appears to be an attempt to deflect attention from these later developments. Fundamentally, then, these films serve to affirm the GDR's decision to close the German-German border, and they cement an alternative narrative as justification. Rather than addressing the economic crisis that the flight of the populace posed, these films assert that the U.S. liberation policy and the fear of some kind of impending Western overthrow were the formal justification for the construction of the Berlin Wall. Indeed, three additional feature films premiered in 1962 and 1963 that also focused on Western plots as a valid justification for the construction of the wall: ... *und deine Liebe auch* (... and your love too; Vogel 1962), *Der Kinnhaken* (The upper cut; Thiel 1962), *Der Sonntagsfahrer* (The Sunday driver; Klein 1963). All three met with limited success (Stöver 2006, 56–59). In the end only *For Eyes Only* is remembered as a successful example of the spy film genre in East German film history.

Notes

I am grateful to Rachel J. Halverson for her insightful reading of earlier versions of this essay, to Dieter Wolf for his willingness to answer questions about the films, and to Birgit Scholz for her assistance locating archival materials at the Filmmuseum Potsdam.

1. See http://www.filmportal.de/film/for-eyes-only-streng-geheim_abb7e1ff 74b640a491db403eceab97e8, accessed October 23, 2017.

2. Details of the Hesse case will be discussed in greater detail later in the chapter.

3. See http://www.filmportal.de/film/chiffriert-an-chef-ausfall-nr-5_df2446 5603024ae98db916e464797429, accessed October 23, 2017.

4. The author of the screenplay, Günter Karau, also wrote a spy thriller titled *Go oder der Doppelspiel im Untergrund* (1983) based on the board game *Go*, in which he incorporated the plot of *Chiffriert an Chef*. Interestingly, the novel,

published by the Militärverlag, was more popular than the film, and it is likely that East Germans familiar with the story read the book.

5. Unless otherwise noted, all translations are my own.

6. See Booth 1990 for an analysis of U.S. and British espionage films.

7. Even more-contemporary portrayals of the GDR such as the television series *Deutschland 83*, continue to perpetuate the Stasi's worldview that an ever-present danger emanates from the West (nrichardsonlittle 2016).

8. Thomas Rogers suggests that the popular television series *Das unsichtbare Visier* drew heavily on James Bond films, while simultaneously remaining true to socialist values. For instance the agents in *Das unsichtbare Visier* "are friends of the working class . . . and abhor anything flashy." Furthermore, "the CIA is shown to be a scheming, evil organization and West Germany is portrayed as materialistic and superficial." See Rogers 2015.

9. James Chapman has argued that Bond films intentionally invoke Great Britain as a superior world power, ignoring the monarchy's declining influence on the world political stage (2000, 274–75).

10. "Bewertung des Films von Klaus Rümmler," 3, Nachlass Dzuiba, Filmmuseum Potsdam.

11. See https://www.fernsehserien.de/das-unsichtbare-visier, accessed October 26, 2017.

12. Incidentally, the show was broadcast specifically to compete with popular West German shows on ARD and ZDF, thus encouraging GDR citizens to choose to watch GDR television rather than Western programming. See Löser 2016.

13. One exception is Kurt Maetzig's feature film *Septemberliebe* (September love, 1960), which depicted a young woman who voluntarily approaches the Stasi to inform on her friend's plans to flee the country. See Löser 2016.

14. Hesse was celebrated in the GDR as a hero, while Wax's role in the theft was not made public until 1996 (Kohl 1996). Several scholars have written about this case; for details see Koehler 1999, 203–21; Mittmann 2002, 75–86; Scherer 2006, 224–36; Stöver 2009, 238–66; and Böhm 2016. These scholars each present slightly different accounts of the actual theft, but all are based on documents, witness accounts, and personal interviews. Böhm's book recounts Hesse's life and espionage activities and compares Hesse's "true" story to the events as portrayed in *For Eyes Only*; it reads simultaneously as an attempt to rescue Hesse's story from obscurity, as well to correct some misperceptions he reads in Stöver's account in *Zuflucht DDR* (2009).

15. Derived from information displayed at the Filmmuseum Potsdam's permanent exhibition.

16. Indeed, the character of Colonel Rock is played by Hans Lucke, who does his own English voice-over because his language skills and accent are so good.

17. See http://www.imdb.com/title/tt0055928/releaseinfo, accessed October 27, 2017.

18. A fatherly Stasi agent also played in Maetzig's *Septemberliebe*. See Löser 2016; Grob proposes that this positive portrayal of a Stasi agent was intentional propaganda (1991, 196).

19. In the documentary portrait *Disco Film 5* Horst Hesse confirms that he had to undergo a lie detector test similar to the episode portrayed in the feature film.

20. Contrary to Löser's (2016) contention that the benevolent Stasi agent was a one-time occurrence in Maetzig's *Septemberliebe*, we see positive portrayals of the Stasi in both *For Eyes Only* and *Chiffriert an Chef*.

21. For an insightful essay on the role of spectatorship in a surveillance culture, see Kapzynski 2014.

22. Heinz Barwich was an East German physicist working as an agent for the CIA. He is one of the few spies who was able to gather intelligence from within the Soviet Union. He defected in September 1964. For details about Barwich's role as a spy and his defection, see Maddrell 2005.

References

Begg, Morgan. 2016. "The Politics of James Bond." *IPA Review* 68 (1): 32–35.

Berghahn, Daniela. 2005. *Hollywood behind the Wall: The Cinema of East Germany*. Manchester: Manchester University Press.

"Berlin Operations." 2015. In *Historical Dictionaries of Intelligence and Counterintelligence: Historical Dictionary of Russian and Soviet Intelligence*, edited by R. W. Pringle, 2nd ed. Lanham MD: Rowman & Littlefield. https://libproxy .library.unt.edu/login?url=http://search.credoreference.com/content/entry /rowmanrasi/berlin_operations/0?institutionId=4982.

Beyer, Frank, dir. 1991. *Der Verdacht*. Feature film. DEFA & Westdeutscher Rundfunk.

Böhm, Peter. 2016. *For Eyes Only: Die wahre Geschichte des Agenten Horst Hesse*. Berlin: Verlag Das Neue Berlin.

Booth, Alan R. 1990. "The Development of the Espionage Film." *Intelligence and National Security* 5 (4): 136–60.

Brockmann, Stephen. 2010. *A Critical History of German Film*. Rochester NY: Camden House.

Bundeszentrale für politische Bildung. n.d. "Source Material: Documentary Film *For Eyes Only—Ein Film und seine Geschichte*." Accessed May 26, 2017. http://www.bpb.de/gesellschaft/kultur/filmbildung/63225/handout.

Carow, Heiner, dir. 1991. *Verfehlung*. Feature film. DEFA & Von Vietinghof Filmproduktion.

Chapman, James. 2000. *Licence to Thrill: A Cultural History of the James Bond Films*. New York: Columbia University Press.

Dueck, Cheryl. 2016. "Secret Police in Style: The Aesthetics of Remembering Socialism." *Seminar* 52 (4): 426–48.

Dziuba, Helmut, dir. 1979. *Chiffriert an Chef—Ausfall Nr. 5*. Feature film. DEFA.

Grob, Norbert. 1991. "Like Puppets on a String: Notizen zum späten Spy Thriller." In *Kalter Krieg: 60 Filme aus Ost und West*, 184–202. Berlin: Stiftung Deutsche Kinematek.

Habel, F.-B. 2017. "Chiffriert an Chef—Ausfall Nr. 5." In *Das große Lexikon der DEFA-Spielfilme: Die vollständige Dokumentation aller DEFA-Spielfilme von 1946 bis 1993; Neuausgabe in zwei Bänden A–L*, mit Inhaltsangabe von Renate Biehl, 134–35. Berlin: Schwarzkopf & Schwarzkopf.

Hake, Sabine. 2005. "Anti-Americanism and the Cold War: On the DEFA Berlin Films." In *Americanization and Anti-Americanism: The German Encounter with American Culture after 1945*, edited by Alexander Stephan, 148–65. New York: Berghahn.

Helwig, Joachim, dir. 1975. *Disco Film 5: Im Zentrum der US—Militärspionage*. Documentary film. DEFA.

Henckel von Donnersmarck, Florian, dir. 2006. *Das Leben der Anderen*. Feature film. Wiedemann & Berg Filmproduktion, Bayerischer Rundfunk, Arte, & Creado Film.

Kapzynski, Jennifer M. 2014. "Surveillance States: Structures of Conspiracy in *Wende* Cinema." In *DEFA after East Germany*, edited by Brigitta B. Wagner, 154–73. Rochester NY: Camden House.

Karau, Günter. 1984. *Go oder Doppelspiel im Untergrund*. 2nd ed. Berlin: Militärverlag der deutschen demokratischen Republik.

Klein, Gerhard, dir. 1963. *Der Sonntagsfahrer*. Feature film. DEFA.

Koehler, John O. 1999. *Stasi: The Untold Story of the East German Secret Police*. Boulder CO: Westview Press.

Kohl, Christiane. 1996. "Donner, Blitz und Teddy." *Der Spiegel*, March 4, 52–68.

Löser, Claus. 2016. "Im Visier des Unsichtbaren: Stasi im Film." October 7. http://www.bpb.de/geschichte/deutsche-geschichte/stasi/229280/film.

Maddrell, Paul. 2005. "The Scientist Who Came in from the Cold: Heinz Barwich's Flight from the GDR." *Intelligence and National Security* 20 (4): 608–30.

Maetzig, Kurt, dir. 1950. *Der Rat der Götter*. Feature film. DEFA.

Mittmann, Elke. 2002. "Der Fall Horst Hesse: Eine Kundschafterkarriere." In *Duell im Dunkel. Spionage im geteilten Deutschland*, edited by Stiftung Haus der Geschichte der Bundesrepublik Deutschland and Zeitgeschichtliches Forum Leipzig, 75–86. Cologne: Böhlau.

Mückenberger, Christiane. 1993. "The Cold War in East German Feature Films." *Historical Journal of Film, Radio and Television* 13 (1): 49–57.

nrichardsonlittle. 2016. "Sympathy for the Devil: Seeing the World through the Eyes of the Stasi in *Deutschland 83*." February 8. https://historynedblog.wordpress.com/2016/01/31/sympathy-for-the-devil-seeing-the-world-through-the-eyes-of-the-stasi-in-deutschland-83/amp/.

Rogers, Thomas. 2015. "The James Bond of East Germany." *BBC—Culture*, October 28. http://www.bbc.com/culture/story/20151028-the-james-bond-of-east-germany.

Scherer, F. M. 2006. "Horst Hesse: A Cold War Military Intelligence Mole." *Intelligence and National Security* 20 (2): 224–36.

Schittly, Dagmar. 2002. *Zwischen Regie und Regime: Die Filmpolitik der SED im Spiegel der DEFA—Produktionen*. Berlin: Christoph Links Verlag.

Scholz, Gunther, dir. 2008. *For Eyes Only—Ein Film und seine Geschichte*. Documentary film. DEFA Stiftung.

Schweitzer, Eva C. 2015. *Amerikas Schattenkrieger: Wie uns die US seit Jahrzehnten ausspionieren und manipulieren*. Munich: Piper.

Spielberg, Stephen, dir. 2015. *Bridge of Spies*. Feature film. DreamWorks et al.

Stöver, Bernd. 2006. "'Das ist die Wahrheit, die volle Wahrheit': Befreiungspolitik im DDR—Spielfilm der 1950er und 1960er Jahre." In *Massenmedien im Kalten Krieg: Akteure, Bilder, Resonanzen*, edited by Thomas Lindenberger, 49–76. Cologne: Böhlau.

———. 2009. *Zuflucht DDR: Spione und andere Übersiedler*. Munich: Beck.

———. 2013. "The Truth, the Absolute Truth: Liberation Policy and DEFA's *For Eyes Only*." Translated by Skyler Arndt-Briggs. Supplementary material with DVD (partial translation of the chapter "Das ist die Wahrheit").

Thiel, Heinz, dir. 1962. *Der Kinnhaken*. Feature film. DEFA.

Veiczi, János, dir. 1963. *For Eyes Only—streng geheim*. Feature film. DEFA.

Vogel, Frank, dir. 1962. *. . . und deine Liebe auch*. Feature film. DEFA.

Weiß, Peter Ulrich. 2006. "Wo das Wolfsgesetz regiert: Amerikabilder in DEFA—Produktionen zu Beginn der 60er Jahre." In *Umworbener Klassenfeind: Das Verhältnis der DDR zu den USA*, edited by Uta A. Balbier and Christiane Rösch, 160–79. Berlin: Links.

Wolf, Dieter. 2013. "Our Own James Bond." https://ecommerce.umass.edu /defa/memories/9892.

9 Breaking Borders

Niklaus Schilling's Critical Spy Drama *Der Willi-Busch-Report*

LISA HAEGELE

A lesser-known figure in the New German Cinema (NGC), the internationally acclaimed art cinema movement in West Germany in the 1970s and early 1980s, Swiss-born filmmaker Niklaus Schilling directed six feature films between 1971 and 1982. His films garnered critical praise upon their premieres, including both spy dramas, *Der Willi-Busch-Report* (The Willi Busch report, 1979) and *Der Westen leuchtet!* (The West glows, 1982, released in English as *The Lite Trap*). *Der Willi-Busch-Report* received the first Max Ophüls Award at the eponymous film festival in Saarbrücken, Germany in 1980, and *The Lite Trap* earned the prestigious German Film Award in Silver for Wolfgang Dickmann's camerawork in 1982 (Jansen 1980; Blumenberg 1982). Despite their achievements Schilling's films—and the director's oeuvre at large—have received little scholarly attention compared to the works of the more celebrated NGC auteurs, including Rainer Werner Fassbinder, Wim Wenders, Volker Schlöndorff, Alexander Kluge, and Werner Herzog.

Like other films in the NGC—Wenders's road movies and Fassbinder's melodramas, for example—Schilling's spy films reappropriate genre conventions in offering critical portrayals of contemporary German society and politics. *Der Willi-Busch-Report*, Schilling's first spy film, addresses the topic of espionage at the inner German border, an issue largely unaddressed in the NGC.[1] Set in a rural West German border town, Schilling's tragicomedic film adapts a genre popularized in Cold War Europe by the phenomenally successful

James Bond films and their numerous spin-offs. While the Bond films offer riveting stories of espionage between real and fictitious world powers, *Der Willi-Busch-Report* represents spying and surveillance in ways that bring into relief nationally specific problems rooted in the historical reality of West Germany in the late 1970s. By linking surveillance—and the climate of paranoia that it generates—to issues in West German media politics, Schilling's film challenges the Cold War borders and binaries that the Bond films tend to reify through their extravagant tales of international conspiracy and intrigue. The film uses irony to demystify Bondian spy fantasies, foregrounding instead the sociopolitical and lived reality of the border in West Germany. I suggest that the film therefore does political work by breaking down the ideological clout of Cold War boundaries and allegiances that popular spy films of the era reinforce.

Ironizing "Popular Geopolitics"

Der Willi-Busch-Report centers on Willi Busch (Tilo Prückner), a reporter named after the famous German poet and satirist Wilhelm Busch (1832–1908), whose rhymes Willi recites to himself throughout the film.[2] Shot in Wanfried, a border town in Hessen, the film is set in a fictitious provincial village named Friedheim on the inner German border. There Willi works for the *Werra-Post*, a local newspaper company that he inherited from his late father and shares with his sister, Adelheid. Since Germany's division the *Werra-Post* has struggled financially, having lost the majority of its readership to the East. Once located at the center of Germany, Friedheim is now a remote, sleepy village on the outermost perimeter of the new West Germany. To sell more copies of his newspaper, Willi devises, stages, and publishes stories that might attract readers. For example he steals telephones from telephone booths and warns readers about a "telephone vandal." After overhearing a little girl recite fairy tales to a flock of sheep, he concocts the story that she is a "miracle child" who has prophesized the reunification of Germany. Later, when his old school friend Arno Rösler dies of a presumed heart attack, he deposits his body at the border, claiming in an article that he was a spy. Soon thereafter two more mysterious deaths occur in Friedheim: the corpse of an Austrian man named Baumbauer washes up ashore, and Sir Henry, Willi's elderly friend and a veteran of the Second World War, dies at a bus station of what appears to be a gunshot wound to the chest. Willi then becomes paranoid, convinced that Friedheim is indeed home to a nest of spies. When he finds that Munzel, his pet rabbit, has gone missing, Willi panics and takes off to the border to find him. Once there he threatens to shoot the helicopters and police who have come to detain him. Despite the attempts of Adelheid and his girlfriend, Rose-Marie, to placate him, he faints, and paramedics load him onto a stretcher and carry him off to an ambulance. In the final shot of the film, a border patrol helicopter flies off into the distance.

In one of the few scholarly treatments of *Der Willi-Busch-Report*, Inga Scharf convincingly analyzes the film's "critical geopolitics," a term that she borrows from Gearóid Ó. Tuathail in his book *Critical Geopolitics: The Politics of Writing Global Space*. The "critical geopolitics" of Schilling's film, Scharf argues, foreground the "constructedness" and shifting nature of geopolitical boundaries (2007, 182). By publishing sensationalist border narratives in the local press, Willi recenters Friedheim from the national periphery by drawing in tourists and facilitating a "new sense of place" in a newly vibrant town (189). In an attempt to counter Friedheim's "sealed geopolitical fate" on the outermost margins of West Germany, Willi shifts Friedheim back to the center by manipulating its image in popular media, portraying it as an important national site full of wonder and intrigue (189). Willi's newspaper thus represents a potentially subversive force in its ability to renegotiate and reset the official political boundaries mapped out by global leaders immediately after the Second World War.

But even though Willi uses sensationalist stories to relocate Friedheim from the nation's margins back to the heart of Germany, his spy stories nevertheless exploit the border between East and West Germany as a site of danger and conspiracy, through which he paradoxically *reinforces* its power in the public imagination rather than undermines it. In an opposite move to its titular protagonist, Schilling's film critiques Cold War popular spy fictions, demonstrating how they reify political borders and binaries by instigating the fear and paranoia to which Willi ultimately succumbs. Adding to Scharf's reading of the film, I argue that the film's "critical geopolitics" therefore are based not only on its staging of the complex shifts and negotiations of political boundaries but also on its ironic commentary on and subversion of "popular geopolitics"—a term I explore below in the context of the James Bond films—in the spy stories circulating in mainstream media. Schilling's film, therefore, demonstrates how the NGC is as much concerned with German national politics, as Scharf notes, as it is with the politics of representation, particularly in the mainstream press and cinema.

Building Borders: "Popular Geopolitics" and the Cold War James Bond Films

At the time the NGC was emerging in the mid-1960s, the spy thriller had become one of the most prominent film genres in Europe and the United States, resulting in the phenomenon known as "Spy Mania" (Classen 2011).[3] More specifically "Bondmania," referring to the James Bond media franchise, quickly spread from the United Kingdom to other parts of the world (Bennett and Woollacott 2003, 20). *Dr. No* (Young 1962), the first British-American film adaptation of Ian Fleming's spy novels, was an immediate and surprising international success, leading to a series of lucrative Bond films and spin-offs in the 1960s and 1970s (Bennett and Woollacott 2003, 20). The James Bond–inspired *Kommissar X* (Commissioner X) and Jerry Cotton series in West Germany—two strands of the European "Eurospy" Bond knockoffs—attracted millions of cinemagoers in the 1960s and continued to enjoy television reruns through the 1970s (Osteried 2016). In East Germany, too, Bond-styled spy heroes worked in the service of their governments in popular films and television productions, such as János Veiczi's film *For Eyes Only—streng geheim* (For eyes only—strictly confidential, 1963, released in English as *For Eyes Only*) and the television series *Das unsichtbare Visier* (The invisible visor; Hagen 1973-79).[4] The James Bond films, as Martin Rubin argues, dominated the spy genre at the time both commercially and conceptually (1999, 132). Bond functioned as the standard by which other cinematic and television spy heroes were defined, whether as his imitations, "mock-Bonds," or "anti-Bonds" (Bennett and Woollacott 2003, 26).

While the spy thriller genre has enjoyed popularity since the late nineteenth century, it witnessed a boom during the Cold War, an era in which secret agents on both sides of the Iron Curtain infiltrated the enemy state to become the subject of media attention and widespread public speculation (Classen 2011). After a spate of relatively unsuccessful and stylistically muted "anti-Communist" spy films in the 1950s, the British-American Bond series embedded its Cold War ideologies in cinematic spectacles that foregrounded action, sexual innuendo, and technological thrills (Rubin 1999, 127). While Fleming's early novels are distinctly anti-Communist—the primary villains are Communists working for SMERSH, a dangerous Soviet counterintelligence agency—the films take a more ambivalent political stance. Following the producers' suggestion that the screen adaptations be "depoliticized" in order to increase their financial viability worldwide, the Bond films "marginalize" the topic of the Cold War, giving it, according to Rubin, a "friendlier, less threatening aspect" (Bennett and Woollacott 2003, 23; Rubin 1999, 130). Replacing the Communists in the novels, Bond's enemies are megalomaniacs driven by a more abstract desire to rule the world. In addition the films take place not in the hot spots of the Cold War but in the exotic and more peripheral locations, such as Jamaica, Switzerland, Venice, the Bahamas, and Japan (Rubin 1999, 130). For Christoph Classen the Cold War functions as a "shadowy backdrop" to the action in the largely "depoliticized" Bond action thrillers (2011).

But the politics of the Cold War crucially shape the narratives of the early Bond films, even if the films refrain from addressing contemporary politics directly. The dualistic conflict between a "good" and an "evil" foreign power, for example, clearly evokes the binary between East and West at the height of the Cold War, an observation that Umberto Eco (2003) made in his famous analysis of the Manichean world order in Bond. The Bond adventures were always, as Klaus Dodds remarks, "sensitive and sensitized by the prevailing Cold War conflict," despite the producers' alleged intentions to "depoliticize" the series (2007, 77). The early Bond films "helped define the Cold War zeitgeist" by introducing various "geographies of danger" that "reflected and anticipated Cold War political allegiances" and adversaries (Hughes 2016, 78).

Far more than mere exotic "backdrops" to action, the locations in the Bond films—though set on the peripheries of the Cold War conflict—"actively contribute to the geo-graphing of the Cold War as a series of Manichean struggles between good and evil" (Dodds 2007, 77). Contributing to and reinforcing the "ideological formation of the two blocs" (Nikitin and Baumgarten 2011), the Bond films engage a form of "popular geopolitics," a term used by Marcus Power and Andrew Crampton to describe films that "provide a way of solving (geo)political uncertainty . . . through building moral geographies and making clear the lines of division between 'us' and 'them'" (2007, 6). The Bond films reinforce Cold War ideologies precisely by encoding their battles between "good" and "evil" within geopolitical terms. "Good" and "evil," in other words, are divided along geographical boundaries that Agent 007 traverses in his missions to protect an "innocent community functioning in a Manichean world" (Lawrence 2011, 339).

Indeed, the early Bond films convey procapitalist and anti-Communist ideologies that would be difficult to overlook in retrospect. Though politically ambiguous Bond's villains nevertheless retain some affiliation to the Eastern Bloc. Hollywood, as Rachel Hughes asserts, rarely passed up opportunities to capitalize on popular perceptions of the Soviet "Evil Empire" (2016, 78). In *Dr. No*, for example, the German Chinese supervillain attempts to sabotage the American space program by disrupting missile launches, recalling in some respects the Cuban missile crisis conflict between the Soviet Union and the United States in 1962. In *You Only Live Twice* (Gilbert 1967), SPECTRE, an unnamed Asian government evocative of "Red China," leads an underground organization modeled after the Soviet SMERSH in Fleming's novels (Rubin 1999, 130). In *From Russia with Love* (Young 1963), the Soviets reprise their role as the primary villains. Never failing to realize his ambitious goals, Bond represents the strength in individualism that lies at the heart of capitalist ideology, while the films promote consumerism by boasting an ever-more riveting display of technological advancements over the course of the decade, from faster cars to more impressive gadgets and weapons. The Bond films reveal Cold War tensions in their heroic portrayal of a Western counterintelligence agent who consistently saves the world from a threat posed by a powerful and ideologically opposing foreign enemy. Emphasizing borders, boundaries, and polar opposites, the Bond films in the 1960s represent and reaffirm Cold War ideologies, even if only implicitly.

Although the Bond films tend to support dominant ideologies, they also incorporate ample scenes of irony and self-mocking quips, which in many genre parodies work to destabilize and break apart the ideological prowess of the original text. Unlike many genre parodies, however, Bond's irony serves to *fix* rather than *upset* or call into question the cultural purchase of the Bond franchise, as Kevin Hagopian (2009) argues. Referring to Dan Harries's notion of the "canonization of parody," Hagopian makes the claim that the "Eurospy" Bond parodies of the 1960s—and the Bond films themselves, which parody the novels—provide contrastive settings to the originals in ways that bring Cold War geopolitics into sharp relief. In this way the films, unlike subversive parodies, reinforce the ideological "stability of the original" (Hagopian 2009, 23). That is, the Bond parodies are "characterized by ironic inversion" but significantly "not at the expense of the parodied text" (26). Hagopian argues that the "self-conscious recruitment of humor [in Bond] . . . opened a space into which parody could insert itself without undercutting what the film denominates as its 'serious' material, that is, its espionage plot, which, however improbable, still obeys rules of causality, norms of character construction, and patterns of suspenseful plotting characteristic of the realistic film narrative" (29). In an ironic twist, irony in the Bond films and their parodies works to secure rather than unsettle the cultural authority of Bond; the films function ultimately as a conservator of the very consumer-capitalist values and Manichean worldview that they mock.

By the time Schilling's *Der Willi-Busch-Report* premiered in West Germany in 1979, the spy film popularized by the James Bond series was a well-established genre. In 1966 Alfred Hitchcock lamented that the espionage genre had already become cliché (Hagopian 2009, 25). Featuring more special effects, impressive technologies, and humorous gags, the Bond films remained popular in the 1970s and early 1980s. In West Germany *Moonraker* (Gilbert 1979) and *Octopussy* (Glen 1983) won Golden Screen awards for attracting at least three million viewers ("Moonraker" n.d.; "Octopussy" n.d.). While Cold War politics inform the narratives of the Bond films in the 1960s, they take center stage in the Bond blockbusters of the late 1970s and early 1980s, reflecting in part an increased hostility in Cold War relations and the reemergence of anti-Communist rhetoric under the right-wing governments of President Ronald Reagan and Prime Minister Margaret Thatcher (Chapman 2000, 203).

In an interview published in the press book to his later espionage drama *The Lite Trap*, Schilling stressed: "For today's German absurdities one needs a lot of irony" (Sprengel n.d., "Sein und Scheinen"). Unlike the irony in Bond, *Der Willi-Busch-Report* challenges the Manichean worldview propagated by its Bond contemporaries through its use of irony. By creating narrative ambiguities and subverting spy film tropes in the mise-en-scène, the film draws attention to the issues of surveillance, hysteria, and paranoia in West Germany shortly after the German Autumn in late 1977, when the Red Army Faction (RAF) conducted a series of terrorist attacks that culminated in the murder of business executive and former SS officer Hanns Martin Schleyer. Schilling's film relocates the conflict from the international to the (West German) national; the problem is not "them" but "us." Indeed, as I argue below, the film frames Cold War "popular geopolitics" as a problem itself within the precarious political climate of late 1970s West Germany. A spy story *about* spy stories, *Der Willi-Busch-Report* reinterprets a genre that it deems grossly at odds with contemporary West German reality.

Spy Fantasies? Narrative Ambiguities in *Der Willi-Busch-Report*

Although Willi's spy stories are fictional, the opening sequence of the film establishes a sense that Willi is in fact being surveilled, which never completely erodes through the course of the film. While Willi dozes in front of the border, a narrator in voice-over introduces us to him, citing his full name, current location, and the day's date. As the narrator lists other important dates and events in Willi's personal and family history, the camera slowly tracks toward and behind Willi as though not to awaken him. The narrator accordingly reduces his voice to a whisper when the camera circles around to face Willi. Concluding his story of how Willi had come to inherit

FIG. 9.1. Willi dozes in front of the border (*Der Willi-Busch-Report*).

the family business, the narrator explains that Willi's parents died in the early 1960s, leaving behind the "burdensome inheritance with their children, Adelheid and Wilhelm Busch." The moment he utters the word "Busch," Willi, startled, sits up and looks around him as though he has heard his name. Finding nothing, he lies back down and looks into the sky, where the opening credits appear.

While the presence of the border already invokes an atmosphere of surveillance, the opening sequence enhances this atmosphere through its use of voice-over and camerawork. From specific dates, names, and places to details about Willi's family history, we realize that the narrator is knowledgeable about Willi and his background, sharing this information with us while observing his "subject." Aligned with the perspective of the narrator, who remarks, "That is Wilhelm Busch," the camera slowly approaches Willi from behind in one long take, creating the effect that the narrator—and by extension, the viewer—is spying on Willi. Narrating Willi's history from offscreen, the voice-over is omnipresent and omniscient, qualities that Mary Ann Doane has attributed to the voice-over technique (2004, 379). Disembodied and not locatable, the voice-over bears authority over the image, thereby enhancing the sense that Willi is being surveilled by an unidentifiable but powerful entity.

Approaching Willi in one smooth shot, the Steadicam camera—at the time a new cinema technology that steadies the camera mounted to the body of its operator—is both embodied and disembodied at once. While it moves freely toward Willi like a body in the diegesis, its movements are conspicuously smooth, as though hovering in air. In this way the Steadicam evokes a drone-like technology. As though operated by the narrator at a different location, the mobile camera enters Willi's nearest proximity but remains unseen by Willi. Playing on popular associations of espionage with technological advancements, the camerawork in the sequence reinforces the impression that Willi's surveillant is an all-seeing authority with a limitless purview. Willi's disembodied "spy" can see everything without being seen. When he thinks he hears his name, Willi immediately looks forward toward the border, a gesture suggesting his intimation that a spy from across the border is watching him.

Appearing on-screen at the end of the opening sequence, the title of the film, *Der Willi-Busch-Report*, implicitly refers either to a surveillance "report" about Willi that the film represents or to Willi's own journalistic "reports" about Friedheim. The title thus reflects the ambiguity that lies at the heart of the film, namely, whether spies are pursuing Willi. Flying off into the distance, the border-patrol helicopter at the end of the sequence serves as a reminder that even if Willi is not being surveilled, the inhabitants of Friedheim are immersed in a climate of surveillance that the border generates. With the constant presence of patrol officers surveying the border both on and aboveground, the border town appears to be a hotspot for espionage activity, whether real or perceived.

Once Willi begins to publish his spy stories, several moments in the film suggest that his spies are not merely imaginary. For example he finds that someone has slashed the tires of his Messerschmitt bubble car; later a driver runs him off the road in a blue Mercedes, a car that he recognizes from an earlier moment in the film. Although the film does not offer a clear motive explaining why either the East or the West German secret service would surveil him, one might surmise that the Friedheim police are observing him to determine whether he is indeed the "telephone vandal" or if he is staging corpses—and perhaps even killing people—for his stories. The film also leaves open several possible explanations for the mysterious deaths of Arno Rösler, Baumbauer, and Sir Henry. Were they really spies? Or are Willi's sensationalist stories creating a climate of fear that is leading to violence? As more tourists come to Friedheim—whose name ironically alludes to peace—to see the "miracle child," is more violence an inevitable result of more people in the town? Or is Willi chalking up mere coincidences as acts of espionage? By refusing to explain whether Willi's spies are simply fantasy, Schilling's film sustains the "(geo)political uncertainty" that the Bond films typically seek to solve. Foregrounding ambiguity over clarity, *Der Willi-Busch-Report* undermines the rigid binaries that undergird the central conflicts in popular Cold War spy films. The film breaks down the border further by drawing attention to the climate of surveillance that invokes Willi's fears in the West, thus connecting lived experiences in East and West Germany.

Schilling's film uses ambiguity to critique the exploitation of spy narratives in popular media during the Cold War. These stories, the film suggests, skew the public's perception of reality, fostering the illusion that one is under threat by a foreign enemy, however vaguely conceived. Like the financially motivated Bond franchise, Willi invents spy stories in order to keep his business running. Soon, though, he is seduced by his own stories, leading him to take up arms against his imaginary enemies at the end of the film. In this respect one might read the final scene as an allegory for the Cold War. Influenced by his fantasies of espionage, Willi prepares to defend himself against an imagined danger, just as the powers of the Cold War—"a war in the mind" (Classen 2011)—waged the war with fictions in the form of propaganda and speculation, leading both sides to prepare for a "hot" war that remained only a threat. Spy stories in popular media, in other words, functioned as ideological warfare, inciting the fears and antagonisms that motivated the Cold War conflict. Initially a purely economic venture, Willi's stories begin to filter his reality as one that is full of imminent dangers, so that he is prepared to use violence against a threat that may or may not actually exist.

Although *Der Willi-Busch-Report* clearly taps into the stories circulating in the West German press about spies from the East, it also evokes the fear and mistrust that characterized the political climate in West Germany at the time of the German Autumn. Released just two years after the national crisis, the film conveys the atmosphere of suspicion and paranoia that arose with the increased presence of police and military forces during the nationwide search for the RAF terrorists. The headline of one of Willi's earlier stories, "Telefonterror" (Telephone terror), implicitly links terrorism to the mood of hysteria that ultimately incapacitates Willi. Easily swayed by his stories within this precarious environment, Willi succumbs to a nervous breakdown at the end of the film. Like Fassbinder in his contribution to the omnibus film *Deutschland im Herbst* (Brustellin et al. 1978, released in English as *Germany in Autumn*), Willi becomes paranoid and fearful to the extent that he becomes physically ill. Just as Fassbinder trembles, cries, sweats, and vomits when he hears the news and police sirens outside his apartment, Willi struggles to catch his breath and stay standing shortly after he reads the latest news. When police cars rush by him in the center of town with their screaming sirens, Willi, on the verge of collapse, leans against his car for support. In both NGC films, the politics of terror pervade the most intimate space of one's body, debilitating it from within (Rentschler 1984).

Der Willi-Busch-Report reiterates the criticisms that the left leveled against yellow journalism in the mid-1970s. Volker Schlöndorff's 1975 film adaptation of Heinrich Böll's controversial novel *Die verlorene Ehre der Katharina Blum oder: Wie Gewalt entstehen und wohin sie führen kann* (1974, translated as *The Lost Honor of Katharina Blum or: How Violence Develops and Where It Can Lead*) starkly criticizes the invasive methods of the press—the Axel Springer publishing company and its widely read *Bild-Zeitung* in particular—and its manipulation of facts for the sake of a good story. Indeed, the logo for the *Tag*, Willi's primary competitor, looks remarkably similar to the *Bild-Zeitung* logo with its white block letters on a red square background. In both Schlöndorff's and Schilling's films, tabloid journalism leads to violence: while Katharina murders the reporter who has violated her personhood with his false and exploitative representations of her, Willi is consumed by his own stories and prepares to defend himself with violence against people he now believes are spies plotting to kill him. Willi becomes a victim of hysteria created by his own sensationalist reportages.

Moments before his nervous breakdown, Willi quickly drives past a crowd of reporters recording him on video. Like Schlöndorff's *Die verlorene Ehre der Katharina Blum* (released in English as *The Lost Honor of Katharina Blum*), Schilling's film criticizes the press by implicitly comparing the invasive methods of reporters to espionage. In his "report" on Willi, the spy-narrator in the opening sequence recounts Willi's history in a manner that is stylistically evocative of journalism, using long, complex sentences and the simple past. Arno Rösler, Willi's friend and chief reporter for the popular national magazine *Ring*, is also a journalist-spy. Before Willi decides to frame him as a spy, he learns that Rösler has intended to steal his story about the prophetic little girl. Posthumously, the *Ring* publishes Rösler's article on the Friedheim "miracle child." Like a spy Rösler refuses to disclose his true motives for visiting Friedheim, claiming that he simply wants to stop by his hometown while on his return trip to Munich. His girlfriend, an attractive and elegant woman who—like the women in Bond—sits on his lap and flatters him, knows Rösler only by his pseudonym Wolf-Dieter Schönborn, or his "cover." Willi's friend is not the person he projects himself to be but rather is "infiltrating" a location under camouflage for the purpose of gathering information and material for his work.

But Willi, too, spies throughout the film in the hopes of discovering a good story. When the teacher Rose-Marie first comes to Friedheim, Willi uses binoculars to observe her from afar as she arrives at work. Later Rose-Marie asks Willi to leave her alone after he surprises her outside her school, circling and snapping photographs of her. In the scene in which they sleep together, Willi pauses to take notes, prompting Rose-Marie to ask him whether he is using her for a "sex report." Disappointed, she hastily gets dressed and looks out the window toward the border with Willi's binoculars. In a binocular shot from her point of view, two guards chuckle and move closer to the border behind a small hill, where they look back at her with their binoculars. The scene implies that both Willi and the border guards alike are "spies" who invade Rose-Marie's personal space to exploit her sexually. While Willi, Rose-Marie assumes, intends to write a "sex report" about her, the border guards spy on her having sex with Willi and then getting dressed. She is caught between the crosshairs of "spies" in the East and the reporter "spies" in the West. The reporter, in other words, is just as invasive as the "spies" across the border, a notion that the mutual spying between Willi and the border guards emphasizes. Looking through their binoculars, Willi and the guards look back at each other in shots/reverse shots throughout the film. Although they have different motives, Willi and the guards spy on each other in mirrorlike images that imply an equivocal relationship between them and their surveilling gazes. Willi is the reporter who acts as a spy, trespassing spaces and violating personal boundaries for the sake of his "reports." Reporters, the film suggests, are the spies who invent the spies.

In comparing reporters to spies, Schilling's film ironizes spy film tropes in the mise-en-scène, in particular the radio cassette player/recorder. As transmitters of secret codes and information, radios and recorders appear frequently in the Bond spy thrillers, where they serve important narrative functions.[5] Though a radio is not a surprising find on a reporter, Willi decides to frame Rösler as a spy upon discovering Rösler's radio cassette recorder, exploiting the trope for his own spy stories. Contrary to the trope, Willi finds nothing remarkable in Rösler's recordings, and lacking the finesse with which Bond handles technological devices, he fumbles with the recorder as it repeatedly ejects the cassette he tries to insert. While Willi is excited by his "discovery," Rose-Marie and Rösler's girlfriend fall asleep in the background, an ironic jab at Willi's exaggerated inventions. Soon, however, Willi is seduced by the trope he initially exploits. When the same radio model he finds on Rösler washes up ashore with Baumbauer, he becomes increasingly suspicious that Friedheim actually does host a nest of spies. He later discovers the same radio model on the corpse of Sir Henry, which leads him to believe that Sir Henry was also a spy and that Friedheim is teeming with spies. In a close-up shot, Sir Henry's radio drips blood onto a copy of the *Werra-Post*, a visual metaphor for the transformation of what was originally Willi's discursive fiction into—at least for Willi—a violent reality. Discovered by Willi with the radio on and newspapers strewn about him, Sir Henry appears to be a murder victim of the stories themselves, which seem to have taken on a life of their own with real and dangerous consequences.

The scene leading to Rösler's death amplifies the ironic undertones of the radio. As Willi leaves his class reunion in a local party hall to check on Rösler, he walks by a poster for *The Green Hornet*, a popular American television show in the 1960s. Originally a radio series, *The Green Hornet* starred the martial arts icon Bruce Lee as the vigilante Kato, who fights crime undercover with his partner, the "Green Hornet." The Green Hornet is Britt Reid (Van Williams), owner and publisher of the *Daily Sentinel* newspaper. Though not spies per se, Kato and the Green Hornet infiltrate crime rings in disguise, working beyond the aegis of the police to ensure the security of their community. In the pilot for *The Green Hornet* (Peerce 1966), the discovery of a radio transmitter leads the vigilantes to the criminal. The tongue-in-cheek reference to the television series implies that on-screen tropes have conditioned Willi's spy fantasies. Willi imagines that Rösler, like the Green Hornet, leads a dual life of a journalist for a successful newspaper and a spy, a secret that Rösler's radio reveals. The *Green Hornet* poster emphasizes the discrepancy between global media culture and Willi's local reality in provincial West Germany. Willi's *Green Hornet*–inspired spy fantasies—and the poster itself, which boasts action and the international film star Bruce Lee—contrast sharply with the sleepy class reunion in which traditional folk music is the entertainment highlight of the event. The film ironically demonstrates how global stories of espionage influence local realities—which in actuality look very different— where they instigate violence, both imagined and real.

After Willi discovers the third radio on Baumbauer, we, the viewers, also begin to suspect that there is something amiss in Friedheim. But when Willi flips through Rösler's story in the *Ring*, he pauses briefly at an advertisement for a shiny silver radio cassette recorder, reminding us of its consumerist function as media image. Despite our temptation to interpret the radios of Rösler, Baumbauer, and Sir Henry as signs of espionage, the advertisement brings back into relief how the press and popular media exploit visual tropes linked to spies and spying for commercial profit. The image of the radio—twice removed as an image in print that the camera captures on film—calls our attention to our own suspicions and expectations that spy stories in the media have created. *Der Willi-Busch-Report* not only emphasizes the dangerous effects of sensationalism in the charged political climate of 1970s West Germany but also debunks fantastical tales of espionage by bringing into focus the seemingly arbitrary relationship between spying and its tropes.

Subverting Border Tropes: Reimagining the Inner German Border

Der Willi-Busch-Report extends its critique of "popular geopolitics" to its representation of borders and the inner German border in particular. While it demonstrates the arbitrariness of geopolitical divisions, the film also emphasizes the discrepancy between the global ideological—that is, imagined—binaries in Bond and the local reality of the border in the heartland of Germany. In the West German border town, the abstract ideological differences of the global Cold War conflict fade into insignificance. By demystifying popular border fantasies, Schilling's film challenges and contests the authority of the "Iron Curtain," whose divisive violence had particularly injurious effects in the country it ruptured.

Mimicking the imagined geopolitical borders between rivals in popular spy fictions, Willi creates his own imaginary borders throughout the film, which separate him from his perceived "spies" and adversaries. Whenever he buys the *Tag* at the local convenience store, he reads it while standing in the middle of the street, crumples it up, and tosses it into a trash can on the sidewalk across from him. The camera focuses on Willi's feet as he lines himself up precisely on the edge of the painted border dividing street traffic. Annoyed when he realizes the *Tag* is stealing his stories, Willi erects an imaginary border in the space of his daily lived experience, tossing his competition over and away onto the other side. In an ironic gesture, the camera reinforces this border by using shots/countershots that do not reflect Willi's point of view. Instead, the camera cuts from a medium shot of Willi to a medium shot of the trash can on the other side. Willi and the receptacle thus appear to be in separate spaces that are too distant from each other to be captured in one shot, even though they are only a few meters from each other.

Before Willi tosses the *Tag* over his "border" for a second time, he notices a well-dressed man on the other side reading the same paper and facing his direction. The soundtrack evokes an air of suspicion, and when Willi returns to the sidewalk, he observes two similarly dressed men in dark sunglasses swiftly cross the street and drive off in a blue Mercedes, the vehicle that drives him off the road later in the film. As soon as the men cross the "border," Willi links them to spies, remarking to a man nearby, "Oh, yes, our BND friends are already here," referring to the West German secret service (Bundesnachrichtendienst). In the following shot, Willi scribbles on a scratch pad the words "Stasi" and "BND," as though trying to determine whether he should frame his new "spies" as either East or West German. He speculates that the men could be Stasi agents rather than BND; after all, they cross the "border" back to the other side. Tellingly, Willi appears to consider these options while sitting in a movie theater, a tongue-in-cheek reminder that moving images have created the "spies" of Willi's imagination. At the same time, the film that Willi is about to watch—an East German propaganda film—indicates the fluidity of the boundary between East and West in the border town, while Willi's consideration of both national secret services implies an equivocal relationship between them, as though they are interchangeable. In the streets of the border town—the very heart of the Cold War—ideological borders and binaries become redundant. The closer one approaches the Iron Curtain, the more muddled it becomes.

Just as Willi perceives "spies" and antagonists across his imagined borders, so, too, does the inner German border stimulate spy fantasies that reinforce its presence and power in the West German national imaginary. In Schilling's film, however, the border town is not a site of action, violence, and intrigue, but rather it is a boring, plain, and uneventful place, a blank slate that Willi must discursively reinvent in order to sell his newspaper. Friedheim is seemingly stuck in time. The inebriated Sir Henry continues to mumble Nazi rhetoric to the annoyance of the barkeeper, and when Willi interviews an elderly couple for advice to share with his readers, they recommend ingesting "Thorn," a product with which Willi and Rose-Marie are unfamiliar. Visitors to Friedheim are sparse: when a small caboose rolls in, Willi and his auto mechanic immediately look up, as though its arrival were a special event for the untraversed town. Ironically, the border has transformed Friedheim into a dull and sluggish village, now at the remote outskirts of the country rather than at its heart and center.

The wire itself dividing East from West is uninteresting, so much so that Willi is able to sleep directly in front of it in the opening scene of the film. A daily sight for the villagers, the "fence" is a mere eyesore, as Rose-Marie remarks: "Darn fence! I can't look at it anymore." Hardly a source of excitement, the border is an everyday object, a "fence" that is more annoying and inconvenient than it is threatening. On an acoustic level, too, the border is unremarkable, as Willi and the other inhabitants of Friedheim do not notice the sounds of flares, gunfire, and grenades that we hear throughout the film. Willi becomes startled at the sound of a flare only toward the end of the film when he believes that he is surrounded by spies. In a scene tinged with moderate black humor, Willi exploits the very lifelessness of the border zone for the sake of his stories when he deposits Rösler's corpse at the border at dusk with no one—not even a border-patrol officer—around to notice.

Der Willi-Busch-Report portrays the inner German border as drab and mundane on a visual level as well. In the opening credits, aerial shots of the border underscore the flatness of the region. While images of the Berlin Wall circulating in West German mainstream media tend to emphasize the verticality of the border as a rigid and formidable divider between two distinct spaces, the images in Schilling's film flatten out the border by drawing attention to the almost mirrorlike reflection of the green forested areas on both sides. The uniformity in landscape and color merge the two areas, whose monochrome hues of greenish-brown impart a dull, lackluster quality to the border zone. Ironically, the border town—in contrast to Willi's spy stories—is nothing other than a no-man's-land with an unsightly "fence" embedded in greenery.

In emphasizing the uneventfulness of the border, the film subverts the Bondian tropes of the binocular shot and the technologically advanced automobile. When Willi observes the border-patrol officers with his binoculars, a binocular mask covers the lens of the camera to mimic Willi's perspective. While Bond frequently uses

FIG. 9.2. An aerial shot shows the lackluster border zone (*Der Willi-Busch-Report*).

binoculars to spy on his enemies—in *Goldfinger* (Hamilton 1964) and *For Your Eyes Only* (Glen 1981), to name just two examples— Willi, unlike Bond, does not discover anything of importance with his device. Contrary to our expectations, the binocular shots in *Der Willi-Busch-Report* pan left and right to follow the guards and trucks, but rather than reveal new and interesting information, they illustrate the monotony and routineness of everyday life on the border. Hardly an indicator of a developing intrigue, the binocular shot of the guards who chuckle as they watch Rose-Marie get dressed merely shows two bored young men taking pleasure in spying on a naked woman.

Willi's Messerschmitt similarly conveys the stagnancy and temporal standstill of the border town in its ironic appropriation. Unlike Bond's sexy, high-speed, intricately designed vehicles, Willi's Messerschmitt, a car that had not been in production since the early 1960s, fails to start in the beginning of the film despite Willi's efforts (Cruz n.d.). Struggling to start the car, Willi pushes it forward along the road when another car—an Italian Fiat—honks and races past him. He then jumps into his worn and ratty driver's seat and successfully starts the car after it backfires several times. Willi proceeds to put on his aviator hat, an ironic gesture in relation to his slow, barely functioning vehicle. This irony becomes more pronounced when the auto mechanic—who knows Willi's "stinky" Messerschmitt well—teasingly refers to the car as Willi's "airplane." In her review of the film, Mareike Sprengel wrote with a hint of sarcasm: "One could almost think it [the Messerschmitt] capable of extending wings and flying into the air like in a James Bond film to fool the GDR border patrol" (n.d.).

As he drives along the border in the opening sequence, Willi scowls at the helicopter flying above him when it quickly overtakes him. Replacing the helicopter's drone, an upbeat synthesized musical score enters the soundtrack when the camera joins Willi in his Messerschmitt, forming an ironic contrast with a vehicle that is hardly as fast as its musical motif implies. Willi conveys his hope that time will speed up with his car in a rhyme: "If you drive a Messerschmitt, time will fly by" (Fährst du auch 'n Messerschmitt, die Zeit vergeht in Sauseschritt). As the company vehicle—*Werra Post* is printed on its side—the outdated automobile ironically points to the demise of a newspaper in a town seemingly stuck in time.

While Bond achieves a virtually limitless range of mobility through his vehicles, traversing through land, air, and water all over and even beyond the globe, Willi can hardly move within his small town with his Messerschmitt. Indeed, his dysfunctional car allegorizes the very spatial limits that are imposed—rather than uplifted—by popular spy stories. The "spies" pursuing Willi literally restrict the space in which Willi can move by running his vehicle off the road, after which it must be towed back into town where it originated. Willi's own narratives of espionage render him immobile at the end of the film when paramedics must transport him to an ambulance. Triggering paranoia spy stories ultimately push Willi up against an otherwise inconspicuous border—to the very "Stop! Border" sign—where he is cornered and vulnerable. Now without a car, Willi stumbles to the border with a visible limp—though we do not see him injure himself—and points his rifle at the people trying to detain him above, in front, and behind him. As the police approach, Willi gestures toward the other side of the border and threatens, "If anyone comes down here I'll go for a walk in the GDR!" Before he can escape across the border, however, Willi collapses, stuck

FIG. 9.3. Willi tries to collect himself after two mysterious vehicles run him off the road (*Der Willi-Busch-Report*).

within the confines of the West. Schilling's film demonstrates the paradox of Cold War popular spy stories that foster the illusion of mobility but ultimately reaffirm borders between East and West, thus delimiting one's spatial range, both physically and as imagined.

Der Willi-Busch-Report does not simply subvert tropes in order to expose the covert ideological functions of popular spy fantasies. Rather, by foregrounding its material reality, the film opens the inner German border up to new meanings and imaginings beyond its dominant discourses. Both the opening and the end sequences of the film emphasize the organic quality of the border zone as a living and lived space that contrasts with its representations in global politics and the media. In the first shot of the film, the press snaps photographs of Stalin, Churchill, and Roosevelt in documentary footage of the Yalta Conference, where the three global leaders drew the new geopolitical boundaries after the Second World War. The following shot shows a map of Europe held directly in front of the camera. A person behind the map begins to cut with scissors along the Iron Curtain—described by the narrator as an "odd line"—revealing the actual border zone in three-dimensional space behind it. The official discourses on the border are visually flat and removed from lived reality: while the Yalta Conference is represented in grainy

FIG. 9.4. Willi is cornered at the border (*Der Willi-Busch-Report*).

black-and-white footage, the map fills the entire frame of the shot, emphasizing its one-dimensionality. By contrast the camera lends a sense of depth and vitality to the third representation of the border in which the film is set, moving easily through the green space in long, smooth sweeps afforded by the Steadicam. Acoustically, too, Schilling's film re-instills a sense of life to the border: as we watch the Yalta Conference, chirping birds fill the soundtrack rather than the snapping of photographs and voices we might expect. By virtue of their incongruity, the unexpected sounds of birds crack open the official political discourse of the border that is evoked visually. By representing it as a living and lived site, Schilling's film depicts the border as a place of change and potential, thus breaking the ideological authority that its fixed dominant discourses enforce.

With its ongoing presentness, the long take in the opening sequence releases the border from the constraints of narrative time, thus granting it an additional charge of political resistance. Summarizing Pier Paolo Pasolini's claims in his famous 1967 essay "Observations on the Long Take," Lutz Koepnick points out that the long take for Pasolini "defied the closure and death imposed by the violence of the cut" and in so doing, "ran up against the very possibility of meaning-making, precisely because our ability to generate meaning . . . cannot do without us actively recognizing the finality that is death and that film allegorizes in the form of the cut" (2013, 196). For the postwar European art filmmakers, the long take represented an act of resistance against the cut, a "method of challenging closure, probing presentness, and thus intensifying realism; of allowing spectators to peruse the screen according to their own measure and will" (196). In Schilling's film the long takes of the border resist the temporal boundaries that give it meaning—and thus its political power—to begin with. In these shots the film asks its viewers to perceive the border beyond the discursive parameters that have framed and thereby legitimized it. Defying the violence of the cut, the long take in Schilling's film *mends* the wound that it represents, namely, the division of Germany. Unlike the Bond films with their rapid cuts that allegorically reinforce the films' ideological demarcations, *Der Willi-Busch-Report* engages a cinematography of suturing rather than cutting, healing rather than wounding. Schilling's long take inspires a reimagining of the inner German border that does not—as opposed to "popular geopolitics"—confirm and perpetuate its divisive violence, but rather it resists that violence through its patient, mending gaze.

As Willi's world becomes increasingly smaller as a result of his growing paranoia, the camera in the final sequence of the film paradoxically lends movement to the border zone, yielding a sense of life and regeneration that contrasts with Willi's immobility and threat of violence. With the camera following him from behind, Willi stumbles through a defunct and overgrown train tunnel as he escapes to the border. Connecting the spaces on each side of the tunnel, the tracking shot of the camera stages a bridging that is rendered smooth and continuous by the Steadicam. Although the camera does not transcend the inner German border, it conveys through its linking of two spaces an underlying potential for unity and oneness at the divided site, a potential that the camera itself discovers with its new technology.

The very strangeness of Willi's attempt to find Munzel, his runaway rabbit, at the end of the film imbues the border zone with a sense of the unexpected and unconventional. As Willi searches for his rabbit with a piece of cabbage in hand, we, too, look for it in binocular shots that slowly and silently pan over the border. Rather than surveil the border for spies, escapees, or some act of conspiracy, we are instead called on to look for Willi's rabbit. These shots thus compel us to read images of the border *differently*, to remove the filter that has shaped our perception of the border. Although the film admittedly does not ask us to look for rabbit fugitives per se, the cue to a rabbit search pushes the limits of our imagination to conceive of new and unanticipated images of the border, which, in turn, undermine the political authority that its popular representations administer. Unusual and peculiar the search for Munzel prompts us to look for hidden inflections and latent possibilities in the images of the border that might inspire its reimagining. While Willi's spy stories reinforce the power of the Iron Curtain, Schilling's film, by contrast, seeks to dismantle that power by presenting it as a site that is not ideologically closed off but rather replete with enigmas and undiscovered potentials, a site that is open to transformation and the prospect of change.

Though relatively unknown among German cinema scholars and cineastes, *Der Willi-Busch-Report* stands out among its contemporaries as a unique historical record of the inner German border in the West German countryside. Forgoing the action and suspense of the more successful espionage thrillers of its day, the film opts instead to critique "popular geopolitics" in particular and the violence of media sensationalism in general in late 1970s West Germany. The film is not as formally or thematically radical as many other films in the NGC, as it tends to follow the storytelling patterns in classical narrative cinema. Nevertheless, it takes on a political valence not only in its sociopolitical critique but also in encouraging new images and perceptions of the border that are no longer predetermined by dominant—and destructive—ideologies. In this respect the film offers a counter-aesthetic not only to the popular spy films of its time but also to contemporary Hollywood-style productions that represent the Stasi, from Florian Henckel von Donnersmarck's Oscar-winning *Das Leben der Anderen* (2006, released in English as *The Lives of Others*) to the RTL television series *Deutschland 83* (Berger and Radsi 2015). While many of the Stasi dramas tend to reiterate Cold War dichotomies in their facile representation of East Germany as the morally destitute and evil "other" to the West, more recent East/West spy dramas—Christian Petzold's *Barbara* (2012) and Christian Schwochow's *Westen* (*West*, 2013), for example—engage more critically with Germany's Cold War past, muddling the binaries that still dominate cinematic retellings of the era since the war thawed (Pinfold 2014). Schilling's film thus represents an important yet overlooked precursor to the more critical German spy films since reunification.

But the political charge to *Der Willi-Busch-Report* is particularly meaningful within the film's historical context of a still-divided Germany. Indeed, in deconstructing border tropes, the film predicts Germany's actual reunification, lending yet another layer of irony to the film that Schilling later takes up in *Deutschfieber* (German fever, 1992, released in English as *Border Frenzy*), the postwall sequel to *Der Willi-Busch-Report*. Demonstrating the subversive power of irony, the film anticipates in some respects the very ironic turn of events on November 9, 1989, when a revision of border regulations in East Berlin led to the full dismantling of the Berlin Wall. Just as "popular geopolitics" reify Cold War borders, so, too, the film suggests, can "critical geopolitics" take them down. Opening East/West German cinematic spy stories back up to inquiry at the time the Berlin Wall still stood, Schilling's film challenges German Cold War politics long before hindsight afforded us the distance for critical reflection.

Notes

1. Reinhard Hauff's *Der Mann auf der Mauer* (The man on the wall, 1982), an adaptation of Peter Schneider's story *Der Mauerspringer* (1982, translated as *The Wall Jumper: A Berlin Story*), is one exception.

2. Ironically, like the works of the real Wilhelm Busch, Schilling's film uses black humor to critique contemporary Germany. See Davidson 2003.

3. Translations here and throughout are mine.

4. See Costabile-Heming's chapter on *For Eyes Only* in this volume.

5. For example, in *Diamonds Are Forever* (Hamilton 1971), Bond attempts to replace the cassette tape that villain Blofeld uses to control his satellite, but his plan fails when Blofeld finds the replacement tape in Bond's suit.

References

Bennett, Tony, and Janet Woollacott. 2003. "The Moments of Bond." In *The James Bond Phenomenon: A Critical Reader*, edited by Christoph Lindner, 13–33. Manchester: Manchester University Press.

Berger, Edward, and Samira Radsi, dirs. 2015. *Deutschland 83*. Television series. UFA Fiction.

Blumenberg, Hans-Christoph. 1982. "Markt des schönen Seins: Ironische Exkursionen in ein Land der falschen Bilder." *Die Zeit*, October 1.

Brustellin, Alf et al., dirs. 1978. *Deutschland im Herbst*. Feature film. ABS Filmproduktion.

Chapman, James. 2000. *License to Thrill: A Cultural History of the James Bond Films*. New York: Columbia University Press.

Classen, Christoph. 2011. "Kalter Krieg im Kino: Zur Konjunktur des Agentenfilms in den 1960er-Jahren und ihren Voraussetzungen." *Bundeszentrale für politische Bildung*, September 9. http://www.bpb.de/gesellschaft/kultur/filmbildung/63102/kalter-krieg-im-kino.

Cruz, Frank da. n.d. "The Messerschmitt Kabinenroller." Accessed June 10, 2017. http://www.columbia.edu/~fdc/germany/messerschmitt.html.

Davidson, John E. 2003. "Crime and the Cynical Solution: Black Comedy, Critique, and the Spirit of Self-Concern in Recent German Film." In *Light Motives: German Popular Film in Perspective*, edited by Randall Halle and Margaret McCarthy, 259–80. Detroit: Wayne State University Press.

Doane, Mary Ann. 2004. "The Voice in the Cinema: The Articulation of Body and Space." In *Film Theory and Criticism*, edited by Leo Braudy and Marshall Cohen, 373–85. New York: Oxford University Press.

Dodds, Klaus. 2007. "Screening Geopolitics: James Bond and the Early Cold War Films (1962–1967)." In *Cinema and Popular Geo-Politics*, edited by Marcus Power and Andrew Crampton, 72–94. Routledge: New York.

Eco, Umberto. 2003. "Narrative Structures in Fleming." In *The James Bond Phenomenon: A Critical Reader*, edited by Christoph Lindner, 34–55. Manchester: Manchester University Press.

Gilbert, Lewis, dir. 1967. *You Only Live Twice*. Feature film. Eon Productions and Danjaq.

———, dir. 1979. *Moonraker*. Feature film. Eon Productions and Les Productions Artistes Associés.

Glen, John, dir. 1981. *For Your Eyes Only*. Feature film. Eon Productions.

———, dir. 1983. *Octopussy*. Feature film. Eon Productions.

Hagen, Peter, dir. 1973–79. *Das unsichtbare Visier*. Television series. DFF.

Hagopian, Kevin J. 2009. "Flint and Satyriasis: The Bond Parodies of the 1960s." In *Secret Agents: Popular Icons beyond James Bond*, edited by Jeremy Packer, 21–53. New York: Peter Lang.

Hamilton, Guy, dir. 1964. *Goldfinger*. Feature film. Eon Productions.

———, dir. 1971. *Diamonds Are Forever*. Eon Productions.

Hauff, Reinhard. 1982. *Der Mann auf der Mauer*. Feature film. Bioskop Film.

Henckel von Donnersmarck, Florian, dir. 2006. *Das Leben der Anderen*. Feature film. Wiedemann & Berg Filmproduktion.

Haegele

Hughes, Rachel. 2016. "Geopolitics and Visual Culture." In *The Ashgate Research Companion to Critical Geopolitics*, edited by Klaus Dodds, Merje Kuus, and Joanne Sharp, 69–89. New York: Routledge.

Jansen, Peter W. 1980. "Halt! Hier Grenze: Der Max-Ophüls-Preisträger Niklaus Schilling." *Frankfurter Rundschau*, July 26.

Koepnick, Lutz. 2013. "Long Takes . . ." In *Berlin School Glossary: An ABC of the New Wave in German Cinema*, edited by Roger F. Cook, Lutz Koepnick, Kristin Kopp, and Brad Prager, 195–203. Chicago: Intellect.

Lawrence, John Shelton. 2011. "The American Superhero Genes of James Bond." In *James Bond in World and Popular Culture: The Films Are Not Enough*, edited by Robert G. Weiner, B. Lynn Whitfield, and Jack Becker, 330–48. Newcastle upon Tyne: Cambridge Scholars Publishing.

"Moonraker—Streng geheim." n.d. *Goldene Leinwand*. Accessed May 21, 2017. https://www.goldene-leinwand.de/filme/moonraker-streng-geheim/.

Nikitin, Nikolaj, and Oliver Baumgarten. 2011. "The Celluloid Curtain: Europe's Cold War in Film." *Bundeszentrale für politische Bildung*, September 9. http://www.bpb.de/gesellschaft/kultur/filmbildung/63060/kuratorentext.

"Octopussy." n.d. *Goldene Leinwand*. Accessed May 21, 2017. https://www.goldene-leinwand.de/filme/octopussy/.

Osteried, Peter. 2016. *Eurospy Helden: Jerry Cotton, Kommissar X, Sumuru*. Munich: Self-published.

Peerce, Larry, dir. *The Green Hornet*. Television series. Season 1, episode 3, "Programmed for Death." Aired September 23, 1966, on ABC.

Petzold, Christian, dir. 2012. *Barbara*. Feature film. Schramm Film Koerner & Weber.

Pinfold, Debbie. 2014. "The End of the Fairy Tale? Christian Petzold's *Barbara* and the Difficulties of Interpretation." *German Life and Letters* 67 (2) (April): 279–300.

Power, Marcus, and Andrew Crampton. 2007. "Reel Geopolitics: Cinematographing Political Space." In *Cinema and Popular Geo-Politics*, edited by Marcus Power and Andrew Crampton, 1–12. New York: Routledge.

Rentschler, Eric. 1984. *West German Film in the Course of Time*. New York: Redgrave.

Rubin, Martin. 1999. *Thrillers*. Cambridge: Cambridge University Press.

Scharf, Inga. 2007. "Staging the Border: National Identity and the Critical Geopolitics of West German Film." In *Cinema and Popular Geo-Politics*, edited by Marcus Power and Andrew Crampton, 182–202. New York: Routledge.

Schilling, Niklaus, dir. 1979. *Der Willi-Busch-Report*. Feature film. Visual Filmproduktion.

———, dir. 1982. *Der Westen leuchtet!* Feature film. Visual Filmproduktion.

———, dir. 1992. *Deutschfieber*. Feature film. Visual Filmproduktion.

Schlöndorff, Volker, dir. 1975. *Die verlorene Ehre der Katharina Blum*. Feature film. Bioskop Film.

Schwochow, Christian, dir. 2013. *Westen*. Feature film. Zero One Film.

Sprengel, Mareike. n.d. "Sein und Scheinen: Mareike Sprengel im Gespräch mit Niklaus Schilling." Accessed June 10, 2017. http://visualfilm.deutsches -filminstitut.de/texte2.html#Sein.

——. n.d. "Wilhelm Busch—der Dichter und Willi Busch—der Lenker." Accessed October 15, 2017. http://visualfilm.deutsches-filminstitut.de/willibusch.html.

Veiczi, János, dir. 1963. *For Eyes Only—streng geheim*. Feature film. DEFA.

Young, Terence, dir. 1962. *Dr. No*. Feature film. Eon Productions.

——, dir. 1963. *From Russia with Love*. Feature film. Eon Productions.

10 Political Ambiguity in Recent Cold War Spy Stories on Screen

CHERYL DUECK

Film, itself a medium of surveillance, is arguably an ideal site for the aesthetic depiction of surveillance mechanisms. A number of films in the second decade of the twenty-first century have effectively employed these aesthetics as a conduit for national stories to travel internationally and thus contribute both to discourses about Cold War surveillance and to those about the current climate of "liquid surveillance" (Bauman and Lyon 2013). As David Lyon puts it, today's surveillance "not only creeps and seeps, it also flows. It is on the move, globally and locally. The means of tracing and tracking the mobilities of the twenty-first century are 'going global' in the sense that connections are increasingly sought between one system and another" (2010, 330). The Edward Snowden revelations of 2013 brought attention to the vast scope of National Security Agency activities worldwide and, in turn, served to reframe representations of Cold War surveillance. As explored here the films about the Cold War in the subsequent years engage more explicitly than previously with a current international preoccupation with blanket surveillance in their aesthetic approach, their thematic content, and their application of plurimedial networking. My analysis of the feature films *Westen* (*West*; Schwochow 2013) and *Bridge of Spies* (Spielberg 2015) and the television series *Deutschland 83* (Winger and Winger 2015) will show how these productions undertake to present political ambiguity through filmic devices such as blurring, framing, and representation of affect, as well as narrative, thus speaking to the climate of fear and mistrust of *all* mechanisms of surveillance.

We live in a heightened era of surveillance anxiety, in which we have learned that the CIA uses camera devices in phones and televisions to spy on people. Indeed, when President Trump's advisor and spokesperson mistakenly told Americans that even their microwaves could be watching them (Timberg, Dwoskin, and Nakashima 2017; Kelly 2017), many likely accepted it as fact. Who is watching whom and why? Since the beginning of cinema, the act of looking has been a preoccupation of filmmakers, a built-in reflexivity. With this in mind, then, spy films are a natural fit and speak to each audience with their own timely concerns about watching and looking. Cinematography and staging are key elements that convey to the viewer the anxieties and motivations of watchers and watched. This chapter will address the Cold War espionage that has featured prominently in film and television of the second decade of this century, not as historical representation but as an engagement with more-contemporary preoccupations with blanket surveillance. In Germany public debate over communications surveillance and protection rose sharply in 2012, as citizens learned that the Federal Intelligence Service (Bundesnachrichtendienst, BND) had been monitoring tens of millions of emails ("Geheimdienste überwachten" 2012). Since Snowden's revelations in 2013 of the extent of the U.S. National Security Agency's reach internationally (Poitras, Rosenbach, and Stark 2013), from laptop cameras to German chancellor Angela Merkel's phone ("Merkels Handy" 2013), international anxieties about surveillance have been at front of mind. Lyon defines surveillance as "collecting information in order to manage or control" (2015, 3). The collection of information by agents that took place during the Cold War had, for the most part, a clear purpose: to understand the activities of an enemy state in order to prevent harm, or to avert counterrevolution from within the state. Surveillance was carried out by individuals on individuals. Lyon explains further that surveillance involves "systematic and routine attention to personal details, whether specific or aggregate, for a defined purpose," and this purpose is "to protect, understand, care for, ensure entitlement, control, manage or influence individuals or groups" (3). While this purpose and definition apply equally well to Cold War and current surveillance practices, the *means* of surveillance have changed, and the anxieties shifted.

A significant difference between Bond-style spy thrillers and films about surveillance in state socialism is, of course, that the Bond-style agents are carrying out surveillance of an enemy state. Creating empathy with a spy who is serving one's own national interests by protecting against a foreign enemy differs from when the enemy is his or her own people. Since the spy may come from within, the spy thrillers that involve internal state surveillance speak compellingly to contemporary anxieties about the kind of "liquid surveillance" that is conducted worldwide through digital monitoring.

Liquid Surveillance in Cinema

The term "liquid surveillance" derives from conversations between Zygmunt Bauman and David Lyon, first used in publication in 2010 (Lyon) and subsequently in a book-length record of their exchanges on the subject (Bauman and Lyon 2013). Bauman's long-standing occupation with surveillance branches out from Foucault's use of the prison panopticon as a metaphor for the power relations of surveillance: a form of self-monitored behavior control contingent on the knowledge that one could be observed at any time by an unseen inspector. In this model there remains a relationship between the watcher and the watched, and the model aims to provide transparency to the watcher and eliminate ambivalence (Lyon 2010, 329). We are now, according to Lyon and Bauman, in a postpanoptical environment, in which those with surveillant power "can at any moment escape beyond reach—into sheer inaccessibility" (Bauman 2000, 11). In liquid modernity change is permanent: structures of the social world are in a condition of constant mutation and are no longer "solid" (Bauman 2000). Connections that have been made are readily severed, identities change, and expectations give way to uncertainty, which means that citizens subject to mass data surveillance may easily become suspects:

> Because of the way that personal data are used, everyone living in so-called advanced societies is routinely targeted and sorted by

numerous organizations on a daily basis, whether applying for a driver's license, paying a telephone bill or surfing the internet. The concept of liquid surveillance captures the reduction of the body to data and the creation of data-doubles on which life-chances and choices hang more significantly than on our real lives and the stories we tell about them. It also evokes the flows of data that are now crucial to surveillance as well as to the "time-sensitivity" of surveillance "truths" that mutate as more data come in. (Lyon 2010, 325)

The flows move in all directions, in turn eliciting "liquid fear," Bauman's term from 2006. The constant mutation of information means that attempts to eliminate ambivalence, or blurred lines, are doomed to fail.

Rapidly flowing images and heightened anxiety are signatures of a good thriller, and all three of the works discussed here fall into the thriller genre: two as feature films, the other as an eight-episode television series. Their plot structures are designed for suspense and enjoyment and to attract diverse international audiences. They vary in the extent to which the historical events depicted are part of a contextualization or didactic purpose, but all make efforts to provide high style diversion. Set in the Cold War, with involvement of East and West Germany, the Soviet Union and the United States, all of them move across East-West borders and provide views of both sides that shift preconceptions of the truths that governments believe they can gain through surveillance. In each case the story is driven by the pervasive question, "who is watching?"

Continuities in Post–Cold War Surveillance and Espionage: Schwochow's *Westen*

Westen is a film by director Christian Schwochow, with a screenplay by his mother, Heide Schwochow. It is based on a bestselling novel with the title *Lagerfeuer* (Campfire) by Julia Franck (2003), who also assisted with details as the Schwochows worked on the screenplay.[1] It premiered at the Montreal World Film Festival in August 2013 and was released more widely in 2014, timed to coincide with the twenty-fifth anniversary of the fall of the Berlin Wall, on November 9, 2014. The film, which received several awards at the German Film Awards and the Montreal Film Festival, tells the story of Nelly, played by Jördis Triebel, a woman who decides to go West with her son, Alexei, in the late 1970s: so-called *Republik-flucht* (flight from the Republic). Nelly is a professional chemist, and Alexei's father, Vassily, was a Russian physicist who traveled often. The film begins with his departure for a conference in the Soviet Union, from which he never returns. She is told that Vassily died in a crash, but his body has mysteriously never been found. Opting for a fresh start in the West, she hires a Western smuggler, who takes her and her son across the border on the pretense that they are getting married. The action is set primarily in the Marienfelde Refugee Transit Centre in West Berlin for a period of months in the late 1970s, where the protagonist is subject to extensive questioning by the CIA and the West German BND, as a potential security risk. An African American CIA agent, John Bird, finds her attractive, and after they begin a discreet sexual relationship, she is able to elicit from him the reason for the intense scrutiny: The Americans believe that Vassily was an agent whose role was to recruit Western scientists, and the West Germans may have faked his death to get him out when he wanted to distance himself. That would mean that he could still be alive and now rogue in the West, and she would be an observation target for the Stasi to track him down. When asked why she left the East, she draws a comparison between the interrogation and surveillance by the Americans and the West Germans with that of the State Security Service (Stasi) in East Berlin: "I'll tell you why I wanted to leave East Germany. Because of questions like these, which insinuate, attack, and keep breaking open old wounds." The film emphasizes a continuity of experience: the similarly bleak cityscape on both sides of the border, the unsettled movement of the camera, and the conspicuous angles with which it "watches" her activities lend an air of constant anxiety to the film. She has difficulty getting work, since the employment assistance office disregards her profession as a chemist with a doctorate, and her son is bullied at school for his East German appearance and different behavior. By the end of the film, she has exited the camp, and set up an apartment and a Christmas tree for her and her son. The film concludes with the camera peering at her brightly lit window from the outside, and we are left wondering who is watching. The mystery of the husband is never resolved—could it be Vassily watching? The BND? The CIA? We don't know, just as those living through it at the time did not know.

A Question of Loyalty: Spielberg's *Bridge of Spies*

A big-budget film directed by Steven Spielberg, *Bridge of Spies* is set further in the past and is based on a historical episode in 1957, in which the lawyer James Donovan served as defendant for the KGB agent, Rudolph Abel, whom the CIA apprehended in New York City. After the Soviets shot down CIA agent Gary Powers's plane in 1960 and then captured him, Donovan was an unofficial government delegate who assisted in the arrangement of a prisoner exchange at the Glienicke Bridge in East Berlin. The opening scenes lead with the character study of Abel, whose cover is as a struggling artist with his easel on the river walk, as he transfers a coded message with the aid of a hollow coin. Soon after we see FBI agents in trench coats and fedoras in hot pursuit, preparing to take him down. Abel gains the audience's empathic response when he is able to evade the agents, walking right past them as he exits the crowded subway station: we are on the side of the Soviet spy from the first moments of the film. Mark Rylance compellingly plays Abel as modest, soft-spoken, and clever. When the agents do catch up with him in his studio, he is able to destroy the coded message with paint, on the pretense of cleaning his palette, and the narrative focalization remains with him as the agents scour the modest room for evidence. The subjective agency lent to Abel is, in effect, mirrored when James Donovan is introduced to the narrative as a principled attorney. His field is now insurance law, but he has been tapped for Abel's defense because he was a prosecutor in the Nuremberg trials and knows criminal law. Although reluctant he adheres to the value of the American justice system that everyone deserves a fair trial and legal representation. Played by Tom Hanks, Donovan begins his defense of the KGB spy with the argument that Abel can't be accused of being a traitor" since he was loyal to his own state. The narrative mirroring recurs when Gary Powers enters the story, portrayed as a naive yet patriotic CIA agent assigned with a small team to a top-secret mission: to fly deep into Soviet territory with the new high-altitude surveillance aircraft—the Lockheed U2—equipped with powerful camera equipment. The commanding officer instructs the agents that they are in no circumstances to fall into enemy hands and gives them each a lethal poison pin inside a silver dollar, for an efficient suicide in the case of impending capture. When the plane is shot down and Powers does not use the pin, his U.S. military superiors consider this an instance of personal failure, inferior in the film's narrative to his Soviet peer. In the second half of the film, when Donovan secretly brokers negotiations for the trade of Abel for Powers in East Berlin, and political machinations of Soviet–German Democratic Republic (GDR) relations enter the fray, the ambiguity established early on devolves into characterization of Eastern Bloc politics as clownish and lacking sophistication. The film, though it concludes with an emotive endorsement of the American justice system and a heroization of the free individual in a democratic society embodied by Donovan, draws a parallel early on between the techniques employed by the CIA, the KGB, and the Stasi. The film is narratively structured to maximize the symmetry of the characters and systems: at the midpoint of the script (Charman, Coen, and Coen 2014, 50), a news bulletin announces the Powers crash and the Supreme Court conviction of Abel on the same day. The focalization of Abel and Donovan's recognition of his individuality and honor counters the demonization of the Soviets that is dominant in the American culture of the time and muddies the waters of political allegiance.

Sympathizing with the Spy: Anna and Jörg Winger's *Deutschland 83*

Deutschland 83 is a TV series set in Germany in 1983, as the title indicates, a year of intense nuclear tension. Our protagonist is a reluctant East German spy for the HVA (Hauptverwaltung Aufklärung [Main Intelligence Directorate]), reassigned from his border-guard duty to infiltrate the office of West German Bundeswehr general Edel at a missile base. NATO is engaging in an elaborate mock nuclear exercise, titled Able Archer, which the East Germans think is the real thing, and a nuclear war is narrowly averted—an event that has a real historical basis.[2] The eight episodes begin with Lenora Rauch, the cultural attaché of the East German Permanent Mission in Bonn, and a Stasi agent, watching Ronald Reagan's now-iconic "Evil Empire" speech on television, in which he warns Americans against the perils of the "so-called nuclear freeze solutions proposed by some," since that would mean ignoring the "facts of history and the aggressions of an evil empire" (Reagan 1983). Alarmed, Lenora picks up the phone from her luxury apartment to coordinate a plan with Stasi headquarters to gain intelligence on NATO plans. From the outset, then, the narrative focus of the story is on the East German response and resists an overly one-sided understanding of the dominant historical narrative that Reagan's anti-Communist rhetoric signifies. Lenora's nephew, Martin Rauch, tagged as a look-alike of a Bundeswehr officer named Moritz Stamm, succumbs to the pressure to take on the role of HVA agent and live in the West, leaving his fiancée and sick mother behind. Lenora ultimately blackmails Martin, promising that if he agrees, his mother (Lenora's sister) will receive a kidney transplant and the medications from the West that she needs. Lenora and Stasi general Schweppenstette drug Martin and transport him to the home of Tobias Tischbier (Alexander Beyer), a professor and a deep-cover HVA agent in Bonn, where he must prepare for his mission. Lenora, in this portrayal, embodies the cold manipulation and cunning of the Stasi and holds the aims of the state above the health of her sister. The juxtaposition of Lenora's position with Reagan's anti-Communist stance underlines how the administrations of the two regimes are fundamentally different, yet the viewer already senses how similar their means of operating can be. Early on Moscow clashes with East Berlin, and West Berlin clashes with Washington, as the military and intelligence agencies respond to Reagan's policy direction. Throughout the series misunderstandings arise over the plans for "Able Archer" that Martin has covertly photographed. Although "Able Archer" is a NATO simulation of a conflict that escalates to a DEFCON 1 nuclear attack, the Stasi reads the classified document as a threat of an actual attack. As events unfold in the eight episodes, and pressure from Lenora continues,

Martin becomes more and more implicated in the misdeeds of the HVA. The son of General Edel, Alex, also in the Bundeswehr but increasingly on the side of the antinuclear protest group headed by Tischbier as part of his cover, kidnaps General Jackson. In covering up for Alex, Martin becomes implicated in the death of the woman Jackson was with and another Stasi agent. Several of Martin's assigned tasks culminate in a death, and he begins to dissociate his identities: he can be Moritz Stamm, have a relationship with Edel's wayward daughter, Yvonne, and grow closer to Edel, while also feeling loyal to his fiancée, who becomes pregnant and wants him to come home (although she strongly supports his duty). The double identity of Martin Rauch and Moritz Stamm serves to underline the compromised integrity on both sides of the border, and as in *Bridge of Spies*, the audience immediately perceives the ambiguity and develops an empathic connection with the spy.

Pluri-medial Networking

In her work on how films contribute to cultural memory, Astrid Erll has pointed to contextual information flows as an essential component. She explains that "intra- and inter-medial strategies are responsible for marking them out as media of cultural memory," but that these strategies must be actualized through reception of all kinds: "Advertisements, comments, discussions, and controversies constitute the collective contexts which channel a movie's reception and potentially turn it into a medium of cultural memory. Moreover, all these expressions are circulated by means of media. Therefore we call these contexts 'pluri-medial networks'" (2008, 396). The effect of pluri-medial networking that Erll describes here determines not only the film's influence on cultural memory but also its impact on perceptions of current issues. After all cultural memory involves a reconstruction that relates knowledge of the past to present circumstances and understanding, as Jan Assmann notes (Assmann and Czaplicka 1995, 130). The filmmakers take pains to exert control over the pluri-medial networking to mobilize their films to the extent possible. For each of these three films, the directors endeavor to establish a biographical connection to their subject matter through related personal memories and experiences in the United States or Germany and thereby claim an authenticity of the story as a vehicle of cultural memory. Reviewers readily draw comparisons to other spy stories, and interviewers are eager to relate the stories to the news of the day.

Deutschland 83 received prerelease promotion as the first German-language television drama series to be screened on a U.S. network, Sundance TV, with subtitles for the American audience (Roxborough 2015). It was developed by RTL Germany and screened there in the same season. Reviewers in the English-speaking media compared it to the popular series *The Americans*, about a Soviet KGB couple under deep cover in the United States, leading an American family lifestyle with two children, also set in the early 1980s (Littleton 2015; Brennan 2015; Tate 2016). Both of these series are unusual in that the audience's sympathies lie squarely with the "enemy"; the narrative focalization leads American and Western European viewers to root for the Communist protagonists, while showing that agents on all sides engage in morally dubious activities to maintain their positions. The two series engage similarly with the current political climate: The *New Republic* says of *The Americans*, "It takes the concrete landscape of 1980s America and pumps it full of the retrospective anxiety of our current political age" (Bennett 2013). The networking connections in the reception of the two series serve to show a pattern that links the Cold War to current anxieties about surveillance and build audience engagement.

While viewers share the knowledge of surveillance concerns of the present transnationally, memories of the Cold War are localized, and creators' claims to historical and biographical authenticity contribute significantly to the pluri-medial networking of these tales of cultural memory. The DVD release of *Deutschland 83* includes a fifteen-minute interview with Anna and Jörg Winger, the co-creators of the series (Winger and Winger 2015, DVD, "Deutschland 83: The Creators," disc 3). Anna Winger is the head writer, and Jörg the executive producer. In speaking about their motivation for creating the series, they emphasized that the series is fictional and entertainment but made authenticity claims by relating an anecdote about the story's inception. They repeated one particular anecdote in a number of interviews to promote the film. Jörg Winger, during his time in the Bundeswehr in the 1980s, was a radio signaler listening in on communications of Russian troops stationed in the GDR, with the use of a wall of recording reels. The signaler would press record upon hearing key words. When around Christmas the troops in question greeted the West German signalers individually by name, the Bundeswehr knew they had a mole among them. Anna Winger said the appeal was that "everyone was listening. It's so bizarre to think that they knew everything all along, on both sides." She went on to observe, "History doesn't repeat itself, but it rhymes. . . . There are parallels, and when you're writing about history, you're always kind of writing about the time you're living in. We were inspired in large part by the debate about metadata and the NSA, which has been a huge political issue in Germany because of the Stasi history. And that was something we wanted to explore: the idea of being listened to, the question of privacy" ("Deutschland 83: The Creators").

Through pluri-medial networking, then, they expressed a form of insider knowledge of the current surveillance issues through personal Cold War experiences. Jörg Winger interjected in the interview that "the Stasi was really good at collecting data, and they had so much data that they didn't know what to make of it. If the Stasi had Google back in those days, they would have been able to make sense of all the data" ("Deutschland 83: The Creators"). The series features comical instances of the race for technology that accompanies the arms race, such as in episode 3, "Atlantic," in which the East Germans are foiled by the ill-gained 3.5-inch floppy disk, when their state-of-the-art Robotron A 5120 can only read the 8-inch kind. To elaborate on the connection between the personal memory of the data collected by listening and physical gathering and the mass collection and analysis of today: the surveillance data can change, become meaningless, or even impenetrable over time. Jörg Winger's firsthand knowledge of the technology, then, helped to bridge the gap between past and present in the promotion of *Deutschland 83*.

In the promotional materials and interviews for *Bridge of Spies*, a strategy to build audience engagement emerges similarly. In interviews Spielberg highlighted his personal memories and the biographical connection to the story through his father, despite the fact that the script originated with Matt Charman—and linked his own past Cold War anxieties to the current politics of surveillance. Charman, who stumbled across James Donovan's story in a footnote in a Kennedy biography, wrote the script and pitched it to DreamWorks. Because of Spielberg's interest in the Cold War, the studio approached him and then brought the Coen brothers on board to further develop the script. At the press conference for the New York Film Festival screening on October 4, 2015, the director expressed concern about cyber-surveillance and noted the topical nature of the surveillance theme: "The cold war was polite in terms of the way we were spying on each other. The way it is today, you just don't know that when you're watching television, is television actually watching you? There are just so many eyes on all of us" (quoted in Smith 2015). There is a nostalgia in this comment, exposed by Cold War history not found on the silver screen—the Cold War was not really polite at all. The filmmakers capitalize on gestures of nostalgia in the film through the use of cinematography reminiscent of internationally familiar Hollywood film noir titles, as well as through costuming and spy film genre tropes. On the DreamWorks website for the film, the commentary begins with Spielberg's biographical connection to the Cold War: his father, Arnold Spielberg, was an engineer who had been part of a General Electric delegation to visit Russia during the year after Gary Powers was shot down, and he had stood in line to see the remains of the U-2 and the flight suit. Their group was asked for their passports and pulled to the front of the line to make a spectacle of them: "This Russian pointed to the U-2 and then pointed to my dad and his friends and said, 'Look what your country is doing to us,' which he repeated angrily several times before handing back their passports" ("Bridge of Spies—Production Notes" 2015). Another anecdote, told to the *Wall Street Journal*, reports Spielberg's fears about surveillance during the Cold War: His father, a second-generation Jewish immigrant to the United States from Ukraine, who spoke Yiddish and Russian, would speak to people in the Soviet Union over ham radio in the backyard shed, and his son (Steven) would ask him, "What if the FBI finds out you were talking to people in Russia over the radio?" (quoted in Calia 2015). Relating *Bridge of Spies* to current politics in the same interview, he said, "A frost has settled between today's Russia and the United States, and it's the kind of frost that I'm very familiar with, having grown up with the permafrost of the Cold War" (Calia 2015). Like the Wingers, then, Spielberg employed the personal and biographical perspective to claim authenticity and convey local specificity for a collective memory.

In the interviews Spielberg connected his distrust of government players with a preoccupation with ever-growing surveillance, and this distrust emerges within his characters, too. Daniel Clarkson Fisher has identified Spielberg's wariness of excessive government power as a motif in his films, in which authority figures often tip to overreaching their license, either legal or ethical, and violate citizens' privacy and civil liberties in a patronizing, corrupt, and often inept manner. This distrust is expressed even in the *Indiana Jones* movies, which he claims to have modeled on B-movies about flying saucers and Martian invaders in the 1950s, phenomena that were "really about government paranoia, cold war fears, and things like that" (quoted in Clarkson Fisher 2017). For *Bridge of Spies*, Spielberg rejected a one-sided story and the facile earmarking of a villain: "One of the things I loved about the story was that everyone you think should be wearing a black hat isn't necessarily wearing that hat, nor did they intend to. It doesn't make it easy to root for someone who is a spy against the national security of our nation.... How could we possibly come out on the other end of this experience caring about this person in the least? But in this case we do, and that was something that made me want to get involved with the project" ("Bridge of Spies—Production Notes" 2015). The political ambiguity in the narrative is therefore at the crux of the project for him and aligns with the contemporary audience member who cares less about the allegiances of those conducting the surveillance now than the fact that surveillance is occurring.

Just as for *Deutschland 83* and *Bridge of Spies*, the biographical connection is a consistent subject of attention in the publicity about *Westen*. The novel by Julia Franck on which it is based, *Lagerfeuer*, is a semiautobiographical tale of a mother who leaves East Berlin and must stay for months in the West Berlin transit camp, an aspect always discussed in interviews with the author. Heide and Christian Schwochow rewrote the multiperspectival novel for the screenplay, reducing the story's narrative core to Nelly and Alexei, whose adapted fictional stories incorporate details from the screenplay writers' lives. The Schwochows applied to leave the GDR in the 1980s, and the question of leaving or staying had always been an issue. Their exit visa was granted on November 9, 1989, the day the border opened (Brady 2015). The sequences depicting alienating incidents for Alexei in the West Berlin school originate in some cases directly from Christian Schwochow's experiences in his new school in Hannover after his family left Berlin. Although the Schwochows may well have had interactions with the Stasi, since Christian's father, Rainer Schwochow, unsuccessfully attempted to escape the GDR in 1970 and subsequently spent a year and a half in prison (Brady 2015), the reception and marketing of this film employed the biographical *not* primarily to address the surveillance practices of West and East Germany. The interviews and press kit shifted instead to the foregrounded subject of the migration experience, being caught in the in-between, and the harm brought about by the oversimplified duality of the presumed better and worse Germany. *Die Zeit*'s Oliver Kaever describes the film as "something between a refugee drama and a suspenseful spy thriller" and praises Schwochow for the "ambivalent discursive space" he created, as the protagonist is caught "between worlds" (2015). The refugee crisis in Europe, precipitated by the refugees flowing out of war-torn Syria, Somalia, and Afghanistan and dying by the hundreds in the Mediterranean in their attempts to reach Europe, was just beginning to intensify in 2014 when *Westen* had its theatrical release. The film was released to theaters in the United States in November 2014 and it began to have screenings at many Goethe Institutes worldwide around the twenty-fifth anniversary of German unification, leading Schwochow to make the connection between the current refugee crisis and the experience depicted in the film more overt in his interviews. In an interview with *IndieWire*, he spoke of his research preparation, which included visiting a refugee center in Berlin for people from Syria and Iraq and getting a sense of their physical and psychological experiences (Aguilar 2014). At the time of the German theatrical release, Schwochow connected the subject matter to the Snowden discussion and the growing awareness of the surveillance of citizens in the West: "We have known at least since Edward Snowden the kind of role that the Western secret services play. My film aims to show, then, that even a Western democracy has very particular mechanisms that, in the first instance, have nothing at all to do with freedom" (Kessler 2014). He repeated the same line before the American premieres and challenged the rhetoric of freedom (Teich 2014; Aguilar 2014). For him the tendency to portray the superior freedom of the West, at the cost of overlooking similar surveillance mechanisms in the West, demanded a corrective.

Cinematography of Blurring

Having established that the narratives and audience development strategies for these thrillers associate personal and collective memories of the Cold War with a critique of present-day surveillance, let us turn to the aesthetic devices employed to this end. As already indicated, the cinematography contributes substantially to the expression of the anxiety that the controlling surveillant eye engenders. When one considers that the video surveillance practices that are now widespread have developed in tandem with the medium of cinema itself, it is fitting that filmmakers use images to investigate how surveillance can blur truth and reality, as well as shed light on it, and how meaning can shift with camera angle and the surveillant perspective. Thomas Levin points out that the pioneering 1895 film by the Lumière brothers, *Workers Leaving the Factory*, could be considered a form of surveillance of the workers (2002, 581). Catherine Zimmer also gives numerous examples of how early cinema produced stories of cameras catching crimes in progress, thereby producing social commentary at the same time as a form of disciplinary enforcement of norms (2015). Films can call the function of the image into question, and filmmakers have historically investigated the capacity of the image to deceive, mask, or blur. The cinematographic technique of blurring dates back to cinema's beginnings, and many have connected blurred or fast-moving images to the anxiety and paranoia of modern life. In 1903 Georg Simmel wrote in "The Metropolis and Mental Life":

> The psychological basis of the metropolitan type of individuality consists in the intensification of nervous stimulation which results from the swift and uninterrupted change of outer and inner stimuli. Man is a differentiating creature. His mind is stimulated by the difference between a momentary impression and the one which preceded it. Lasting impressions, impressions which differ only slightly from one another, impressions which take a regular and habitual course and show regular and habitual contrasts—all these use up, so to speak, less consciousness than does the rapid crowding of changing images, the sharp discontinuity in the grasp of a single glance, and the unexpectedness of onrushing impressions. These are the psychological conditions which the metropolis creates. With each crossing of the street, with the tempo and multiplicity of economic, occupational and social life, the city sets up a deep contrast with small town and rural life with reference to the sensory foundations of psychic life. (1950, 410)

With reference to the innovative 1927 film *Berlin: Symphony of a Great City*, Ágnes Pethő describes the sequences of images of the metropolis, pulsating and flowing with the rhythm of the music, as a representation of the "liquid city" (2011, 103). "Such a musical (video-clip like) rendering of the flow of the traffic and the clustering of (illuminated) skyscrapers has," she points out, "already become one of the running clichés of television series" like *CSI* or *Law and Order* (103). There is a connection of the urban environment to the anxiety and paranoia of modernity, as expressed through the rapidly moving images, blurring, and lack of separation. Joachim Paech, in turn, establishes that blurred, defocused, or vague (*unscharfe*) images are always dependent on "norms of correct seeing" and are therefore relational (2008, 345). He considers especially the intermedial aspects of blurring, such as painted films or paintings in films, and talks about the dissolution of demarcation lines between art forms. The relational reception of the images involves "psychophysical code" that filmmakers instrumentalize. Kathrin Rothemund, in her study of how filmmakers use surveillance footage in several feature films, articulates that the blurred footage expresses "images in crisis" as well as "images of crisis" (2016, 1). The focused and blurred images "constantly negotiate the interrelation between fact and fiction, between subjectivity and objectivity, between dream and reality, between time and place. Images between vagueness and acuity should be dealt with according to their visual, temporal or movement density, the superimposition of perceptive attention and the creativity of interpretive approaches" (1). She goes on to point out that this is an issue of technology as well as aesthetics. In cinema, there are numerous tools and strategies that can bring about blurring or vagueness, which include the technologies of the camera and material—she lists lenses, depth of focus or depth of field, soft focus and diffusion, focus shift, the graininess of film material (16 mm/8 mm), various filters, double exposure—and can extend to weather and atmosphere or physical barriers in the mise-en-scène that obscure or partially block the view of the narrative subject.

The three productions addressed in this chapter make extensive use of all these forms of defocus and blur, instrumentalizing them for "connotative surplus value," as Paech terms it (2008, 359). In surveillance films blurred footage can signify authenticity because lower-quality footage that could come from constantly looping security tapes or nonprofessional camera work signals a kind of mechanical objectivity. These various forms of blurring have become pronounced in many recent works, especially in the films that deal directly with surveillance politics, such as Oliver Stone's *Snowden* (2016), to cite a prominent example. In the films addressed here, a dominant use of the blurring is to convey political ambiguity, both in a shifting understanding of historical developments and with respect to the climate of surveillance now: who is watching and why, and how do we judge the practices and the recordings?

Certainly, in *Deutschland 83* the camera movements, blurring, and framing are key devices in the creation of political and moral ambiguity. Constantly presented in duplicate in mirrors, windows, and doorways and peered at in grainy surveillance footage, the undercover Stasi agent Martin Rauch confronts daily the fragility of his ideological position. He does what the Stasi asks him to do but finds himself developing close relationships with the West German targets, and he often unwittingly uncovers the weaknesses and morally questionable acts of high high-ranking players on both sides—for example, he accidentally shuttles explosives from the East to Carlos the Jackal, resulting in mass casualties, to his great dismay, and sympathizes with General Edel, who worries about his renegade son. The television series draws on *Mad Men*–style nostalgia aesthetics and shifts between the use of familiar tropes and the deconstruction of political and moral binaries. In the first episode, "Quantum," the fast pace and blurring techniques employed by cinematographer Philipp Haberlandt bombard the senses with the disorientation of the protagonist, the split identities of West and East Germany in 1983, the agitation, tension, and jangled nerves of the nuclear arms race. The blurring reveals how covert observation is happening on both sides, and the visual representation of surveillance conveys the inner inquietude that it causes. The images of doubling begin before the opening credits, with Martin's mother and his aunt, Lenora, embracing at the same time as Martin and his girlfriend Annett, and Lenora peering through the window-like kitchen pass-through at Martin. When Stasi general Schweppenstette arrives to recruit Martin, the viewer position is on the other side of a wrought-iron divider in the living room, and we observe Martin's reaction to recruitment through a grid, with his face half in shadow and framed by the backs of the heads of Lenora Rauch and Schweppenstette. The position of the camera obscures the view, and the bifurcation of both the scene and the protagonist's face suggest shady, or unclear, motives and decisions (fig. 10.1).

The scene cuts to a slow zoom on his mother and Lenora in the kitchen, through a bead curtain—another form of obstruction—in the doorway. Martin's last words are "I won't do it," before he blacks out from the sedative in the tea and wakes up in Bonn. Looking through the window, he sees a dreamlike, blurred, and distorted view of Bonn. This compelling sequence is replete with blurring: Martin passes through a doorway, soon to emerge

FIG. 10.1. Martin's recruitment viewed through wrought-iron room divider (*Deutschland 83*).

as Moritz Stamm, and a reflection appears as a haunting, ghostly apparition, as the beveled glass of the door further fractures the clarity of Martin's image (see fig. 10.2).

His identity is divided before our eyes. He then stands in a second doorway, framed by beveled-glass doors and a beveled-glass half-circle window over his head, his small figure slightly out of focus, as he asks the question, "Where am I?" As Lenora Rauch and Tobias Tischbier, in sharp focus, tell him his assignment, he becomes angry, and the background blurs as the camera draws his face into shallow focus. After Martin has reluctantly changed into his Western brand-name Puma T-shirt, jeans, and Adidas shoes, Lenora views with satisfaction from a shadowy doorway across from him, his face, in turn, halved by the shadow in the opposite doorway. He turns to sprint down the spiral staircase, through the seemingly endless doorways and gates of the house and property, where the cinematographer employs blurring of rapid movement, accompanied by a racing soundtrack, to express psychological disorientation, as in *Berlin: Symphony of a Great City*. He pauses briefly at an electronics store where Bundesrat president Franz Josef Strauß speaks from multiple televisions about the million deutsche mark loan provided to the GDR (fig. 10.3), preceding his meeting with General Secretary Erich Honecker—a use of archi-

FIG. 10.2. Martin refracted (*Deutschland 83*).

val footage to layer the questions of representation of reality and of political position as they shift over time.

The camera points from the inside of the store to the corner of the display window, such that we see three televisions, a reflection of a television in the windowpane and, projected onto Martin's Puma T-shirt, a close-up image of Strauß, followed by an image of Erich Honecker on the television screen as he shakes hands with Strauß. The sensory overload of Western culture is visually and physically impressed on his body, and his understanding of the environment is blurred. The multiple screens echo the multiplicity of perspective, just as the camera angles in the sequence emphasize that he is being watched. The historical reference made by the archival television footage reveals the public face of détente and diplomacy, which serves to hide from view the espionage activities, driven by fundamental distrust. The CSU chair Strauß, an avowed anti-Communist who had lost in his bid for the chancellorship in the 1980 election, negotiated a billion deutsche mark loan to prop up the failing East German economy. His big business friend Josef März brought him in contact with his negotiating partner, Alexander Schalck-Golodkowski, East German international trade minister and a Stasi colonel. Strauß, whose tactics and approach found disfavor among many, including in his own party, answered in these negotiations only to the new chan-

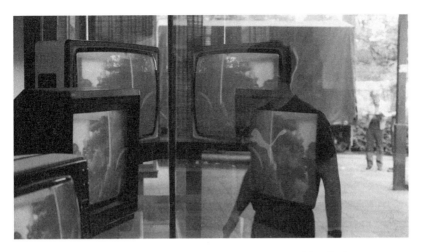

FIG. 10.3. Martin on the run in the capitalist West (*Deutschland 83*).

cellor, Helmut Kohl, keeping his other government colleagues in the dark. He claimed credit for a GDR humanitarian concession, the removal of the automatic firing devices at the so-called death strip, which turned out later to be a ruse: Honecker had announced plans to dismantle these already a year earlier, but Strauß did not know this (Wiegrefe 2017). The cinematography of this sequence serves to externalize the layers of secrecy, calculation, and espionage that lie beneath these television images and Martin Rauch's initiation into this world.

A frantic Martin runs on, into the supermarket, where hyper-real colorful shelves of goods frame him, as he stops in his tracks, overwhelmed by Western consumer culture. Indeed, material culture is a thematic core issue for surveillance that speaks to the contemporary viewer: it is the global online consumer and social media activity that generates the most personal information about individuals and in turn influences behavior.

In *Westen* the cinematographer uses the hand-held camera and its position to emphasize the surveillant gaze: unsteady footage, suboptimal views partially obscured by trees or buildings, with subjects sometimes out of focus, reveal the human observer behind the lens. The film opens with a view from across the street: a poorly exposed view of a gray apartment block partially obscured by blowing snow, with two small figures in the

FIG. 10.4. Nelly across the border (*West*).

window. We are briefly introduced to Nelly, Alexei, and Alexei's father, Vassily, bidding a tender farewell before Vassily leaves. The same across-the-street point-of-view shot recurs in quick succession, with the title "three years later," this time without Vassily. The frontal view cuts to an obscured shot in which the surveillant camera is concealed behind the foliage in the foreground. Immediately upon crossing the border, the camera draws attention to itself once again, as it captures the sun's glare on the lens in Nelly's moment of relief (fig. 10.4).

Although she is unaware that someone is watching her here, too, the viewer is already on guard. The covert observation from afar is present at every moment, before, during, and after her stay at the transit camp.

In figure 10.5 the window frame and the view over the shoulder of the CIA agent emphasize the constant framing by the surveillant gaze—by the human eye or the eye of the camera. When Nelly has finally passed through the threshold of interrogation and is free to come and go as she pleases, she celebrates with her son in the park, and the position of the camera signals surveillance yet again, from behind a tree at a distance, then zooming in to a yellow blur as the camera suggests that someone is monitoring mother and son in an intimate moment of playful wrestling in the leaves. Nelly is all too aware that someone may be watching her at any time and the degree to which information is concealed from her. While in *Deutschland 83*, Martin appears as a double or a

FIG. 10.5. John Bird watches Nelly from a window (*West*).

ghost of himself (fig. 10.2), Nelly is haunted by visions of her lover, Vassily, who may be living or dead (fig. 10.6). The partial obstruction by the window, the unfocused shot, the reflection, and the position of the eyes—Nelly's gaze from behind and the camera's (surveillant) gaze from the fore—contribute to the anxiety and uncertainty of her position.

Like Vassily, Hans, a fellow resident of the transit camp, has a haunting presence. He has been there for a long time, befriends her son, and tries to befriend her. After a warning from another camp resident to watch out for the Stasi, who are everywhere, it is clear that she suspects that Hans may have connections to the Stasi, and she tries to keep her son from him. He seems to appear randomly and too coincidentally when she is in distress. By the film's conclusion, he has been redeemed in her eyes after he explains his dissident past and has helped her and her son; he is at the door to join them for Christmas dinner in the final scene observed from a surveillant position outside the building. Nelly appears to accept the level of uncertainty and ambiguity that she has been dealt. After Hans points it out, she sees that her escalating paranoia, signaled by increasing camera movement, backward glances, and close-ups of her distressed face, is hurting herself and her son. In subsequent scenes the camera movement slows, Nelly smiles calmly, and she unhesitatingly answers the apartment buzzer to welcome Hans.

In *Bridge of Spies*, the cinematographer uses less camera blur-

FIG. 10.6. Nelly sees a ghost (*West*).

ring to work with the theme of political ambiguity, although this is certainly present in many of the stylized noir scenes, such as when someone is trailing Donovan on a dark and rainy night (fig. 10.7), or when the blurred stream of subway passengers in trench coats and fedoras allows Abel to evade the agents in pursuit.

In the rain sequence, shown in figure 10.7, Donovan is out of focus in the foreground, while the rain and dark obscure the features of the trailing agent, adding tension and anxiety to the scene. Since the camera dwells on this scene to build suspense, and the identity of the figure is revealed minutes later as an American—an FBI agent—the sequence undermines the notion of the hostile *foreign* surveillant. *Bridge of Spies*, however, more heavily employs the technique of doubling, or even tripling, images, extending the model even to the narrative structure. In figure 10.8, in the film's opening sequence that introduces us to Abel and begins to provide character development, the camera shows him from behind in triplicate (painting, person, and mirror reflection) in a noir-style image of fragmented identity and an illustration of Paech's intermedial blurring.

The shot draws the audience affectively to the face, and together with the title of the film, it prompts us to begin to speculate about the multiple identities of the character—one with whom we immediately begin to empathize. How does he see himself, and how do others see him, in the mirror and on the canvas? Which one, if any of them, is "real"? In the fade-in transition shown in figure 10.9, the blurred image of Abel appears as an uncanny—even

Dueck

FIG. 10.7. Donovan trailed by FBI agent (*Bridge of Spies*).

ghostly—double with Powers and strongly suggests an equiva-
lence of their positions. The repeated pairing of images underlines the narrative question of why the American U-2 surveillance
pilot should represent a superior ethical or national position to
that of the Soviet agent.

Political Ambiguity on Screen

The three productions described here, *Westen*, *Deutschland 83*,
and *Bridge of Spies*, share the dual objectives of cultural memory and a close examination of the current seen and unseen risks
of mass surveillance. Their approach to the memory of the Cold
War marks a shift from previous narratives in that they emphasize
political ambiguity: the individual characters become enmeshed
with the questionable deeds and collective fears of whole regimes.
The characters in these stories have no alternative but to live with
the intrusive cameras and eyes that watch them, but the films
challenge the audience to consider their willing participation in
the omnipresence of surveillance. The transnational filmmaking
and marketing address the fact that there are Cold War transatlantic stories, located at the Berlin nexus of East and West, that
are as relevant to us today as ever, but which take on new meaning
in a globalized environment in which nation states have arguably
yielded much power over social and political spheres to corpora-
tions. Online sales will draw the spy stories themselves into forms
of digital surveillance to sell the DVDs and streaming versions,
along with products that will be marketed on these sites, and pro-

FIG. 10.8. Triple image self-portrait of Rudolph Abel (*Bridge of Spies*).

motions of other movies by the same directors and actors: "Customers who bought this item also bought." The film *Westen* calls on audiences to reexamine the notion of the "better Germany" in the Federal Republic of Germany, to show that ideologically motivated suspicion and fear were not unique to the GDR and aspires to convey the displacement migrants experience in the modern and now the liquid modern era. In terms of funding and marketing, *Westen* is predominantly German-funded, but with the support of the MEDIA Program of the European Union, and it has targeted the international audience beginning with its Montreal premiere. With its 1980s soundtrack and attractive young cast, *Deutschland 83* has a lighter touch and a pop-culture nostalgia that nonetheless aims for a transatlantic reexamination of the Reagan/Brezhnev era, both in its noteworthy binational television funding and release and in its East German perspective. *Bridge of Spies*, though German input is significant, through the coproduction by Studio Babelsberg and the casting of German actor Sebastian Koch of *The Lives of Others* fame as the East German negotiator, culminates in an indubitably American ending: the film presents Donovan as the story's hero and champion of the American justice system. Nonetheless, the narrative, structural, and cinematographic features of the film serve to shift the viewer's empathic perspective and muddy the waters of Cold War history. Concerns with the penetration of state surveillance into the private sphere and its consequences, then, are a preoccupation of all these screen stories, and

FIG. 10.9. Faces in parallel: Abel and Powers (*Bridge of Spies*).

they reframe, complicate, and mobilize memory of the Cold War in a context of acknowledged political ambiguity.

Notes

1. The novel was translated by Anthea Bell after the release of the film, with the title *West*, published by Vintage in 2015.

2. In 2013 Mark Kramer published research that refutes the notion that the Soviets failed to recognize that Able Archer was an exercise, not the real thing (Kramer 2013, 129–50).

References

Aguilar, Carlos. 2014. "Beyond the Wall: Dir. Christian Schwochow on His Intriguing Historical Drama 'West.'" *IndieWire*, November 18. http://www .indiewire.com/2014/11/beyond-the-wall-dir-christian-schwochow-on -his-intriguing-historical-drama-west-171799/.

Assmann, Jan, and John Czaplicka. 1995. "Collective Memory and Cultural Identity." *New German Critique* 65:125–33.

Bauman, Zygmunt. 2000. *Liquid Modernity*. Cambridge: Polity.

———. 2006. *Liquid Fear*. Cambridge: Polity.

Bauman, Zygmunt, and David Lyon. 2013. *Liquid Surveillance: A Conversation*. Cambridge: Polity.

Bennett, Laura. 2013. "The Spies Next Door: *The Americans* Is a Cold War Thriller for Our More Ambiguous Age." *New Republic*, January 30. https:// newrepublic.com/article/112284/fxs-americans-reviewed.

Brady, Martin. 2015. "West Q+A with Christian Schwochow: 04 June 2015." BFI *YouTube Channel*, June 11. https://www.youtube.com/watch?v=mOyxDf49zGo.

Brennan, Matt. 2015. "'Deutschland 83,' 'The Americans,' and the End of an Era in TV Drama: A Tale of Two Spy Stories; 'The Americans' Has Two Seasons Left, but 'Deutschland 83' May Shape TV's Future." *IndieWire*, June

23. http://www.indiewire.com/2015/06/deutschland-83-the-americans-and
-the-end-of-an-era-in-tv-drama-trailer-186944/.

"Bridge of Spies—Production Notes." 2015. DreamWorks Animation LLC, Storyteller Distribution Co. LLC. http://dreamworkspictures.com/films/bridge-of-spies#production_notes.

Calia, Michael. 2015. "Steven Spielberg Remembers the Cold War in 'Bridge of Spies'; Steven Spielberg recalls the Cold War; Tom Hanks plays a lawyer defending a Russian spy." *Wall Street Journal*, October 8. https://www.wsj.com/articles/steven-spielberg-remembers-the-cold-war-in-bridge-of-spies-1444145673.

Charman, Matt, Ethan Coen, and Joel Coen. 2014. *Bridge of Spies: Final Shooting Script 12.17.14.* DreamWorks. http://dreamworksawards.com/download/BOS_screenplay.pdf.

Clarkson Fisher, Daniel. 2017. "Spielberg and Surveillance." Video essay, February 17. https://vimeo.com/204631958.

Erll, Astrid. 2008. "Literature, Film and the Mediality of Cultural Memory." In *Cultural Memory Studies: An International Handbook,* edited by Astrid Erll and Ansgar Nünning, 389–98. Berlin: De Gruyter.

Franck, Julia. 2003. *Lagerfeuer.* Köln: Dumont.

"Geheimdienste überwachten mehr als 37 Millionen E-Mails." 2012. *Spiegel Online,* February 25. http://www.spiegel.de/politik/deutschland/schlagwort-fahndung-geheimdienste-ueberwachten-mehr-als-37-millionen-e-mails-a-817499.html.

Kaever, Oliver. 2015. "Warten auf die Freiheit: Christian Schwochow hat Julia Francks Roman 'Lagerfeuer' verfilmt; Im Notaufnahmelager muss eine DDR-Bürgerin lange auf ihre Weiterreise in die Freiheit warten." *Die Zeit,* March 24. http://www.zeit.de/kultur/film/2014-03/westen-film.

Kelly, Mike. 2017. "Kellyanne Conway Suggests Even Wider Surveillance of Trump Campaign." *USA Today,* March 12. https://www.usatoday.com/story/news/politics/2017/03/12/kellyanne-conway-surveillance-trump-campaign-wider/99109170/.

Kessler, Tobias. 2014. "Interview mit Christian Schwochow über seinen Film 'Westen.'" *Saarbrücker Zeitung Kinoblog,* March 27. http://www.meinsol.de/blog/show.phtml?cbid=36688.

Kramer, Mark. 2013. "Die Nicht-Krise um 'Able Archer 1983': Fürchtete die sowjetische Führung tatsächlich einen atomaren Großeingriff im Herbst 1983?" In *Wege zur Wiedervereinigung: Die beiden deutschen Staaten in ihren Bündnissen 1970 bis 1990,* edited by Oliver Bange and Bernd Lemke, 129–50. Munich: Oldenbourg Wissenschaftsverlag.

Levin, Thomas. 2002. "Rhetoric of the Temporal Index: Surveillant Narration and the Cinema of 'Real Time.'" In *CTRL[SPACE]: Rhetorics of Surveillance from Bentham to Big Brother,* edited by Thomas Levin, Ursula Frohne, and Peter Weibel, 578–93. Cambridge MA: MIT Press.

Littleton, Cynthia. 2015. "SundanceTV *Deutschland 83* Breaks Cultural Barriers with Cold War Chiller." *Variety*, June 17. http://variety.com/2015/tv/news /deutschland-83-sundancetv-german-language-drama-1201522499/.

Lyon, David. 2010. "Liquid Surveillance: The Contribution of Zygmunt Bauman to Surveillance Studies." *International Political Sociology*, no. 4, 325–38.

———. 2015. *Surveillance after Snowden*. Cambridge, UK: Polity Press.

"Merkels Handy steht seit 2002 auf US-Abhörliste." 2013. *Spiegel Online*, October 26. http://www.spiegel.de/politik/deutschland/nsa-ueberwachung-merkel -steht-seit-2002-auf-us-abhoerliste-a-930193.html.

Paech, Joachim. 2008. "*Le Nouveau Vague* oder Unschärfe als intermediale Figur." In *Intermedialität, analog/digital: Theorien, Methoden, Analysen*, 345–60. Munich: Fink.

Pethő, Ágnes. 2011. *Cinema and Intermediality*. Cambridge: Cambridge Scholars.

Poitras, Laura, Marcel Rosenbach, and Holger Stark. 2013. "NSA überwacht 500 Millionen Verbindungen in Deutschland." *Spiegel Online*, June 30. http:// www.spiegel.de/netzwelt/netzpolitik/nsa-ueberwacht-500-millionen -verbindungen-in-deutschland-a-908517.html.

Reagan, Ronald. 1983. "Remarks at the Annual Convention of the National Association of Evangelicals, March 8, 1983." Online by Gerhard Peters and John T. Woolley, *The American Presidency Project*. http://www.presidency .ucsb.edu/ws/?pid=41023.

Rothemund, Kathrin. 2016. "Traversing Media—Blurring Images: On the Interrelation between Moving Images of Crisis and Blurred Aesthetics." Paper presented at the Network of European Cinema Studies Conference, Brandenburgisches Zentrum für Medienwissenschaft, Potsdam, July 28–30.

Roxborough, Scott. 2015. "FreemantleMedia International Takes German Series *Deutschland 83*." *Hollywood Reporter*, January 15. https://www .hollywoodreporter.com/news/fremantlemedia-international-takes-german -series-763994.

Schwochow, Christian, dir. 2013. *Westen (West)*. Feature film. Zero One Film.

Simmel, Georg. 1950. "The Metropolis and Mental Life." In *The Sociology of Georg Simmel*, edited and translated by Kurt H. Wolf, 409–24. Glencoe IL: Free Press.

Smith, Nigel M. 2015. "Steven Spielberg: Compared to Today's Surveillance, the Cold War Was Polite." *Guardian*, October 5. https://www.theguardian .com/film/2015/oct/05/steven-spielberg-tom-hanks-bridge-of-spies -cyber-hacking-torture.

Spielberg, Steven, dir. 2015. *Bridge of Spies*. Feature film. DreamWorks et al.

Stone, Oliver, dir. 2016. *Snowden*. Feature film. Endgame Entertainment.

Tate, Gabriel. 2016. "Deutschland 83: 'A Lot of People Were Happy in East Germany.'" *Guardian*, January 3. https://www.theguardian.com/tv-and-radio /2016/jan/03/channel-4-cold-war-drama-deutschland-83.

Teich, David. 2014. "Interview: Christian Schwochow (Director—'West')." *Indiewood Hollywouldn't,* November 6. https://indienyc.com/interview -christian-schwochow-director-west/.

Timberg, Craig, Elizabeth Dwoskin, and Ellen Nakashima. 2017. "WikiLeaks: The CIA Is Using Popular TVs, Smartphones and Cars to Spy on Their Owners." *Washington Post,* March 7. https://www.washingtonpost.com/news /the-switch/wp/2017/03/07/why-the-cia-is-using-your-tvs-smartphones -and-cars-for-spying/?utm_term=.66874f095a4e.

Wiegrefe, Klaus. 2017. "Die Legende vom listigen Franz Josef." *Der Spiegel,* January 19. http://www.spiegel.de/spiegel/ddr-wie-erich-honecker-csu-chef -franz-josef-strauss-austrickste-a-1130208-druck.html.

Winger, Anna, and Jörg Winger, dirs. 2015. *Deutschland 83.* Television series. RTL. Freemantle Media International, DVD.

Zimmer, Catherine. 2015. *Surveillance Cinema.* New York: New York University Press.

CONTRIBUTORS

Carol Anne Costabile-Heming is a professor of German in the Department of World Languages, Literatures, and Cultures at the University of North Texas. She received her PhD in German from Washington University in St. Louis and has distinguished herself as a scholar of twentieth- and twenty-first-century German literature and culture. She has published widely on *Wende* literature and post-*Wende* Berlin, including (with Rachel Halverson and Kristie Foell) *Textual Responses to German Unification: Processing Historical and Social Change in Literature and Film* (De Gruyter, 2001) and *Berlin: The Symphony Continues; Orchestrating Architectural, Social and Artistic Change in Germany's New Capital* (De Gruyter, 2004). She has also published essays and book chapters on the authors Volker Braun, F. C. Delius, Jürgen Fuchs, Günter Grass, Günter Kunert, Erich Loest, Peter Schneider, and Christa Wolf, as well as on censorship and the Stasi in the GDR. Most recently she coedited (with Rachel Halverson) the volume *Taking Stock of German Studies in the United States: The New Millennium* (Camden House, 2015). In 2018 the Southern Conference on Language Teaching awarded her the Educator of Excellence Award.

Cheryl Dueck is an associate professor of German and senior academic director international at the University of Calgary, Canada. Her areas of research are Central European cinema; GDR and postunification literature and film; cultural memory; surveillance; and cultural and gender politics. Recent work includes articles and book chapters on German, Hungarian, Polish, and Czech films, such as *The Lives of Others, Little Rose, In the Shadow, The Exam, Yella, Jacob the Liar, November Child, Winter Daughter,* and *American Rhapsody.* Her current project, together with Balázs Varga (ELTE, Budapest), is titled "National Pasts-Transnational Presence: Post-Socialist Cinema of Central Europe." She is the author of *Rifts in Time and in the Self: The Female Subject in Two Generations of East German Women Writers* (Rodopi, 2004).

Julie Fedor is a senior lecturer in modern European history at the University of Melbourne, Australia. She is the author of *Russia and the Cult of State Security* (Routledge, 2011); coauthor of *Remembering Katyn* (Polity, 2012); contributing coeditor of *Memory, Conflict and New Media: Web Wars in Post-Socialist States* (Routledge, 2013) and *War and Memory in Russia, Ukraine, and Belarus* (Palgrave, 2017); and coeditor of *Memory and Theory in Eastern Europe* (Palgrave, 2013). In 2010–13 she was a postdoctoral researcher on the Memory at War project based in the Department of Slavonic Studies at the University of Cambridge (www.memoryatwar.org). She has taught modern Russian history at the Universities of Birmingham, Cambridge, Melbourne, and St. Andrews. Her research on memory and authoritarianism in Putin's Russia was funded by an Australian Research Council Discovery Early Research Award.

Valentina Glajar is a professor of German at Texas State University and an accredited external researcher at the Romanian CNSAS (National Council for the Study of the Securitate Archives). She is the author of *The German Legacy in East Central Europe* (Camden House, 2004) and coeditor (with Bettina Brandt) of *Herta Müller: Politics and Aesthetics* (University of Nebraska Press, 2013), (with Jeanine Teodorescu) *Local History, Transnational Memory in the Romanian Holocaust* (Palgrave Macmillan, 2011), (with Domnica Radulescu) *"Gypsies" in European Literature and Culture* (Palgrave Macmillan, 2008), and *Vampirettes, Wretches, and Amazons: Western Representations of East European Women* (East European Monographs; Columbia University Press, 2004). She has also translated (with André Lefevere) *Traveling on One Leg* (Northwestern University Press, 1998; 2nd ed., 2010) by the Nobel Prize laureate Herta Müller. Glajar's latest book, coedited with Alison Lewis and Corina L. Petrescu, is *Secret Police Files from the Eastern Bloc: Between Surveillance and Life Writing* (Camden House, 2016). As a fellow of the American Council of Learned Societies, she is currently working on a monograph, "The Afterlife of Files: Herta Müller's Story of Surveillance."

Lisa Haegele is an assistant professor of German at Texas State University. She completed her PhD in German and comparative literature at Washington University in St. Louis in 2014. Her research covers postwar through contemporary German cinema with a special focus on West German genre films in the 1960s and 1970s. Her work has appeared in the special issue "1968 and West German Cinema," edited by Christina Gerhardt, in *The Sixties: A Journal of History, Politics, and Culture* (2017), *Berlin School Glossary: An ABC of the New Wave in German Cinema* (Intellect, 2013), and *The Berlin School and Its Global Contexts: A Transnational Art-Cinema*, edited by Marco Abel and Jaimey Fisher (Wayne State University Press, 2018). She is currently working on a monograph on violence and politics in West German genre films in the "long 1968," in addition to an article on the aesthetics of 1970s feminist underground comix in Ziska Riemann's *Lollipop Monster*. Her research has been supported by the Berlin Program for Advanced German and European Studies.

Axel Hildebrandt is an associate professor of German at Moravian College in Bethlehem, Pennsylvania. His research topics include GDR literature and film; contemporary German literature, film, and politics; questions of memory; and transnational studies. His coedited volume *Envisioning Social Justice in Contemporary German Culture* (with Jill E. Twark) was published by Camden House in 2015.

Alison Lewis is a professor of German in the School of Languages and Linguistics at the University of Melbourne, Australia. She has published widely in the areas of modern German literature and German studies, mainly on gender, literature and politics, the German

Democratic Republic, German unification, and the history of intellectuals. She is the author of numerous journal articles and book chapters, as well as three single-authored monographs: *Subverting Patriarchy: Feminism and Fantasy in the Works of Irmtraud Morgner* (Berg, 1995), *Die Kunst des Verrats: Der Prenzlauer Berg und die Staatssicherheit* (Königshausen & Neumann, 2003), and *Eine schwierige Ehe: Liebe, Geschlecht und die Geschichte der Wiedervereinigung im Spiegel der Literatur* (Rombach, 2009). Her coedited book with Valentina Glajar and Corina L. Petrescu, *Secret Police Files from the Eastern Bloc: Between Surveillance and Life Writing* (Camden House, 2016), has been well received. She recently coauthored a monograph with Birgit Lang and Joy Damousi, *A History of the Case Study: Sexology, Psychoanalysis and Literature* (Manchester University Press, 2017). She is coeditor of the Australian yearbook for German studies *Limbus* (Rombach) and the monograph series Transpositionen with Röhrig-Universitätsverlag and currently serves as president of the German Studies Association of Australia. She has just completed a monograph on secret police informants, *A State of Secrecy: Stasi Informants and the Surveillance of Culture in East Germany* (forthcoming with the University of Michigan Press). In 2018 she was a fellow of the Internationales Kolleg Morphomata, a center for advanced studies at the University of Cologne.

Jennifer A. Miller is an associate professor of modern European history at Southern Illinois University, Edwardsville. She has published on postwar guest-worker immigration to Germany and is the author of *Contested Borders and Hidden Lives: The First Generation of Turkish Guest Workers in Postwar Germany* (University of Toronto Press, 2018). Her research has been supported by the DAAD, Fulbright, and the Berlin Program in Advanced German and European Studies, among others.

Corina L. Petrescu is an associate professor of German at the University of Mississippi. She is the author of *Against All Odds: Subversive Spaces in National Socialist Germany* (Peter Lang, 2010) and of various articles on Volker Braun, Eginald Schlattner, representations of 1968 in the Romanian media, and Yiddish theater in Romania. She is the coeditor with Valentina Glajar and Alison Lewis of *Secret Police Files from the Eastern Bloc: Between Surveillance and Life Writing* (Camden House, 2016) and of the *Monatshefte* special issue "Archive und Geheimdienstakten: Dialogisches Erinnern an Verfolgung und Zensur im Ostblock" (2018). She is a fellow of the Alexander von Humboldt Foundation at the University Potsdam, Germany, working on a cultural history of the Jewish State Theater Bucharest from 1948 to the present.

Mary Beth Stein is an associate professor of German and international affairs at George Washington University. She has published on Berlin, the Berlin Wall, East German memory culture after 1989, and Florian von Donnersmarck's film *Das Leben der Anderen*. She is currently working on a book-length monograph, "The Lives of East Germans: Experience, Identity and Memory after the Wall," and has written a recent article on narratives of detention in the tours at the Stasi prison of Berlin-Hohenschönhausen.

INDEX

border (*continued*)
294, 295; lackluster, *297*; patrolling of,
265, 281, 288, 296, 298; tropes, *294-303*
border crossers: about, 19; and border-
pass agreement, 204-5; and Communist Party, 205; implications related
to, 223-24; income generated through,
205; and intimate relationships, 198-
200, 207, 210; and Iron Curtain, 223-24;
"position" of, 197; and Stasi, 206-7, 213-
24; suspicion about, 207, 210. *See also*
guest workers; Turkish nationals
bourgeois lifestyle, 40, 140, 142, 145
Brandin, Wolf (fictitious character),
267-72
Bridge of Spies (movie), 255, 312-13, 317-
20, 329-33
Bundesnachrichtendienst (BND), 5, 255,
295, 308, 311, 312
Busch, Willi (fictitious character), 280-82,
286-302, *287, 300*

capitalist systems, 8, 222, 224, 266, 284
Caspar, Günter, 106, 107, 122, 123
censorship process, 100-105, 107, 108,
111, 119
Charman, Matt, 313, 318
Cheka, 18, 181, 185, 187n6
chekist: about, 5, 18, 82, 187n6; and Cold
War, 164-65; as guardian angel, 177-86;
identification with, 178; and prisoners,
180-81; and repentance, 171-72, 174-75.
See also secret police
Chiffriert an Chef (movie), 256, 258, 260,
267-73
CIA: about, 4, 7, 10; and DEFA films, 255,
257, 267, 268, 270, 271; and Ion Mihai
Pacepa, 14; and Radio Free Europe,
67n37, 82
cinematography, 308, 318, 321-31
civil liberties, 172, 319
classified information, 112, 261, 267, 314
CNSAS, 153n2
Cold War: about, 1; and chekist, 164-65;
and cinematic topography, 257; collaboration during, 19-20; covert operations
during, 10-11; culture and ideology of,
11-12, 162; and DEFA films, 255-73; defi-

nition of, 6; and enemy types, 6, 10;
fear and mistrust during, 12, 22; and
foreign policy, 7, 10, 22, 23; and intelligence agencies, 10, 14; and Iron Curtain, 3; and James Bond films, 283-86; as
knowledge race, 13; making sense of, 10;
and Markus Wolf, 89, 95; and morality,
218-19; news analysis of, 11; and NGC
movies, 279-303; population movements during, 9; post-, 1, 7, 21-24, 202,
310-12; propaganda, 6-11, 236-37, 241
Cold War stories. *See* spy stories
Communism: East German, 80, 84;
fall of, 13; and Markus Wolf, 76, 83;
"sources" used during, 139, 153n2
Communist autobiography, 77-80, 96
Communist Party: and border crossing,
205; German, 73, 84; Romanian, 29, 30,
140; and Samuel Feld, 32, 34, 36, 59
contract workers. *See* foreign workers
counterespionage, 29, 59, 67n36, 263
counterintelligence work, 10, 81, 83, 84,
163, 283
counterrevolutionary stance, 115, 117,
118, 119
"critical geopolitics," 281, 282, 303
Critical Geopolitics (Tuathail), 281
cross-border relationships, 198-200,
207, 210
Cuban missile crisis, 8, 21, 261, 284
cultural authorities, 144, 147, 285
cultural memories, 247, 248, 315, 316, 331
cultural politics, 100, 109, 116, 118, 120, 122
currency exchange, 205
curtain of lies, 11-13

Das unsichtbare Visier (TV series), 260,
274n8, 282
declassified files, 1, 100, 102, 163, 229
DEFA films, 255-73
defectors, 14, 107, 176, 256
Der Westen leuchtet! (movie), 279
Der Willi-Busch-Report (movie), 279-81,
286-94, 296-97, 299-303
Deutsche Film-Aktiengesellschaft
(DEFA) films, 255-73
Deutschland 83 (TV series), 22, 274n7,
307-8, 313-16, 323-24, 331

Stasi informer(s): about, 16–17; as experts, 103; Hermann Kant as, 101; motivation of, 106; Peter Edel as, 121; recruitment of, 99, 103; and sense of belonging, 127–28; types of, 103; Werner Neubert as, 121

Stern, Herbert J., 238–39, 245, 249n6; *Judgment in Berlin*, 230, 231, 239

Stiller, Werner, 14, 71, 107–8

Stockholm syndrome, 178

storytelling, 1, 2, 32, 40, 137, 302

Strittmatter, Eva, 117–18, 130n12

Strubel, Antje Rávic: *Tupolew 134*, 230, 247, 248

superpowers. *See* Soviet Union; United States

surveillance: about, 9–11, 20–22; Ana Novac under, 153n4; anxiety about, 308, 310, 318; blanket, 307, 308; and border, 287; and civil liberties, 319; current politics of, 318; and data flow, 310; definition of, 308; domestic, 82, 83, 271; Ingrid Ruske and Horst Fischer under, 231–32, 243–44; movies representing, 280, 286, 321; Paul Wiens under, 109, 110; post–Cold War, 310–12. *See also* espionage

target identity, 17, 138, 139, 148, 152

terrorism, 20, 238, 243, 290

Third Reich, 80, 84, 249n6

Tiede, Hans Detlef Alexander: about, 229; arrest of, 236; sentence of, 240; and travel documents, 233; trial of, 237–41

totalitarian regimes, 10, 103, 153n2, 184, 185, 200

tracing and tracking. *See* surveillance

transit camp, 320, 328, 329

travel documents, 233–34, 241

Tuathail, Gearóid Ó.: *Critical Geopolitics*, 281

"Tunte" and "Number 279594" episode, 216–17

Tupolew 134 (Strubel), 230, 247, 248

Turkish nationals: about, 19, 197; border crossing by, 198; and East-West confusion, 206; files related to, 198–99; intimate relationship with, 212–15; and social exclusion, 213–14; suspicion of,

218; tracking of, 215–17; transgressions by, 201–2, 218–19; from West Berlin, 199–200; working for Stasi, 201, 220–23

United States: about, 4; and BND, 5, 255, 295, 308, 311, 312; foreign policy of, 7; and hijacking trial, 238; position of, during Cold War, 257

U.S. Department of State, 239

Vassily (fictitious character), 328, 329

Voice of America, 7, 12, 65

Warsaw Pact, 8, 23, 255

Wax, Hans, 260, 274n14

Wegner, Bettina, 117

West, 9, 12–13, 114–15

West Berlin: about, 19, 140; sightseeing tour through, 237; social exclusion in, 213–14; Tiede and Ruske trial in, 237–41; Turkish nationals from, 199–200

Westen (movie), 303, 307, 310–12, 320, 327, 331–32

West Germany: about, 8, 21; and border, 202; and guest-worker program, 200, 204; and Markus Wolf, 74, 81, 83; and Samuel Feld, 57, 59; and secret services, 288, 295

Wiens, Paul, 109–13, 123, 130n7, 130n9

Winger, Anna, 316, 317

Winger, Jörg, 316, 317

Wolf, Konrad, 74, 76

Wolf, Markus: about, 14, 16; and admissions of guilt, 87–88; at Alexander Square rally, 76–77; books written by, 72, 76, 95–97; and Communism, 76, 83; comparison of, to James Bond, 91–92; and credibility, 85–90; death of, 77; and disclaimer about omissions, 86; early life of, 73–77; in East Berlin, 74; and Erich Honecker, 84, 85; as fan of spy fiction, 90–91; and GDR, 74, 84, 85, 88; as head of espionage, 82–83; as ladies' man, 91; life story of, 72, 85, 87, 91, 95, 96; *Man without a Face*, 79, 80, 82, 85, 93, 94; marriage of, 73–75; memoirs of, 79, 80; narrative strategy of, 76, 81, 86, 90; *On My Own Behalf*, 76; personnel file of,

Wolf, Markus (*continued*)
  97n3; remorse and shame of, 87, 89, 93; resignation letter of, 75, 79; retirement of, 74–75, 84; rumors about, 90–97; and secret services, 80, 92, 96; and SED, 84, 90; sentence of, 79; and socialism, 74, 83, 89, 95; in Soviet Union, 77; *Spionagechef im geheimen Krieg*, 79, 86, 93, 94; and Stasi, 5, 71, 88, 93; as storyteller, 80–85; on trial, 78, 79; and "Troika" project, 75; and victimization, 89–90; views of, on boss, 83–84; as wanted man, 94
Workers Leaving the Factory (movie), 321
World War II, 179, 239, 249n6, 255
writers: about, 99–100; Ana Novac, 139–53; Bettina Wegner, 117; Erich Loest, 17, 111, 114, 122; Eva Strittmatter, 117–18, 130n12; Franz Fühmann, 111, 116, 119, 122, 123; Günter Casper, 106, 107, 122, 123; Günter Kunert, 100, 114, 121, 125, 130n10, 130n14; Klaus Poche, 17, 111, 114–15, 125; Lutz Rathenow, 17, 111, 116; Monika Maron, 17, 111, 115, 122, 125, 131n18; monitoring of, 101; Paul Wiens, 109–13, 123, 130n7, 130n9; and peer reviews, 99, 104, 111, 112, 129; Peter Edel, 121; repression of, 125; Sarah Kirsch, 111, 121–25, 127, 130n15; secret war on, 125–26, 129; Wolf Biermann, 107, 119–22, 130n13; Wolfgang Hilbig, 17, 111, 115–16, 125. *See also* Berger, Uwe; censorship process
Writers Guild, 107, 109, 119, 121–24
Writers Union, 143, 144, 147, 155n17

xenophobia, 204, 215, 216, 225n3

Yalta Conference, 299, 300

Zionist movement, 40, 58
Zionist organizations, 38, 47, 58, 66n30